MW01130724

The Dallas Story

The North American Aviation Plant and Industrial Mobilization during World War II

Terrance Furgerson

Number 16 in the War and the Southwest Series

University of North Texas Press
Denton, Texas

10 9 8 7 6 5 4 3 2 1

Permissions:
University of North Texas Press
1155 Union Circle #311336
Denton, TX 76203-5017

The paper used in this book meets the minimum requirements of the American National Standard for Permanence of Paper for Printed Library Materials, z39.48.1984. Binding materials have been chosen for durability.

Library of Congress Cataloging-in-Publication Data

Furgerson, Terrance, 1960– author.
The Dallas story : the North American Aviation plant and industrial mobilization during World War II / Terrance Furgerson.
    pages cm
Includes bibliographical references and index.
ISBN-13 978-1-57441-893-4 (cloth)
ISBN-13 978-1-57441-901-6 (ebook)
1. LCSH: North American Aviation—History. 2. Airplane factories—Texas—Dallas—History—20th century. 3. Aircraft industry—Military aspects—Texas—Dallas—History—20th century. 4. World War, 1939–1945—Economic aspects—Texas—Dallas. 5. North American airplanes (Military aircraft)—Design and construction—History. 6. Industrial mobilization—United States—History—20th century.

F394.D2157 F87 2023
338.4/762913334097642812–dc23
                          2022048760

The Dallas Story is Number 16 in the War and the Southwest Series.

The electronic edition of this book was made possible by the support of the Vick Family Foundation. Typeset by vPrompt eServices.

Contents

List of Illustrations

Preface

The origin of this book began in 2012, when I was a student in Dr. Randolph Campbell's graduate seminar class at the University of North Texas. The theme of the course was local history and each student was required to select a topic, preferably one associated with Texas. The goal was to produce a research paper of approximately thirty pages, incorporating local archival sources where possible. There was limited time available to accomplish this task, so grandiose projects were unrealistic. I therefore picked what seemed like a simple undertaking. I was aware that North American Aviation (NAA) had operated an aircraft factory in Dallas during World War II, manufacturing the famed P-51 Mustang fighter, but other than that I knew nothing about the facility. Thus, I set out to learn what I could over the course of the semester, only to discover that no comprehensive history of the plant was available. I had stumbled across a story that needed to be told. What was intended to be a ten-week project became an eight-year endeavor to discover everything I could about the aircraft factory, and then assemble the information into a presentable format.

The first step was to gain an understanding of why the Dallas aircraft factory had come into being. This required studying the industrial mobilization of the United States during World War II. There are numerous works on this subject, including *Arsenal of World War II: The Political Economy of American Warfare, 1940–1945*, by Paul A. C. Koistinen, and *A Call to Arms: Mobilizing America for World War II*, authored by Maury Klein. Koistinen's work is primarily intended for academic readers, while Klein targets a more general audience. Both look at mobilization from a broad perspective.

Ultimately, the two works most utilized for this project were found within the official government series collectively titled the *U.S. Army in World War II*. These were *Chief of Staff: Prewar Plans and Preparations*, by Mark Skinner Watson, and *Buying Aircraft: Material Procurement for the Army Air Forces*, by Irving B. Holley Jr. These two volumes provided foundational knowledge about industrial mobilization, and the citations within them pointed toward additional useful resources. However, neither work provided specific details concerning Dallas, meaning that additional research was required.

Another book that helped shape the direction of this project was *Planning the Home Front: Building Bombers and Communities at Willow Run*, by Sarah Jo Peterson. This work examines the factory where the Ford Motor Company mass-produced B-24 bombers. Peterson, with a background in urban planning, only briefly relates the process of industrial mobilization that led to the creation of the Willow Run facility. She focuses on the building and operation of the plant, with an emphasis on the demand created for housing in the surrounding area. The book provided insights into how the construction of a large factory could strain the infrastructure of surrounding communities. Peterson's work offered a template on how the story of a specific plant could be presented as local history, suggesting the use of a similar approach with the Dallas factory.

The remaining pieces of the research puzzle involved the search for primary documents dealing with the factory. This effort was hampered by the fact that NAA no longer exists as a corporate entity, and no repository was located for records from the company. Nevertheless, a limited amount of company documents were discovered by scouring through archives located from Seattle to Austin and Austin to Washington, DC. The quest for government documents was more productive, especially within the records of the Defense Plant Corporation (DPC), located in the National Archives at College Park, Maryland. Materials were eventually obtained from thirteen different archives, ten of which the author visited in person. While continued effort could have uncovered additional materials, there came a point where it became necessary to conclude the research phase and begin writing. This started in the latter half of 2017, when the early chapters started to appear as rough drafts.

Questions remained as to what approach to take with the narrative. An early decision involved the timeline of events. The original graduate paper had traced the beginnings of the Dallas plant to May 1940. It soon became obvious that a proper historical study was needed to examine the process by which Franklin D. Roosevelt initiated the industrial mobilization of the United States. This required expanding the timeline back to the year 1938, when the President first gave serious thought to the issue. This topic eventually consumed two complete chapters of the manuscript.

Other considerations continued to move the work in a new direction. The initial seminar project had been intended as a piece of local history about a largely forgotten aircraft plant. The title of the paper reflected this limited goal: *The Dallas Story*. It was a throwaway name inspired by a magazine advertisement publicizing the opening of the factory. To convert the paper into a book-length manuscript would require expanding the study into something more substantial. The preliminary idea was to focus on the government's role in financing and building the plant, through the actions of the DPC, a government entity created to facilitate the defense buildup prior to Pearl Harbor. It was to be a scholarly work based on government documents; the sort of tedious product typical of academic writing. What was discovered during research was that the DPC records concerning the Dallas plant offered scant material, insufficient for pursuing that course. A broader history of the DPC was also not an option, as historian Gerald White had authored such a study in *Billions for Defense; Government Financing by the Defense Plant Corporation during World War II*.

As the writing phase progressed, it became clear that the Texas operations of NAA could best be presented as local history. The project had come full circle, returning to its origins; it truly is "the Dallas Story." Yet at the same time it is a story set against the backdrop of national issues. With this realization the final vision for the project emerged. The concept was to examine why one specific factory came into existence, how it operated, how it affected the community, and what problems were encountered along the way. The goal was to create a microhistory to serve as an example of how the fabled "Arsenal of Democracy" was created. The efforts undertaken in Dallas and the problems encountered along the way were also present in other locations throughout the nation as the United States mobilized itself for industrial warfare.

This book incorporates elements of different types of history into one presentation. The goal was to merge aspects of business, military, political, and social history, and weave them into a single useful narrative. Whether the attempt has been successful must be decided by the reader, for the creator is too invested in the project to be a dispassionate judge. Ultimately, the interpretations and conclusions presented are the personal opinions of the author. Likewise, any factual errors found in the work are his responsibility alone.

In 1941 the citizens of Dallas effectively went to war. This is their story.

Acknowledgments

The process of completing this work has been challenging and time consuming. The effort has been aided along the way by archivists and librarians across the nation, from College Park, Maryland to Seattle, Washington. These individuals are too numerous to list, and indeed many of their names are unknown, but their contributions have made this work possible.

Gratitude is owed to friends and colleagues who assisted in different ways. Andrew Galloway, Millard Baxley, and Nina Christman all provided useful books. Keegan Chetwynd, director of the Military Aviation Museum in Virginia, provided knowledge and insights in the research phase of the project. Dr. Mervyn Roberts, a colleague since graduate school, offered encouragement, advice, and feedback throughout the journey. I am also thankful for help provided by Michael Lombardi, Senior Historian for Boeing, who facilitated the use of photographs.

I wish to express my appreciation to the members of my doctoral committee at the University of North Texas (UNT) for their support. Most especially to Dr. Richard B. McCaslin, who has served as an excellent mentor to a neophyte author. He assisted in acquiring photographs as well. Ronald Chrisman at UNT Press made the publication a reality, and Jill Kleister at UNT was helpful with the intricacies of putting the manuscript into the proper format.

Finally, I must express eternal love to my long-suffering wife Sherry, who has stood by my side during this endeavor. She has stoically endured my preoccupation with this project, and without her support this work would not have been conceivable.

Chapter 1

Introduction

It was the first weekend of April 1941, and it was Palm Sunday. While Christians associate the day with a triumphant procession, the events this Sunday were of a secular nature. In its one-hundred-year existence, the city of Dallas had never seen a procession like this. The citizens of Texas came by the thousands, traveling toward a common destination. Some pilgrims traveled from outlying towns such as Denton, located more than forty miles to the north—a substantial distance in the era before interstate highways. Their automobiles clogged the main east-west route from Dallas, even though Jefferson Avenue was designated a one-way street for this special event, and traffic stretched back for two miles. Fortunately, authorities had planned ahead, and thirty state troopers had been tasked with controlling the traffic flow, aided by deputies of the Dallas County Sheriff's office. Dallas police were also on the scene, as well as two hundred enlisted military personnel. Their assignment was to help direct visitors toward the proper areas. Soon the designated parking zone had been filled, despite calculations that it could accommodate twenty thousand vehicles. Drivers resorted to parking in remote areas and walking for miles to reach their destination. Dallas Mayor Woodall Rogers was caught in the jam as well. As a result, he barely arrived in time for a scheduled 3:30 p.m. radio broadcast.[1]

1

Planners had expected that twenty-five thousand people might attend the scheduled four-hour event. There were at least that many on hand when the gates opened at 2:00 p.m. and more continued to arrive. Faced with this unanticipated crowd, a command decision was needed; it fell on James H. Kindelberger, an aviation engineer turned executive who was ultimately responsible for the whole affair. "Let 'em come in until there isn't a crowd anymore," was his decree. An afternoon rainstorm failed to drive away the masses, and when the gates were finally closed at seven o'clock there had been an estimated sixty thousand people in attendance.[2]

These common citizens had been drawn to the outskirts of Dallas to attend an open house of a brand-new factory designed to manufacture aircraft for the United States military. Operated by North American Aviation (NAA), the multiple buildings at the site covered more than a million square feet. The most impressive of these was a large edifice that spanned approximately 900 by 950 feet, billed as the largest industrial room in the world. Visitors to the open house began their odyssey at a giant machine shop. Here they could observe how parts were fabricated and then mated with other components and transformed into subassemblies. These in turn were fed toward the main assembly area, which ran along an east-west axis, located on the northern side of the structure. As the guests exited the building they could look down the length of the final production line, where wings, tails, and center sections were assembled into flyable military aircraft. It was a process that was certainly unfamiliar to most of the massive crowd.[3]

Much of the curiosity about this new factory was inspired by economic concerns. The giant facility would employ thousands of workers, a significant matter in a country struggling through the Great Depression. Furthermore, the opening of the aircraft plant would help transform the city of Dallas into an industrial manufacturing center. There was also a public awareness of the importance of the factory to national security. World War II was raging in Europe and China, and Americans were increasingly mindful of the dangerous international situation. There was interest in the plant because it signified the beginning of the defense buildup that eventually created the fabled "Arsenal of Democracy."[4]

The Texas division of NAA is arguably the premier example of the manufacturing phenomena that helped the United States win World War II. During
fifty-three months of operation, NAA Dallas was tasked with the production
of three important types of aircraft: trainers, fighters, and multiengine bombers. And produce them it did, delivering a reported 18,784 planes during its
wartime operations. This made it the most prolific aviation factory within
the United States. To put this figure into a larger perspective, one official
monograph reports the American military procured 304,139 aircraft during
the years 1939–45. Based on this information, the Dallas NAA plant was
responsible for just over 6% of the military aircraft acquired during the
period. This represents a substantial contribution to the war effort. But despite
these impressive numbers, the story of NAA Dallas, and its significance to
history, has been largely forgotten. The passage of time has claimed most of
the wartime generation that fabricated the steady stream of aircraft rolling out
of the massive overhead doors. A visitor to the factory site in the year 2017
found a group of largely empty buildings, offering a Sphinx-like enigma to
passersby. Nearby residents no longer heard the roar of radial engines, or the
bark of machine guns being test fired. There was not even a historical marker
at the location to explain its role during the war.[5]

The lack of public knowledge concerning NAA Dallas is not particularly
unusual. What is surprising is how little notice has been paid to the subject
by professional historians. An examination of several books on the history
of Dallas found scant information about the factory. Shifting focus to works
dealing with World War II aviation produced a similar lack of results. Even
works that ostensibly deal with NAA give the Dallas facility only passing
mention. Searches of library and academic databases have located no scholarly histories focused on the Texas operations of NAA. Clearly, there is room
for such a study.[6]

The question can be asked, however, whether there is a need for such
a study. There are numerous books available that deal with the subject of
industrial mobilization during World War II. Many of these are comprehensive and broad in scope, providing detailed information and critical
analysis. Studies of this nature typically concentrate on the role of the
federal government and other national issues. They fail to present a local

perspective,and seldom offer details about how a particular factory was built and operated. But is there any actual worth to a history of one specific aviation facility? One noted historian, when approached with the topic, commented that the factory was just a building where they once constructed airplanes. This is not an unreasonable reaction when given only a morsel of information. But upon further examination, it is obvious that the story of NAA Dallas offers opportunities for a multifaceted historical approach. For example, the facility was financed by the federal government under the auspices of the Defense Plant Corporation, and then leased to a private business to facilitate the industrial buildup during the period immediately preceding the attack on Pearl Harbor. This cooperation between the national government and business leaders was a major factor in industrial mobilization during the war, so an analysis of North American's efforts in Dallas can offer a useful case study of this symbiotic relationship.

Additional aspects found within the story are the roles of local governments and businessmen in attracting major industries to an area. These civic leaders then had to deal with the rapidly changing needs of the community as large numbers of individuals went to work in the plant, causing difficulties with traffic and issues with housing. Another problem arose in the fast speed in which massive programs at the plant were instituted, leading to delays and accusations of waste. These accusations eventually prompted a Congressional investigation, bringing discord to both NAA and the Dallas area. Thus, there are many factors suggesting a comprehensive history of the facility is a worthwhile endeavor, incorporating aspects of military, government, industrial, and social history.

The importance of the North American plant to the mobilization of the aviation industry certainly demands scholarly attention. But another consideration provides additional justification for studying the construction and operation of the factory, and this is its significance to the economic development of Dallas. Currently there are no works available that offer a detailed explanation of how the factory affected the surrounding communities. Even works dealing with the local history of Dallas offer few details about NAA, and the existence of the factory appears to be largely unknown among the modern citizens of the city. Even encyclopedic sources devoted to the history of Texas largely underplay the existence of NAA. For example, the Texas State Historical Association maintains an online resource known as the *Handbook of Texas*. A search of this database provides few details about the factory. Snippets of information can be found within the entries on Grand Prairie, Aeronautics, Dallas, and Urbanization. However, at the time of this writing the *Handbook* appears to have no dedicated article about NAA, a glaring omission indeed.[7]

Given the current state of the historiography, and its absence from public memory, the NAA factory at Dallas is a prime candidate for scholarly study. The fact that the facility was the single largest producer of military aircraft is reason enough for such an effort. An additional factor to consider is the marriage of the federal government and private enterprise in establishing a new, large-scale manufacturing industry in the Dallas area. There are also the problems that arose from the influx of the workers into the area, which taxed the housing and infrastructure of the surrounding communities, thus offering another rich area of study. The shift of local political and business leaders from trying to lure NAA to coping with its presence can be a useful model for case studies of similar communities all over the United States during World War II. And finally, there is the fact that the story of NAA Dallas has been largely forgotten by the citizens of the city, leaving a glaring hole in the history of the local area. This is a significant oversight in need of correction, and this book seeks to fulfill that need.

Admittedly, this work is attempting to succeed at a multitude of tasks. It seeks to explain the national topic of industrial mobilization, while at the same time looking at the issue through a local perspective. It is a product of scholarly research, yet it employs a narrative format designed to reach beyond a purely academic audience. Lastly, the author hopes to present a compelling story of people at war, while also providing a useful case study of how the United States prepared itself for a global conflict of unprecedented scale. For in the end, *The Dallas Story* is an American story as well.

Chapter 2

Genesis, 1938–39

How did Dallas—a city with no preexisting aircraft manufacturing industry—become the location of a factory producing airplanes during World War II? The beginning of the answer is found in the international situation in early 1938. In Europe, Nazi Germany was a growing threat due to Adolph Hitler's expansionist goals. Asia was also in turmoil, as Japanese aggression in China had led to open warfare beginning in July 1937.

President Franklin D. Roosevelt was concerned over conditions in both Europe and China, and he recognized the need to improve the military readiness of the United States. The President apparently developed these thoughts over time, as overseas events became increasingly troublesome. Roosevelt's desire to upgrade American capabilities led him to initiate a sequence of decisions that would eventually result in the building of the North American Aviation (NAA) plant at Dallas. A complete examination of Roosevelt's decision-making process is outside the focus of this historical study, but a basic knowledge of events can provide a better understanding of the situation. Therefore, this chapter will provide a summary of measures and issues that were under consideration at the time.[1]

Having been the commander-in-chief since 1933, Roosevelt certainly had an awareness of the military situation within the United States. But the ongoing Great Depression demanded most of his effort during his first term of office. After he won a second term in 1936, he was forced to devote more attention to foreign relations. Various pronouncements he made early in 1938 offer a useful starting point for discussing the American military buildup. In his annual State of the Union address on 3 January 1938, Roosevelt acknowledged the troubled international situation, warning of "future hazards" and declaring that "the acts and policies of nations in other parts of the world would have far-reaching effects." While he did not call for increased military spending in this address, the President referred to "a world of high tension and disorder," in which "stable civilization is actually threatened." Therefore, Roosevelt stated, "we must keep ourselves adequately strong in self-defense."[2] The President followed with specific ideas on 28 January, when he made seven recommendations to Congress regarding increases in military spending. Roosevelt wanted legislators to appropriate funds for a multitude of purposes. He requested greater funding for the Navy, the building of two battleships, additional ammunition for the Army, an increase in antiaircraft materials, and more than six million dollars to be used to manufacture tooling needed to produce materials for the Army. Nothing was explicitly stated regarding aviation at this time.[3]

The momentum for improved military readiness accelerated after Germany annexed Austria in March 1938. Evidence is found in a letter written to Roosevelt by presidential advisor Bernard Baruch, dated 29 April 1938—mere weeks after the *Anschluss* of Germany and Austria. Baruch had been the head of the War Industries Board during World War I and was acquainted with issues involving industrial mobilization. In this short letter, he addressed a variety of concerns, writing, "You are aware of the condition of the American Navy and of the Army. Everyone knows what it is, except the American people, for surely the foreign governments know." Baruch called for the acquisition of industrial machinery to produce gunpowder, as well as the manufacture of antiaircraft and antitank artillery, semiautomatic infantry rifles, and "Then airplanes and more airplanes."[4]

White House files suggest an interest in military aviation during the months that followed, but the subject does not appear to have been foremost in the President's mind. The need for a military buildup was common throughout the armed forces, and aviation was just one component of the overall problem. What accelerated the process was the situation in the Czechoslovakian Sudetenland, which reached the crisis stage in the autumn of 1938. After listening to a speech by Hitler on 12 September, Roosevelt directed his trusted advisor Harry L. Hopkins to "go out to the Pacific Coast and take a look at the aircraft industry with a view to its expansion for war production."[5] Given the nature of this order, it is obvious that Roosevelt was aware of the challenges to be faced in building up America's air forces. At the end of September came the Munich Conference, in which the leaders of France, Italy, Great Britain, and Germany met to negotiate the infamous pact that partitioned Czechoslovakia to satisfy Hitler's demands. Emboldened by the weaknesses of the western democracies, and backed by the *Luftwaffe*, Hitler intimidated the French and British into allowing the Germans to occupy the Sudetenland. It represented the supreme folly of appeasement and started the final countdown to World War II.[6]

The capitulation at Munich increased concern at the White House. Although President Roosevelt had been calling for an increase in military readiness since the beginning of 1938, the European situation had become critical. October brought additional developments, including a briefing by William C. Bullitt, the US ambassador to France. Bullitt returned to Washington on 13 October and met with Roosevelt to report on conditions in Europe. Bullitt offered insights into the mindset of French officials:

> The French military chiefs attributed Hitler's confidence to his possession of an air force already large and still capable of rapid expansion by means of the huge German aircraft factories already in operation. What impressed the French the most was the existence of a German bomber fleet much larger than that of France and Britain combined.

The French thought the answer to this problem could be found in utilizing American production to counter that of the Germans, and Roosevelt agreed:

> Through Mr. Bullitt's recital of French fears and desires, duplicated to a degree by reports of similar anxieties in Great Britain, President

Roosevelt became convinced for the first time that American airplane production should be greatly stimulated with all possible speed.[7]

Ambassador Bullitt's information describing French worries was considered credible by the President, who accepted the idea of American industry as the solution to the dilemma.

The question remains as to whether the French concerns, and their endorsement of American airpower, were well-founded. Certainly, they were sincere in their beliefs that the Germans possessed a greatly superior air force. This is shown by a French order for one hundred Curtiss Model H-75 fighters on 13 May 1938, with an option to purchase another hundred if the airplanes were satisfactory. The French clearly saw a need for more aircraft and were unable to wait for their own industry to provide them. Roosevelt would have been aware of this order, in fact, he had facilitated it by allowing a French pilot to test fly a P-36 fighter, which was the Army version of the H-75.[8]

Fortunately for Roosevelt, there were additional sources of information supporting the assertion that Germany was far ahead of other European nations in terms of air power. The American government had already started to explore the large-scale manufacture of military aircraft, even as the Czechoslovakian debacle increased the urgency. One step in doing this was to examine the production facilities of other countries. This prompted representatives of the American aviation industry to visit Europe to investigate the situation. These men were trained observers, who "grasped the implications of what they saw in the German factories they visited."[9] Two such individuals were Glenn L. Martin, who headed his namesake company, and James H. Kindelberger, president of NAA. Both men played significant roles in the production of airplanes for the American military. Martin's observations were summarized in a War Department memorandum on 23 June 1938 with a warning that "Germany is obviously thoroughly organizing from standpoints both of men and machines to utilize to the maximum the destructive power of the airplane."[10]

Another visitor was Lawrence Bell, of Bell Aircraft, who toured facilities in Germany, Italy, France, and Great Britain during July and August of 1938. On 12 September 1938—the same day as the previously mentioned speech by Hitler—Bell submitted a twenty-seven-page confidential report to the War Department about his European visit. This report reached Assistant Secretary of War Louis Johnson, who forwarded it to Roosevelt on 31 October. The date of Bell's report places it at the height of the ongoing discussion concerning the production of aircraft. Roosevelt had already established a committee on 25 October, tasked with reporting on the necessary steps for increasing aircraft production. The members included Assistant Secretary of War Johnson, Assistant Secretary of the Navy Charles Edison, and Aubrey Williams, the Deputy Administrator of the Works Progress Administration (WPA). Given the timing, it would be inaccurate to say that Bell's report initiated Roosevelt's desire for increased production. But Bell's observations support the information provided by Ambassador Bullitt, and likely reinforced Roosevelt's opinions. A detailed examination of the document is worthwhile, as an example of the information that was reaching the President.[11]

Bell had started his tour in Germany, where he spent the last two weeks of July 1938 visiting eleven aviation facilities, including aircraft factories, subcontractors, and research laboratories. During his travels he observed the construction of different aircraft that would soon become familiar names: the Dornier Do 17 and Heinkel He 111 bombers, the Junkers Ju-52 transport, the Junkers Ju 87 dive bomber, and the Messerschmitt 109 and 110 fighters. Bell made notes regarding the various designs such as crew requirements, weapons, engines, and other assorted specifications. He was also interested in the actual physical construction of the aircraft, including what materials were used and what techniques were employed in assembly. He paid special attention to the Messerschmitt 109, remarking that it "held more interest to me than any other plane in Germany."[12]

Bell was impressed by the aircraft factories themselves. He found the German facilities to be of recent construction, observing that most were from two to three years old and "strictly modern with the finest of production equipment." He also observed camouflaged factories equipped with bomb shelters, and that buildings were dispersed and were staggered "as a protection against bombardment." Seeing large quantities of airplanes under construction in modern plants with defensive features made a great impression upon Bell. His assessment of German facilities was reinforced as his European visit continued in countries with less aviation capabilities. After visiting Germany, he traveled to Italy, where he visited the Breda factory in August 1938. Having visited only one Italian factory, Bell reported with minimum observations. Still, he concluded that their "general workmanship was good" and that the workers "appeared both capable and industrious." The factory itself, however, had "departments badly cut up and extremely poor natural and artificial light."[13]

Having toured the two fascist countries, Bell moved west to inspect the French aviation industry. As an aircraft manufacturer himself, he seemed appalled by conditions in that country. There was apparently little activity for him to witness, as he claimed that "the entire aircraft industry was either on holiday or just completing holidays at the time of my arrival." The plants themselves were unlike their German counterparts. His first stop was the Amiot factory near Paris. He noted that "the plant is very poor, low head-room, inadequate light, untidy and most of the equipment is obsolete, no really modern production equipment or methods." His next stop was at the Potez factory, which was "considered the show plant of France." Bell found that this showcase plant was utilizing a large amount of "old and obsolete" equipment, although more modern machinery was starting to be introduced. Workmanship at Potez was of "high quality" and Bell was impressed by the technique by which wings were fabricated. But the plant was suffering from an inadequate supply of engines, and some unfinished planes were stored due to a lack of power plants. Even if the plant had been able to obtain the necessary engines, it still only had a production capacity of one aircraft per day when working one shift. This did not bode well for increased output in case of mobilization.[14]

The final plant that Bell visited in France was the Morane—Saulnier facility near Paris, where the M.S. 405 and 406 models of pursuit planes were constructed. Bell found the process of producing these aircraft employed "practically every known type of construction." He wrote that the airplane's design made it "almost impossible" to achieve quantity produc-tion. He added, "The external workmanship is very poor, although a fine finish is obtained by using large quantities of glazior's [sic] putty to fill up bad workmanship."[15] Bell was critical of the factory itself, citing "old type construction, low headroom, poorly lighted, very poorly equipped." Discipline was poor, and the workers had low morale and lacked industriousness. At this point Bell had visited three manufacturing plants in France and was not impressed. He declared that if these facilities were typical examples, "the state of the military aircraft industry in France is pretty low." Overall, Bell wrote, "The status of the French military aircraft production appeared to be pathetic in view of the possible need of this equipment," and it would take years for the French to produce an air force equal to that of the Germans.[16]

Bell finished his journey by visiting the British aircraft industry during the fourth week of August 1938. His first stop was the Vickers Aviation factory, where the new Wellington bomber was under construction. This airplane was noted for its geodesic method of construction, akin to a basket weave. Bell observed that the Vickers plant manager had done a "masterly job" of overcoming the difficulties inherent in the use of this method, but that it was a "tremendously expensive" way to build an aircraft. Bell reported that "No material advantage of this type of construction is apparent to me." The facility itself was "well equipped with modern machine tools" and featured an "especially fine drop forge and heat treat plant."[17]

Moving on to the Hawker Aircraft plant, Bell witnessed the building of Hurricane fighters. This plane became a key component of the Royal Air Force during the Battle of Britain in 1940. Being largely fabric covered, the Hurricane was built with "a great deal of hand work," which Bell wrote could have been better done with more use of machinery. The Hurricane was "considered definitely inferior to the Spitfire," and the Hawker plant was "old and not very impressive," with "low headroom and old type equipment."[18]

A trip to Vickers Supermarine gave Bell a glimpse into what would become the most important British fighter of World War II—the Spitfire. This aircraft was just then beginning production, with only five examples having been delivered at the time of Bell's visit. The factory itself was small, and parts of the airplane were manufactured by subcontractors and delivered to Vickers Supermarine for final assembly. It was anticipated that output at the plant would eventually reach nine to twelve planes per week. Meanwhile, the British had started construction of a new factory to deliver an order of one thousand Spitfires. Bell also visited the Rolls Royce plant that was constructing the Merlin engine that powered both the Hurricane and the Spitfire. "Rolls Royce," he wrote, "appears to be doing an excellent job." The British government was also building a second factory to produce Merlin engines.[19]

It was obvious to Bell that Great Britain was in much better condition than France, with superior factories and better aircraft. However, the Germans were still well ahead of the other countries. Bell quantified his findings in a ratio, rating Germany as a 10, England as a 5, Italy as a 2, and France merely at 1. Germany, he estimated, produced "not less than 8,000 to 10,000 planes per year," with "high efficiency and without confusion." The British had the potential to close the gap, he wrote, noting that "England is stronger than a ratio of 5 but will certainly require at least another year to reach anything that could be considered minimum defense in the air against Germany." In the meantime, "it is evident that England cannot at this time defend itself in the air against the German Air Force."[20]

Bell concluded his findings with some useful advice. After explaining that "Great Britain has apparently made tremendous mistakes in endeavoring to build up its aircraft production during the past few years," he added, "It is my strong recommendation that our government examine carefully what has happened in this British effort to get emergency aircraft production if the same mistakes are to be avoided here in the event of a similar emergency."[21]

Bell's detailed report offered valuable insights into the European aviation industry. This information was no doubt presented to Roosevelt and his top advisors. But there was also a need for an evaluation of the manufacturing situation within the United States. As stated earlier, the President asked for this information after Hitler's speech of 12 September 1938. Roosevelt ordered Hopkins to examine American aircraft production on the west coast, where a large portion of the industry was located. Whether Hopkins personally traveled to the area is unclear, but he worked to obtain the requested information. This is shown by a seven-page memorandum written to Hopkins by Major Alfred J. Lyon of the United States Army Air Corps. Since Lyon's report is written on stationery from the Los Angeles office of the WPA, which was headed by Hopkins at the time, it seems likely that Hopkins assigned the task of visiting the manufacturers to Lyon. Dated 3 November 1938, the report provides a summary of the aircraft manufacturing capacity of the United States at that time, as well as projections for growth. The location of this memorandum within White House files suggests that Roosevelt viewed it and used the information to help formulate decisions regarding the expansion of American air power. An examination of the Lyon report is therefore warranted.[22]

Although Hopkins was initially tasked with gathering information on the west coast, the memorandum he received from Lyon also addressed the larger national picture. Lyon found that there were twelve manufacturers "experienced in the production of Army types of military aircraft." The firms operating in southern California were NAA, Douglas, Consolidated, and Vultee, while Boeing was based in Seattle, Washington. Companies in the eastern part of the country were Curtiss, Martin, Stearman, Bell, Grumman, Brewster, and Sikorsky (soon to merge with Vought). The last three listed were "primarily builders of Naval types of aircraft" but were "capable of building Army types." Lyon also mentioned a thirteenth company, Lockheed, which was just starting to enter the military market. These companies, experienced in building military aircraft, could provide a nucleus for industrial expansion. The report suggested, "smaller manufacturers producing commercial types ... should be considered as sources for contributory parts and for sub contracts."[23]

Lyon believed the existing aviation facilities on the west coast could produce "a potential maximum rate of 315 Army aeroplanes per month, when the requirements of the Navy are neglected." Adding the manufacturers in the east to the program would roughly double production to six hundred aircraft each month. "Therefore," Lyon wrote, "the maximum production rate for all existing facilities is approximately 7,500 aeroplanes per year." The industry at the time was operating way below its actual capacity, with an estimated twelve hundred aircraft produced in

1938. This meant production could be increased by a factor of six before it outgrew the capacity of the current factories. This clearly could not be done immediately, as additional materials and tooling would have to be obtained, and new employees would have to be recruited and trained.[24]

These numbers, while based on experience, were of course speculative. The types of aircraft to be produced were a definite variable. For example, North American was producing both trainers and observation planes (the O-47). The trainers required roughly seven thousand labor hours per airplane, while the more complicated O-47 needed twelve thousand hours. This meant that 120 trainers could be assembled per month, as compared to only 80 of the observation craft. Larger multiengine bombers would require even more man hours. Another important factor to be considered was the size of contracts. The process of designing new aircraft imposed a good deal of engineering costs, often including the expense of building a working prototype by hand. To put designs into quantity production required expenditures for additional tooling, plus the training needed to familiarize employees with the new model. These front-loaded costs had to be factored into the cost of the final product. With military expenditures limited during the Great Depression, military contracts tended to be for relatively small numbers of aircraft. However, if the numbers were to be increased it would provide an economy of scale, allowing the per-unit production costs to be driven downward. Another benefit could be found in faster production times in the latter part of the contract; as employees became more familiar with the designs the manufacturing process would become more efficient. Donald Douglas, the head of Douglas Aircraft, provided the following hypothetical example regarding production of a "B-18 type" bomber (Table 2.1):

Table 2.1 Douglas Aircraft Hypothetical Example of B-18 Type Bombers

Production Timeline	Aircraft Delivered
January 1939–July 1939	35 Airplanes
January 1939–January 1940	500 Airplanes
January 1939–July 1940	1,000 Airplanes
January 1939–January 1941	1,500 Airplanes

If his calculations were correct, a two-year production run could potentially yield three times more aircraft than a one-year effort. If the United States wanted large numbers of airplanes, it would be best to commit to these numbers at the beginning, rather than to keep adding small quantities into the equation.[25]

Based on his inquiries, Major Lyon reached a series of conclusions regarding aircraft production. First, it was best to select "proven types" for production if maximum numbers were needed. It was also desirable to place orders of at least two hundred airplanes at a time; this would allow manufacturers to plan accordingly in the acquisition of materials, tooling, and personnel. Lyon opined that "Production at maximum rate must be made a definite objective in procurement policies governing purchase of standard types of airplanes." Finally, he wrote, "designs should be "frozen," that is, changes and modifications eliminated during the construction period for any order." All these factors could come into play when working to increase production.[26]

Ultimately, if military aircraft production were required beyond the current capacity, it would be necessary to construct additional factories. This is where complications could arise. Operating in the atmosphere of the Great Depression, aviation companies would be hesitant to expend capital building new facilities that might ultimately prove unneeded. If increased procurement proved to be a short-term affair, then the industry could find itself burdened with expensive plants sitting idle. One possible answer was for the government to construct its own aircraft factories, thus excluding private enterprise from the plan. This approach would be problematic, as many aviation companies depended on military orders to stay in business. If the government started building its own aircraft this would cause financial hardship in the aviation industry, on which any large production program would greatly depend. Another problem was that the government lacked experience in designing and manufacturing airplanes on a large scale.[27]

The solution supported by the aircraft industry, according to Lyon, was for the federal government to construct "shadow factories" that would be operated by private firms. These plants could be constructed near those already in operation and equipped with government-supplied machinery.

Aircraft manufacturers could then use their expertise to operate these plants when needed to meet increased demand. Lee Atwood of NAA and Charles Van Dusen of Consolidated were specifically mentioned as being in favor of this concept. Lyon reported:

> All manufacturers' interviewed were definite in their statements that they believed that the additional facilities produced should be made available to and managed by the parent aircraft company. In other words, they visualize the government erecting a plant adjoining their own at a cost of $3,000,000.00. In the event of emergency production he [sic] would manage and direct production in the new plant and manufacture certain parts in the privately owned parent plant.

At the same time, the manufacturers made it clear that they were not enthusiastic about the government establishing its own production capability:

> All manufacturers interviewed were unfavorable to any scheme whereby the government would own and operate aircraft facilities. The representatives of the Consolidated Company appeared to be of a conviction that the establishment of Government plants would not be a means of reducing cost or improving the merit of aircraft.[28]

Aviation industry leaders were more interested in having the federal government build plants for their companies to operate, rather than constructing government-operated facilities. The latter could have deprived the industry from participating in a program that might produce immense amounts of profit. Another consideration was the labor force. Lyon reported approximately 13,700 people employed in aircraft production in the Los Angeles—San Diego area. But manufacturers were not concerned about maintaining their labor supply at this time, as the need for skilled workers was lower than might have been anticipated. Lyon's memorandum pointed to current practices in which workers were trained to operate in groups. "In general," Lyon wrote, "ten percent of the manufacturing personnel should have a considerable degree of training. The balance, constituting ninety percent of the manufacturing personnel, do not require special skill or experience." A more important factor, according to aircraft industry representatives, was that "only executives and managements experienced in aircraft production can produce satisfactory airplanes." Manufacturers also believed that the Army's procurement procedures would need to be changed to increase output.[29]

The impact of Lyon's memorandum cannot be ascertained. However, knowing that President Roosevelt specifically ordered Hopkins to obtain this exact information, it seems reasonable to conclude the President carefully read the report and absorbed the content. In the meantime, Roosevelt's aircraft committee was also working on the problem. On 28 October 1938—only three days after it was created—the group suggested questions for further study and a call to increase production capacity to fifteen thousand aircraft annually within two years. The committee advocated building of additional aircraft production facilities by the government, with these plants capable of manufacturing sixteen thousand planes per year. A follow-up letter on 2 November identified seven government-owned properties that could be sites for such factories and suggested fifteen additional areas as possible locations for new plants. One entry on the list was the Dallas–Fort Worth metropolitan area. Jointly signed by Johnson, Assistant Secretary of War, and Edison, Assistant Secretary of the Navy, the letter provides an early indicator of official interest in Dallas as the location of an aircraft factory.[30]

Clearly, a great deal of activity was occurring in the weeks immediately after the Munich conference. Roosevelt was obtaining information from a variety of sources regarding military aviation both at home and abroad. He evaluated this evidence and acted upon it, calling a meeting for the middle of November 1938—just six weeks after the Czechoslovakian debacle. This gathering would prove a significant step forward in the expansion of the aircraft industry. Held at the White House on 14 November, it was attended by key administration officials, including Roosevelt, Hopkins, Johnson, Secretary of the Treasury Henry Morgenthau Jr., and others. Military officers were also present, notably Army Chief of Staff Malin Craig, Deputy Chief of Staff George C. Marshall, and Major General Henry H. Arnold, who had become the Chief of the Army Air Corps on 29 September. The subject was aviation, and various sources agree that Roosevelt was in control of the conversation.

Historian Mark Watson relates, "The President did most of the speaking, as if his mind had been made up by earlier discussion and appraisal." According to historian Irving B. Holley Jr., Roosevelt "did not ask for advice, he laid his positions on the line."[31]

Roosevelt was concerned about the weakness of the Army Air Corps and wanted to dramatically increase its strength. He already had numbers in mind, calling for "an Army air force of 20,000 airplanes and an annual productive capacity of 24,000." There were political considerations, however, as Congress would need to appropriate a lot of funds. With the economic depression still ongoing, and with isolationist sentiments common among many Americans, Roosevelt initially decided to request a less ambitious goal:

> He therefore wished the War Department to develop a program for 10,000 planes ... of which 2,500 would be training planes, 3,750 line combat, and 3,750 reserve combat planes. His stated broad objectives were: (1) production over a two-year period of 10,000 planes as described, of which 8,000 would come from existing commercial plants and 2,000 from new plants to be built with government funds and (2) the creation of an unused plant capacity for producing 10,000 planes annually.[32]

The program as envisioned by Roosevelt would have the government build seven aircraft factories, of which two would go into operation to produce the two thousand planes specified above. The remaining five plants would be held in reserve until needed. This would provide the capability of a much larger aircraft program than the ten thousand units then being proposed. The President clearly wanted the industrial capacity to handle a far greater number of airplanes, should the need arise.[33] These numbers can be put into perspective by considering that in 1938 the statutory strength limit of the Air Corps was understood to be 2,320 aircraft (although Air Corps officials had been working to have that interpretation increased). Even this number does not provide clarity, for squadrons were often underequipped or used obsolescent models.[34]

A better appreciation of the situation might be found in a lecture to the Army War College on 1 October 1938. The speaker was Major General Frank

M. Andrews, commander of the General Headquarters Air Force. During his presentation, Andrews provided the following numbers regarding Air Corps strength as of 30 June 1938:

1. 114 single-seat fighters, of which only 54 were the most modern designs (P-35 and P-36)
2. 115 single-seat A-17 attack planes
3. 107 twin-engine bombers, of which 24 were the obsolete Martin B-10
4. 12 four-engine B-17 bombers[35]

Now, five months later, President Roosevelt was announcing his desire for ten thousand new aircraft to be built within two years. It was an audacious goal.

As 1938 drew to its conclusion, the Roosevelt administration was focusing attention on military aviation. The President had started the year calling for increased defense spending in several areas, especially the Navy. However, his attention had increasingly turned to airpower. There were various factors that contributed to this. Advisors such as Baruch were lobbying for more aircraft. There were insightful observations from individuals such as Bell, who had documented a well-organized and productive aircraft industry in Germany. Then there was the personal report of Ambassador Bullitt, who related that the French and British had been intimidated at Munich by the strength of the German *Luftwaffe*. Confronted with these realities, Roosevelt had called for a substantial increase in the number of aircraft procured, to be supported by an expansion of manufacturing capacity.

Roosevelt's call for ten thousand airplanes quickly ran into complications. Detailed plans needed to be formulated if the program were to go into effect. There were a variety of concerns, many of which had been explored in the Lyon report. One was the concept of government-built factories. Some officials envisioned them as "aerial arsenals," operated by the government as needed. This was not embraced by the aviation industry, which feared a loss of military contracts. Manufacturers also believed the government lacked the necessary skills to operate aircraft factories. What the industry favored was for the government to finance the construction of reserve plants to be operated by private firms during an emergency. This would relieve the manufacturers of the financial risk of funding their own expansion.[36]

Another area of concern was that there could be repercussions to the aviation industry if the military bought ten thousand airplanes, and then the national security situation changed. If war was avoided, the Army Air Corps could potentially possess a large reserve of aircraft. Surplus equipment could deter additional contracts for the foreseeable future. This could damage the industry, leading to manufacturers having to lay off skilled workers, or even going out of business. This scenario was one of the worries of Arnold in his capacity as Chief of the Air Corps, and he told a colleague that "we must find a way to lick that problem."[37] This also corresponded with what an industry spokesman insisted to Lyon: sustained steady production was better than start and stop contracts. There was also the possibility that too rapid of a buildup could leave the Army in possession of thousands of obsolescent aircraft. There was a need for aircraft to be sure, but a slower rate of acquisition would allow for improvements along the way.

Roosevelt's emphasis on sheer numbers of aircraft presented logistical problems as well. These ten thousand planes would be of little value without the apparatus needed to support such a force. The most obvious need would be pilots, but an air force also requires mechanics to keep the planes operational. Multiengine bombers would need navigators, bombardiers, and aerial gunners; these men would need to be trained in their roles. Schools would be needed to teach all the jobs listed above. All this would cost enormous sums of money. Military administrators were tasked with developing a workable expansion plan and determining how much would be needed to pay for it all. This process was underway in the weeks after the White House meeting of 14 November 1938, as the Air Corps and Assistant Secretary of War Johnson worked to turn Roosevelt's ideas into actual plans. In a memorandum to the President on 1 December, Johnson sent the numbers on what it would take to implement the ten thousand-plane program. The amount came to a staggering $1,289,000,000 over a course of two years. This included an estimated forty-two million dollars to be spent constructing seven government aircraft factories. This document also contained a recommendation from the Chief of

Staff that called for increases in the Army ground forces. Roosevelt wanted airplanes, but his War Department was endorsing a more comprehensive approach.[38]

Whichever way the President decided to go, it was going to be expensive. The biggest obstacles would be political and economic, as legislation was required to provide the necessary funding. To obtain it, the President needed to overcome strong isolationist sentiment among many members of the Congress, as well as the fiscal concerns of other conservative-minded legislators. Roosevelt would have to convince a hesitant Congress to support his program, and he set about making his arguments. In his State of the Union message on 4 January 1939, the President opened his address with a reference to "storm signals from across the seas." Alluding to the Munich Agreement, he declared: "A war which threatened to envelop the world in flames has been averted; but it has become increasingly clear that world peace is not assured." American neutrality alone could no longer protect the nation, for "the world has grown so small and weapons of attack so swift that no nation can be safe in its will to peace so long as any other powerful nation refuses to settle its grievances at the council table." Against such nations, "weapons of defense give the only safety," and Roosevelt warned that "survival cannot be guaranteed by arming after the attack begins—for there is new range and speed to offense."[39]

As he had done the previous year, Roosevelt followed his State of the Union address with more specific details. On 12 January 1939 he communicated again with Congress, this time concerning defense appropriations. Roosevelt believed that the United States was as unprepared for war as it had been upon its entry into World War I in 1917. Furthermore, unlike the previous war, "we cannot guarantee a long period free from attack in which we could prepare," because of the offensive capabilities of potential adversaries. America could no longer rely on the vast oceans as adequate protection against enemy nations, and it would be necessary to be prepared in advance should hostilities commence.

I have called attention to the fact that "We must have armed forces and defenses strong enough to ward off sudden attack against strategic positions and key facilities essential to ensure sustained resistance and ultimate victory." And I have said, "We must have the organization and location of these key facilities so that they may be immediately utilized and rapidly expanded to meet all needs without serious danger of interruption by enemy attack."[40]

Roosevelt provided the figure he sought; approximately $525,000,000, of which $210,000,000 would be spent in the upcoming 1940 fiscal year. The majority of the funds—$450,000,000—would be spent on the Army, the military branch most in need of attention.[41]

The President in his second communication paid special attention to matters concerning aviation, calling for "a complete revision of our estimates for aircraft." He continued:

> No responsible officer advocates building our air forces up to the total either of planes or of productive capacity equal to the forces of certain other nations. We are thinking in the terms of necessary defenses and the conclusion is inevitable that our existing forces are so utterly inadequate that they must be immediately strengthened. It is proposed that $300,000,000 be appropriated for the purchase of several types of airplanes for the Army. This should provide a minimum increase of 3,000 planes, but it is hoped that orders placed on such a large scale will materially reduce the unit cost and actually provide more planes.[42]

Roosevelt argued that the need for more aircraft was heightened by advances in technology, adding that "Military aviation is increasing today at an unprecedented and alarming rate. Increased range, increased speed, increased capacity of airplanes abroad have changed our requirements for defensive aviation." And although the President was mostly focused on the Army, he also called for an additional $21,000,000 for Navy aviation, as well as a program to train civilian pilots who could be mobilized for military service if needed.[43]

The numbers given by Roosevelt in fact hide his true intentions and can probably be considered as political sleight of hand. Only two months previously he had expressed a desire for twenty thousand planes, although his plan was to only ask for ten thousand at the outset. Now he was referring to an increase of some three thousand planes with the possibility of additional units.

Various factors played into this, the most important of which was the need to get the program through Congress. A lesser consideration was the possibility of buying a considerable number of aircraft only to have them become obsolete. So, the President went with a more moderate request to start with, to get expansion under way. Roosevelt was aided in this goal by the fact that the Europeans had started to order American aircraft during 1938. For example, Great Britain ordered two hundred patrol planes from Lockheed in June of 1938. That summer also brought a British contract for two hundred trainers built by NAA, and these numbers later increased. The French were buyers as well. As previously mentioned, they purchased fighters from Curtiss in 1938. Additional French contracts came in the new year; on 26 January 1939 they awarded a contract for 115 twin-engine Martin Model 167 bombers. This was followed by another order on 15 February, this time for one hundred Douglas DB-7 twin-engine bombers. The French Navy needed aircraft too, ordering forty Vought V-156 dive bombers on 22 February.[44]

The effect of foreign orders was beneficial. The French and British helped stimulate the American aviation industry, giving companies the impetus and capital to expand. This improvement in industrial capacity would be useful at a future date, if Roosevelt's larger plans were enacted. In the meantime, there was the possibility that a supply of American aircraft might strengthen French and British defenses to where those countries could successfully stand up to Germany. This could alleviate the need for the United States to get involved in a potential European conflict. There was one possible obstacle to be faced: under the Neutrality Act of 1937, sales of weapons to countries at war were prohibited. If war were to arrive, Roosevelt might be forced to stop the delivery of aircraft to belligerent countries, depriving the British and French of badly needed equipment. If conflict did arise, it might be possible to get Congress to alter the law to allow weapons sales to continue, but this could not be counted upon. It would be best to get as many American airplanes shipped as possible before war started.

In the weeks and months after Roosevelt's request, Congress discussed the matter while quizzing military leaders about the specifics. Arnold recalled that "In the spring of 1939, I was still having to defend the estimates for additional airplanes in Congress." The ebbs and flows of this political debate are outside the scope of this narrative; suffice to say that on 3 April 1939 Congress approved an expansion of the Air Corps, authorizing a strength of up to six thousand aircraft. This was a substantial increase over the existing force, which at the end of 1938 was just under eighteen hundred planes. The legislation also authorized up to $300,000,000 to cover the cost of aircraft and the associated logistical support. Once the necessary funding was in hand, the Air Corps could set into motion an expansion program. Conspicuous in its absence were appropriations for building government-operated aircraft factories. The idea of the aerial arsenals, according to one historian, "simply faded away."[45]

There are differing interpretations regarding why the President backed down from his original call for ten thousand aircraft. Some analysts believe that Roosevelt started with the higher number to encourage military and government officials to start thinking in larger terms. Others suggest that Roosevelt focused too much on airpower at the neglect of other needs, only to have his proposal challenged by military leaders who advocated a more balanced approach. The latter argument appears to be made by Mark Watson, who authored the official Army history concerning pre-war planning by the Army Chief of Staff. According to Watson, the Chief of Staff sought to capitalize on Roosevelt's 1938 defense concerns to bring about a more comprehensive and balanced program. Watson explains that "Even while the President was interested wholly in airplanes, [War Plans Division] was pressing for three other objectives." These included "improvement of the Regular Army in continental United States, to include the creation of an expeditionary force," along with "improvement of American defenses in the Canal Zone, Puerto Rico, Hawaii, and Alaska," and last but not least, an increase in the strength of the National Guard by twenty-seven thousand men. This proposal led to a meeting between the President and his advisors about the situation, leading to a "careful and thorough discussion of the armed forces' low state and, more particularly, of the futility of producing planes over a long period without producing trained pilots and crews and air bases at an appropriate pace." This resulted in Roosevelt agreeing to a more balanced approach, and he lowered his goal to three thousand combat aircraft, which is the figure he submitted to Congress in his 12 January 1939 message.[46]

An alternative premise is offered by historian Irving B. Holley Jr., who wrote the official Army study on aircraft procurement. Holley maintains that "The transitions from 10,000 to 3,000 to 6,000 airplanes was the essence of the President's political art." It should be recalled that Roosevelt originally talked to his inner circle about twenty thousand airplanes. Knowing that Congress would never approve such a program, he went with the number ten thousand, which he presumably would have accepted if he could get it. But the Army advocated for a more balanced program, with spending spread across more areas. As the cost estimates for the ten thousand-aircraft program reached staggering numbers, Roosevelt agreed to a 5,500-plane program formulated by the Air Corps. Considering the aircraft on hand and already ordered, the President formally requested three thousand planes in his message to Congress on 12 January 1939.[47]

Holley thus believes that Roosevelt's fluctuating numbers were "perhaps deliberate, and not haphazard planning." He explains that:

> The President's 10,000-airplane goal may have served as a most useful trial balloon. Carefully "leaked" to the press, it gave the president an opportunity to provoke discussion on the point, an opportunity to accustom the public in general and congressmen in particular to the immense increases in air power that he sought. Once the critics had fired all their ammunition at this trial balloon, the President could then ask for somewhat less and appear moderate in so doing.[48]

This strategy, writes Holley Jr., "was exceedingly adroit, as events proved."

> His request for 3,000 won him support from the very people who had been most alarmed by the rumors of 10,000 or more emanating from "usually reliable sources" and undenied at the White House. Yet even as his request for 3,000 was made, Air Corps officers were readying a bill asking for a ceiling of 6,000. This, of course, would not bear the White House label and in any event by the time it appeared the President would have already garnered the dividend of his apparent moderation.[49]

Holley obviously believes that Roosevelt was committed to an expansion of the Army Air Corps, and he employed his considerable political skills to achieve his goals, directly or indirectly.

As can be seen, Roosevelt's actions during the closing months of 1938 and early 1939 have resulted in two different historical interpretations. Watson, writing in 1949, would have his readers believe that the President sought an unbalanced military buildup focusing almost entirely on aircraft. This plan was challenged by the Army planners, who successfully diverted Roosevelt into a wider program. Holley, working in 1962, embraced the idea that the President deliberately worked to get the Army and Congress thinking in terms of the thousands of aircraft that would be needed in wartime, as opposed to a peacetime mindset that approved procurement only of smaller numbers. Both scenarios are plausible, and there are probably elements of truth in both. However, it is worth remembering that Roosevelt had been Assistant Secretary of the Navy during World War I, and he presumably retained a basic understanding of the logistical support needed to field an effective combat force. This suggests that Watson has the weaker argument. Surely Roosevelt would have realized the necessity to increase the infrastructure of the Air Corps to handle the numbers of warplanes he ultimately desired. But training barracks and mechanic schools were not the sort of things that would stir up excitement in the Congress, so the President went with the item that would draw the most attention—the airplanes that provided the actual military strength. Whichever interpretation is believed, Watson and Holley agree that it was Roosevelt who set into motion the expansion of American air power. The actual number of planes at that moment was perhaps irrelevant; what was important was to start the process of industrial mobilization of the aviation industry. Congress voted to spend the money, and NAA and Dallas would reap the benefits.

The military moved quickly, ordering 571 airplanes worth approximately $19,000,000 almost immediately after the initial appropriations were authorized. Additional money became available in July 1939, and on 10 August the Air Corps contracted to buy another $86,000,000 worth of aircraft. It was "the largest single day of business in the history of the industry up to that time." In fact, the orders exceeded a normal year's worth of business prior to 1937.[50] Three weeks later, Germany invaded Poland. World War II had begun.

Chapter 3

Awakenings, 1939–40

Upon the outbreak of World War II the Neutrality Act of 1937 went into effect, which stipulated that the United States would not sell arms to belligerent countries. This left the French and British in a difficult position. Both countries had ordered large quantities of aircraft from American manufacturers, with many of the planes yet to be delivered. Under the law, these aircraft were now subject to being embargoed. President Franklin D. Roosevelt formally invoked the provisions of the act on 5 September 1939, effectively cutting off the flow of American weapons to Great Britain and France.[1]

This was problematic. For one thing, orders from Europe were helping to fund mobilization of American aviation companies, and this increased manufacturing capacity would be needed if the United States entered the war. A halt to foreign orders could slow the expansion which was currently underway. It was also realized that the embargo would harm the British and the French, while doing nothing to deter Germany. This led Roosevelt to advocate for a change in the laws, which he had first requested in July 1939. Now, with the war underway, the need for revision was urgent. On 21 September Roosevelt traveled to the Capital to address a joint session of Congress. During the speech he laid out his arguments for modifying the Neutrality Act:

> We have learned that when we deliberately try to legislate neutrality, our neutrality laws may operate unevenly and unfairly—may actually give aid to an aggressor and deny it to the victim. The instinct of self-preservation should warn us that we, ought not to let that happen anymore.[2]

The President avoided naming any specific countries, but it takes little imagination to cast Poland in the role of victim, with France and Great Britain as would-be rescuers, and Germany as the aggressor.

To sway the opinion of an isolationist-minded public, Roosevelt needed to show how the current law could hurt the United States, and he expanded on that point:

> These embargo provisions, as they exist today, prevent the sale to a belligerent by an American factory of any completed implements of war, but they allow the sale of many types of uncompleted implements of war, as well as all kinds of general material and supplies. They furthermore, allow such products of industry and agriculture to be taken in American flag ships to belligerent nations. There in itself—under the present law—lies definite danger to our neutrality and our peace.

He added:

> From a purely material point of view what is the advantage to us in sending all manner of articles across the ocean for final processing there when we can give employment to thousands by doing it here? Incidentally, and again from the material point of view, by such employment here we automatically aid in building up our own national defense.[3]

Roosevelt provided several examples of the ways in which the embargo of war materials was somewhat ambiguous. For example, he argued that airplane wings might be treated different than sheets of aluminum.

What Roosevelt was saying was that even if American weapons and munitions were embargoed, other nations might still be able to purchase the materials needed to manufacture such products on their own. Thus, America would still be contributing to the aggressive actions of other countries, albeit indirectly. Furthermore, these raw materials might be shipped on American-flagged cargo ships, leading to the possibility of such vessels entering war zones.

This could lead to incidents where American ships were lost to hostile action, leading to the sort of escalation that preceded the United States' entry into World War I. The only way an embargo might work would be if it were total, as attempted in 1808. This was, according to Roosevelt, "a disastrous failure" which caused economic ruin to the country while failing to prevent war. It was better, he asserted, for the United States to manufacture the weapons and sell them to the belligerent countries and reap the economic benefits. To prevent foreign entanglements, purchasing countries would be extended no credit and would be obligated to transport any purchased war goods in their own cargo freighters.[4] This policy was known as "Cash and Carry," and Congress assented to Roosevelt's request and modified the Neutrality Act to allow the sale of military items to countries at war.[5]

While Roosevelt's urgings helped bring about the desired changes to the Neutrality Act, his arguments were slightly disingenuous. Certainly, there was truth in what he said regarding the economic advantages of selling goods to countries at war, and prospects of employment opportunities would have resonated with many United States citizens. But there seems to be little doubt the President's primary goal was to aid the French and British in their fight against Germany. Roosevelt was counting on the combination of the French Army and British Navy to beat Adolph Hitler, and if American munitions could further that effort then it was an obvious choice to make. The fact that foreign cash was helping to finance an expansion of the American aviation industry was a welcome bonus.[6]

And so, with the implementation of new rules in 1939, the short-lived embargo against weapons sales to the western European democracies was lifted. With war now underway, France and Great Britain bought still more aircraft from the United States. For instance, both countries wanted more Curtiss fighters, with France ordering another hundred planes on 5 October 1939. New orders continued into 1940. In April the French agreed to purchase 170 Bell Model 14s (P-39), and in May the British ordered 560 Curtiss P-40s. This was followed by a British order for 667 Lockheed fighters in June. This is just a partial accounting of incoming orders, as other European countries were starting to look toward the United States as well. Norway had ordered twenty-four Curtiss Hawk 75s in September 1939, and Belgium had contracted to purchase the Model 339B from Brewster. The Europeans were willing to purchase almost anything that could fly, and Asian contracts were being signed as well. For example, China and Thailand ordered American-built fighters. Suffice to say that the aviation industry was booming in the United States, as countries all over the world prepared for conflict. At some point, the existing factories would be unable to keep up with the demand, and it would be necessary to construct new facilities. The questions were who would build them, and where would they be built?[7]

As it happened, the question of potential locations had already been considered as part of mobilization planning. In November 1938, the Assistant Secretary of War had presented the President with a list of potential sites for proposed aircraft factories to be owned and operated by the federal government. As previously noted, these plans for "aerial arsenals" had been discarded. However, the logic behind the site selections was still valid in 1940, and it seems likely that the list was consulted when new facilities began to be considered. At the very least the parameters were similar, as several communities on the 1938 list eventually became the locations of new aircraft factories. Various factors were taken into consideration when selecting sites for the manufacturing plants. One of the most significant was the desire to spread the aircraft industry across a wider area, to lessen the risk of possible attacks. The West Coast was particularly vulnerable, with Douglas, Lockheed, North American Aviation (NAA), Ryan, and Consolidated all operating plants in Southern California. These locations were all potential targets for attack by enemy aircraft carriers. This was also true of the Boeing factory in the state of Washington. Some aircraft factories on the East Coast were also exposed; the Martian company was in Baltimore, and Grumman and Brewster were on Long Island. But aircraft plants were not the only concern, as two of the most important engine factories were also located close to the eastern seaboard. East Hartford, Connecticut, was home to Pratt & Whitney, and Wright Aeronautical was in Patterson, New Jersey. All these plants could be within range of carrier-launched aircraft.[8]

Even plants further inland were not necessarily immune from attack, for multiengine land-based bombers were improving with each new generation. This was demonstrated by the United States Army Air Corps in February 1938, when a group of six B-17 bombers made an ostentatious flight from Langley Field, Virginia, to Buenos Aires, Argentina. The journey was billed as a "goodwill mission," with the flyers attending the inauguration of the new president of Argentina. In reality, the primary motive of the Air Corps was to demonstrate the capabilities of the newly acquired B-17. The longest leg of the flight, from Miami, Florida, to Lima, Peru, spanned more than twenty-six hundred miles but was completed in less than sixteen hours. This showed that the protection offered by distance was becoming less certain. The US government had to consider the possibility that hostile nations could acquire air bases within the western hemisphere, and the Roosevelt administration started to tout the idea of "hemisphere defense" as one justification for enlarging the military.[9]

These security concerns explain the desire to locate new aviation factories outside the traditional production areas. Many of the twenty-two possible sites were in the central part of the United States, farther from potential danger. Among the cities listed were Chicago, Illinois; Kansas City, Missouri; Indianapolis, Indiana; Atlanta, Georgia; Wichita, Kansas; Nashville, Tennessee, and Dallas–Fort Worth, Texas. Some of these were eventually chosen as locations for aircraft plants. Examples include facilities in Atlanta and Wichita, which became involved in building B-29 bombers. Nashville was assigned to the production of dive bombers, and Dallas and Fort Worth would both be selected to host large aircraft factories.[10]

Factors other than security also influenced the selection of sites. If the only criteria had been to protect production facilities from air attacks, it might be desirable to locate new plants in remote rural areas far from the nation's borders. But there were other concerns to be taken into consideration. Aircraft factories required plentiful and reliable electric service to

operate the machinery. Railroad access would be useful to bring in materials to construct the actual plant, and then to carry in heavy equipment to
be installed within it. Rail transportation could also deliver raw materials
such as aluminum, and aircraft components like tires and engines would have
to be shipped in from subcontractors. An airfield would be necessary from
which to fly the finished aircraft, and moderate weather would assist in that
regard. Finally, there needed to be an available pool of workers to operate
the factory. These employees in turn would need housing and transportation.
These requirements were essential for the efficient manufacture of large
numbers of airplanes.[11]

The requirements listed above were satisfied by the city of Dallas, Texas.
The only thing lacking was a large pool of trained industrial workers, for in
1940 the city of Dallas was anything but a major industrial center. With a
population of 294,734, the potential workforce numbered 125,475. Of this
figure, only 20,682 workers (16.5%) were classified as being engaged in
"manufacturing." Some of these laborers were employed by Ford Motor
Company, which operated an assembly plant on East Grand Ave, one of the
few major factories within the city. Industrial jobs such as these represented
only a fraction of the overall jobs in the area. One report summarized the
situation by observing "Prior to the war, Dallas was regarded chiefly as a
distribution center. Manufacturing did not occupy an important place in the
city's industrial makeup." Instead, the largest employment category at the
time was in "wholesale and retail trade," which accounted for 35,165 jobs,
equaling 28% of the workforce.[12]

Among the factors in favor of Dallas was its healthy economy, a function in part of its location as the hub of several railroads. A significant
example of its wholesale trade can be seen in the cotton market, which
had been a key component of the economic life of the city for many years:
some 31% of Texas cotton was produced within a one-hundred-mile radius
of Dallas. However, while cotton was an important commodity, it had
become less significant than oil. Discoveries in East Texas and the Permian
Basin had made Dallas into a major center for the petroleum business, as
hundreds of companies tied to the industry set up operations in the city.
Visual proof of the importance of oil was demonstrated by the headquarters of

the Magnolia Petroleum Company, located in a skyscraper towering over the downtown landscape. The Magnolia building was topped at its zenith with a large neon-lighted sign representing the mythical Pegasus, erected in 1934 when the American Petroleum Institute held its annual meeting in Dallas. The business district harbored department stores such as Sanger Brothers, A. Harris, Neiman Marcus, and Titche-Goettinger. But the most significant retail operation was found south of downtown on Lamar Street. This was the location of the Sears & Roebuck distribution center, a large, multistory red brick building where merchandise was warehoused to service mail orders from the ubiquitous Sears catalog. The city was also a banking center, home to the headquarters of the Eleventh District of the Federal Reserve Bank, located on Akard Street.[13]

In summary, it seems accurate to say that Dallas had a reasonably healthy economy, at least by the standards of the era. The fact that no single industry dominated the community helped smooth out the highs and lows that can plague cities focused on one endeavor. At the same time, the oil industry gave Dallas financial stability, as even during economic hard times there was still a need for petroleum products. This has led one local historian to declare that "This injection of fresh money into the economy helped the city escape the worst aspects of the Depression being felt so severely in other parts of the nation."[14]

The financial climate inspired Dallas business and civic leaders to seek companies that might be convinced to expand operations to their city. One entity that was particularly desired was the aircraft industry, and city leaders had been working on this effort for over a decade. As a relatively new technology, aviation had a great deal of growth potential, and forward-thinking businessmen wanted to establish Dallas as a leader in the field. A key early step was the purchase of Love Field by the city in 1927, to ensure the continued existence of the airport after the United States Army ceased using the facility. This made the city one of the first to own and operate a municipal airport. The city followed up by declaring the airfield as a "free port" so that aviators could avoid paying landing fees. This was designed to encourage use of the airfield, and soon Love Field was in use by passenger airliners and aviation schools.[15]

Plans for growth continued in 1928, when the Dallas Chamber of Commerce made recommendations on how to increase the role of aviation in the economy of the city. One suggestion was to convince two aircraft factories to begin operations in Dallas. Another key recommendation was that Dallas should acquire a second airport to accommodate the military. This would keep Army aviation units operating in the city, while allowing Love Field to continue to grow as a commercial airport. What the Chamber of Commerce advocated was "the formation of a continuing and aggressive aviation policy" for Dallas. The second airfield was acquired in 1929, but there was no success in securing a major manufacturing facility after the onset of the Great Depression. But the city's efforts were about to finally bear fruit, as the national defense program accelerated into high gear in 1940.[16]

Although the Dallas–Fort Worth area had been identified as a potential location for an aircraft factory in a 1938 note sent to Roosevelt, the exact method by which Dallas was selected remains uncertain. Perhaps aircraft manufacturers were given a list of recommended sites and allowed to choose from among them. It could be that local leaders were informed that their cities were under consideration and took it upon themselves to lure aviation firms to their communities. Another possibility is that the national government served as a matchmaker, bringing together cities and aviation firms into arranged partnerships. If so, it is likely that politics might have played a role in the selection process. But why did Dallas become the home of the first expansion factory built by the federal government? Pending the discovery of currently unknown evidence, the exact answer is uncertain. However, some facts are known, and the information offers insights into the selection process.

One certainty is that the outbreak of war in September of 1939 accelerated the ongoing mobilization of the American aircraft industry. The Roosevelt administration was committed to supporting the Allied nations while at the same time building up this country's own air power. The time was at hand to start building new factories. What would happen in the first half of 1940 was a series of events that led to the construction of the NAA plant. Given the short time period involved, it appears likely that decisions being made were based on shared knowledge between national and local governments, as well as the aircraft industry.

This exchange of information is indicated by a Congressional visit to Dallas on 13 November 1939. The visit brought Senators and Representatives to examine Hensley Field, the second airfield purchased by the city as part of the 1928 aviation plan. The facility was leased to the US Army for use as an airbase. The group reportedly consisted of five Senators, including Harry S. Truman of Missouri, eight Representatives, and a number of Air Corps officers. The visitors were greeted at Hensley Field by members of the Dallas Chamber of Commerce, including President J. B. Adoue Jr., Vice President J. Ben Critz, and B. B. Owen, the chairman of the aviation committee. The visit was part of a planned five-week inspection tour of Army Air Corps facilities, to assess the needs of that service.[17]

It is unclear whether the Chamber of Commerce knew that Dallas was being considered as a location for an expansion aircraft factory. It seems likely they were, for Texas was politically well-connected. Vice President John Nance Garner was a Texan, as was House Majority Leader Sam Rayburn. It does not require a great stretch of the imagination to conclude that the Chamber of Commerce delegation took full advantage of the opportunity to brief their visitors on the advantages of locating an aircraft factory in Dallas, on vacant land alongside Hensley Field. It is possible, of course, that it was someone in the Congressional delegation that alerted the Dallas aviation committee about the upcoming Air Corps expansion. In the end it does not really matter which is correct. What is important is that as the calendar moved into 1940, the Chamber of Commerce was working to bring an aircraft factory to Dallas.

The opening months of the new year were apparently busy ones for the Chamber, as the organization worked to achieve its goal. Unfortunately, conflicting information makes the exact sequence of events difficult to establish. According to historian Eugene C. Barksdale, the first steps in the process involved the Consolidated Aircraft Corporation. Barksdale bases his assertion on information he obtained from Andrew W. DeShong during an interview in 1957. DeShong was publicity director of the Chamber of Commerce in 1939, as well as the editor of the *Southwest Business* magazine, which was published by the Chamber. According to DeShong, officials from Consolidated visited Dallas late in 1939, selecting a site just west

of Hensley Field as a location for a new factory. This led the Chamber of
Commerce to secure land options on the needed acreage. Given his involvement in the management of the Chamber, DeShong's version of events is
credible. Furthermore, DeShong served as public relations director for the
Dallas branch of NAA beginning in April 1941, which suggests he would
have intimate knowledge of the whole course of events. Realistically, the
fact that he was being interviewed about affairs from eighteen years prior
raises the possibility that his recollections could have been faulty. However,
DeShong's assertion concerning land options is substantiated by the *Dallas
Morning News*. In September 1940, the newspaper reported that one-fourth
of the land needed for an air plant was held in trust by Critz, Vice President
and General Manager of the Dallas Chamber of Commerce.[18]

Historian Robert B. Fairbanks offers a slightly different timeline, writing
that "Chamber of Commerce leaders had seriously courted airplane manufacturers since March of 1940. They emphasized the city's good weather,
'open shop' traditions, and the willingness of officials to cooperate with
the company's needs." According to Fairbanks, Critz and banker Robert L.
Thornton flew to California and visited with officials from both Consolidated
and NAA, working to attract a factory to Dallas. However, Fairbanks fails to
clarify the date of the trip, leaving the timing of events uncertain.[19]

The process by which the leaders of NAA became interested in Dallas
instead of one of the other suggested locations remains unknown. It is
possible that the persistent recruitment efforts of the Dallas Chamber of
Commerce captured the attention of executives at NAA. Officials from the
other potential sites would certainly have worked to convince aviation firms
that their cities were the logical choice, but the Dallas Chamber was not about
to be outdone. It is reported that the organization sent out information in
March 1940 to "every possible prospect" about what the city had to offer.
The Chamber also invited firms to send representatives to their city for a
visit. NAA would certainly have been a prospect but the question remains:
what factors prompted NAA to narrow its selection to Dallas?[20]

One possible answer is that the top two executives at NAA both had
connections to Texas. James H. Kindelberger, president and general manager
of the company, had spent a brief period in Dallas during May 1918. At the

James Howard Kindelberger, President of North American Aviation.
North American Aviation. Copyright ©Boeing. Used by permission.

time Kindelberger was a member of the Army Air Service, and he was assigned
to Love Field to undergo preliminary flight training. It is unclear whether the
city made a favorable impression upon the young cadet, but Kindelberger at
the least would have had an awareness of the area. This knowledge of the
city might have caused him to listen to those individuals who advocated for
Dallas as an expansion site.[21]

The second executive was John L. Atwood, the vice-president and
assistant general manager of NAA. He had been born in Kentucky in
1904, but his family later moved to Plainview, Texas, where he went to
high school. Afterward, Atwood attended Wayland College, a small private
school in Plainview. He attended Hardin-Simmons College in Abilene and
the University of Texas, where he earned a Bachelor of Science in Civil

Engineering. Atwood later left Texas to work as an engineer for the Army at Wright Field in Dayton, Ohio. He eventually migrated to California, where in 1930 he took a position with the Douglas Aircraft Company. Here he came to the attention of Kindelberger, who was at that time the chief engineer at Douglas. While at Douglas the two men were part of the team that developed the DC-1 and DC-2 aircraft, which represented a new generation of passenger airliners. Kindelberger left Douglas in 1934 to be the president of General Aviation Manufacturing Company, which soon underwent a name change to become NAA. He brought Atwood along as his number two man, and together the pair worked to build the company into a major aviation firm.[22]

It is obvious that "Dutch" Kindelberger thought highly of "Lee" Atwood, given the fact that the elder engineer had recruited his younger colleague to join the top management at NAA. Knowing this, it seems reasonable to assume that Atwood's opinions would have carried weight with Kindelberger. The unanswered question is whether Atwood advocated for the selection of Dallas as the location for NAA's expansion. Considering Atwood's Texas roots, it is plausible to believe that he sought to bring jobs to the state by locating an aircraft factory in Dallas. Whether this was the case is uncertain; however, it is known that NAA responded to the March invitation from the Dallas Chamber of Commerce. In April, Robert A. Lambeth, the treasurer and comptroller of NAA, paid a visit to Dallas. At the same time, Consolidated continued to explore Dallas as well; company president Reuben Fleet visited the city in mid-May 1940, with two more trips thereafter. Thus, there were two firms with an interest in the city; Consolidated and NAA. The question was whether either company would follow through with their plans. What was about to come was a period of fast-paced activity. The catalyst for this frenzy was found in the person of President Roosevelt, who was about to kick over a proverbial anthill in the aviation community.[23]

As previously discussed, Roosevelt had desired a strengthening of American air power since the time of the Munich Crisis in the autumn of 1938. His efforts had borne fruit in the form of increased federal appropriations and a program to enlarge the Army Air Corps. Along with these actions had come a surge in America's industrial mobilization. Indeed, it was this buildup that had prompted both NAA and Consolidated to investigate the possibility of expanding operations into Texas. These initial efforts were soon accelerated by events in Europe. After the defeat of Poland in 1939, World War II entered a period of relative calm, as the participants waited out the winter and contemplated their next moves. As the spring of 1940 progressed, Hitler seized the initiative. Germany attacked both Norway and Denmark in April. The Danes succumbed after a few hours of feeble resistance, while the Norwegians fought for sixty-two days before capitulating. In May the Germans attacked the neutral nations of Belgium, Luxemburg, and the Netherlands. German units moved through the low countries and into France, overwhelming the defenders. French Prime Minister Paul Reynaud telephoned his British counterpart on 15 May with the news that "We have been defeated. We are beaten; we have lost the battle."[24]

On the other end of the telephone line with Reynaud was Winston Churchill, who had only become Prime Minister on 10 May 1940, just as the Battle of France was commencing. He was surprised by Reynaud's assertion, asking the French leader "Surely it can't have happened so soon?" Attempts by Churchill to provide hope were futile, and Reynaud repeated his lament; "We are defeated; we have lost the battle." This conversation occurred about 7:30 in the morning; by that evening Churchill had sent a communication to Roosevelt informing the president of the military situation. Churchill suggested various means by which the United States could offer support to Great Britain, with the most urgent request being "the loan of forty or fifty of your older destroyers." Churchill also stressed another immediate need, asking for "several hundred of the latest types of aircraft, of which you are now getting delivery." This communique was received in Washington just before 1:00 p.m. Given the critical situation, it must have been immediately delivered to the President.[25]

The rapid advance of the Germans through the low countries was certainly sobering, but Belgium and the Netherlands were not major military powers. The more startling developments were occurring in France. Even though the French high command had been at war since the previous September, they seemed ill-prepared as their large and well-equipped army struggled to mount an effective resistance.[26] As it happened, the Roosevelt administration was considering another increase in the aerial strength of the United States, beyond that which had already been authorized. The situation in Europe was on Roosevelt's mind as he prepared a presidential address regarding defense issues. He delivered it in person, addressing a joint session of Congress on 16 May 1940.

Roosevelt began by pointing out the speed at which modern warfare was operating. "Motorized armies," he observed, "can now sweep through enemy territories at the rate of two hundred miles per day." Parachuting troops threatened rear areas, and long-range aircraft could strike against a nation's industrial centers. With these developments in mind, he stated, "The clear fact is that the American people must recast their thinking about national protection." The Atlantic and Pacific oceans alone could no longer be relied upon to provide safety: it would take a stronger and more prepared American military, one that was "ready and available to meet any lightning offensive against our American interest." To upgrade the armed forces, Roosevelt wanted Congress to appropriate the funds necessary to procure essential new equipment, as well as to replace older items. This would require American production facilities to be "ready to turn out munitions and equipment at top speed."[27]

Many areas needed improvement, but throughout his speech Roosevelt emphasized the requirement for aviation assets. The President alluded to Germany when he observed that "one belligerent power" possessed more planes than its combined opponents. Furthermore, this unspecified country appeared to have a production capacity that surpassed that of its adversaries. Because of this threat, Roosevelt declared the United States most pressing aviation need was the establishment of "additional production capacity." He then called for previously unseen numbers. In November 1938 he had talked in terms of twenty thousand aircraft. Now Roosevelt wanted a program that would provide the military with fifty thousand planes. Furthermore, he wanted an industrial capacity capable of producing fifty thousand planes a year. Not only did Roosevelt want a lot of military planes in inventory but he also wanted to get there quickly and establish the means to replenish the inventory as needed. Having made his arguments, the President asked for "an immediate appropriation of 896,000,000 dollars," with most of the funds to be divided between the armed services. However, he requested that $100,000,000 be allotted to him so that he could provide funding for emergency defense situations. Roosevelt explicitly stated that he anticipated that these funds would be "used principally for the increase of production of airplanes, anti-aircraft guns, and the training of additional personnel for these weapons."[28]

Although Roosevelt covered a variety of issues during his address, his emphasis on airpower was notable, especially his call for fifty thousand aircraft. This number greatly exceeded all previous proposals; in fact, it surpassed the needs anticipated by military planners at that time. So how did the President arrive at that number? Historians are uncertain. One version of the story is offered by Eugene Wilson, who was an executive at United Aircraft. This entity controlled different aviation firms, including Pratt & Whitney, a major engine manufacturing company. United Aircraft also owned Vought and Sikorsky, as well as Hamilton Standard, the most important source of aircraft propellers. Wilson relates the story that Roosevelt mentioned a figure of twenty-five thousand planes to Lord Beaverbrook, director of aircraft production in Britain. Beaverbrook allegedly replied, "Why be a piker; 100,000 makes better headlines." Roosevelt responded by increasing his request to fifty thousand. Wilson was certainly well-connected in the aviation industry, but he offers no evidence to back up his story, which he describes as "gossip."[29]

A differing account is given by Secretary of State Cordell Hull. In his memoirs he recalls meeting with Roosevelt in May 1940, when the French were nearing collapse. Hull recalls that Roosevelt discussed his upcoming address to Congress in which he would be calling for increased military spending. Hull had received a cable on 13 May, in which Ambassador William Bullitt stressed the role of the German air force in the invasion of France. With this information in mind, Hull maintains that he "thereupon suggested to the President that he tell Congress that the United States should aim for a production of 50,000 planes a year." According to Hull, Roosevelt "was literally speechless, for 50,000 planes was ten times our current annual production."[30] It is certainly possible that Hull made such a suggestion, and historian Irving B. Holley opines that Hull's origin story is "no more bizarre than the Beaverbrook anecdote." Indeed, the two stories are not mutually exclusive: Roosevelt was probably getting advice from multiple angles at this time. Apparently, neither story can be substantiated by official documents, for Holley quotes Hull and Wilson rather than government sources. The fact that this official history cites anecdotal evidence suggests there is no definitive answer as to where the fifty thousand-plane figure originated.[31]

In the end, it was Roosevelt who made the actual request for the dual fifty thousand figures, calling for that number of aircraft to be built, with a matching capacity for annual production. These are separate but equally important goals. The President could have asked for a smaller procurement of aircraft while still requesting a larger reserve production capacity. But that still leaves unanswered the basic question of where the figure originated, since military leaders had never envisioned such a number. In reality, it appears that the fifty thousand number was determined by mostly political considerations. Historian Holley argues:

> The 50,000 figure finally used was neither an Army nor a Navy figure—it was a Presidential figure concocted by the President and his political associates. The President's big round number was a psychological target to lift sights and accustom planners in military and industrial circles alike to thinking big.[32]

Donald M. Nelson, the head of the War Production Board from 1942 through 1944, later wrote that Roosevelt "really saw the magnitude of the job ahead." Nelson maintained that military leaders and legislators alike "thought of the defense program as only a means for equipping ourselves to keep the enemy away from the shores of the United States." Nelson credited the President with having the foresight to envision a worldwide struggle against both Germany and Japan, and for taking the necessary measures.[33]

One thing was clear: Roosevelt wanted aircraft, and aircraft factories. The question of what kinds of aircraft was unanswered, as details of the program had yet to be determined. Also unknown was who would build these aircraft, and where it would be done. In Texas, the members of the Dallas Chamber of Commerce were working to make sure that their city would be part of the answer.

Chapter 4

Maneuvering for Position, 1940

Business leaders in Dallas had been working to attract the aviation industry to the city for many years by 1940. The purchase of Love Field by the city in 1927 likely prevented that facility from closure and allowed commercial aviation service to develop. This was followed by the establishment of Hensley Field in 1929, intended for use by the military. The Chamber of Commerce also created an aviation committee to promote the potential of the city to aircraft companies. However, efforts to attract an aircraft manufacturer to the area had been fruitless. The effects of the Great Depression presumably hindered their chances of success. But the outbreak of World War II stimulated the expansion of the American aviation industry. As 1940 progressed, it appeared that Dallas was finally in the position to acquire the long-desired prize. The city had been courting two different companies even before President Franklin D. Roosevelt's call for fifty thousand aircraft. Now, with the President advocating for a massive building program, the momentum was increasing. But could Dallas seal the deal, or would another location lure away the potential suitors?

On Tuesday, 18 June 1940, the directors of the Dallas Chamber of Commerce met in a special meeting to consider the situation. It had been just over four weeks since the President had issued his call to action, and mere days since representatives of Consolidated Aircraft had discussed their needs with members of the Dallas city government and the Chamber of Commerce. Attendees at the session included several prominent individuals, some of whose names would be familiar to later generations of Dallas residents, including John W. Carpenter, (president of Texas Power and Light), and realtor Henry S. Miller. Also, present by invitation were key city officials: Mayor Woodall Rogers, city manager James Aston, and Clyde Wallis, manager of the Industrial Department.[1]

During the meeting, Chamber president J. B. Adoue explained the details, stating that officials at Consolidated Aircraft had "virtually agreed" to select Dallas as the location of a factory. The company would require the use of a four-hundred-acre airport, a two-hundred-acre industrial site, and improvements to Mountain Creek Lake to make it useable for seaplanes. Adoue noted that other cities had already agreed to meet similar requirements, including Fort Worth, Houston, and New Orleans. J. Ben Critz, vice-president and general manager of the Chamber, briefed the attendees. He believed that Consolidated was ready to come to Dallas if the city would cooperate. He thought the necessary land could be acquired for about $100 per acre. It would also be necessary to clear obstacles from Mountain Creek Lake and dredge the lake to the depth required for seaplanes. This work would necessitate from $35,000 to $40,000. The costliest item would be airfield improvements, which were estimated to cost between $200,000 and $250,000. Up to 75% of this amount could be covered by the Works Projects Administration (WPA) as part of the defense expansion program. However, this expenditure might be avoided entirely if the Army was willing to grant permission for Consolidated to utilize Hensley Field.[2]

There were concerns that this opportunity might be lost without decisive action. One Chamber member in attendance was Nathan Adams, the president of the First National Bank in Dallas. He declared "Dallas is in danger of losing this important industry if the Chamber of Commerce leaves [the] decision up to the City Council." Adams suggested that the businessmen of Dallas should obtain the needed land and deed it to the city with the insistence that the city then obtain the needed assistance from the WPA to build the required improvements. Critz pointed out the potential benefits that were expected

for the city if Consolidated located its facility in Dallas. The company anticipated employing five thousand workers in jobs that would pay from four
to fourteen dollars per day. This would be a payroll of somewhere between
$750,000 and $1,000,000 a month. Given the ongoing effects of the Depression, it was an incredible opportunity to boost the local economy. With this in
mind the group called a recess until the following day, to examine the costs if
the Chamber followed Adam's suggestions.[3]

The directors reconvened the next day, this time with Robert L. Thornton
in attendance. Thornton was a former president of the Chamber of Commerce,
and president of the Mercantile Bank.[4] Mayor Rogers once again attended,
bringing five members of the city council, so they could understand the situation. Critz informed the group that he had been in telephone contact with
officials at Consolidated after the prior session, and that "the company had
told him that it must have Dallas' decision today." Whatever was going to be
done, the clock was running out. Critz recapped the financial costs that he had
explained the previous day for the benefit of the council members who had
not been present. The exact cost to the city government could not be determined, pending decisions on the airport situation, but estimates put the city's
share at approximately $130,000. Rogers, presumably hoping to share the
expense, suggested that the county government might be brought into the
deal as well. This was problematic to some attendees because Consolidated
needed an answer right away; involving other entities would only compli-
cate the situation. Eventually a proposal was made in which the city would
commit to participate in 50% of the cost up to $150,000, with the Chamber of
Commerce agreeing to cover the remaining costs of Consolidated's requirements. Mayor Rogers agreed that he and the councilmen present would advocate for this plan to the remaining members of the city council, providing it
passed legal scrutiny.[5]

Adams, who had been vocal about his lack of trust in the city to close
the deal, suggested that the Chamber of Commerce "should take no chances
on working out the proposal with the City, but that it should immediately
make the necessary commitments" to ensure that Consolidated would come
to Dallas. He insisted that it was one of the "biggest opportunities in the
history of the city," and that the Chamber could not afford any delays that

might put the project in jeopardy. He wanted the Chamber to commit to underwrite the cost of the operation, no matter what the city government decided. If the city government were to balk, Dallas businessmen would close the deal if Consolidated contributed a minimum of $3,500,000 toward the cost of the project.[6]

Adam's motion was unanimously approved by the Chamber directors. If Critz could obtain an assurance that Consolidated would locate a plant in Dallas, then the Chamber would "proceed at once to obtain options for the necessary land." The task would be undertaken by Miller, who stipulated that he would waive any realtor commissions involved in acquiring the acreage.[7] With that, the meeting adjourned. According to the minutes, eighteen members of the Chamber board of directors were present. These Dallas businessmen committed themselves to bringing an aviation factory to Dallas, either with or without financial cooperation from the city government. Two of these men, Adoue and Thornton, would later be elected as Mayors for Dallas. This is indicative of the powerful influence that the business community wielded in the city during the middle decades of the twentieth century.[8]

On Friday, 5 July 1940, the *Dallas Morning News* featured the story of the Chamber decision on its front page, with a banner headline declaring "$8,000,000 Plane Factory, Employing 5,000, to Be Built Here." The plant would be "the largest single plant in Texas." The announcement was made in San Diego, California, by David G. Fleet of Consolidated Aircraft, and in Dallas by the Chamber of Commerce. The exact site of the factory had yet to be determined, with the article listing White Rock Lake, Lake Dallas, and Mountain Creek Lake as possible sites because Consolidated needed a lake for seaplanes, as well as an airstrip for regular planes. But with Hensley Field being located next to Mountain Creek Lake, it offered that location a strong advantage, and the paper chose to illustrate that scenario by including an aerial photograph of the area. The article stipulated the plant would be erected for the Hall-Aluminum Aircraft Corporation, a small company which was named as a subcontractor for Consolidated. The exact reason for this switch is unclear, as the Chamber of Commerce consistently referred to negotiating with Consolidated, and it was Consolidated that made the announcement. Consolidated did absorb Hall-Aluminum a few months later, so it is likely that the declaration tied in with the eventual merger of the two firms.[9]

It is notable that the Chamber of Commerce took the lead in releasing the news in Dallas, rather than the city government. Further proof of the leading role played by the Chamber was the inclusion in the news article of a picture of Critz, whom the writer credited with playing a key role in "obtaining this important industry for Dallas." The city government was scarcely mentioned other than a comment that the mayor and council had pledged their cooperation in providing water and airport facilities. This nondescript commitment took on more substance the following day when the newspaper reported that the city had informally discussed an expenditure of up to $75,000 for the project.[10]

The announcement of the Hall-Aluminum factory coming to Dallas was certainly major news. And with the prospects of five thousand workers and a million-dollar-a-month payroll, it was surely viewed as good news. But, as events progressed, it turned out to be inaccurate news. The announced Hall-Aluminum facility was never built, and the reasons for this were due to decisions made within the federal government.

For some time, federal leaders had been contemplating how to finance rapid expansion of the aviation industry, a problem that had been lurking since the days of the Munich Crisis. Now, with the President's call for fifty thousand aircraft, the need to resolve this issue became paramount. Various concepts were explored by the National Defense Advisory Commission, including tax amortization schemes and a program allowing for an Emergency Plant Facilities (EPF) contract. The latter was "specifically designed to lure private capital into emergency construction work." As envisioned in this plan, manufacturers would build whatever facilities the government required. In return, the government would buy the facility over the course of sixty monthly payments, thus avoiding an immediate strain on War Department appropriations. The military entered into some EPF contracts for aviation facilities, but for a variety of reasons the concept was not totally successful. One troublesome aspect was that lenders feared that Congress might fail to appropriate the needed funds to reimburse them for the costs of the plants.

Because of this, "the conservative banking community insisted upon writing in safeguards to the point where EPF financing became cumbersome if not unworkable." By the end of the war, the majority of the contracts had been canceled or modified in some way.[11]

The more important source of federal government funds—and the one that eventually impacted Dallas—was the Reconstruction Finance Corporation (RFC). It had been established during Herbert Hoover's administration as a device to combat the Great Depression by offering low-cost loans to businesses. Historian Gerald T. White observes that the "RFC had independent borrowing authority and was not dependent upon Congress for its funds. During the last two weeks of May 1940, following the "50,000 planes" speech, there was a frequent utterance of the belief that the RFC could play a role in defense financing. Congress passed legislation allowing the RFC to lend money for defense efforts, with the measure being signed by President Roosevelt on 25 June 1940.[12]

Having agreed to finance industrial expansion, the national government took control of which facilities and companies received top priority. With both Consolidated and NAA eyeing Dallas, it became necessary to choose one company over the other. With the announcement that Hall-Aluminum (Consolidated) was building in Dallas, it would appear that the company held the upper hand. However, the leadership at NAA was not going to surrender without a fight, and company executives engaged in a concerted effort to sway the decision in their favor. On 11 July 1940, Vice-President Lee Atwood sent a letter to the Chief of the Army Air Corps, Henry H. Arnold, in which Atwood pointed out that NAA had been considering the Dallas location for many months. In fact, NAA president James H. Kindelberger had discussed the situation with Arnold around the middle of May. At that time, NAA was informed that the War Department was not actively engaged in the selection process, and the company was advised to wait for the impending appointment of a Defense Commission that would oversee these matters. This group, the Advisory Commission to the Council of National Defense (commonly referred to as the National Defense Advisory Commission (NDAC)), was appointed by Roosevelt on 28 May. During the first week of June Kindelberger discussed expansion plans with William S. Knudsen, president of General Motors and a member of the NDAC. At that time NAA had been advised to approach the RFC about financing, the details of which were being worked out in the legislation being discussed in Congress. NAA therefore sent a telegram on 2 July to Jesse Jones, the former chair of the RFC who still had a role in administering loans (he would become the Secretary of Commerce in September 1940).[13]

Focusing on the fact that NAA had been in contact with government officials since May 1940, Atwood wrote, "We feel as a result of this activity that we should be given preference in the allocation of this area for new facilities." Furthermore, he argued that the NAA advanced trainer was already a well-developed model of aircraft, which would allow NAA to "establish quantity production much sooner than any other company."[14] Atwood was not the only NAA executive lobbying to secure the Dallas location. On 20 July 1940, Kindelberger crafted a letter to the Secretary of War in which he requested that the War Department allow the company to use Hensley Field to support operations at the proposed factory. He followed up on 23 July with a detailed letter to Assistant Secretary of War Louis Johnson in which he articulated the steps that his company had already undertaken to increase the production of the AT-6 trainer. NAA had ordered the materials and tooling needed to construct more than six hundred additional trainers and had authorized the construction of additional floor space at the NAA plant in Inglewood, California. What was really needed, however, was an additional factory. This letter added that NAA had started examining possible locations in the fall of 1938, when the military first approached the aviation industry about expansion during the post-Munich period.[15]

The immediate problem, according to Kindelberger, was that construction of the proposed facility was delayed until federal arrangements for financing, such as methods of amortization and depreciation for tax purposes, were finalized. Rather than delay construction any longer, he wanted to work with the military to obtain funding, an idea he had gotten from a War Department spokesman:

Colonel Burns of the War Department office, in discussing this matter with a representative of this Company, stated that the War Department was favorably disposed toward the construction of a plant or plants along the lines outlined by the War Department two years ago wherein the plant would be built for the Government by the contractor and leased to the contractor by the Government.[16]

Kindelberger stipulated that NAA "would be very glad to cooperate with the War Department on the construction of a plant along such lines." He envisioned a facility of about eight hundred thousand square feet of actual manufacturing space, with another one hundred thousand square feet devoted to offices and other supporting functions. The cost estimate for the plant and necessary equipment was $5,500,000, for which the government would get a factory that could produce up to 250 AT-6 trainers per month. Kindelberger suggested another possible option for the facility: NAA would be responsible for the design and construction of the plant for the government, which in turn would lease the facility to the company for a nominal fee. The details could be worked out between the two parties, but the pressing concern was to get the process started. An agreement between the War Department and the company would allow the construction to begin earlier than possible under the proposed legislation, which was still being debated in Congress.[17]

The letter-writing campaign continued on 26 July 1940, when Leland R. Taylor of NAA wrote a detailed letter to Brigadier General George H. Brett, the chief of the Material Division for the Army Air Corps. In this letter, Taylor referenced the earlier letters from Atwood and Kindelberger and stated that he was the company representative who had held the discussion with Colonel Burns on 22 July. Taylor was writing to provide additional information requested by the Air Corps. The letter offered details about the proposed new plant: it would employ about ten thousand workers working on two shifts, with a capability of turning out three hundred trainers a month. This figure could be increased in the future if required. The plant would occupy three hundred acres of land, which cost approximately sixty thousand dollars and was currently under option by the Dallas Chamber of Commerce. Improvements to the land and construction of the buildings themselves would cost two million dollars, with tooling and machinery accounting for another three million dollars.[18]

The selected location had numerous advantages. Utility services for the factory were sufficient, with the main generating station for Dallas Power and Light located nearby and a fifteen-inch gas main adjacent to the site. Transportation of materials and parts could be provided by a rail line running across the street from the plant, and a nearby highway would also facilitate deliveries. Climatic conditions were typically favorable for operating aircraft, which would need to be flown out upon completion. Geographically, the Dallas factory was located seven hours flying time from NAA headquarters in California, which would allow NAA executives to shuttle between the two factories when needed. And finally, with a population of two million people within a one-hundred-mile radius of the plant, there was an adequate supply of workers. Having presented all this information, Taylor stated that NAA wanted to obtain funding from the RFC along the lines suggested in the earlier communication of 23 July. He closed his letter with the request that the proposed facility "be given prompt and favorable consideration."[19]

With extensive lobbying from NAA executives underway, the pressure on government and military officials for a decision mounted. A flurry of communications at the end of the month indicated that North American's arguments were finding favor. On 31 July, Assistant Secretary of War Robert P. Patterson crafted a memorandum to Knudsen of the NDAC. In this, Patterson referred to the NAA project in Dallas, recommending that it be cleared to proceed. At this time the source of funding was still undetermined, but there was $93,480,000 available from the War Department that had been designated for an expansion of aviation manufacturing capacity. Patterson broached the prospect that the plant might instead be funded by the RFC under the revised statutes, but in the meantime the project should be approved. He also mentioned that the Chief of the Air Corps, Arnold, had endorsed the building of the plant and the awarding of the Dallas location to NAA.[20]

That same day, 31 July 1940, Brigadier General Brett produced a memorandum as well. His note went to Colonel H. K Rutherford of the Ordnance Department, and it concerned the NAA project in Dallas. Brett reiterated arguments that by then must have been common knowledge. He also pointed out that the appropriate officials had cleared the use of Hensley Field for use by NAA. Brett observed that the NAA Board of Directors were meeting the following day, and that Kindelberger was urgently requesting that the decision be finalized on the location of the plant and the utilization of Hensley Field. The only possible conflict, wrote Brett, was in the plans by Consolidated to use the site for its proposed plant. However, that firm had explored Fort Worth as an option before announcing their interest in Dallas. The president of Consolidated, Reuben H. Fleet, helped to resolve the dilemma by declaring that either location would be satisfactory to him. Brett observed that Consolidated had yet to make a written application for the Dallas location. With such matters now being decided by federal government action, these factors undoubtedly strengthened the position of NAA. Brett therefore urged that the decision be expedited.[21]

Arnold as the chief of the Army Air Corps contributed to the communications as well. On the first day of August 1940 he sent a memorandum to the Assistant Secretary of War, in which he recommended "that the project and site location be approved." Arnold wanted NAA to be authorized to proceed with its construction of the plant, pending approval by the NDAC.[22]

As stated previously, this agency had been appointed by President Roosevelt on 28 May 1940. The enabling statute to form this group was still on the books from World War I, enabling the President to recreate it without waiting on Congressional action. The NDAC consisted of seven advisors, each of which concentrated on a specific area. In this case the key individual was Knudsen, who had been briefed by Kindelberger in June. Knudsen was the president of General Motors but had taken a leave to become a member of the NDAC, where he was tasked with overseeing industrial production. Historian Paul A. C. Koistinen offers this explanation of Knudsen's responsibilities:[23]

> Knudsen's Production Division had the task of facilitating the manufacture of munitions not normally produced by the economy. That meant gathering or estimating military requirements, establishing the productive capacity of the economy for specific goods, and determining whether new plant and equipment were necessary. In order to maintain the nation's industrial balance, the division had

to play a role in locating or expanding productive capacity. It also had to have some voice in negotiating contracts with manufacturers and ensuring that they delivered quality goods on time.[24]

Although these appear to be rather heavy duties, Knudsen's committee had limited authority. Koistinen observes that "with only advisory powers, NDAC was limited in what it could do and easily kept under presidential control." In fact, the NDAC eventually faded away in 1941 as more formal administrative structures were established. But during the initial phases of the defense build-up, Knudsen's approval was crucial. Legislation from Congress in late June 1940 authorized the Secretaries of War and Navy to "enter into contracts only upon the recommendation of the Council of National Defense, and the Advisory Commission thereof, and with the approval of the President." The Council of National Defense consisted of six members of Roosevelt's Cabinet, a group unlikely to challenge his ideas. In fact, the NDAC worked directly with Roosevelt. Since the funding for the NAA plant was envisioned as coming from the government, it was necessary for the NDAC to approve the project. Since Knudsen had jurisdiction over industrial matters, his opinion would effectively decide the issue, sending the issue to the President for final approval. On 1 August, Knudsen wrote Assistant Secretary of War Patterson, conveying his approval for NAA to construct a plant in Dallas.[25] Thus, it appears that the decision was close to being finalized on 1 August 1940. The NAA plant in Dallas would be the first project undertaken by the War Department as part of the aircraft expansion program. Brett, writing in a 21 August memo, placed the cost of the factory at $6,500,000. By 25 September the amount had been revised to $7,183,605, and Roosevelt approved this amount on 3 October 1940, by which time construction was already underway.[26]

Meanwhile, word of the planned facility was made public. On Saturday, 17 August 1940, the afternoon *Daily Times Herald* featured a front-page headline declaring "DALLAS GETS BIG PLANE FACTORY" in all capital letters. The news had arrived that morning via a telegram from Kindelberger to Critz. The newspaper stated that the plant would start construction in thirty days. The following day, the *Dallas Morning News* broke the news to its Sunday readers on the front page of the local section, announcing the impending construction of the North American factory next to Hensley Field. The plant would cost seven million dollars, and construction would be started within twenty days. The article proclaimed the facility would "be first of the new emergency plants to begin production," and capable of building three hundred planes a month within a year. Both newspapers suggested that trainers, fighters, and bombers might be built at the facility. In the meantime, it was reported that NAA had an option on an unspecified downtown building, which could be used to train personnel and start the manufacture of parts.[27]

Having previously announced the proposed construction of the Hall-Aluminum plant on 5 July 1940, it was necessary to clarify why NAA had displaced Hall from the chosen site. The reason, explained Critz, was because "North American demonstrated to the satisfaction of the government that it would be able to get into production far sooner than anyone else. So the government gave North American the right of way." There was still the possibility that Hall-Aluminum (now identified as a subsidiary of Consolidated) might locate a factory near Hensley Field at a future date, as the Chamber of Commerce held options for additional farmland that could be used for a second facility. Other companies were supposedly eyeing Dallas as well; on 20 August the *Morning News* reported that both Boeing and Lockheed were "studying sites in the Dallas vicinity." Thus, it appeared that the city might attract yet another aviation firm. As it happened, none of these other companies built a factory in Dallas, although Consolidated did operate a bomber plant in Fort Worth. The closest Dallas came to a second airplane factory was a facility built in neighboring Garland by the Southern Aircraft Corporation. This plant was originally intended to build biplane trainers, but eventually ended up producing aircraft subassemblies for larger firms.[28]

Describing how the decision was made for NAA to build in Dallas leaves unanswered the question of why the military favored NAA over Consolidated. Aside from NAA's arguments about who was first to express interest in Dallas, the reason is likely due to the types of planes for which the two firms had contracts. At that time Consolidated's main products consisted of flying boats for the Navy, most notably the PBY Catalina. The PBY was in demand for maritime patrols, and the Navy had ordered two hundred of the aircraft in December 1939. Orders for the Catalina had also come from the British and French. These planes were certainly needed, but that did not necessarily give Consolidated the highest priority. Consolidated was also developing a new bomber, the B-24, which would eventually become the most produced American combat aircraft of World War II. But the prototype B-24 had first flown only in December 1939. It was not a mature design in the summer of 1940 when the plant decision was made. There were legitimate concerns about putting newer designs into mass production before lessons could be learned from the war in Europe, as this could result in building large numbers of deficient aircraft. It would be better to develop production of unproven combat types a bit more slowly.[29]

In contrast to Consolidated, NAA was engaged in manufacturing the AT-6 trainer. This plane was in use by several nations, as well as the US Army and Navy. The aircraft was a mature design, and as Atwood pointed out in his July 1940 letter to Arnold, it would be possible to set up production in Dallas without major delays. And since trainers do not become obsolete as quickly as combat planes, there was little danger of buying large numbers of outdated aircraft. Probably the most important consideration was the anticipated enlargement of military aviation. If Roosevelt wanted fifty thousand airplanes, there would be a corresponding need for pilots. This meant that the military would need to mobilize a massive training program for aviators. During the war the United States would operate many different fighters, attack planes, bombers, and cargo aircraft. But whatever type of plane they eventually flew, the student pilots had to start in trainers. Given these factors, it made perfect sense to give trainers a high priority during the opening stages of the defense buildup. At the time the most significant products of NAA were trainers because the military needed large numbers of them. Now the company would build them in Dallas.

Chapter 5

Dallas

Saturday is a day normally devoted to shopping, household chores, or recreation. But 28 September 1940 was not a typical Saturday in Dallas. Instead, it was a day focused on business, industry, and the hovering specter of World War II. It was the day of the ceremonial groundbreaking for the North American plant, a significant step in the mobilization of the aviation industry. It marked the beginning of a new era for Dallas, as the city looked toward a significant role in manufacturing, a business category in which the city had not previously excelled.

In the weeks prior to the big event, the wheels of bureaucracy turned as final approvals were obtained from Washington. Uncertainty remained on how the plant would be financed. Initially the War Department was a likely source of funding, but legislation passed in June had created the possibility of loans through the Reconstruction Finance Corporation (RFC). The RFC eventually funded a significant number of wartime defense expansion projects, but in September 1940 the future remained murky. On 13 September the *Dallas Morning News* reported that financing for the plant was assured, but that it was still undetermined exactly what method would be used.[1]

Locally, the North American Aviation (NAA) facility was a big news story. After the first articles announcing the plant in August, area residents started driving to the outskirts of Dallas to see the location of the factory. As reported in the *Dallas Morning News*, viewing the site soon became "one of the major outdoor sports in these parts." The *News* interviewed G. Harry Turner, the Mayor of Grand Prairie, who encouraged visitors to see his community, which was just down the highway from the future plant. Grand Prairie, with a population of 1,581 in the 1940 census, stood to reap financial benefits from the presence of North American. Mayor Turner was in the real estate business, and the potential for growth presumably stimulated his realtor instincts.[2]

Meanwhile, the physical work needed to make the plant a reality started in late August. Earth-moving equipment began preparing for an extension to the Texas and Pacific Railroad. An existing rail line was located on the north side of Jefferson Avenue, which ran alongside the factory location. New tracks would be laid to allow building materials to be brought directly to the construction site. Later the tracks could be used to bring in industrial machinery to be used within the plant, as well as aircraft components once production started.[3] Other infrastructure projects were less visible. Southwestern Bell Telephone ordered equipment that would double the size of the Grand Prairie telephone exchange. Dallas Power and Light was already capable of handling the electrical needs of the plant, through its nearby Mountain Creek Lake generating station. The NAA officials anticipated that the plant would require a constant and reliable supply of 6,500 kVA, which the *Morning News* equated to the needs of a city of thirty thousand residents. This would consume approximately 5% of the utility's generating capacity.[4]

As the various pieces started to come together, plans were finalized for a celebratory groundbreaking event. Key executives from NAA would be present, including Ernest R. Breech, chairman of the Board of Directors. Breech also served as a vice president for General Motors Corporation, which held a financial interest in NAA, leading to his dual roles. Breech arrived at Love Field, reportedly at 12:31 a.m. on Friday, 27 September, when he was met by J. Ben Critz and taken to the Baker

Hotel in downtown Dallas. NAA president James H. Kindelberger was scheduled to fly into Fort Worth on the same day, along with his right-hand man Lee Atwood and other company executives. Kindelberger and his entourage arrived in Dallas at 9:30 a.m. Presumably they met with Breech before attending a 12:15 p.m. luncheon at the Baker Hotel, hosted by Nathen Adams of the First National Bank. Meet and greet activities continued later in the day, with Kindelberger visiting with members of the press at 5:30 p.m., followed by a radio interview. There was a strong sense of excitement about the plant, which was to be the largest industrial employer in Texas.[5]

Public ceremonies were scheduled to commence at 4:00 in the after-noon on 28 September 1940. The forecast for the day called for fair weather, with mid-day temperatures predicted in the seventies. It was good flying weather, and the event was accompanied by a flyover of Army aircraft manufactured by NAA. In front of an estimated crowd of over five thousand spectators, the executives of NAA joined with civic and business leaders from Dallas for the event. Chamber of Commerce President J. B. Adoue Jr. served as the master of ceremonies, which featured speeches by Kindelberger, Dallas County Commissioner Vernon Singleton, and Mayor Woodall Rogers. Breech served as the principal speaker, wrapping up the hour-long event. He spoke about the ability of "a democratic people to rise to the occasion" in the interest of the nation's security. He also heralded the quality of American aircraft, which he ranked among the "finest types" in the world. Breech encouraged the citizens of Dallas to consider the plant their own, but he also observed that the long-term future of the facility was uncertain.[6]

> There is no question in my mind that after the first big spurt of defense building, not only for this country but for export, there will be a period of let-down, whether that be in five years or less. For the time being, therefore, I urge that you look on this plant as an emergency plant. I urge that you far-seeing businessmen of Dallas, as represented by your chamber of commerce, be giving thought to how these conditions will be met when that let-down comes. Now is the time to begin planning for that period. We shall cooperate with you.[7]

In retrospect, Breech's words were prophetic. He clearly realized that the huge build-up in aviation manufacturing facilities would likely result in excess capacity once the needs of the military were met. There was, of course, the possibility that the Dallas facility would find postwar use. However, the use of government financing left the issue uncertain. If NAA were to stay in the factory after the war, the company might need to purchase the facility from the government. All this was undetermined at this time, as the specifics were still being worked out. Meanwhile construction would get underway, as time was critical. Mayor Rogers warned "Democracy is now on trial for its life. The mad bandits of Europe are on the march of death." Rogers pledged the city would contribute whatever "time, service, and talents" were needed to ensure success.[8]

As the ceremony concluded, Rogers presented Breech with a ceremonial silver shovel, which the NAA chairman used to break ground in the black prairie soil. Breech solemnly declared, "I hereby dedicate this plant to the preservation of the American principles of freedom and the principles of American peace." To add a touch of state pride, the Southern Methodist University band played "The Eyes of Texas are Upon You." The event ended with the national anthem and the raising of the American flag. With that, the crowd started dispersing, with the dignitaries scheduled to reconvene at 7:00 p.m. in the Crystal Ballroom of the Baker Hotel. There the Dallas Chamber of Commerce hosted a banquet, with NAA executives as their guests. This was open to the public, at a cost of five dollars per plate.[9]

This event appears to have been extremely cordial, as various business and civic leaders heaped praise and trinkets upon the visitors. Robert L. Thornton, the first speaker at the banquet, called for applause for the guests from NAA, which drew a standing ovation from the crowd. Thornton praised the attitude demonstrated by the company officials, declaring they were "really wonderful people and we love them." Fort Worth Mayor L. M. McCrary attended the event as well, putting aside the normal rivalry between the two cities by pledging cooperation "in these trying times." Mayor Rogers declared the NAA executives to be honorary citizens of Dallas, presenting each of them with a packet tied with a ribbon. This entitled them, he said, to the keys to the city, including "both the front and the back doors."[10]

The executives from NAA responded warmly to the kindness shown to them. Breech stated that the representatives of Dallas were the "most gracious hosts I've ever seen." Kindelberger echoed his accolades, declaring he would have a hard time expressing just how much he enjoyed visiting Dallas. Kindelberger mused that if he were to collapse in a dead faint, his hosts might begin to appreciate just how good of a time he was having. Turning to a more serious topic, he discussed the German aircraft industry, with which he was familiar due to his visits in the pre-war period. German aircraft factories, he observed, "were magnificently planned, executed, and utilized." The Germans, however, had copied their production methods from those found in the United States. The implication was that American manufacturing was perfectly capable of competing with the Germans. This idea was reinforced by NAA chief engineer Atwood, who declared that "What we are doing in this country is fully the equal if not far ahead of anything being done anywhere else in the world." If the attitudes of Kindelberger and Atwood were representative of their peers, it appears American aviation executives were confident they could meet the German challenge.[11]

In addition to good feelings, Kindelberger brought gifts as well. He presented Mayor Rogers with a scale model of the AT-6 trainer; the airplane that was to be manufactured in Dallas. The model was substantial in size, large enough that the two men could hold on to it simultaneously. Kindelberger promised that full-size versions of the aircraft would be flying over the city by the spring of 1941. There was an additional gift to be presented as well. Chamber president Adoue summoned a surprised Ben Critz to the front of the gathering, where Kindelberger expressed his appreciation for the efforts the chamber manager had made in bringing NAA to Dallas. Kindelberger presented a fine gold wristwatch to Critz, who apparently was overwhelmed by the gesture. Described as "almost speechless," Critz managed to squeeze out a response, stating, "This is just more than I expected. Thank you Dutch."[12]

With the niceties of ceremony behind them, the managers of NAA could focus on the task at hand: the construction of the aircraft factory. The architectural work was assigned to Allen & Kelley, an Indianapolis company. J. Floyd Allen was in Dallas during the first week of October 1940 to confer with Rollins & Forrest, a local engineering firm. Orders were signed for cement, and Allen was working on bids for the required steel, planning to award the contract on 12 October. Meanwhile, crews began clearing the land for construction.[13] The factory would be designed according to blackout standards, without windows that could allow the escape of light or shatter during aerial attack. With no windows, it was necessary to air condition the plant. The *Dallas Morning News* observed that this would allow for filtering the air in case of a potential gas attack, but a more practical benefit was the ability to keep the plant bearable during the oppressive summer heat.[14]

As the architects and builders finalized their plans, other personnel were preparing the labor force to operate the factory. To do so, NAA acquired a four-story building located at 3221 Commerce Street, slightly east of downtown Dallas. The structure had at one time had been used by Chevrolet but had most recently been offices for the Farm Security Administration. The building would serve as a local headquarters pending the completion of the actual factory near Hensley Field. The interim headquarters also doubled as a teaching facility, where newly hired workers were trained in the manufacturing of parts. When describing the facility Kindelberger explained that the parts would be fabricated primarily for educational purposes, and that he anticipated most of them would be destined for the scrap heap. The plan was to start hiring workers around 15 October 1940, with one thousand individuals undergoing training at the Commerce Street facility. These workers were to serve as the nucleus of the labor force once the main manufacturing plant started operations. It was expected that twelve thousand employees would eventually be needed when the factory reached peak production.[15]

Regarding the training facility, Kindelberger issued a public notice that all hiring would be done by NAA. This was presumably in response to a series of advertisements that had been appearing in the newspaper offering training in aviation manufacturing. The NAA president stipulated that "No agency or school is authorized to serve as an agent of this firm in any way in arranging for employment of personnel." He added that the company intended to only bring in a few key managers from California, with the rest of the workforce being recruited locally. This would have surely been welcome news to a community dealing with the Great Depression.[16]

Work on converting the Commerce Street building proceeded rapidly under the supervision of Walter C. Smeton, an NAA executive from the firm's headquarters in Inglewood, California. Equipment started to arrive on Monday, 21 October 1940. That same day Charles E. Kindelberger arrived in Dallas as well. Charles, sometimes referred to as Ed, was the younger brother of the NAA president and shared the title of Assistant Plant Superintendent with Smeton. Scheduled to arrive near the end of the month was E. J. Rivers, who was managing the training plant. The actual training of workers was due to begin at the beginning of November 1940.[17]

Meanwhile, as preparations gained momentum, the federal government was hammering out financial arrangements to pay for the construction of the factory. A variety of proposals had emerged on how to fund the plant during the weeks immediately after President Roosevelt's call for fifty thousand planes. Records indicate that initially the money was scheduled to come from the War Department, but eventually the RFC was granted the authority to participate in the national defense buildup. To facilitate this, the RFC established four subsidiaries, each with a specific focus. These were the Rubber Reserve Company, the Metal Reserve Corporation, the Defense Supplies Corporation, and the Defense Plant Corporation. The DPC was tasked with building facilities for the defense program.[18]

The DPC appears to have made a preliminary decision regarding NAA on 21 October 1940, when the DPC authorized a lease agreement between the two entities. More formal action occurred on the afternoon of 14 November, during a meeting of the DPC directors held in Washington. At that time they adopted a resolution outlining the specific details of the arrangement. This document acknowledged a number of facts: that the federal government had contracted with NAA to produce 1,880 advanced training planes; that to produce these aircraft the War Department had advised establishing a manufacturing facility in Dallas, to consist of 1,022,400 square feet; that the Advisory Commission to the Council of National Defense had approved the project as necessary; and that NAA had acquired or obtained options on one hundred and fifty acres of land for the plant site. Furthermore, the negotiated price for the training aircraft included no charges to cover the construction of the needed plant facilities.[19]

Therefore, the DPC and NAA entered into a complex agreement regarding the Dallas facility. The document spanned thirteen pages and contained twenty-six clauses. A detailed examination of the lease is outside the scope of this narrative, but certain key elements are worth considering. First, NAA would complete the acquisition of the land needed for the plant, the title to which would then be transferred to the DPC. NAA would also be responsible for the design and construction of the Dallas factory, and for acquiring the equipment and machinery needed to operate it. The firm would be required to provide the DPC with "complete plans, designs, specifications, and schedules for the construction and the equipment of the plant." In return, the DPC would then "advance the funds necessary for carrying out the construction program." The DPC would also pay for major equipment, which would be considered property of the DPC and marked accordingly. The initial authorization specified DPC expenditures would not exceed $7,700,000.[20]

In sum, the federal government assigned NAA the task of designing and constructing the aircraft plant at Dallas, providing the expenditures were first cleared through the DPC. This was a logical approach, as it was NAA who knew how to build the facility and what would be required to make it operational. In return for financing the plant, ownership of it would be vested in the DPC. NAA would lease the plant from the government for one dollar per year. The lease document stipulated what obligations NAA had for maintaining the plant and the provisions by which either party could terminate the agreement. The initial lease was slated to expire on 30 April 1946, unless other developments required it to be modified. The agreement also specified different scenarios by which the plant could be transferred or sold at the end of the defense emergency, including an option by which NAA could buy the Dallas facility from the DPC.[21]

The financing for the NAA Dallas facility thus reflects a complicated series of stages that seem to defy easy characterization. War Department records show that the construction of the plant had been approved prior to the creation of the DPC, although there was certainly an awareness that new legislation had authorized the RFC to become involved in the defense program. Pending resolution of this issue, it appears that the War Department was prepared to cover the cost through its own appropriations. This conclusion is supported by the previously referenced memorandum of 31 July 1940 in which Assistant Secretary of War Robert Patterson referred to the Dallas project as having been reviewed and approved by the necessary officials. The unanswered question, according to Patterson, was whether financing would be accomplished through RFC loans, War Department appropriations, or some other method. Air Chief Henry H. Arnold, writing on 1 August 1940, apparently had more exact information, specifically stating that the plant would be financed through the RFC. This was still three weeks before the establishment of the DPC. The NAA factory was thus announced as the first project in the defense program even before the financial details had been firmly decided.[22]

A War Department memo, dated 2 January 1941, offers insights into the chain of events. The document refers to an arrangement having been reached between NAA and the DPC for funding the Dallas facility. The memo states that the War Department had originally designated $7,183,605 for the project. Since that time, with the DPC becoming involved, an agreement had been reached where the War Department would provide $3,101,000 for the venture. This left the Air Corps with $4,082,605 of the original appropriation, and the January memorandum requests that those funds be reallocated to other facilities in the expansion program. Thus, it seems apparent that the War Department was originally intending to fund the plant entirely if necessary. However, the establishment of the DPC left that entity with the primary responsibility for the factory by bankrolling three-fifths of the costs. With that established, the plant became the property of the DPC, as stipulated in the lease agreement. With the approval of the lease, the final obstacle was overcome, and construction accelerated on the facility, with the project referred to as "Plancor 25," in DPC records.[23]

An internal document from NAA states that the final approval of the DPC lease allowed the project to begin to move "at top speed." A general contractor for the plant was announced on 1 November 1940, with the job awarded to James Stewart & Company of New York City and work scheduled to begin on 13 November. Concrete was poured before the end of the month, and upright steel started being put into place on 2 December. NAA personnel began to move into the incomplete factory by 20 January of the new year.[24] Their primary task was to prepare it for production. A staggering amount of machinery and tools were needed to transform the empty building into an operational unit. As mentioned, the lease stipulated that NAA had to supply the DPC with the plans, construction schedules, and equipment inventories related to Plancor 25. Because of this, it is possible to consult DPC archival records to obtain a remarkably detailed representation of what went into the NAA plant at Dallas. These records are subject to fluctuation, as equipment lists were modified, or construction overruns occurred. However, a preliminary itemization dated 4 April 1941 offers insights into the initial costs of the factory in the days immediately before it became operational. A twenty-page document describes the situation in detail, beginning with the acquisition of land valued at $65,000. As to the plant, the summary lists six buildings: an office, the main factory, a foundry, a drop hammer building, a paint storage building, and a hangar for storing finished aircraft. These various structures were listed at an estimated cost of $1,788,150.[25]

Costing almost as much as the actual factory buildings were the many improvements around them. There were various utilities and environmental controls that were required to make the plant function: lines for air and gas for $16,000; sprinklers and hydrants at $193,900; electrical lines at $572,378; assorted plumbing at $242,300; heating and air conditioning at $364,750; and fluorescent lighting for the windowless plant at $273,185. All these expenditures accounted for $1,662,513. Also itemized were improvements to the area surrounding the factory, including the railroad spur line, parking lots, roads, and fencing, totaling $143,950. Another $130,000 covered architect fees, accounting, travel, and various other incidental expenses. Thus, the total cost for the actual factory buildings was tabulated at $3,724,613.[26]

The federal government, and NAA, got an impressive facility for their money. The main factory building was approximately 950 by 900 linear feet and ran parallel to Jefferson Avenue oriented on an east-to-west axis.

Finished airplanes would leave through a massive door measuring 150 feet wide and 25 feet tall, located on the eastern side of the building. Further east was the hangar building, which could hold finished aircraft. Concrete taxiways connected the plant to nearby Hensley Field, allowing for planes to be flown for testing and delivery.[27]

These buildings, impressive as they might sound, were empty shells without the equipment that would be required to manufacture aircraft. Almost three million dollars in equipment went into the factory. The collection was immense, consisting of dozens of lathes, scores of welders, hundreds of drill presses, and a variety of bench tools. Other machinery was more massive, including two hydraulic presses rated at three thousand tons, costing $150,000, and eight drop hammers costing a total of $82,522.25. Even the smallest hand tools were specified: the plant needed five grease guns, thirty jacks, and 2,165 electric drills, with the drills alone costing $75,775. Some items were not industrial tools, such as nineteen Singer sewing machines, fifteen vacuum cleaners, and an unspecified amount of first aid equipment worth $4,500. Fire extinguishers alone cost $15,000, with office equipment and furniture requiring another $60,000. The factory had its own tow vehicle for use on the flight line, and four Chevrolet trucks valued at $3,500.[28]

All told, the estimated start-up cost for NAA's Dallas facility was officially tabulated at $7,961,349. Later additions enlarged the factory, increasing the price of the entire endeavor. There was a human cost as well, for at least two workers were killed during the construction of the plant. Rainy weather also caused delays, forcing crews to work overtime to make up lost time. But as 1940 drew to a close, the initial stages of the project were reaching completion, with concrete foundations and steel frameworks taking shape on the Texas soil. By the end of December, approximately 50% of the steelwork had been completed on the main building as the factory started to rise from what had been cotton fields.[29]

Chapter 6

Housing, 1941–42

As 1941 began, construction crews labored to complete the aircraft factory at Dallas. Meanwhile, local leaders and businessmen turned their attention toward an impending need: housing the thousands of people who would be employed by North American Aviation (NAA). Those who already resided in Dallas would have accommodations, but newcomers would be in search of habitation. The facility was on the outskirts of Dallas, and Jefferson Avenue provided direct access into the Oak Cliff neighborhood. Developers responded by planning new houses in that area, with an estimated five hundred homes scheduled to begin construction in January 1941. This was just the beginning, and assistant building inspector A. Fred Robbins predicted that "the section west of the Trinity [River] will experience the greatest home-building activity in its history during 1941." Robbins estimated that up to two thousand new homes would be built during the year, with the majority constructed in Oak Cliff.[1]

While this new construction in Dallas would be useful, there was still the issue of transportation. Jefferson Avenue was limited as to how much traffic could be carried quickly and safely. Bus service to the plant could ease congestion, but it would be advantageous to have housing closer to the plant. This could provide for the influx of newly arriving workers and reduce the numbers of commuter vehicles. One answer was to look west-ward, to the nearby town of Grand Prairie. This small community was liter-ally across the highway from the factory and stood to benefit from the large number of employees who would soon be part of the NAA operation. Payroll dollars from the plant would surely spread out into the city through stores, service stations, and restaurants. The real prize, however, might be found in the creation of housing in the area surrounding the NAA plant. This led to numerous efforts within the city, as investors and officials evaluated different approaches toward the situation.

There was an opportunity for profit here, and private developers set about the task of providing housing. One example can be found in the Fairview neighborhood, which originally lay just to the east of Grand Prairie prior to being annexed into that town. This neighborhood serves as a representative sample of the kind of growth that occurred near the North American plant. It seems reasonable to assume that investors recognized the possibility of housing developments as soon as construction of the NAA aircraft factory was announced. In the case of Fairview, two key investors were Dallas City Councilman M. M. Straus and Gus Cook, a vice-president at Oak Cliff Bank and Trust. The two men acquired a thirty-two-acre tract to be used for the project, which was announced in the *Dallas Morning News* on 11 April 1941, just days after the NAA plant was completed. The development was budgeted at $500,000 dollars and was intended to provide 162 residences. Utilities were to be supplied by the community of Grand Prairie.[2]

The Fairview Addition, which still exists today, is located just north of Main Street and south of the current Interstate Highway 30. The neighbor-hood is roughly defined as being between Fifteenth Street on the west and Seventeenth Street on the east, with the numbered streets running on a north-to-south orientation. The east-to-west streets are named after trees, includ-ing Pine Street, in the middle of the development. A house located on Pine Street is approximately one mile from the aircraft factory. This allowed an easy commute by car or foot. The houses were of the frame variety, small by today's standards at around one thousand square feet, some with just two bedrooms and one bath. But in the Great Depression they must have seemed almost palatial. Prices were planned to range from $2,500 to $4,000, with the average price point anticipated to be $3,000. Furthermore, the financing of the homes was attractive, due to Federal Housing Administration (FHA) policies designed to enhance residential opportunities in defense areas. Potential residents could buy a house on an installment plan with no down payment, meaning that recently hired NAA employees would be able to move in based on the potential of their newly acquired paychecks. However, this would be slightly in the future, as it would take time to prepare the land and install roads and utilities.[3]

As it developed, the dwellings were constructed by a variety of builders rather than a single firm. On 21 September 1941, the *Dallas Morning News* reported that no fewer than four different contractors were at work in the Fairview Addition. This practice apparently continued into the new year, as suggested by a classified advertisement that appeared on 18 January 1942. This was addressed to builders, announcing that ninety "Title VI FHA defense housing lots" were available in the "Fairview Addition No. 2," with utilities, curbs, and improvements already installed. These lots were specified as being within five blocks of the NAA plant. The advertisement mentioned that one hundred homes had been completed in the previous sixty days, indicating that construction was well underway on the project. Another advertisement that same day targeted potential homeowners, offering "twenty brand-new two-bedroom residences," for rent or sale, with special FHA terms available to NAA employees. Similar announcements appeared throughout the early half of 1942, later with the stipulation that homes could be financed with a down payment of just fifty dollars. The units in Fairview Addition No. 2 seem to have been mostly purchased by the beginning of summer, when an advertisement announced that there were only three two-bedroom homes still available.[4]

The sort of growth demonstrated by the Fairview neighborhood was underway in other areas around the NAA factory. To the west was the Robin Hood Park development, located just south of E. Grand Prairie Rd. and nestled between 10th Street to the west and 14th Street to the east. An announcement appeared in the *Dallas Morning News* in September 1941, which reported that 170 homes were planned on the seventy-acre parcel. By February 1942 there were five model homes available for inspection, with fifty units to be completed within three weeks. By now the anticipated number of houses had increased to 319, as several developers worked to meet the housing needs of the expanding NAA workforce. Built on lots that averaged 59 by 169 feet, the Robin Hood Park structures were of frame construction on concrete slabs, utilizing mass production methods such as precut lumber. The floorplans had two bedrooms, a living room, kitchen and dinette, and one bathroom. There was also a garage, which could be either attached or detached, depending on the specific design. Developer Roscoe Dewitt told the *News* that a unique feature of the homes was that the bedrooms had outside entrances, which would allow homeowners to rent out a room if they wanted to. A large advertisement appeared in the Sunday newspaper on 8 February, promising "handsome and convenient homes just west of the North American Aviation plant," allowing employees to walk to work. Advertisements in March announced the homes were under construction and at the end of June the Sunday newspaper was advertising the opening of "The most beautiful, the best planned and best-built group of homes for defense workers in America." Potential buyers could tour a demonstration house furnished by the Sanger Brothers department store. The response was apparently strong, with thirty-four homes sold within nine days of the opening.[5]

If the Fairview Addition and Robin Hood Park developments are to be considered as representative samples of commercial real estate offerings, then it is obvious that private investors were eager to provide housing for the burgeoning NAA workforce. It is also clear that many of these offerings were not available until 1942, almost a year after the opening of the NAA factory. The need for additional housing would be present as soon as the plant became operational. A streamlined process was needed to fill this need, and the solution was found in an interesting and innovative project known as Avion Village.

While private investors labored to arrange home construction, in the early months of 1941 another entity was on the move: the federal government. February witnessed the arrival of field agents from the Public Buildings Administration (PBA). This was under the control of the Federal Works Agency (FWA), an umbrella organization that oversaw various programs, including the Works Projects Administration (WPA). The field agents included Irving Porter, who had formerly been a government architect in Dallas, giving him knowledge of the metropolitan area. The PBA was examining potential locations for a government-built housing project to serve the NAA plant. Two different municipalities were lobbying to become the site of the proposed development. The Fort Worth Chamber of Commerce wanted the federal housing project to be in Arlington, which was several miles west of the NAA facility. This location was also supported by Congressman Frederick "Fritz" Lanham, who represented the Twelfth Congressional District, which included Tarrant County. Representative Lanham, the son of former Texas Governor Samuel W. T. Lanham, was the chairman of the House committee on public buildings and had been instrumental in the passage of the National Defense Housing Act in October 1940. As originally proposed, this legislation provided $150,000,000 to "expedite the provision of housing in connection with the national defense program." Under this act the government eventually provided almost one million housing units for families of military personnel, civilian employees of the military, and defense contractors. Having pushed this legislation through Congress, Lanham wanted some of the funds spent in his district.[6]

One argument for Arlington as a site was that the housing could eventually be used by the North Texas Agricultural College (now University of Texas—Arlington) after the defense emergency had passed. If the NAA factory closed at some future time, the government could be left with unneeded housing near that facility, whereas the Arlington site offered a possible alternative use for the structures. Therefore, Fort Worth leaders believed that the Arlington location was the best choice. However, the long-standing rivalry between Fort Worth and Dallas cannot be discounted when considering this issue, and both cities certainly wanted the influx of federal spending that would come with such a development.[7]

Other potential locations were within Dallas County, where the NAA plant was located. One promising site being contemplated was within two miles of the aircraft factory. This was certainly valuable if only the immediate defense needs were taken into consideration. Having workers living within walking distance of the plant could reduce automotive traffic in the area, reducing congestion on the roads during shift change. Grand Prairie Mayor G. H. Turner traveled to Washington to persuade federal officials that the housing should be placed on this property, which was near the southern limits of his city.[8]

The choice was eventually made in favor of the Grand Prairie location, which was officially announced on the first day of March. Newspaper reports indicate that the final decision was in the hands of Lawrence Westbrook, a Texas native with a long career in state politics. Often referred to as "Colonel," due to his status as a reserve officer, Westbrook had served as General Manager of the Waco Chamber of Commerce during the 1920s. He resigned that position in 1928 to campaign for a seat in the Texas Legislature to represent McLennan County. He won this seat and served two terms, during which he chaired the House Committee on Agriculture. After leaving the legislature, Westbrook became the director of the Texas Rehabilitation and Relief Commission, with the responsibility of representing Texas in matters related to the Reconstruction Finance Corporation. The creation of the New Deal gave him additional duties as the state relief director for Civil Works Administration projects. His work in Texas brought Westbrook to the attention of Harry L. Hopkins, who named the Colonel to a position in the WPA. The two men became more than just colleagues, with Hopkins serving as best man for Westbrook's wedding in March 1937. It has been suggested that Westbrook was a friend of Congressman Sam Rayburn, a relationship that was probably beneficial to Westbrook's success.[9]

Westbrook had previously been involved in the construction of Woodlake, an experimental community in Texas constructed with funds from the Federal Emergency Relief Administration. During this project he became associated with David R. Williams, a Texas architect with Dallas connections. Williams designed many high-end homes, some of which still survive in University Park. He also served as the chief architect of the National Youth Administration (NYA), giving him a connection to the New Deal as well. Westbrook and Williams worked together on several projects before becoming involved in defense housing for Dallas. Williams was joined by two other architects: Roscoe P. Dewitt and Richard J. Neutra. Together the three men would be responsible for the design of what was eventually christened Avion Village, utilizing the French word for airplane.[10]

The Avion project was orchestrated by Westbrook under the auspices of the Mutual Ownership Defense Housing Division, which was a part of the FWA. Westbrook envisioned a planned community initially financed by the federal government, with the residents buying into the housing as part of a cooperative. Historian Kristin M. Szylvian provides a summary of the concept:

> Under terms of this Plan, residents formed a non-profit corporation called a mutual home ownership association. Each family purchased equal shares of stock in the association, in exchange for which they received a life-long lease to their dwelling unit, called a perpetual occupancy agreement.[11]

Under the plan, the ownership association leased the development from the FWA, with an option to purchase the property at a future date. One advantage to the residents was that it simplified any potential moves. If a worker needed to relocate, there was no need to deal with selling a home. Instead, the association would maintain ownership and a new family could be brought into the association. It was an unusual and unorthodox solution to the problem of providing quality housing on short notice to a potentially nomadic group of workers.

While the ownership model was innovative, the actual design characteristics of Avion Village were also outside the norm. It was more than just a housing development, for the project was designed to provide a sense of community. The boundaries of the neighborhood formed a teardrop-shaped area, with an open greenbelt park in the middle. The total number of one-story dwellings numbered 216, with a mixture of single units and duplexes. An additional 84 residences were built as apartments, located in 21 buildings that formed the western edge of the community, intended to serve as a buffer between the main housing and a busy street known today as Beltline Road. Houses were arranged so that they faced toward green areas, with automotive access coming into the rear of the homes. Footpaths through the green areas allowed residents to avoid crossing roads, a legitimate concern with children residing in the complex. A community center was located on the southern end of the property, providing room for administrative offices as well as recreational facilities and a nursery. Residents could keep informed of activities by way of a neighborhood newspaper known as *The Prop Wash*. Through such measures the designers of Avion Village sought to encourage a collective spirit among the residents, creating a community where none had previously existed. The goal, according to Westbrook, was to encourage "the development of those neighborly relationships which are characteristic of village and small town life."[12]

All these ideas seem somewhat utopian in concept, which is not necessarily bad. But the demand for housing was a pressing one, and time was critical. Construction of the buildings was contracted to Henry C. Beck, a Dallas builder who served as president of the Central Contracting Company, described as "one of the largest builders of government projects in the South." The contract was announced on 15 March 1941 by John Carmody, the administrator for the FWA, which oversaw the project. Beck's contract was awarded on a cost-plus fixed fee basis for $712,500, with Beck's fee slated to be $37,000. Work on the site began on 19 March, less than a month before the NAA plant was to become operational. Final drawings were approved on April 9, with the first eight foundation slabs poured that same day. A force of over twelve hundred workers was eventually assigned to the task, starting ten new units each day. The total cost of the housing project was reported to be one million dollars, which breaks down to just under $3,400 per dwelling.[13]

The announced budget apparently did not include the needed infrastructure, as reports indicate that the city of Grand Prairie applied for $319,117 in WPA funding to pay for the construction of streets, as well as water and sewage service for the seventy-five-acre development. The necessary paperwork was submitted at 4:00 in the afternoon on Thursday, 20 March 1941, the day after work commenced on the development site. The WPA district manager Gus W. Thomasson quickly sought approval of his superiors headquartered in San Antonio, with a request to have the plans air-mailed to Washington by Friday afternoon. The approval process was expedited because the project was related to national defense.[14]

While the government wheels turned at the WPA, Central Contracting was turning earth and laying foundations. The community center was largely finished by 31 March 1941, allowing the builders to move their construction office into that structure. The first residences built were the two-story apartments that formed the western boundary of the property. Meanwhile, contracts were bid for the materials needed for the houses that would compose most of the neighborhood.[15] To facilitate rapid construction, the designers of Avion Village embraced the use of prefabrication techniques. Much of the work was done on site, in three large circus tents which were erected in the open area slated to serve as the central park within the community. Walls and roof sections were produced within the tents before being moved on rails to the construction area. Work on the prefabricated sections began on 21 April 1941, with the goal of finishing the three-hundred-unit development by the early part of June.[16]

The efficiency of these methods was demonstrated by a publicity stunt held on Friday, 16 May 1941, when opposing teams competed to build a house in the fastest time. Construction workers were divided into two fifty-man groups, a "white" team and a "blue" team, with the men wearing color-coded uniforms and numbers on their backs like athletes. The sports motif also included a zebra-striped referee, who fired a revolver into the air to start the competition. Building upon previously laid concrete foundations, the two teams rushed to erect the frames of the homes, install plumbing and wiring, and paint the walls before moving in furniture to stage the house for occupancy. A pretend "family" awaited, ready to portray residents in the home. The goal of the contest was to produce a finished house with "a girl in the bathtub in less than an hour." The entire process was captured in photographs for inclusion in *Life* magazine, which documented the contest in a three-page spread featuring a dozen illustrations. The article noted that "Colored and white workmen worked together on both teams," co-operating "smoothly and efficiently." The result was a win by Jim Bruno's white team, which completed the assignment in 57 minutes and 58 seconds. Charlie Nelson's blue group lagged by twenty minutes, meaning their house was assembled in under ninety minutes. The contest attracted a crowd of spectators, including the mayors of both Dallas and Grand Prairie. Also on hand was Westbrook, who was photographed smiling as he approvingly observed model Veneta Perry, the promised girl in a bathtub. Strategically placed bath bubbles hide what was presumably a swimsuit, and Westbrook's smile is theoretically due to his satisfaction with the building process. This conclusion is admittedly speculative, but there is no doubt that the contractor demonstrated the speed by which the prefabricated homes could be erected.[17]

Ultimately, the desired completion date for Avion Village was not met. The weather was one problem; rainy days in May and June hampered construction. Two inches fell on the Dallas area on Friday, 6 June 1941, and by Sunday the Trinity River crested at thirty-three feet, four feet over the flood stage. High waters blocked Jefferson Avenue, forcing traffic to the NAA plant to divert through Grand Prairie and turning Avion Village into "a huge mud puddle" that slowed activities.[18] Another delay came from labor unrest. Union workers for Central Contracting went on strike, in protest of the use of WPA workers on the project. Here the union leaders may have made a tactical error. Given the general friendliness of the Roosevelt administration toward labor, the workers might have assumed their actions would resolve their complaints. What happened instead was that Central Contracting notified the government they would be unable to complete the work due to "circumstances beyond their control." This resulted in Westbrook flying to Dallas, where he terminated the contract with Central and signed a new agreement with Ballard Burgher & Company. The new contractor declared that the project would become an open shop, with the company utilizing its own nonunion crews. Union laborers would be welcome as well, if they wished to participate, and union pay scales would be maintained. Company president Ballard Burgher stated, "I do not wish to stir up a labor controversy, but I have been awarded a contract and I intend to carry it through."[19]

As for Westbrook, he went on record as saying that he had "no quarrel with organized labor in any fashion." The government, he stipulated, had no interest other than completing the project, which by this point was "90 to 95 per cent finished." Labor union leaders apparently had no public comment on the situation. They possibly overplayed their hand, failing to realize that the national defense attributes of the project would override the concerns of organized labor, especially with the project so close to completion. One possible explanation is that the strike might have been intended to influence policies at a second defense housing project, which was just starting at the beginning of July. Like Avion Village, this development was overseen by the FWA, with Central Contracting serving as the builder. It is conceivable that Westbrook sought to send a strong notice to labor unions that defense housing was a national priority, an essential part of the industrial mobilization then underway.[20]

Regarding Avion Village, with a new contractor on hand the project moved toward completion. Burgher had eighty men on the job by 1 August 1941, working hard to finish the project under signs urging "Let's Get the Job Done!" Meanwhile, female workers from the NYA posed for pictures in a furnished unit, depicting what life would be for future residents. Formal dedication ceremonies took place on Saturday, 16 August, featuring the usual speeches and obligatory barbeque dinner. The highlight of the evening was a marriage ceremony uniting Marjorie M. Sullivan with Floyd L. Jackson, a milling machine operator at NAA. The ceremony was performed on the grounds at Avion Village, with the mayor of Grand Prairie, G. H. Turner, giving away the bride. Sam Roberts, the head of the housing committee at NAA, served as best man. With the ceremony concluded, the newlywed couple moved into their new three-room apartment on Waco Place. The dinner, wedding cake, and many of the gifts were paid for through the courtesy of business interests in Grand Prairie. On a more serious note, G. Gresham Griggs represented the national government as a principal speaker. Griggs opined that the twelve defense housing projects being constructed nationwide were "just as important as housing of machinery for defense."[21]

At this point Avion Village was open for business, although scattered improvements continued as the WPA put finishing touches on the development. The last house was officially declared completed on 23 September 1941, when project manager Ray Holder and Mayor Turner hung an "O.K. House Completed" sign on the final unit. "We didn't have any speaking," Holder told the *Dallas Morning News*, "We just shook hands and congratulated one another." By this time there were families living in the complex. With more than three thousand employees then at NAA, it was certain that the three hundred residences would be filled. The personnel department at

NAA worked to help workers with the process, and the plant newspaper reported on 18 September that 195 families had been approved as residents, of which 92 had already moved into their new homes.[22]

The growing workforce meant more housing would be required. The debate was over how this housing would be provided. Private developers were working to construct dwellings in the proximity of the NAA facility, as shown by the Fairview Addition. These efforts continued, and by 27 May 1941 there were five different projects either underway or in the planning stages, with the potential to create 912 dwellings. This was apart from the government-funded units under construction at Avion Village, as well as a similar government project that was working its way toward approval.[23]

It was this second project that started to create noticeable complaints from the private sector. The announcement of Avion Village does not appear to have generated much conflict; it might not have seemed to be a threat because it was unique. But then the FWA considered another such development, and Dallas businessmen feared that continuation of these projects could suppress private-sector initiatives. This would result in profit-minded investors competing against the unlimited resources of federal administrators. This led local businessmen to organize against the idea of the government getting into the large-scale construction of housing in the Dallas area.

The effort began in earnest on Monday, 28 April 1941, with a meeting scheduled at the auditorium of Dallas Power and Light Company. Lawrence T. Beck, a spokesman for the group, told the *Dallas Morning News* that it would include "Real-estate operators, members of the Real Estate Board, builders, lumbermen, mortgage bankers, landowners, title companies, every conceivable phase of the real-estate business." The *News* regarded the gathering as the start of "An all-out effort by Dallas real-estate men to form a coordinated defense housing program and make the construction of more government housing projects unnecessary." This meeting resulted in the creation of an executive committee to deal with the situation. The members, led by Beck as chairman, met with officials from Washington who were in Dallas to examine the state of affairs. Beck and his team hoped to derail the second government project by offering plans for private investors to build housing. Strategies were discussed at a meeting held on 15 May, during which the businessmen prepared for their scheduled meeting with the government officials, including Westbrook. One of their proposed projects was slated to build 311 homes, with a subsequent expansion of an additional hundred units. This program would be discarded, argued a member of the Building and Housing Association of Dallas County, if the federal government proceeded with a second development after Avion Village.[24]

Holmes Green, a member of both the Building Association and Dallas Chamber of Commerce, had a more positive outlook toward the government housing projects. Earlier in May he told the *Morning News* that the government "definitely wants each locality to build all possible housing for defense workers by its own initiative." But Green also recognized the usefulness of the federal projects. At the meeting on 15 May he declared, "When the snow begins to fly you're going to need those houses." He said the second government project ought to be allowed to proceed, but that his Association should stand firm in opposing any additional government projects.[25]

Despite protests, the site selected for the second development was tentatively approved by federal authorities on 22 May, with the location being near the convergence of Cockrell Hill Road and the Fort Worth Pike (US Highway 80), some four miles east of the NAA plant. The announcement of the decision stirred more opposition, and the Building and Housing Association called the project "unnecessary, undesirable, and a waste of the taxpayers' money." Political leaders also expressed concern, with Mayor Turner of Grand Prairie stating that "Private enterprise is being held back by the fear that the government will construct more housing units. If it should be announced definitely that no more units would be constructed, private capital would jump in and take care of the situation."[26]

These protests failed to stop the new government housing project. By the beginning of July 1941, the first structure was being erected at what press reports initially called a "second Avion Village." Like the first, this development was slated to provide three hundred residences, and once again the Central Contracting Company was the contractor. This neighborhood was eventually christened as "Dallas Park," and construction continued into autumn. By November, however, Westbrook was offering hope to private developers, announcing that "No further authorization for defense housing projects in this area have been received by our agency, and I don't know whether any others are being considered." After November, press coverage of the construction largely disappeared. Presumably the rush of war news pushed aside coverage of more mundane matters such as construction updates.[27]

In the end, no more Dallas-area housing projects came about through Westbrook's program. With the attack on Pearl Harbor in December 1941, defense housing shifted away from the social-engineering ideals of a permanent Avion Village. Instead, a more utilitarian model was adopted, often focusing on temporary housing. One wartime observer summarized the shift thusly:

> During the period when materials and labor were plentiful, opposition from many quarters blocked the full development of the public war housing program. Now, on the ground that the material shortage makes it difficult to build sound buildings anyway, the temporary program has been expanded to include practically all the public home building."[28]

Furthermore, there were concerns in Congress about the management and expenditures of the Mutual Ownership Defense Housing Division. Eventually the whole concept was discarded, with only eight projects being completed across the nation. Indeed, sources disagree on whether the Dallas Park development was even part of the program, though it definitely was a government project. It is possible that the involvement of Westbrook in the site selection for Dallas Park led to erroneous assumptions that the Division was overseeing the development. It is conceivable that Westbrook was merely involved in the site location due to his frequent visits to Dallas to supervise the construction of Avion Village. The somewhat cryptic story of Dallas Park could be the subject of further research, but the particulars are inconsequential to the task at hand.

In conclusion, both private and public construction contractors worked throughout 1941 and 1942 to provide housing for the thousands of workers that were expected to be employed by NAA. In the process, the city of Grand Prairie exploded in population, from 1,581 in the 1940 census to approximately 5,000 at the start of 1942. This rapid increase left the city scurrying to upgrade utilities, roads, and public services such as schools and fire protection. Fortunately for the municipal government, the increased population brought taxes from new residents, and the national government provided financial aid to provide infrastructure in support of defense housing.[29] As for Avion Village, as of 2022 it is still operating as a mutually owned housing cooperative—over eighty years after the first residents moved into the complex. It serves as an interesting juxtaposition between the social progressivism of the 1930s and the defense-minded purposefulness of the early 1940s. At Avion Village, the New Deal intersected with efforts to be the Arsenal of Democracy, creating at least one unique legacy of the efforts by NAA to build warplanes in North Texas.

Chapter 7

Plains to Planes

The months after the groundbreaking ceremony were busy ones as crews worked to construct the aircraft factory. They struggled against torrential rains in November 1940 that transformed the blackland prairie soil into a morass of mud. According to J. Gordon Turnbull, the consulting engineer, it rained for no less than thirty-four days during the construction period, totaling 14.2 inches. These heavy rains hindered construction, creating what one reporter termed a "mudkrieg."[1] Nonetheless, the plant opened ahead of schedule, the first of its kind in the nation, and delivered its first planes in April 1941.

Frank H. Shaw was the supervising engineer for the Defense Plant Corporation (DPC), with an office in a temporary structure on the job site. Known as the "blue shack," the L-shaped frame building served as a headquarters for representatives of the DPC, the contractor, the architects, and the consulting engineer. The staff worked long hours, often past midnight, as they attempted to keep on schedule. The rain did not help, and Shaw later recalled that "Many is the day where we had to wade [through] mud almost knee deep to get in and out of the building."[2]

While the construction teams went about their tasks on the western fringes of Dallas, an equally vital operation was underway on the eastern side of the city. At the North American Aviation (NAA) interim headquarters on Commerce Street, executives rushed to hire and train employees for the massive factory. It was projected that as many as twelve thousand workers might eventually be needed, but some jobs did not require mechanical skills. There was plenty of clerical work to be done, involving requisitions, timekeeping, payroll, and a host of routine tasks. Some unskilled workers would engage in physical labor such as unloading incoming materials and supplies. A security force was needed to guard against sabotage, secretaries had to be hired at all levels, and maintenance men had to be available to repair broken equipment. And even a modern aircraft factory was still in need of janitors to keep things orderly. None of these positions were directly related to building airplanes, but all of them were necessary to keep a large manufacturing plant productive.

The real challenge was to train the cadre of skilled workers required to build aircraft. Machine operators would be needed, probably enough to consume the pool of experienced machinists in the area. Other skills were more specific to aviation and were likely to be rare among the available labor pool. Such skills could be taught, and the Commerce Street facility was tasked with teaching them. The intention was to begin by hiring one thousand workers for training. These employees could form the core of the workforce when the main plant became operational. Executives for the firm desired to hire these workers locally, rather than transfer individuals from California. Attempting to staff Dallas with transferees would have robbed the Inglewood factory of trained labor, at a time when it was engaged in full production. As the training facility was being prepared, there was a great amount of interest from potential workers. This was so pronounced that the company declined to accept applications at the temporary headquarters. Individuals seeking jobs were directed instead to visit the Texas State Employment Service, located at 1605 Ross Avenue. This agency then sorted through the applications to refer qualified candidates for interviews with NAA.[3]

Efforts began small. The first training class reportedly contained just twenty-five men, scheduled to begin during the latter half of October 1940. This process was anticipated to last "from two and a half weeks to one month, depending on the type of training given." It appears the class did not actually start until November, possibly due to delays in receiving necessary equipment.[4] With no records available, it is impossible to determine what type of individuals made up the early training classes. It seems reasonable to assume that many of the first trainees were people with prior experience as machinists, assembly workers, or other industrial trades. People with this level of knowledge should have been able to quickly absorb the nuances of aircraft manufacture. These employees could then serve as instructors for later classes, working with trainees who might have no previous history of industrial employment. Using this tactic, it would be possible to enlarge the size of later training classes, steadily increasing the number of available workers as the aircraft factory moved toward completion.

This training reaped benefits beyond just creating a competent workforce. It allowed NAA to identify potential shop foremen and other supervisors. This was a critical need because on the assembly line it was not necessary for the average employee to be a trained aviation engineer. All that was needed was for each worker to be skilled at their specific assignment. But the process did require the presence of certain highly qualified employees who could oversee and guide operations on the factory floor. NAA officials were pleased to find some of their recent recruits capable of taking leadership roles.

Of course, not every experienced machinist was a potential foreman. Conversely, some workers with no previous industrial experience might have a talent for supervision. One such person was Fayron L. Croom, age 27, whose story was told in the Sunday newspaper in April 1941. In October 1940, Croom had been working as a foreman on a ranch located thirty miles outside of Mineral Wells, Texas. In the middle of the month he traveled to Dallas to seek employment at NAA and was put in a ten-day training class at the Commerce Street facility. The class, according to the news report, was intended "to ascertain an applicant's abilities." It was also reportedly unpaid, which must have indicated how seriously a candidate desired a job. Croom, who did have some mechanical experience in his background, must have demonstrated an aptitude for assembly work. By 2 December he had been assigned to work on the center section subassembly of the AT-6 fuselage. Within two weeks he had moved up again, this time to lead a group of five workmen. Soon after he was named an instructor, handling classes of sixty students as he taught riveting techniques and sheet metal work.[5]

Such rapid advancement brought Croom to the attention of E. James Rivers, the head manager for NAA in Dallas. "Jim" Rivers was born in 1887 in Harrisburg, Pennsylvania, before the invention of the airplane. He was an early participant in the fledgling business of aviation, working for the Dayton-Wright aircraft firm during World War I. Afterward, Rivers spent the next eighteen years shuffling between different companies in the ever-fluctuating aircraft industry. He eventually became an engineer and superintendent for NAA, joining the firm in 1937. Rivers arrived in Dallas in November 1940 to oversee operations at the temporary facility."[6]

Faced with the task of recruiting industrial workers in an agrarian region like North Texas, Rivers "worried a bit about the prospects of making cogs for industry from the citizenry of an agricultural center." But his worries apparently faded as men like Croom worked through the training process. On the first day of February 1941, Rivers summoned Croom to his office. The former ranch hand arrived in his white NAA smock, wearing cowboy boots. Rivers and Croom posed for pictures together while they inspected a fuselage for the benefit of a photographer. It was undoubtedly a public relations maneuver, as the experienced engineer and his newly trained apprentice inspected the skeletal framework that lay within an AT-6.[7]

Statements from various NAA sources supported the message that the training programs were productive. The most authoritative of these came from the highest echelon of the company. Some five months into the training period, NAA president James H. "Dutch" Kindelberger publicly commented on his satisfaction with the progress made in preparing the workforce. He believed that Texans had mechanical aptitude learned from keeping farm tractors and Model T Fords running. "The program at our Commerce Street plant here," Kindelberger stated, "has resulted in the training of welders and other workers in exact mechanical trades in the fastest time I have even heard of."[8]

Due to the efforts at the Commerce Street school, there were enough trained employees on hand to start production at the aircraft factory once construction was complete and the machinery installed. By early February 1941 there were approximately a thousand workers at the temporary plant, and it was estimated then that some three thousand would be available when the larger factory was finished. Furthermore, operations at the interim plant had gone beyond merely training, and the workers were producing useable parts that could be used in production at the permanent location. Throughout the four-story temporary building there were men working on wings, tails, and other components. On the second floor was a partially finished trainer, and the final assembly process was being studied. It was certainly not the type of mass production that would take place in the larger plant. Rather it must have been like old-school aircraft manufacturing, with groups of workers building pieces of airplanes almost by hand. Nevertheless, parts were being fabricated, under the watchful eye of government inspectors. It was expected that there would be enough parts ready to support the assembly of the first one-hundred airplanes to roll out of the NAA Dallas plant.[9]

As winter turned to spring, construction crews endeavored to finish the massive factory alongside Hensley Field. By 20 February 1941 the superintendent of construction, Joseph Cunningham, reported that the six-inch thick roof of the main building was 60% completed, and the three-and-a-half-inch thick walls were expected to be in place within two more weeks. Cunningham anticipated being able to turn the structures over to NAA as early as the beginning of April 1941, slightly ahead of the 10 April deadline.[10]

Unfortunately, complications arose. There were delays in getting many of the fixtures required in the main plant because the nationwide buildup of the defense industry was causing shortages of basic items. Seeking a solution, consulting engineer Turnbull decided to manufacture some of the equipment on site. Thus, workmen set about building work benches, storage racks, and other low-tech items, presumably using equipment that had already been delivered to the factory. Some items were more complex, such as a nickel and chromium plating tank that would have taken six months to obtain through commercial sources. A large electric furnace was also fabricated, avoiding a ten-month wait. Some of the more complicated devices were designed by engineers from NAA, who had exact knowledge of just what sort of equipment was needed to manufacture airplanes. According to Turnbull, the use of this "factory within a factory" brought huge benefits. He claimed the lack of equipment would have delayed the plant reaching full production until the following winter. Turnbull boasted, "When we first decided that these things should be made here, we were told it couldn't be done—and it has been." He maintained that "We not only have saved valuable time, but we have saved thousands of dollars."[11]

Eventually everything started to come together. NAA employees had been at the main plant since January 1941, presumably setting up equipment. Manufacturing operations in that facility started on 8 March, possibly to support the fabrication of needed items. On 19 March the company moved an unfinished fuselage from the interim plant on Commerce to the new factory, where it was completed to become the first Dallas-built AT-6. This plane was test flown on Sunday, 30 March, by test pilot Roy Bodeen, who had come from California for the occasion. The aviator was impressed by the ship, which he said performed better than the last fifteen AT-6 aircraft he had flown at Inglewood. Bodeen revealed that he was able to take his hands off the controls and allow the plane to fly itself for fifteen minutes, "and she cruised along smooth as honey." It is almost a certainty that this aircraft was retained by NAA for a ceremonial delivery scheduled for 7 April, the day their new main plant at Dallas was slated to be formally dedicated. With the factory approaching full operation, NAA executives and city leaders worked to arrange a two-day celebration to mark the occasion. It was to be a Texas-sized event to honor a Texas-sized factory.[12]

To make a comparison, the average duration of a human pregnancy is forty weeks. Coincidently, forty weeks had passed since the original announcement that Dallas had been selected as the location for an aircraft plant. A baby conceived in July 1940 would have arrived at about the same time as the formal dedication of the NAA facility. It had been a hectic gestation period for the sprawling new aircraft factory. The first month after the announcement of the plant had seen the replacement of Hall-Aluminum (Consolidated) by NAA. There was also the debate over the financing of the project, which was ultimately assigned to the newly established DPC. Afterward was the ceremonial groundbreaking in September, the opening of the interim plant on Commerce Street, the assigning of contractors, and an ongoing struggle with above-average rainfall. Then there was the shortage of fixtures for the factory, which had been dealt with by manufacturing the items on the scene. And while a human baby has but two parents, the newly constructed factory was a child with a lineage that had many branches, the most important being NAA, the DPC, the War Department, and the Dallas Chamber of Commerce. All of this was driven by the mobilization agenda of President Franklin D. Roosevelt, as he worked to prepare the United States for military conflict.

The public birth announcement for the long-anticipated factory appeared in the two major Dallas newspapers on Sunday, 6 April 1941. If any residents of the city had somehow missed the continuing coverage during the previous months, the papers that day brought them up to speed. Both featured special sections focusing on the impending dedication of the aircraft factory. Articles explained the construction of the buildings, the history of NAA, information about the AT-6 trainer, and the key individuals responsible for bringing this industry to the city of Dallas. Numerous photographs accompanied the stories, as well as large advertisements in which local businesses welcomed NAA to the area. Clearly something big and important was occurring in the city. One full-page headline in the *Daily Times Herald* declared "Plane Factory Heralds New North Texas Industrial Era." Underpinning it all was an awareness that this new industry was born of troubled times, with the military purpose obvious to all. "World's Eyes on Dallas as N.A.A. Gives Army Day Meaning," read the headline on the first page of the *Times Herald* special section, with the article beneath bearing the title "New Factory to Help Arm Democracies."[13]

The *Dallas Morning News* special section was especially effusive in its coverage of the new NAA plant. The section consisted of twenty-four pages, with more than forty articles and thirty illustrations, along with numerous congratulatory advertisements directed toward NAA. Many of these ads were sponsored by companies long associated with Dallas, including retailers such as Neiman Marcus, A. Harris & Co., Sanger Brothers, and Titche-Goettinger. Advertising also featured the Interstate Theater chain, which at that time operated sixteen area movie theaters; the Baker Hotel, where many of the NAA executives had stayed; Cabell's Dairy, which would supply products to the NAA cafeteria, and Wyatt Food Stores, which would be operating that cafeteria. All these businesses were household names in the city of Dallas.[14]

It is not surprising that local businessmen welcomed a new major employer into the area; that is a typical Chamber of Commerce courtesy. What is common in many of these advertisements is the recognition that Dallas was taking a major economic step forward. The text from Mrs Baird's Bread Company observed that the arrival of NAA "pioneers an important trend in the industrialization of our Lone Star State." Cabell's Dairy declared the establishment of the factory signaled "the real beginning of industrialization of the Southwest!" And the Fidelity Union Life Insurance Company hailed "the coming of this great enterprise as one of the most important steps in the industrial expansion of Texas." In the eyes of many businessmen, the opening of the NAA factory signaled a significant step toward a more diverse and modern economy in Dallas and North Texas.[15]

But the excitement for the economic opportunities presented by the NAA plant took place under the looming specter of an impending war. For twenty months Europe had been in conflict, and a subscriber who read the *Dallas Morning News* that celebrated the arrival of NAA was also presented with large-type front page headlines announcing the invasion of Greece and Yugoslavia by German forces. It was after all the actions of Germany that had precipitated the mobilization of America's aviation industry. The deadly serious purpose behind the plant permeated the special section, both in articles and in advertising. An ad from Neiman Marcus expressed admiration for the aircraft workers "playing their gallant part in the defense of America." The Titche-Goettinger company declared "From coast to coast, our new purpose is National Defense," and the A. Harris Department Store claimed that Dallas was "proud to be part of the great national defense program upon which our American heritage of freedom depends." The clothing manufacturer Haggar stated that "North American's Dallas plant is indeed an important cog in the machinery of our preparedness program," and the Baker Hotel also used the cog analogy. Reddy Kilowatt, representing Dallas Power and Light, assured readers that a newly installed sixty-thousand-volt transmission line was ready to provide "Abundant Power for National Defense," during "America's time of need."[16]

Perhaps the most stirring prose was offered by the Texas Textile Mills, a business with branches in Dallas, Waco, and McKinney. Bearing the names of

six executive officers, including treasurer (and future Dallas Mayor) Robert
L. Thornton, the advertisement stated its case:

> The defense lines are forming. Uncle Sam has rolled up his sleeves
> and gone to work. The butcher ... the baker ... the aeroplane
> maker ... all have a common cause—the preservation of the American
> Way of Life.[17]

Based on the underlying tone of these ads, and the accompanying articles,
it is apparent something was happening in the country. American public
opinion in the interwar years is usually perceived as isolationist. This factor,
combined with the economic depression, led the United States to neglect
military spending throughout the 1930s. However, the newspaper coverage
of the NAA opening indicates that Americans were thinking seriously about
national defense. That does not necessarily mean the public was embracing
an interventionist mindset. But clearly the citizens were realizing the need for
increasing the country's military readiness.

North American, for its part, also reached out to the citizens of Dallas in
the April special editions. The company paid for the inclusion of a full-page
organization chart showing the names and titles of key executives, along with
their photographs. This was presumably to add a human connection to what
might otherwise be a faceless corporation. This effort was aided by a piece
written by NAA President "Dutch" Kindelberger, in which he recounted the
process by which the location was chosen for the NAA expansion. Certainly,
there were logistical considerations, as well as the need to decentralize the
aircraft industry. But Kindelberger also gave a great deal of credit to the
community spirit found in the city of Dallas:

> Seldom in industrial history has a welcome as cordial as that given to
> North American Aviation by Dallas been extended to a firm moving
> into a new region. By word and by deed, residents of Dallas and neigh-
> boring communities have demonstrated that they want an aircraft
> industry and will go out of their way to keep it.[18]

This level of support influenced the final selection. "North American chose
Dallas," wrote Kindelberger, "and we find the choice was a happy one."[19]

Given the substantial press coverage since the summer of 1940, it can be assumed that public awareness of the new plant in April 1941 was considerable. Awareness had also raised a level of curiosity. Now there was tangible evidence in the form of a modern industrial facility, and NAA was eager to invite the neighbors to visit. An open house at the factory was planned for Sunday, 6 April 1941. Numerous details had to be sorted out, with much of the work handled by Ronald L. Burla, who served as an assistant to President Kindelberger. Also working on the preparations was Andrew DeShong, who had left his position at the Dallas Chamber of Commerce to become the director of public relations for NAA–Dallas. Given Deshong's familiarity with the city, it is likely he was tasked with contacting local officials. Authorization also had to obtained from the War Department and the Army Air Corps, as the factory was engaged in military production. Final clearance was not received from Washington until Wednesday, 2 April, with Buria making the announcement that evening, too late for that day's newspapers. Preliminary details appeared in the Thursday edition of the *Dallas Morning News*, with a follow-up article on Saturday, the day before the open house.[20]

It was impossible to determine how many people planned in advance to go to the open house. Many must have done so. Others might have made the decision to attend on short notice, inspired by the extensive coverage in the Sunday newspapers. Whatever the case, the organizers of the event had planned carefully. The main route to the plant was down Jefferson Avenue, which had been designated a one-way street for the afternoon. Departing traffic was to be routed west through Grand Prairie and onto the Fort Worth pike for the return to Dallas. Visitors to the factory were directed to park on the west side of the plant, pass through a security gate, and then enter the main building from the southwest. No cameras, packages, or handbags were allowed into the facility. Attendees had to sign a statement attesting that they were citizens of the United States and giving their names and addresses. These forms were collected when they entered the property. Visitors then proceeded through about a quarter of the length of the plant, passing through an area where parts were fabricated, which was said to be the largest machine shop found between Detroit and the west coast. Afterward the tour path made a left turn and headed north through the building, into the area where subassemblies were made. Making a final turn to the west, the crowds would see the main bay where the final assembly of aircraft occurred, before exiting the building.[21]

Dozens of law enforcement officers were on hand to control traffic and provide security. They were assisted by NAA security officers, and by numerous military enlisted men tasked with directing visitors to the proper areas. According to one count, the total number of security and military personal totaled 368. They were expected to handle an anticipated twenty-five thousand visitors.[22] As the time approached for the open house, the roads to the NAA complex became congested. The event was scheduled to run from 2:00 to 6:00 p.m. But when the gates were opened at two o'clock, an estimated twenty-five thousand people were already waiting, and still more cars were on the way, backing up traffic for two miles. The required forms avowing citizenship were depleted, and the NAA printing department had to quickly run off additional copies.[23]

On the scene was broadcaster Hal Thompson, working a live remote for KGKO radio, located at 570 on the AM radio dial. The station had scheduled thirty minutes of coverage beginning at 3:30 p.m., offering listeners at home the opportunity to experience some of the occasion. Using recently rediscovered archival recordings, it is possible to reach back through time and listen to the actual broadcast, which began with an explanation of what was transpiring:

> Good afternoon ladies and gentlemen, this is Hal Thompson speaking to you from the Grand Prairie plant of North American Aviation Inc. of Texas, where open house for the public is being held this afternoon on the eve of tomorrow's formal dedication of this seven-and-a-half-million-dollar airplane factory. This is truly a history making occasion, for North American's plant—12 miles from the heart of Dallas—is the first major new airplane factory to be built since the national defense program was launched.

Thompson's first order of business was to interview Major A. H. Denison, who served as the Air Corps representative at the factory. The two men engaged in the back-and-forth style typically used in radio. Thompson posed the question, "Major Denison, what do you think of the public's response to the invitation to visit the North American factory?" Denison replied:

> I think that the thousands of men and women who have already visited the plant this afternoon—and the highway patrol tells me that thousands more are on the way, walking down to the plant from where they had to park their cars, a long distance—are impressive evidence of America's interest in the defense program. These people have come here this afternoon, not just because it is a big new industry for Dallas and for Texas, but because the average man has a vital concern in his country's defense efforts, and is tremendously proud of the progress that has been made.[24]

The interview wandered away from the immediate subject at hand, morphing into Air Corps braggadocio, before the interviewer refocused the topic to NAA. Thompson requested "for the benefit of our radio listeners who are unable to attend this open house at the factory, would you please carry us on a brief word tour of the plant Major?" The officer, sounding somewhat uneasy on the radio, replied "Well, it is such an immense thing, I hardly know where to begin." Thompson reassured the Major, stating "I'll try not to put you back of the eight ball by asking you to tell us all about it, but tell us something about it will you?" Denison had a lot of facts prepared as part of his response:

> Alright, I'll try. Well, the fact is North American Aviation of Texas adjoins Hensley Field. This is a Dallas owned airport leased to the Army for reserve training and service use. Our plant site is 180 acres, just east of the little town of Grand Prairie, Texas. The main factory building is said to be the biggest room in the world, 900 by 950 feet. It has been designed for directed flow of production. By that, I mean that materials move directly into the fabricating department from the receiving room. As they are manufactured into airplane parts, they pass from south to north across the building. Running in the opposite direction, from east to west, across the north end of the building is the main assembly floor—950 feet long and 150 feet wide. The assembling of the airplane begins at the left end of the floor and moves eastward, until the completed ship is towed through a big door with a clear opening of 149 feet at the east end of the building, and out onto the concrete ramp which leads to Hensley Field. By directed flow of production we mean

that each subassembly reaches the assembly floor from its fabricating department at the exact spot where it will be needed to go into the airplane. There is no waste motion.

After some comments regarding the size of the plant, Thompson fed a set-up line to Denison: "By the way, our radio audience might be interested in some statistics. I'm reasonably sure you have them right on the tip of the tongue." The Army Air Corps officer responded:

> Not too many Mr. Thompson, but I'll try to give you a few. There are 855,000 square feet of floor space in this main building. Other buildings on the plant property increase the floor space of this factory to 1,024,000 square feet. In addition to the main building, there are the hangar, foundry, drop hammer, and paint storage buildings; a stand-by generating plant; a sewage treating plant, a million-gallon water reservoir. Five thousand tons of structural steel went into the construction of this factory. And I understand enough concrete was laid to have built a sidewalk three-feet wide from Dallas to Houston, Texas. There are seven thousand florescent lighting units in the plant. As one of the building contractors said, he had done a great deal of building, but this was the first time he had ever built by the acre.[25]

After almost ten minutes with Major Denison, Thompson switched to interviewing bystanders. The first person he spoke with was Bob Coleman, a Hoosier from Mishawaka, Indiana. Coleman, age 22, had taken classes in mechanical drawing at college, and worked for the Studebaker Corporation. He had started to California to find work in the aircraft industry but stopped in Fort Worth to visit relatives. He learned of the NAA factory being constructed in Dallas, so he applied. He was hired, and assigned to the subassembly department, working on wing fillets and other items. He had been with the company for four months, and he told Thompson that he considered it to be "a fine place to work."[26]

Thompson then spoke to Agnes Samson. She worked for J. Gordon Turnbull, the consulting engineer for the NAA project. Thompson, in what would be considered cringe worthy questioning today, began by asking Samson if she had imagined what it would be like to try to keep

a 900 by 950 room clean. Samson—perhaps playing along—did observe
that the plant was clean, saying she had asked a guard how it was kept
spotless. Levity aside, Thompson did ask about her impressions of the
factory, with Samson responding, "I knew it was big, but not this big.
It makes me feel good to know that America can do things like this.
To build such a big plant in such a short time and get right down to the
job of making airplanes."[27]

Dallas Mayor Woodall Rogers next approached the microphone. He had
been delayed by the heavy traffic. Rogers observed that the factory was bigger
than he expected. He commented that "it was Dallas' one-hundredth birthday,
and this new industry was quite a birthday present." He said that Dallas had
become acquainted with NAA over the course of six months, and "they are
just our kind of folks." Thompson then turned the microphone over to Grand
Prairie Mayor G. Harry Turner. Like all the other interviewees, Turner was
impressed by the size of the plant, even though he had watched it being built
and should have not been surprised. Turner stated, "the place is so big you
can't even imagine it until you get inside." He noted "practically everybody
in Grand Prairie is right here this afternoon."[28]

At this point the broadcast was halfway through the allotted time.
Having allowed the politicians to speak, Thompson turned his attention
back to workers and visitors. The next person before the microphone was
Fayron Croom, the cowboy turned aviation worker who had been profiled
in the *Daily Times Herald*. Thompson made note of Croom's west Texas
drawl, and verified he had been a cowboy, before asking "Fayron, do you
like it here?" "Sure do, we all do," Croom replied. Thompson commented,
"North American's proud to hire all Texas boys I understand." The broadcaster followed up by asking a leading question: "Why do you like it so
much? I mean, I know the air-conditioned factory is a going to be a nice
place to work, it's got good lights for your eyes and all of that, but there
must be more to it, it isn't just that is it?" "No Sir," Croom responded,
"I guess the one reason is that aviation is such a young industry, and most of
us think it has a great future." Croom saw the factory as a real opportunity
for "a lot of fellows like me. It's not just a job, it's a job where you feel you
are really doing something."[29]

Because of his exposure in the newspaper, the appearance of Croom on the radio broadcast suggests it was planned. There were thousands of employees working for NAA by this date, and it seems an odd coincidence that Croom just happened to be near the KGKO microphones during the thirty-minute broadcast. This invites speculation that the North American public relations department was promoting Croom as an example of how Texans could make the jump from agricultural jobs to industrial ones. NAA officials, notably Dutch Kindelberger, had repeatedly stated that the new plant was a Texas operation. What better way to demonstrate that than highlighting the example of a cowboy who had become an aircraft builder?

A notable aspect of the interview with Croom was that Thompson specifically mentioned the air-conditioned environment at the factory, as well as the good lighting. While both were accurate, it seems peculiar that Thompson felt the need to mention them. The likely goal was to portray the factory as a compelling place to work, with pleasant conditions and long-term growth potential. There were only 1,276 employees at the time of the dedication, and it would be in NAA's interest to present the factory in the best possible terms to encourage applications from potential workers. It seems reasonable to deduce that the exchange between Thompson and Croom was an opportunistic mix of public relations and recruiting outreach.[30]

After Thompson finished with Croom, he talked to six more individuals. The visitors repeated familiar themes, finding the factory to be large and clean; one woman even called it magnificent. The broadcast also featured consulting engineer Turnbull, who observed that building the NAA plant was hard work, but everyone had cooperated to get the job done on schedule. Thompson also spoke with Paul Carrington, the president of the Dallas Chamber of Commerce at the time. Carrington provided details about the Monday dedication ceremony. The public was invited to the event, which would be held in the storage hangar.[31]

The archived recordings of the open house broadcast reveal a multifaceted event. The program was a mix of patriotism, public relations, recruitment tool, and civic pride. After thirty minutes, the KGKO broadcast went off the air at 4:00 p.m., two hours into the event. Before signing off, Thompson told the listeners that twenty-five thousand visitors had already

Administration building of North American's Dallas plant.
North American Aviation via Aircraft Manufacturer's Collection,
History of Aviation Collection, Special Collections and Archives Division,
Eugene McDermott Library, The University of Texas at Dallas.
Copyright ©Boeing. Used by permission.

Aerial view of North American's Dallas plant as it appeared in 1941. *North American Aviation via Aircraft Manufacturer's Collection, History of Aviation Collection, Special Collections and Archives Division, Eugene McDermott Library, The University of Texas at Dallas. Copyright ©Boeing. Used by permission.*

been through the plant according to figures provided by NAA. The open house event still had two hours to go, and the numbers had already overtaken the anticipated attendance. But Thompson's figures were lagging behind. When the live remote ended at 4:00 p.m. there had been forty-six thousand visitors, and still there were people waiting to see the factory. Intermittent drops of rain failed to drive away the crowd, nor did a shower that passed overhead at 5:30 p.m. When six o'clock arrived, there were still crowds waiting, and Dutch Kindelberger made the decision to extend the event. The gates were finally closed at seven, by which time approximately sixty thousand visitors had toured the aircraft plant.[32]

It was indeed a busy Sunday on the outskirts of Dallas. And it was only the first day of the two-day event. The next day, Monday, was the formal dedication of the plant, and the delivery of the first Dallas-built AT-6 trainers. But for the moment the activities were halted, and it seems likely that the planners and coordinators of the NAA open house were looking back on their day of labor. Some of them were perhaps excited, some were surely exhausted, and some might have been a combination of both. But they probably went to bed that night with satisfaction from a job well done.

Thirty-five Sundays later would be 7 December 1941.

Chapter 8

Dedicated to National Defense

August 1940 had been an eventful month in Dallas. The announcement of the construction of a facility to build airplanes for North American Aviation (NAA) had brought exciting news to the city. In the short term, the erection of the plant provided an economic stimulus by employing construction workers, electricians, plumbers, and a host of other tradesmen. Looking forward, the new plant would provide thousands of well-paying permanent jobs. There was a sense of civic pride because Dallas would be playing a significant role in the rejuvenation of America's military defenses. All indications suggest the citizens of the city embraced the task with enthusiasm and a sense of purpose. This was not necessarily the case in some parts of the United States. While workers in Dallas were laboring to open a defense plant, labor forces in other cities were threatening to close their own factories until their demands were met. Such developments worried leaders in many parts of the country, but those celebrating the opening of the NAA plant at Dallas in April 1941 made it clear that labor unrest would not be allowed to derail the national war effort.

According to one historical monograph, "the year 1940 was one of comparative peace on the industrial front." However, with the launching of the defense program, huge government contracts were awarded to manufacturers. Organized labor saw an opportunity to reap financial rewards for their union members. This resulted in an upswing in disputes between labor and management. Again, according to one study, "The most severe strains and stresses were in the aircraft industry. A new and rapidly expanding industry, it was not only suffering from a shortage of facilities but was also in the throes of being unionized."[1]

Unrest in the aviation industry started to show in August 1940, around the same time as the announcement of Dallas as the location of the new NAA plant. The labor problem first manifested at the Boeing factory in Washington, where workers threatened a walk-out over a wage dispute. This endangered the supply of B-17 bombers, an aircraft that was to become the foundation of the Army Air Corps strategic bombing force. Although this strike was averted, further trouble was forthcoming. This occurred at the Vultee facility near Los Angeles, California, where the firm was constructing the BT-13 basic train-ing airplane. A strike was called by the United Automobile Workers (UAW), which picketed the plant starting in mid-November 1940. With five thousand men off the job, work ceased on eighty million dollars' worth of aircraft orders. This strike eventually ended after a twelve-day shutdown. But other aviation companies in Southern California were soon hit by union demands, including Ryan Aeronautics in San Diego, and NAA in Inglewood. Another UAW strike broke out on 14 March 1941, at the Harvill Aircraft Die Casting Corporation, a contractor that "supplied practically every aircraft manufacturer on the west coast." This stoppage, if extended, posed a threat to the delivery of military aircraft. Nor was the problem confined to the aviation sector. A particularly worrisome strike began on 22 January 1941, when the UAW stopped work at the Allis-Chalmers Manufacturing Company, a Wisconsin-based firm which held millions of dollars' worth of defense orders. This was especially problem-atic for the Navy, as the company produced "turbines for warships, generators, shafts, pumps and gun mounts," which were needed for new naval construc-tion. The work stoppage also delayed machinery needed for a gunpowder plant being constructed in Radford, Virginia.[2]

Frustrated with the situation, Secretary of the Navy William F. "Frank" Knox, along with William S. Knudsen of the Office of Produc-tion Management (OPM), appealed for an end to the strikes for reasons of national defense. Some workers did comply by returning to the job, but they encountered hostility from their union brethren. Police on the scene at Allis-Chalmers maintained that picketers had harassed workers leaving the factory and alleged that strikers had attempted to overturn automobiles. In response, the police drove an armored car into the mob of protesters, from which they fired tear gas into the crowd. The strike at Allis-Chalmers eventually lasted seventy-six days, with full production not resuming until 8 April. By that time $45,000,000 worth of defense contracts had been delayed.[3]

With so many labor disputes underway, "it had become apparent that 1941 was going to be a turbulent year for American industry." Government sources report that the first quarter of 1941 witnessed fifty-seven strikes that affected defense production. Companies caught up in the unrest included Ford, International Harvester, and the Aluminum Company of America. Affected industries included steel, aluminum, coal, lumber, and shipyards, to name but a few. Manufacturing workers were not the only concern. Construction workers had gone on strike on a project at Wright Field, the large Air Corps base in Dayton, Ohio. The cumulative effect of these work stoppages could potentially derail, or at least delay, the defense program.[4]

These delays tried the patience of many military and government leaders, and some politicians sought to address the issue through legislation. Texas Governor W. Lee O'Daniel advocated such action, and the Texas legislature responded by passing a law to ensure defense plants stayed operational. A key provision of the law was intended to deter violence against strikebreakers, by making such action a felony. Texas might not be able to prevent defense workers from going on strike, but the state wished to protect those who were willing to continue working, or who might fill vacated jobs. Union leaders were unhappy about the new law, but supporters pointed to violence that had occurred during the recent strikes, including the ongoing struggle at Allis-Chalmers. There was also fear that defense work could be disrupted by outside agitators. Senator John Lee Smith of Throckmorton, during debate on the bill, stated, "The new airplane plant in Dallas is being undermined by Communist groups from the North."[5]

This type of fear was not exclusive to Smith. Evidence is found in the advertising that welcomed NAA to Dallas on 6 April 1941. The best example is found in the ad from the Texas Textile Mills. It warned of "people whose business is sabotage," observing that "they come not in the form of organized troops but as organized spreaders of dissension, uncertainty and fear." Whether such a statement was valid is debatable, but that does not negate the fact these ideas existed. Apprehensions about Communists aside, the public was showing irritation with the ongoing strikes. Gallup polls released in March 1941 indicated that 53% of the public believed that production of war materials and weapons was not proceeding fast enough. Unions fared poorly in the survey; 68% of respondents felt that labor union leaders were not doing enough to support the defense program, and 72% thought that the government should forbid strikes in defense industries.[6]

While the national political atmosphere was turbulent, the mood in Dallas was calm on the day of the great dedication of the NAA plant. The weather forecast for 7 April 1941 was for mild temperatures and partly cloudy skies. No rain was predicted. It looked like a fine day for a ceremonial event.[7] A group of dignitaries converged from across the nation for the occasion. From California came a contingent of NAA executives, headed by President James H. "Dutch" Kindelberger and his right-hand man Lee Atwood. From the north came Ernest Breech, the NAA Chairman of the Board who had broken ground for the plant on 28 September. Texas Governor O'Daniel served as the official host for the occasion, with Breech serving as the master of ceremonies. The Army Air Corps was represented by Major General George H. Brett. The featured speaker for the event was Knudsen of the OPM. The magnitude of the guest list indicated the significance of the occasion to both local and national leaders.[8]

Widespread media coverage given to the event also showed its importance. Naturally, newspapers across Texas reported on the NAA plant opening. But publications throughout the country announced the dedication of the factory, albeit in brief snippets. Examples are found in small-town newspapers in Edwardsville, Illinois; Jefferson City, Missouri; Neosho, Missouri; and Camden, Arkansas, all of which had information about the opening of the factory. Coverage literally spanned from coast to coast.

News of the dedication made the Stanford University newspaper, and the *New York Times* featured quotes from the keynote speech.[9] Attention to the dedication also came from the other major news source. As on the previous day, there were remote radio broadcasts originating from the plant. Station KGKO, AM 570, which had covered the open house, arranged to transmit from a preliminary luncheon between 1:00 to 1:30 p.m. Station WRR, AM 1310, was scheduled to cover the dedication ceremony from 3:00 to 3:30 p.m. Station KRLD, AM 1080, was also planning on carrying fifteen minutes of the event, starting at 3:00 p.m.[10]

The day began with "an informal reception for the visiting dignitaries during the morning," followed "by a tour of the plant for the official party." This was followed by the luncheon for two hundred guests, held near the end of the assembly line and hosted by Breech and Kindelberger. Shortly before noon Brett and Knudsen arrived at Hensley Field, from where they traveled over to join the banquet.[11] The dedication ceremony itself was slated to begin at two o'clock, on the east side of the plant in and around the aircraft hangar. Inside the hangar, a speaker's platform had been constructed along the northern wall, where the featured guests were seated. Others present were Dallas Mayor Woodall Rogers, Grand Prairie Mayor G. Harry Turner, Amon G. Carter of Fort Worth, and Merrill Meigs, chief of aircraft production for the OPM. The group was described as a "small army of distinguished aviation, civic and government leaders."[12] Individuals in this "distinguished army" were all in Dallas to commemorate the start of production at the NAA factory. Actually, the plant had been easing into operation for some time, as materials and employees transferred from the training factory on Commerce Street. Three planes had already been completed and were ready for delivery to the Air Corps. The transfer of these aircraft was to be the culmination of the day's events.

Archival recordings of the radio broadcasts have preserved most of what was said from the podium that day.[13] The invited guests who attended the luncheon were welcomed by Breech as master of ceremonies. Introducing the dignitaries seated at the head table, Breech explained that not everyone seated at the table would speak, due to the constraints of time. He stressed the nature of the remarks, stating, "It's not a prepared talk,

everything here today is extemporaneous. Everyone is so busy with his
shoulders to the wheel in the defense program that neither he or his assistants have had an opportunity to write speeches." Audio recordings of the
speeches support this assertion, as speakers occasionally paused to gather
their thoughts or repeated themselves.[14]

The first speaker was Knudsen of the OPM, who was to be the main
speaker at the formal dedication ceremony later that afternoon. For the luncheon speech he employed a more conversational tone. In a talk lasting just over
ten minutes, he reminisced about his background in the automotive industry,
where he had worked for Henry Ford, prior to his time with General Motors.
All of this changed however when he received a phone call:

> And finally, one day I was sitting back in Detroit, having a wonderful
> time, and the telephone rang, and somebody said "You were drafted.
> Come on down to Washington. You aren't going to get any pay, but you
> better get to work." That was last June, around the first of June.
>
> Now I had the advantage, in getting into the defense program,
> in that I have quite a wide circle of acquaintances. In fact, I knew
> a person who makes guns, I knew a person who makes shells.
> I knew a person who makes a gun carriage, and even a bomb sight.
> But I was particularly fortunate in knowing Dutch Kindelberger here,
> who knows something about airplanes.
>
> So, the first thing I did, I got a hold of him, and some of the other
> gentlemen in the airplane industry, and I said, "Now how many airplanes
> can we make and how soon?" He said "Well, what kind of airplanes are
> you talking about?" "Well, I don't know, but we need an awful lot of
> planes." I had to stall for time because I didn't know about the models
> yet. But after a short time, I was able to find out about what the Army
> and Navy wanted.

Knudsen relied heavily upon the expertise of aviation industry executives,
stating that "with the help of these gentlemen we laid out a program." British
and French orders aided the process, but in the end, it was American dollars
that mattered. "Congress," said Knudsen, "has been very kind to us and given
us the capital."[15]

One key to mass production was to divide aircraft into smaller pieces.
Knudsen had learned it was possible to split an airplane into as many as
thirty-two separate subsections, such as wings, tails, and center sections.

These could be constructed apart from each other, then brought together for final assembly. A second requirement for mass production was to design factories to utilize these methods. The Dallas plant had been set up in this manner. Because of such methods, Knudsen observed, "the airplane program today is now in the stages that we are going to make them in pieces and put them together. When you get to that stage, we really don't have to worry too much about quantity. What you have to worry about is quality. That's the all-important part." The answer to that concern was to have a trained and efficient workforce. Knudsen was optimistic in that regard:

> The industry was foresighted enough to start training a whole lot of people in the most important parts of the parts manufacturing in airplanes. And I look forward today with quite a little bit of comfort towards next year when we have all these plants done and all the men working on planes, we've heard a lot of cock and bull stories about what other nations can make in the way of airplanes. I have been over there and I've seen them—some of them are pretty good, but when it comes to make anything, manufacture anything that requires skill and accuracy, I'm still betting on the old United States.[16]

As he concluded, Knudsen moved away from aviation, reflecting on the nature of the conflict ravaging Europe:

> When I was a kid my old man went to war, but there weren't any women or children in that war. They were men that fought—they fought for the protection of women and children. In this damn war—excuse me—the women and children are here from the first. Countries are depositing war right on their doorstep, in order to break the nerve of the menfolk. That's not going to happen here. That kind of warfare is going to be outlawed. We are still going to remain men in the United States, and we are going to fight—if we have to—for our women and children and try to protect them as much as we can. Thank You.[17]

Breech, retaking the microphone, praised Knudsen for his work. He offered the listeners these insights:

> I visited Mr. Knudsen in Washington on business in connection with this plant last summer, and after the business was over, he remarked to me, when I asked him how he was getting along, was he sorry he took

the job? He said "never." Now bear in mind he had worked twenty years with the company for which he was then the head. He had reached that top in that company. He could have settled back for years to come and enjoyed the fruits of his work. But he said to me, in his homey everyday language, "Mr. Breech," or Ernie, as he calls me, "everything I have today I owe to the United States of America. The least that I can do, to repay, in only a small way, what I owe my country, is to serve it the remaining years of my life if necessary."[18]

Breech then introduced Governor O'Daniel, who had recently signed the legislation intended to deter strikes in defense industries. Breech lauded it as a positive move, "designed to protect this property from those who might try to sabotage our national defense efforts." O'Daniel was keen to talk about the new law, but like all good politicians, he began with a story:

Thank you, Mr. Breech. Friends, I've got most all that I want to say contained in a little speech I am going to do later this afternoon at three o'clock, so I won't take up much time speaking here. I do want to clear up one little matter before I make any other remarks. Of course, you all know the old saying that you can take the boy out of the country, but you can't take the country out of the boy. That applies also to anyone who ever lived in Fort Worth. You can take him out of Fort Worth, but you can't take Fort Worth out of the boy. And so, it was with a little sad heart that I came up here at the invitation of the Dallas Chamber of Commerce to take part in the dedication of this great new industry for Texas. But my task grew a little brighter as we started out the Fort Worth highway heading west from Dallas. And as I entered this great building here and admired this building I couldn't help but think of Fort Worth. But my heart rejoiced when I travelled and travelled and traveled until I reached the western terminus of this building and looked out and there's Fort Worth. And then when I got back here I found Amon Carter shaking hands with everybody that came in.[19]

O'Daniel recounted how he had spent many years "broadcasting the wonderful possibilities and opportunities of this grand and glorious state of Texas for industrial development." He stated, "since becoming governor I have continued to broadcast and to advocate that Texas is the greatest—has the greatest industrial possibilities of any state in the entire union." O'Daniel was happy to see this potential finally starting to develop, accelerated by the defense program, which he said could bring 350,000,000 dollars into the Texas economy.[20]

What O'Daniel most wanted to talk about was the labor situation. He explained the antistrike legislation that had passed just days before the opening of the NAA plant at Dallas. He argued that the law protected the rights of all workers:

> And that is exactly the same position that we are taking here in Texas. That those who labor have a right to the jobs which they are holding, they have a right to organize and join any association they want, they have a right to strike, they have a right to quit their jobs. But in this great nation of ours, we find that there has been another great right of freedom overlooked, and that is the right of the man to take the job when they lay down the tools and go to work.

The Governor was confident that the men hired to work the plant were up to the job. All they needed was to be left to do it in peace:

> Now here in Texas I noticed as soon as I walked through this great factory, I recognized the faces of some of these boys working here, they're the same old boys that have been running these filling stations and garages around over this section of the state. I know them because I think I have broken down at almost every point in Texas and had to have my car fixed. Those boys know how to run these machines here. They are skilled because they have learned from the ground up. They learned on the old Model T how to take her apart and put her back together with a monkey wrench and a screwdriver at midnight out on the range. They are trained and they know how to do that work. And they are here to peacefully conduct their work and that's the kind of people we have here in the state of Texas. We're not worried about the labor here in the state of Texas—what we are worried about is these wild-eyed labor agitators and racketeers that we hear about in other states. And we don't want them to come to Texas and try to blow up the work and stop us down here. We think we are treading on sound ground when we enact a law such has been enacted, which only means that no one is to use force or violence, or the threat of force or violence, to prevent any American citizen from working at a job which he wants to work at.[21]

O'Daniel declared that workers had the right to take a job without the risk of "being beaten over the head with a club or shot." He added that he felt so strongly about this legislation that he had forwarded copies to the governors of the other forty-seven states for consideration. All of this was intended to keep defense industries operating and support the national government in the enormous task ahead. He concluded:

> I'm going to quit now, thanking you very much, and extending to these folks who have invested their money and placed this great plant here, thanking them for coming to Texas, assuring them we are going to prove worthy of the faith they have placed in this grand Lone Star State. Thank you.[22]

Breech, resuming his role as master of ceremonies, read a congratulatory telegram from Secretary of Commerce Jesse H. Jones, a Texan who had previously headed the Reconstruction Finance Corporation. Jones expressed regret at being unable to attend the dedication but stated "I am confident that the people of Dallas will do their full share in making the plant an effective unit in our defense program."[23]

Speaking next was Major General Brett, who stated the obvious—the NAA plant had been built to produce airplanes. He explained the problem facing the Air Corps:

> It's not just a production problem, it is not a luxury problem. It is a question where I, at the present time, am trying to train 7,000 pilots a year. That's 600 a month. By November I've got to increase that production—and I speak of it as production—to 1,000 a month. By the first of April next year I've got to build that up to 2500 trained pilots a month. Now that is a problem within itself, it cannot be done unless we have airplanes.

It was critical that the community around the factory support the effort. Brett told the audience, "You people of Dallas have got to see that it carries through."[24]

Breech then introduced Kindelberger to the crowd. By this point "Dutch" was probably familiar to many of the distinguished guests. He reminisced about the previous summer, when NAA was exploring the possibility of locating in Dallas. He recalled a luncheon where he was the guest of the Chamber of Commerce:

> They didn't know anything about North American or anything else at that time, very much. We came down and sat in with them and plotted this thing and talked it all over and laid it all out. And then time went on, due to the fact that the machinery in Washington was just being organized, we had quite a time here getting our contract started and getting everything lined up, and in the beginning this gang here, being bankers, wanted to see a little collateral, they wanted to see a contract. I told them "What the Hell, all they were going to do was say yes," and as far as we were concerned we were going out and buying steel without a contract. They thought, well if that was good enough for us it was good enough for them and they really got to work. And I want to say that nobody anywhere has ever had the cooperation, the help, the friendly interest, that we have had here in Dallas. We've had help just beyond all ordinary good sense, the people go to work here and they stay up day and night doing anything we want done. They've helped us locally anyway they possibly could, they've helped us nationally, and we're just proud and happy that our end of the job has got itself done as well as your end I hope.

Kindelberger related the difficulties that had been faced due to the weather, stating:

> In building this plant here, we had a great deal of difficulty. It was built in a mud hole, because Texas turned on more rain than it had ever saw before. I came down here last December and they were probing for tractors with sounding rods. It rained twenty inches down here in the forty days they were trying to get the steel up.

He particularly praised the contractors who had brought the project to completion, observing that they were:

> ... unstinting in their patriotic efforts to go beyond the scope of the contract. The men that were working on the job didn't have to go out here and paddle through mud, and in most places, they wouldn't have done it. And the contractors didn't have to get out here and spend extra money as they did on overtime to get this place done on schedule. And the men who

were working and controlling this thing here, practically broke themselves
down in health just to get this plant done when they said it would, in spite
of all the dew that was dropping on the place continuously.

The NAA president had special praise for consulting engineer J. Gordon
Turnbull, who had entered the project after there were unspecified problems
with the original architect. Turnbull had done fine work designing the steel-
work for the plant, and he eventually came to Dallas to oversee the construction. Kindelberger also spoke kind words about Frank H. Shaw, the engineer
representing the Defense Plant Corporation (DPC). Both men were presented
with watches as tokens of Kindelberger's appreciation.[25]

Kindelberger then took the luncheon in what might have seemed a
surprising direction. An expected speaker might have been Dallas Mayor
Rogers, or a representative from the DPC. Instead, Kindelberger reached
out to a prominent businessman noted for his animosity toward Dallas:

> I'm going to take over a little of Ernie Breech's job for just a second.
> About three weeks ago I was over in Fort Worth having dinner with
> gentlemen over there. I met one of your distinguished Dallas citizens
> over there, fellow named Thornton. Mr. Amon Carter was the host,
> and it was very nice to see Mr. Thornton over there. Mr. Thornton
> and Mr. Carter threw hatchets all evening—it was a wonderful show.
> Now, Mr. Carter is over here today, and we're very happy to see
> him. And I think since he has come all the way from Fort Worth—on
> gasoline bought in Fort Worth—that he should get up and just say a
> few words to his friends in Dallas, because in spite of all the hatchet
> throwing, I've never seen anybody with more friends in the land of
> the enemy than Amon Carter has in Dallas.[26]

Carter began with pleasantries, thanking the hosts and having fun playing his
adversarial role, declaring, "Naturally I'm delighted to have an opportunity
to be over here and join in with all you gentlemen in helping Grand Prairie
celebrate the location of this magnificent plant," a comment that drew laughter
and applause from the crowd. He informed the audience that his mother had
been born a few miles south of Grand Prairie, and he used to pass through the
city "in the old horse and buggy days." Since then the town had grown a lot,
he observed, "without any assistance from me in any way, shape, or form."[27]

Continuing in a more serious manner, Carter praised Knudsen as "a great guy," and hard worker. Carter also was complimentary of OPM official Merrill Meigs, with whom Carter had traveled "to China and South America and all over the country with." Turning to the subject of the labor situation, Carter "was fairly impressed by what the governor had to say." He opined:

> People working in a place, if they don't like it they shouldn't prohibit somebody else from working there. You find a lot of people in this country criticizing it continually. They don't like the president, they don't like this, they don't like that. I feel about all these people who don't like this country, why don't they go some other place where they can do better?

Carter clearly had no patience for anything that might delay the defense buildup.

> But you take a million and a half or two million mothers and fathers, that have youngsters in the war - I'll have one in there in June— when they get in there, working for twenty-one dollars a month, doing their bit, these mothers and fathers don't like to have some-body get up and interfere with their progress and development of the equipment and things necessary for them to do the job. It's an outrage and the public are not going to stand for it. No one feels any more kindly to labor than I do. I think they have a fine opportunity to do a great job. And the real honest labor people are not behind all this trouble. It's the promoters and racketeers who are misleading them on this thing that is getting them in trouble. And they sooner or later will wake up to the fact this is a pretty good country, we owe our allegiance to it, we owe everything we have. We owe the freedom, freedom of speech, freedom of press, and everything else, to this country. Therefore, we owe an allegiance to it, and if we find anybody in the country, no matter how big or small they are, how many of them they are, that's not working for this country, then something desperate should be done about it if necessary.[28]

In his closing remarks, Carter returned to the rivalry between Fort Worth and Dallas, taking some shots at the larger city. Still, he appreciated being asked to attend, stating, "I want to thank you again for giving me the opportunity to come over and attend this opening. It's a grand thing.

A little later on, 8 or 9 months, we are going to invite you all over to Fort Worth. We're going to have us a little plant over there." By this he was referring to the Consolidated Aircraft plant, for which ground would be broken on 18 April 1941. Carter thought that the dual plants "will be a great asset to the state, a great asset to the nation, and I'm delighted to be over here and accept your hospitality."[29]

As the luncheon concluded, Breech returned to the microphone to close out the event. Activities were to resume at the hangar building, where more speeches would be made. Breech ended with a literary flair, evoking poet Edgar Guest:

> Somebody said that it couldn't be done,
> But, he with a chuckle replied
>
> That "maybe it couldn't." but he would be one
> Who wouldn't say so till he'd tried.
>
> So he buckled right in with the trace of a grin
> On his face. If he worried he hid it.
>
> He started to sing as he tackled the thing
> That couldn't be done, and he did it.[30]

With the luncheon over, most of the crowd probably stayed for the official dedication activities. Those dignitaries who were to speak made the short journey from the factory over to the aircraft hangar, where the formal speeches were delivered. At three o'clock, radio engineers worked their magic, and the dedication ceremony went out across the Mutual Broadcasting System. Listeners could tune in on WPAY in Portsmouth, Ohio, while residents of Portsmouth, New Hampshire could tune into station WAAB out of Boston. In Jefferson City, Missouri, the programing could be heard on KWOS. The Mutual network had, according to one announcer, some 157 affiliates. Exactly how many of these chose to carry the live feed from Texas cannot be determined. But it was clearly a nationwide story, reaching far outside the borders of the Lone Star State. Other affiliates planned to broadcast the event on a time delay. One of Mutual's flagship stations was WOR, AM 710, operating out of New York City. This station had a powerful signal that could reach into neighboring states. According to radio program guides, WOR was to rebroadcast selected parts of the dedication speeches, specifically Knudsen's comments, starting at 11:20 p.m. and running for thirty minutes. This rebroadcast could have reached a large audience. It was also reported that parts of the program were to be transmitted via shortwave radio to South America.[31]

Many out-of-state listeners were likely unfamiliar with the situation in Dallas. For their benefit, announcers for WRR of Dallas (AM 1310) dutifully described the scene:

Good Afternoon. Today the great plant of North American Aviation Inc. joins forces with the other airplane factories of the nation, thus bringing a little closer to completion the network of national defense projects. The armaments needed for complete national preparedness. Through the facilities of WRR in Dallas, the special events department of the Mutual network has placed a barrage of microphones on the speaker's platform in one of the large hangars, in order that you may hear the ceremonies attendant to today's formal opening. This North American Aviation plant is located in Grand Prairie, Texas, just on the outskirts of Dallas. Yesterday was open house, and sixty thousand people were conducted through the vast expanse of this most modern defense unit. The crowd was all-American, and interest ran high. And it was an interest that didn't start yesterday, and neither did it stop. It started way back, when the United States first began to plan a defense program. (unintelligible) Our part of the nation is just like yours. It's all American, and it was only natural that yesterday's thousands could feel and show a great pride as they witnessed this magnificent stone and steel guardian of America's liberty. We have seen these acres of black land, where King Cotton fought the boll weevil, change almost miraculously into a great wall of shining defensive armor that will stand between this land of liberty and dictatorship. From the four corners of the nation have come these materials that men have molded into an American monument. Not merely a lifeless monument built in memory of, but one that was built, and which will be dedicated today, to the future safety of America's freedom. It's a monument that lives and produces implements for the protection of construction, not implements built for the purpose of destruction. Now to the formal ceremonies, which are opened with the playing of our national anthem.[32]

After the anthem, Breech introduced the first speaker, Governor O'Daniel, whom he mistakenly identified as the governor of Kansas, which elicited a great deal of laughter from the audience. Backtracking, Breech offered a *mea culpa*: "My apologies, because we are now building a plant in the state of Kansas, but I'm happy to say we have built this plant in the great state of Texas." For his part, O'Daniel seemed unfazed. He observed that "any state in the American union and any community of this land, would rejoice over its selection as the location for what the distinguished president of North American Aviation Incorporation has promised will be, the finest airplane plant built anywhere." He lauded the economic benefits that would come from the factory, adding, "I trust I may be pardoned for displaying considerable enthusiasm over this material blessing which has been bestowed upon our Lone Star State of Texas."[33]

For most of his speech, O'Daniel discussed the economic potential of Texas, citing raw resources, affordable power, favorable climate, and available labor. Much of this had been covered in his earlier remarks at the luncheon, but now he had a larger audience courtesy of the radio. Like any good politician, he wanted to brag about his state, and boast about his own accomplishments as governor. But amidst the positive feelings, he could not ignore the harsh reality that surrounded the plant. He observed, "It is hard to turn our thoughts to the grim consideration of death and destruction throughout the world, and the potential dangers to our own land. But we must face the grave reality, we must not flinch." Speaking for Texas, O'Daniel pledged "all the facilities at our disposal" to help the nation during "this day of tragic trials."

Invoking the martyrs of the Alamo, O'Daniel added that "a pledge of Texas is an all-out pledge." This "does not mean closed factories and idle men—it means operating factories and busy men." The Governor then touted the recently enacted antistrike legislation that intended to keep factories in operation, declaring:

> Now, let any wild-eyed labor leader agitators and racketeers from distant states or foreign countries, come to Texas and attempt by force or violence, or the threat of force or violence, to slow down or stop work at this airplane factory, or any other industry in Texas, and they

will have plenty of time to rue their folly while they pick cotton on our Texas prison farms.[34]

As O'Daniel saw it, these steps were justified by the need to deal with the national emergency and keep the armaments flowing, "because the mothers and the daddies of our brave Texas soldier boys are enraged by knowing that their sons at Camp Bowie Texas are training with wooden sticks and tree branches instead of real guns, because many factories in other states are closed down on account of strikes."[35]

While it is reasonable to accuse O'Daniel of hyperbole, there is no doubt that he was sincere in his closing statement, when he proclaimed:

With faith in God to guide us through this storm to the sunshine of future happy days, as Governor of Texas, I am happy to participate in the dedication of this great new airplane factory of the North American Aviation Corporation at Grand Prairie, Texas, to the defense and protection of the United States and as encouragement and hope for the peoples of all other God-fearing and God-loving democracies of the world.[36]

This elicited a round of applause from the audience, while Dutch Kindelberger assumed the microphone. The North American president visited what was by now familiar territory for him, stating that it was a Texas plant, and that NAA wanted to be part of the community. He was happy about how the labor situation had worked out, pointing to the success of the training school on Commerce Street in preparing about fourteen hundred–fifteen hundred workers to build airplanes. He was particularly happy at how many men had proven qualified to become supervisors, for "if you have enough top sergeants you can have an army of a million tomorrow."[37]

Kindelberger in turn introduced a man he had known for years, his friend Major General Brett. The General's comments were brief and to the point, lasting less than three minutes. He basically repeated his points from the earlier luncheon. The military needed to train thousands of pilots, and "we cannot train pilots without airplanes. Therefore, the operation of this plant is practically the foundation of the pilot training for the United States Army Air Corps, and it must operate efficiently and without interference." He called upon the power of the local community to ensure that the factory was properly supported. Brett then introduced the primary speaker, Knudsen of the OPM, whom Brett considered a "born organizer," and "a remarkable man."[38]

Taking the lectern, Knudsen echoed the earlier speakers, offering his congratulations to NAA for "finishing this beautiful factory for the United States government." It was, he said, "really the first complete airplane unit of many which will make it possible to expand the production of airplanes," for both the United States and "our friends across the sea." The United States, he observed, had invented the airplane and continued to develop improvements. But American production had been limited, bolstered by orders from Great Britain and France. "It was only when their Dunkerque opened the eyes of everybody, and the fall of France, that we really got busy on airplanes." As production czar, Knudsen was familiar with the numbers. Around the first of June 1940, shortly after Germany invaded France, there were "somewhere between three and four thousand airplanes on order from American manufacturers." Within four months that number had risen to thirty-three thousand aircraft. "Since then," he said, "we have again expanded our program, and by the time we get through we will have something like 80,000 planes on order, and a couple of hundred thousand motors to go with them." Knudsen was confident that the program would succeed, as he believed that the United States had "the greatest technical organization in the world," along with "the greatest management and engineering talent," backed up by "the best skilled labor in the world." With these assets available, he assured the audience that "we will meet, and even go beyond, the requirements and furnish the most and best planes that anybody in the world can produce."[39]

The key to building large numbers of aircraft, Knudsen told the audience, was not speed. Accuracy was required. "That's what makes mass production possible. When you can make pieces so accurate that you can multiply—make thousands of thousands the same way that will go any place where it is supposed to and fits—that is mass production. Yet large numbers of planes alone were not the answer. Knudsen related the tale of one man who "came and told me we ought to build 500 airplanes in one day." The problem, said Knudsen, was that a variety of aircraft were needed, including trainers, observation planes, and different types of bombers. Merely producing a single type would not meet all the needs of the military. It was for that reason the defense program had been initiated. Knudsen related that "a little over twelve billion dollars' worth of work" had been ordered. Some fourteen thousand primary contractors were involved, with perhaps as many as fifty thousand subcontractors. When added to British orders, it would require "about eighteen billion-man hours" just to produce what had already been contracted. If the program were to be expanded by 60% (as might be required if the United States went to war), then the total labor requirements could go as high as twenty-eight billion-man hours. Despite these daunting figures, Knudsen was confident that the country could meet the challenge. He held a "firm conviction that the United States of America is the greatest industrial producer in the world."[40]

Knudsen closed by addressing the workers assigned to the monumental task ahead, stating, "To the men who are going to build the planes, now that the plant is finished, I want to say just these few words. We are depending on you, we need your skill, we have every faith that you are capable and able to finish the job on time, just like the plant was finished on time." He proceeded to thank the citizens of Texas, as well as the United States, for "backing up our industrial efforts in order to secure the freedom, your freedom, your independence in the future." In total, he spoke for approximately seventeen and a half minutes. All indications point toward the Mutual Network coverage ending at 3:30 p.m., meaning stations down the line missed the latter portion of his address. However, WRR continued to broadcast the event locally in Dallas, and it is possible that the live feed continued out across the nation. If so, stations outside of Texas might have had the opportunity to extend the program. This is impossible to determine, but there were certainly listeners in other states that had the opportunity to hear at least some portion of the dedication ceremony.[41]

As Knudsen finished, Kindelberger returned to the microphone to share a few parting words, concluding the formal speeches. The ceremonies moved out to the flight ramp, where Brett was to accept delivery of the first three Dallas-built aircraft. Things apparently bogged down, as various dignitaries posed with airplanes for the benefit of still photographers and

William Knudsen speaking at the formal dedication of NAA-Dallas.
Acme Newspictures, copyright © Getty Images. Used by permission.

Formal delivery of the first Dallas-built AT-6 trainers. On the far left
is William Knudsen. Second from the left is Dutch Kindelberger.
Third from the left is Major General George H. Brett.
Acme Newspictures, copyright © Getty Images. Used by permission.

newsreel cameras. This left the radio announcers of WRR with time to fill, which they did by relating myriad statistics about the factory. Eventually the planes were officially turned over to the military, although this occurred off microphone. The three aircraft took off from Hensley Field and returned to circle over the crowd. Reports indicate that ship number one was later flown to Wright Field in Dayton, Ohio, with the other two going to Kelly Field in San Antonio.[42] It had been 192 days since the groundbreaking ceremony, and the Texas division of NAA had delivered its first aircraft. It was just the beginning.

Chapter 9

Dis-Organized Labor

By 1940 many large manufacturing firms employed a unionized workforce, the most notable example being the automobile industry. In contrast, the relatively new aircraft business did not have a strong tradition of union activity. This was starting to change as the industry grew larger during the defense buildup. Labor leaders, empowered by the passage of the National Labor Relations Act (also known as the Wagner Act), were working to organize aircraft workers. Given that the North American Aviation (NAA) factory in Dallas was a brand-new entity, it might have seemed an obvious target for labor activists. However, there appears to have been only a minor amount of union activity during the early years of the factory. The delay in unionizing the plant can perhaps be partially attributed to the lack of strong union sentiment in Texas. But other factors entered the equation as well, including far-away events on the west coast. This chapter will examine two unrelated labor situations which were occurring as the Dallas NAA facility began production. These events demonstrate some of the issues involved in any potential unionization of the factory.

Mere weeks after the opening of the Dallas plant there were rudimentary efforts to establish a union presence at the facility. On 10 May 1941 the *Dallas Morning News* reported that the two major unions had plans for

NAA, as well as the future bomber plant in Fort Worth. The more organized effort appears to have been by the American Federation of Labor (AFL), with representatives planning a meeting for 14–15 May to plan strategy. The rival Congress of Industrial Organizations (CIO) was also eager to organize aviation workers. The CIO was the weaker of the two unions in Dallas, having made an unsuccessful attempt to organize workers at the Ford assembly plant a few years previously. The competition between the two unions could lead to "Dallas' long-threatened war of rival labor organizing." There were open feelings of hostility between the two groups. One AFL leader, A. J. Essary, disparaged the efforts of the CIO, warning that "the threat of their un-American penetration is there." The CIO was involved in many of the strikes plaguing defense industries at this time, and Essary was proud of "the non-participation of A.F. of L. affiliated unions in antidefense riots and slow-downs." The AFL did not agree with such actions, standing "for conservatism in labor, for arbitration and for 100% Americanism."[1]

Clearly there was bad blood between the AFL and the CIO, and public irritation with the latter group was heightened by strikes against defense industries. With antiunion sentiment present in Texas, an opportunity existed for a more moderate group to enter the fray. This came in the form of the Federated Independent Texas Unions (FITU), a new organization that had just been chartered on 9 April 1941. The goal of this group was to unite the independent unions in Texas, in which there were an estimated four hundred thousand members. The president of the federation was A. W. Powell Jr. of Houston, who had previously been a publications editor for the AFL. Leadership of the new group also included members who had shifted from the CIO, including secretary-treasurer R. C. Kinzer, a Fort Worth oil worker. Powell told reporters that "The past and present record of the national unions has convinced the working people of Texas that they will fare better and the state will make more progress under a federation of Texas unions." The FITU in fact was, according to the *Dallas Morning News*, "organized to combat the A. F. of L. and the CIO." Leaders of the FITU were critical of the two large unions for opposing the recent Texas legislation that sought to curb labor violence. Vice-president W. P. Colburn Jr. opined that "The Texas antiviolence law is not an antistrike law. It was enacted to protect workers and employees from the use of strong-arm squads." These arguments apparently resonated with some workers; by mid-May twelve charters had been granted to unions wishing to affiliate with the FITU. It was also anticipated that some oil worker unions would leave the CIO and shift their allegiance to the FITU.[2]

Leaders of the FITU saw potential members within the ranks of the NAA workforce. On Thursday 22 May, union representatives "distributed about 750 copies of the *Texas Labor Record*, FITU publication, to North American plant workers," before the NAA security force reportedly stopped them. This action was criticized by Powell, who maintained that "The papers were being distributed a quarter of a mile from the plant on the other side of the railroad tracks." Nevertheless, the union apparently got its message out to enough workers to gain attention. Plant employment at the time was approximately 2,000 workers, so 750 copies of the union newsletter could have reached a substantial percentage of the workforce. An informational meeting was scheduled for 29 May 1941 at the Jefferson Hotel, located in downtown Dallas. Turnout appears to have been light; the morning paper reported "a small group of North American Aviation factory and other workers" as being in attendance. Union officials were on hand to explain their goals and principles. Secretary Kinzer stated the union could "do anything for any Texas workingman that the A.F. of L. or the CIO can." Kinzer made it clear that "This organization positively will not tolerate Communism, force or coercion and is not trying to railroad anybody into joining." Attendees were given literature to distribute to interested co-workers.[3]

These efforts yielded results. On 24 June 1941 a union charter was granted to NAA workers at another meeting at the Jefferson Hotel, during which some twenty-five employees signed membership cards. By 30 June the FITU had received one hundred applications for membership in what was called the "Aircraft Workers Local Union." But it is unclear whether the FITU made any further inroads at NAA. The effort to increase membership might have been harmed by internal dissent within the larger FITU organization. On 21 July the *Dallas Morning News* reported that Powell had been removed as president of the FITU. The article included the cryptic announcement that the board had "instructed the union's legal counsel to stand ready to assist public prosecutors in prosecution of anyone found guilty of extorting funds from businessmen through the use of union position." This did not go unchallenged by Powell, who charged that the vote to remove him had been a violation of the union's by-laws, in that there were an insufficient number of directors present at the meeting, thus no quorum. Because the vote was invalid, Powell maintained that he still held his position. Furthermore, he insisted that fraudulent votes had been cast, based on phone calls he had received from fellow union members. He resented the implication that he was "shaking down businessmen through my union connection." Powell apparently intended to fight it out at an upcoming meeting of the directors, scheduled for 25th July. Whether or not this happened is unclear, for no mention of the meeting is found in the *Dallas Morning News*. Whatever the outcome of this dispute, it is reasonable to speculate that the situation was a distraction to efforts to grow the FITU.[4]

While NAA workers were considering their options for unionization, it seems certain that company management was monitoring the labor situation. Powell had charged that NAA security guards had improperly prevented the distribution of literature, even though the union representatives were not on company property. If this did occur it could have put NAA in violation of the Wagner Act, which prohibited employers from interfering in the formation of unions. Lacking internal records, it is impossible to firmly establish how company officials viewed the potential unionization of the Dallas workforce. However, the company was dealing with labor issues at its Inglewood unit at this time, and this may have influenced management's outlook toward unions in Dallas. It is therefore desirable to provide a synopsis of the situation in California during this period.

The labor conflict at the NAA plant in Inglewood originated with an order issued by the National Labor Relations Board (NLRB) in January 1941. On the heels of a "bitter representation contest" between the AFL and CIO, the NLRB ordered an election to select which union would act as the sole bargaining representative at the factory. A preliminary vote offered workers a three-way choice between the AFL, the CIO, or no union at all.

This vote resulted in the "no union" option being eliminated, and in a run-off on 13 March the local chapter of the United Auto Workers (UAW) of the CIO won the right to act as the negotiating agent for roughly 7,700 NAA workers. Negotiations began on 16 April, with the union presenting a proposed contract. Management felt that the union demands were excessive, and the two sides argued for a month without coming to an agreement. This resulted in NAA President James H. "Dutch" Kindelberger contacting the Department of Labor on 21 May, notifying John R. Steelman (the Director of Conciliation) that negotiations were at an impasse due to the demands of the union. On 23 May a vote was taken by the union, and the workers chose to strike. The walkout was scheduled for 28 May. Faced with an impending strike, the government stepped in, calling the two parties to appear before the National Defense Mediation Board (NDMB). This entity was barely over two months old, having been established by President Franklin D. Roosevelt on 19 March 1941 via an executive order. The meeting was held on 27 May, and the parties accepted an agreement that backdated benefits to 1 May, which included a no-strike clause to remain in effect during the time the case was being heard by the NDMB.[5]

That same day, Roosevelt issued a proclamation declaring an "unlimited national emergency." As part of this declaration, he appealed to the patriotism of American citizens:

> I call upon all the loyal citizens engaged in production for defense to give precedence to the needs of the Nation to the end that a system of government that makes private enterprise possible may survive.
> I call upon all our loyal workmen as well as employers to merge their lesser differences in the larger effort to ensure the survival of the only kind of government which recognizes the rights of labor or of capital.[6]

That evening Roosevelt took to the radio for his seventeenth "fireside chat," during which he spoke to the American public regarding his proclamation. The radio address had a wide reach, with an estimated 65,650,000 listeners, representing 70% of the potential audience. This qualified the address as "an all-time radio high," rated "eleven points higher than for any other program

ever measured." Citizens were obviously interested in what Roosevelt had
to say. He painted a dire picture, declaring that the "world war for world
domination" threatened the western hemisphere and pointing out that enemy
forces could gain control of territory within aerial range of the United States.
There was also a naval threat, as evidenced by the ongoing attacks of German
submarines against ships in the Atlantic Ocean.[7]

Because so much was at risk, it was vital that industries operated
unimpeded. Roosevelt declared:

> When the Nation is threatened from without, however, as it is today,
> the actual production and transportation of the machinery of defense
> must not be interrupted by disputes between capital and capital, labor
> and labor, or capital and labor. The future of all free enterprise—
> of capital and labor alike—is at stake.

After admonishing industrial leaders against profiteering, he continued:

> A Nation-wide machinery for conciliation and mediation of industrial
> disputes has been set up. That machinery must be used promptly—
> and without stoppage of work. Collective bargaining will be retained,
> but the American people expect that impartial recommendations of
> our Government conciliation and mediation services will be followed
> both by capital and by labor.
>   The overwhelming majority of our citizens expect their government
> to see that the tools of defense are built; and for the very purpose of
> preserving the democratic safeguards of both labor and management,
> *this Government is determined to use all of its power to express the
> will of the people, and to prevent interference with the production of
> materials essential to our Nation's security.* (Italics added)[8]

Given Roosevelt's plea for cooperation between labor and industry, it seems
likely he would appreciate the no-strike agreement between NAA and the CIO.
Any satisfaction must have turned to annoyance when the UAW chapter at
Inglewood ignored his wishes. On 5 June a picket line went up around the NAA
plant, even while negotiations were still underway before the NDMB.[9]

This action was in violation of the no-strike agreement that had been
signed by CIO representatives. Roosevelt was unhappy with this development.

He reportedly made a flippant suggestion that some of the labor agitators be loaded onto ships, "putting them off on some distant beach with just enough supplies to carry them for a while." Roosevelt's irritation was shared by high-level officials in the CIO. The union had pledged not to strike while negotiations were under way, and now the local chapter was engaged in a rogue operation. For the CIO to retain credibility, the organization needed to control its members and honor its agreements. Attempting to bring the local into line, Richard Frankensteen of the CIO traveled to Los Angeles to investigate the situation. Frankensteen met publicly with the strikers on Sunday, 8 June 1941, stepping into a hostile environment where he was "disrespected, mocked, and jeered." The CIO official was frustrated by the whole affair; he "issued a public statement denouncing the strike as unsanctioned and unauthorized by the CIO." Speaking later on the radio, "He accused the local leadership of irresponsibility, and declared that the strike was Communist-inspired, called for the purpose of impeding the National Defense program."[10]

Whether or not the strike was instigated by Communists is ultimately irrelevant, for the leaders of the strike met a superior force in the person of President Roosevelt. His declaration of an unlimited national emergency gave him enhanced powers in matters of national defense. Roosevelt was also backed by public opinion. His radio address of 27 May 1941 had prompted "A torrent of letters and telegrams," of which "95 percent" supported "President Roosevelt's unlimited national emergency." Such strong senti-ments "cheered him and it appeared certain that it would strengthen his hand for the series of executive orders or directives' by which he will invoke the full powers of the Presidency under the unlimited national emergency."[11]

On Friday, 6 June, the Associated Press reported that "a high government official" verified the government would take over the NAA plant if the strike continued. The unnamed source stated the "patience of the President has been taxed and broken" by the situation. If the workers did not return to the plant on Saturday, the government would act on Monday. The Roosevelt adminis-tration might have leaked this information to influence recalcitrant strikers to return to work. A more explicit warning was issued in a United Press report on 7 June, in which White House Secretary Stephen T. Early reported that the necessary orders were ready for the President's signature. In response, NAA issued a statement from Kindelberger declaring "In accordance with the publicly expressed desire of the President of the United States that full production in the North American Aviation plant be resumed immediately. All employees are hereby notified to report for work at their regular starting times, Monday, 9 June."[12]

By this point it should have been obvious to labor leaders at Inglewood that they were isolated and lacking support. Polling earlier in the spring had shown that 72% of the American public felt that strikes should be forbidden in defense industries. Furthermore, the CIO had disavowed the strike, which Frankensteen labeled as "The irresponsible, inexperienced, and impulsive action of local leaders." And now government officials were threatening to put a halt to the work stoppage. Yet local union leaders seemed oblivious to the weakness of their stand. Elmer Freitag, a member of the strike committee, reported that "It is the unanimous opinion of the committee that the workers stay out until the 75 cent (per hour) minimum wage and the 10 cent an hour general raise are obtained."[13]

Roosevelt, having reached the limit of his patience, issued a statement on 9 June 1941 outlining the sequence of events that had halted production at the plant, which was "essential to national defense." He then issued Executive Order 8773, directing the Secretary of War to "immediately take possession of and operate the said plant of North American Aviation, Inc." To fulfill the task, the Secretary was empowered to "employ or authorize the employment of such employees ... as are necessary to carry out the provisions of this Order." Roosevelt also directed "the Secretary of War to take such measures as may be necessary to protect workers returning to the plant."[14] That same morning, many NAA employees attempted to return to work, only to discover that "picketers, agitators, and other hotheads used intimidation to block the plant entrances." When fighting began, the Los Angeles Police Department used tear gas to try to disperse the strikers. Union members threw the canisters back over the fence, and LAPD officers retreated "under a hailstorm of rocks and bottles."[15]

At this point the Army entered the fray. The commander on the scene, Lieutenant Colonel Charles E. Branshaw, ordered some twenty-six hundred troops into action. The soldiers were in full battle gear, complete with helmets, rifles, fixed bayonets, and tripod-mounted machine guns. Confronted with this show of force, the strikers fell back, and about twenty of them were taken into custody by the Army. By noon the gates were opened, and about three thousand workers returned to their jobs. Military reinforcements arrived later Monday evening, bringing the total number of soldiers to about thirty-five hundred men, and Branshaw instituted military patrols to prevent any violence against those workers who had returned to the factory. The troops settled in for a long stay, and "tents, mess kitchens and field headquarters were being set up in open territory near the plant."[16] The disgruntled strikers found the military to be unsympathetic toward their demands. When union leaders asked that striking workers be allowed to march back into the plant as a body, the request was denied by Branshaw, who made it clear that "The Army is not bargaining with the workers." When some union members demanded that the troops be removed as a condition for the workers to return, a perceptive union executive observed that "it would be silly to tell the Army what to do." Other strikers suggested that sympathy strikes be called at Vultee and other aircraft plants "until every defense factory in southern California is tied up."[17]

Eventually the facts of the matter convinced even the most persistent strikers that their situation was untenable. On Wednesday, 11 June 1941, Branshaw declared the strike was over and the factory was fully manned. It was anticipated that the plant would be in full operation within two days. A handful of men were suspended from their jobs, including eight officers of the North American chapter of the UAW. These men filed a grievance with the NLRB, charging that their suspensions violated the Wagner Act. If they hoped to win support from the CIO, they were probably disappointed, as Frankensteen announced that the local UAW chapter "would be reorganized completely and irresponsible officials purged." Frankensteen, who served as aviation director for the CIO, would lead a new committee in the union's negotiations before the NDMB. These negotiations were resumed on 17 June, with a contract signed on 18 July. In the interim, the Army troops departed, leaving the plant on the morning of 3 July.[18]

The strike at NAA's Inglewood plant might appear, on the surface, to have little direct effect on operations in Dallas. However, the situation in California must have affected the potential unionization of the Texas factory. An antistrike sentiment was already evident in the state, as witnessed by the recent legislation meant to deter strike-related violence. The actions of the federal government in seizing the Inglewood facility presumably gave further pause to prospective union members. Clearly public opinion was against the strikers. An NAA internal document—admittedly biased—argues that "the tremendous wave of national indignation which arose during and after the strike was directed solely against the strikers and those assumed to have influenced them in their course of action." All these factors probably worked together to delay the implementation of a collective-bargaining agreement in Dallas until 1943.[19]

In the interval, Texas workers were perhaps placated by the fact that NAA tied wages in Dallas to those in California, giving Texas workers the benefit of the higher wages that came with the 18 July 1941 contract that had been mediated by the government. Notice of the pay raise was made on 24 July, while the NAA board of directors met in Dallas to review operations at the factory. President Kindelberger announced that new employees would start at sixty cents an hour, with production workers receiving a five cent an hour raise every four weeks until they reached seventy-five cents an hour. Second- and third-shift workers would receive a nickel-an-hour shift differential. Employees would also receive a week of paid vacation after one year of service, and salaried workers earning less than $200 a month would receive a $16 raise. These raises were to go into effect beginning in August. Chairman Ernest Breech suggested that the raises were justified by the work being done in Dallas, stating "We believe our workers understand the necessity of an all-out effort for national defense. Certainly, the work which we saw at the factory convinces us that they are making that effort." By all indications this was true, but the company might also have used the raise to forestall union activity from gaining momentum in Dallas.[20]

To summarize, it seems reasonable that the tense labor situation in California provided extra motivation to get the Dallas factory into production as quickly as possible. NAA held contracts for large numbers of trainers for both the American and British governments. Kindelberger and his executives must have been concerned about a prolonged work stoppage at Inglewood, which developed as the NAA Dallas plant neared completion. If a protracted strike were to occur in California, NAA would need to rely on its Texas division to maintain some sort of delivery schedule. In the end this did not come to pass, due to President Roosevelt's declaration of an unlimited emergency. This was followed by his executive order for the Army to seize the Inglewood plant and end the wildcat strike by the UAW. Having narrowly averted a production disaster in California, Kindelberger and his managers presumably did everything possible to ensure that operations in Dallas proceeded in a timely and efficient manner, without the interruption of labor unions, which pleased Texas political and business leaders as well.

Chapter 10

Training Planes and Teething Pains, 1941

If the United States military was going to improve its aerial strength, it needed more than just airplanes. There would be a need for ground support workers such as mechanics, armorers, and medical personnel. Multiengine heavy bombers required navigators, bombardiers, radio operators, and gunners. Single-engine aircraft required less manpower, anywhere from one to three men. In the case of the Army, single-engine aircraft were almost always single-seat fighters. The Army did have some multiseat, single-engine models in inventory during the defense build-up. These faded from the scene very quickly after Pearl Harbor, and very few such aircraft saw combat. The Navy, with specialized requirements, operated single-engine, multiseat designs throughout the war. All these different aircraft, whatever their design or mission, needed pilots. And that is where North American Aviation (NAA) made its first great contribution to the effort to win World War II: producing AT-6 training aircraft to prepare pilots for combat.

Pilot training for the military varied over the course of the war. Periodic adjustments were made to speed up the process, improve efficiency, or to correct deficiencies in training.

Although the length and exact sequence was fluid, there was a three-stage process in which prospective aviators moved up through progressively more complex aircraft. Thus, there were different models of primary trainers, such as the Stearman PT-17, which was a biplane, and its monoplane counterparts, the Fairchild PT-19 and Ryan PT-22. All three of these aircraft had fixed landing gear and open cockpits. Pilots would then transition to the basic trainer, the most common being the Vultee BT-13 (designated as the SNV by the US Navy). The Vultee had a more powerful engine than the primary trainers, which allowed for higher speeds. Like the primary trainers, the BT-13 had fixed landing gear, but the student operated from an enclosed cockpit. The last plane in the sequence was the NAA AT-6, which the Navy designated the SNJ. This aircraft had many of the characteristics of warplanes, such as retractable landing gear. And while most AT-6s were unarmed, the aircraft could be equipped with machine guns for weapons training. After a pilot graduated from the AT-6, he might be trained in multiengine aircraft, to prepare for flying bombers or cargo planes. Aviators destined to become fighter pilots were often assigned to a specific type of combat aircraft, for training in that model. Others might fly obsolescent fighters, to continue honing their skills before moving to more modern equipment. The exact process varied over the course of the war, as conditions changed and new aircraft models entered service, but almost everyone flew an AT-6.[1]

The lineage of the AT-6 aircraft can be traced back to July 1934, when James H. "Dutch" Kindelberger assumed the role of president and managing director of the company then known as General Aviation. Kindelberger left Douglas Aircraft in California to take the position, driving across the country to the General Aviation facility in Dundalk, Maryland. General Aviation was owned by North American Aviation, a holding company that originally controlled various interests, including air transportation companies and manufacturing firms. Federal legislation passed in 1934 required a divestiture of assets, and North American Aviation, or NAA, became a nameplate for aircraft manufacturing, effective 1 January 1935.[2]

As president, Kindelberger redirected NAA. He saw that older companies like Douglas and Boeing already dominated the market for large airplanes. He therefore abandoned work on an airliner that his company had been developing. Instead, he put his designers to work on a trainer for the military. The result was the NA-16, the prototype of which "was designed and built in a breathtaking sixty-two days." The plane first flew at Dundalk on 1 April 1935, and was later ferried to Dayton, Ohio, for testing by the Army. The NA-16 had a fabric-covered fuselage and fixed landing gear, but it was also described as having "modern attributes." These included "an all-metal cantilevered wing attached low on the fuselage, with no external bracing," a design which would be used on later NAA models. The NA-16 outperformed rival designs and NAA was rewarded a contract worth around one million dollars, with an initial order of forty-two aircraft. The modified design was given the Army designation BT-9, signifying its use as a basic trainer. It was the first in what became a series of trainers that NAA produced for the military.[3]

A second design developed at Dundalk was an observation plane that initially bore the company designation GA-15. A prototype of this single-engine plane with a crew of three was delivered to the military in 1936. The Army adopted it as the O-47, ordering 109 aircraft on 19 February 1937, with follow-up orders later. These planes were in service when the United States entered the war, but they were relegated to secondary uses. The primary accomplishment of the O-47 was that it was a financial success for NAA, which by that time had relocated from Maryland to Inglewood, California. This move took place in January 1936, giving the company a brand-new modern facility in which to construct the BT-9 and O-47.[4]

As war clouds threatened in Europe, NAA started to receive orders for trainers from foreign governments. The British ordered a sizable number, as did the French. By the time the war began in September 1939, NAA had completed four hundred airplanes for the British, and was working on orders for the French. These were in addition to the orders from the United States military and a few small orders from other countries. Added together, these orders kept NAA busy. An internal document states that the company had delivered 1,075 trainers by September 1939.[5]

With the trainer business going strong, the original NA-16 design progressed through many modifications that finally resulted in the AT-6 for the Army, Navy SNJ series, and the Harvard trainers utilized by the British Royal Air Force.[6] Even within the AT-6 series there were variations, as design modifications were made throughout the service life of the aircraft. The initial model produced by the Dallas plant was the AT-6A. The airplane weighed 3,900 pounds empty, and 5,700 pounds loaded. It had a wingspan of 42 feet, a height of 11 feet 9 inches, and an overall length of 29 feet. A Pratt and Whitney R-1340-49 Wasp radial engine delivered six hundred horsepower, which enabled a speed of 210 mph at five thousand feet. Its service ceiling was 24,200 feet, and the operating range was 750 miles. Weight and performance specifications varied, but the general airframe remained more or less consistent. The aircraft has been described as "A pilot's airplane ... designed to give the best possible training in all types of tactics, from ground strafing to bombardment and aerial dogfighting." It could be outfitted with guns, bomb racks, cameras, "and just about every other device that military pilots had to operate."[7]

In the weeks after the dedication ceremony, the management and employees of NAA at Dallas set about their task of building AT-6A aircraft. Any major operation is likely to have problems during the startup phase, and there is no reason to doubt that NAA had production issues to address. Documentation of these is sparse but reports in local newspapers provide some details regarding operations at the plant, and other information can be gleaned from the company's own in-house publications.

One problem was a short-term instability in upper management at the plant. The exact nature of this situation is uncertain, but it is indicated by news reports over a period of just a few weeks. The first indication of trouble appeared in March 1941, when an article announced that E. J. Rivers had been named as the factory manager for NAA in Dallas. According to the report, the position had originally been given to Alexander Burton, but Burton had instead been assigned to Washington to serve as a representative in the capital for NAA. Rivers had been the manager of the interim facility on Commerce Street, so elevating him to direct the new factory seemed a logical step. It appears to have been intended as a permanent position, for the NAA advertisement that appeared in newspapers on 6 April 1941 listed Rivers as the manager of the plant, and he authored a column that appeared in the special NAA section of the *Daily Times Herald*.[8] But his tenure proved to be extremely short. When the first issue of the plant newspaper appeared, it revealed that H. F. Schwedes had been appointed as factory manager on 12 May. Schwedes had originally been announced as the manager for the NAA plant under construction in Kansas City, but he had been reassigned to Dallas. Robert McCulloch, factory manager at the Inglewood plant, had been in Dallas for ten days supervising operations pending the appointment of a permanent manager. This backdates the vacancy to at least the end of April. The article gives no explanation for the change.[9]

Further information is found in a short news article that appeared in July 1941, after Rivers filed a lawsuit in the 116th District Court. Rivers disclosed that he had been recalled to Inglewood, where he was "discharged wrongly," by Kindelberger, effective 14 April. The lawsuit sought $182,000 in damages. Further details were disclosed later, with Rivers charging that NAA executives "had conspired to deprive him of his employment by fraudulent schemes and devices to make it appear that he was not a faithful employee and true citizen of the United States." The exact outcome of this suit is unknown, but obviously Rivers and NAA did not part on amicable terms. Also uncertain is what affect the firing had on operations at the factory, but it was probably disruptive in some way, if only for a short period.[10]

Aside from the leadership change, an examination of news coverage detected no major setbacks in the process of getting the NAA plant into full operation. Instead, there seems to have been steady progress in finishing construction and setup work. A particularly interesting source is the plant newspaper, *Take Off*. This first appeared on 15 May 1941, just over a month after the factory officially went into operation, and its pages offered detailed information regarding operations in the plant. For example, near the end of May workers started installing a three-thousand-ton hydraulic press, the single largest piece of equipment in the factory. This press weighed 357,000 pounds and stood as tall as three men. Once the press was operational, it could be used to stamp rough cut parts, which would then be finished by workers in different departments. Prior to the installation of this press, rough cut parts were fabricated by the Inglewood factory then shipped to Dallas for finishing. NAA production manager J. S. Smithson toured the Dallas facilities and stated that "the rapid installation of the hydro presses and other additional equipment for detail parts fabrication makes it certain that in the near future the Dallas factory will be a completely self-supporting unit." Meanwhile, production was already ahead of schedule, with Smithson noting that this provided "a nice margin over the company's manufacturing schedules, but [a] rapid increase in production is still ahead."[11]

Other final touches were underway. The air handling system was already operating, moving fresh air throughout the plant, but the much-heralded air-conditioning was awaiting the completion of the Freon compressors. The system was slated to be finished by the end of June 1941, making the plant the largest air-conditioned factory in the world. The employee cafeteria—operated by Earl Wyatt—was expected to be operational by the middle of July (although it apparently did not open as scheduled). The last major project was the administration building, which was attached to the plant on the north side. This structure was partially opened in August, providing offices for the accounting, purchasing, and public relations departments. There were also offices for use by Frank H. Shaw and E. A. Davis of the Defense Plant Corporation, as well as offices to be used by Dutch Kindelberger and his vice president, Lee Atwood. A flight test building and a garage were scheduled to be finished by 1 October, by which time the plant would be basically complete.[12]

While the plant management worked to get everything functioning, the employees were working both to build planes, and to establish some sense of community within the workforce. At this time the number of employees was still relatively small, with a figure of 2,173 reported on 28 June 1941. These workers were split into two production shifts, with a third shift handling maintenance at night. These numbers probably facilitated the opportunities to establish social groups among the employees. The relatively small number of employees likely meant that an individual could know most of the members within his or her assigned department. Yet at the same time there were enough employees to provide a wide range of interests. This led to a variety of clubs and sports teams being formed almost as soon as the factory was operational.[13]

All of this was reported in the plant newspaper, which featured numerous stories covering leisure activities at the facility. The first issue documented that many teams had been formed within a month of the plant opening. Indeed, the company softball team played its first game on 7 April 1941, the day that the plant was formally dedicated. In a night game played at Fair Park in Dallas, the NAA "Aviators" lost 8-6 to a team representing the Texas and Pacific Railway, the rail company that serviced the aircraft factory. There were also intramural sports between departmental teams, including bowling, tennis, softball, and golf.[14]

Clubs were popular, and the pages of *Take Off* presented a steady stream of announcements from employees interested in forming different groups. One such individual was Bobby Chapman, who wished to form a flying club. He hoped to attract enough members to pool resources and purchase an airplane to be shared by the group. Chapman eventually was designated as the flight instructor for the club and was pictured standing beside a Piper Cub in the 31 July 1941 issue of *Take Off*. One club that attracted interest quickly was a horseback riding club initially known as the Flying Horse-men, which listed thirty members by 1 June 1941. Included in the ranks was the ubiquitous Fayron Croom, the former cowhand who had attracted media attention earlier in the year. A women's riding club was also proposed, organ-ized by Maxine Bowling, a one-time Iowan who had done some professional modeling prior to her job at NAA. Given the popularity of horses in Texas, it is probably safe to assume that this group acquired enough members to be viable. Other employees expressed interest in forming groups centered on model airplanes, harmonica playing, fencing, and figure skating. Some with musical skills were assembling a swing band, although the ensemble was still short of saxophones at the end of August. All these clubs were being promoted and or established in the first few months of operations and indicate a concerted effort to build personal relationships within the workforce.[15]

Those employees who had no interest in organized hobby clubs had other opportunities to interact with their fellow workers. On 21 May 1941 there was a "get acquainted" dance held at the Bagdad; a lavish nightclub located in Grand Prairie. The dance was well attended, enough so that Personnel Director Nate Molinarro scheduled a second dance for Friday night, 20 June. Admission was fifty cents for men, with free admission for women, and the proceeds were earmarked for the NAA Employees' Welfare Fund. There were also activities for families. On 18 May the jig department sponsored a picnic at Kidd Springs Park, located in the Oak Cliff area. The picnic drew about one hundred people to enjoy lunch and games.[16]

The various activities, and the coverage given to them in the plant newspaper, indicates that NAA management wished to create a pleasant atmosphere for the workforce. This could be due to high-mindedness on the part of company executives, but another possible motive was to develop a sense of teamwork among the employees. There is also great value in having a contented workforce instead of a dissatisfied one. It takes time and effort to train industrial workers, and experienced workers can produce items more efficiently. Therefore, it was in the best interests of the company to create an attractive place to work, in the hope of retaining skilled employees and maintaining an effective workforce. Evidence suggests that NAA sought to develop and maintain a friendly working environment, to further the task at hand.

The task, of course, was to produce airplanes. By all indications this was happening, slowly at first as the plant worked up to speed, then faster as the employees gained experience and new machinery came into operation. Exact numbers are difficult to establish in the early days of production, but aircraft were being completed. The first issue of *Take Off* proudly featured a photograph of five AT-6 trainers flying in formation over Hensley Field. The date of the image is unknown, but it had to have been taken prior to the publication date of 15 May 1941. Another undated photograph appeared in the *Dallas Morning News* on 22 May, showing five trainers (possibly the same ones) lined up outside the factory building. By July production was well underway. A team from the *March of Time* newsreel series arrived during the month, filming inside the plant. One shot shows workers moving a wing assembly, with at least two dozen completed wings stored behind them. The film crew also visited the flight line, where nine to ten airplanes were parked. The footage was incorporated into a report titled *Thumbs Up, Texas!* and appeared in theaters in August 1941.[17]

More visitors arrived later when the NAA board of directors held their monthly meeting in Dallas on 24 July 1941. Eight members came to the city, giving some their first opportunity to view the factory. They toured the plant and inspected the one-hundredth aircraft produced in Dallas. This averages out to about twenty-five planes a month, and Dutch Kindelberger reported that production was two and a half months ahead of schedule. This output would continue to increase, eventually reaching four hundred trainers a month. There was plenty of work to be done, as the plant had received orders totaling $108,000,000.[18] Conditions in Dallas were apparently satisfactory, for a major announcement came about three weeks after the directors meeting. On 15 August 1941 the Inglewood plant delivered its last AT-6, and the Dallas factory took full responsibility for producing the aircraft for the United States military. The California factory was still building the "Harvard" trainer for the British, but that contract was scheduled to be completed late in the year. The shut-down of production in Inglewood made Dallas the sole source of the critically needed trainers. Henceforth, Inglewood would concentrate on building twin-engine B-25 bombers, as well as a new fighter that had been ordered by the British Royal Air Force. The fighter was later adopted by the United States as the P-51 Mustang.[19]

Word of the production shift arrived when the country was focused on more critical matters. On Saturday, 16 August 1941, the front page of the *Dallas Morning News* carried news that more than three hundred British bombers had attacked Germany. In Soviet Russia, the Germans had launched a new offensive against Leningrad. To some Americans, the most significant news that day was that President Franklin D. Roosevelt was expected to return to the United States after an absence of several days. He had supposedly been on a fishing trip aboard the presidential yacht *Potomac*. In reality, he had surreptitiously traveled to meet with Winston Churchill near the coast of Canada. In a series of meetings on board the HMS *Prince of Wales* and the USS *Augusta*, the duo had signed a joint declaration of principles, outlining their objectives for a postwar world. This became known as the Atlantic Charter.[20]

With so much important news, the announcement that trainer production was being moved was possibly little noticed outside Inglewood and Dallas. The information appeared in the *Dallas Morning News* on 16 August—just two days short of one year since that paper had disclosed that NAA was coming to Texas. It merited only a short three-paragraph report on the first page of the local section, yet it was substantial in its own way. In less than a year the NAA plant had gone from being approved, through construction, and into production. Now, after only four months of operation, the factory was the sole source for the AT-6 trainer. Whether this was due to skilled planning on the part of NAA, or a testament to the Texas workforce, is difficult to determine. It was likely a combination of the two. But company spokesmen consistently praised the Texas employees, often pointing out the 95% of the workers had been recruited locally.[21]

On the first day of September 1941 the Dallas plant achieved another milestone, completing the first aircraft assembled totally out of parts fabricated in-house. The initial planes had utilized components supplied by Inglewood to aid in the start-up process. But as machinery like the hydraulic presses came into use, Dallas became less reliant on outside parts. From September 1941 forward the factory was totally self-sufficient, with 98% of the required machinery and equipment in place. Furthermore, the company reported that Dallas was 23% ahead of schedule. By this time employment had surpassed thirty-five hundred workers, with an anticipated employment of eleven thousand, slightly below original projections. Peak production was to be reached in November 1942.[22]

That date was still a year away, and the autumn of 1941 appears to have been relatively calm, as the plant settled into a daily rhythm. Coverage of the plant dropped off noticeably in the *Dallas Morning News* because major developments were few. The plant newspaper, *Take Off*, kept workers informed of births, marriages, club meetings, and sports activities. Human interest stories appeared weekly as well, many of which focused on hobbies or employee accomplishments. Sometimes these reports were out of the ordinary. For example, two members of the NAA security force left their jobs to play professional football for the Chicago Cardinals. William Davis, a native of Grapevine, was a tackle who had attended Texas Tech. Johnny Hall hailed from Kaufman and had been a star halfback at Texas Christian University. Interestingly, both men had played for the Cardinals during the 1940 season, then returned to North Texas. Their football player physiques must have made them intimidating security officers.[23]

"Plains to Planes" advertisement appearing in national publications during October 1941. *North American Aviation. Copyright ©Boeing. Used by permission.*

Other members of the security force had different types of excitement. Guard Thomas Terry was on patrol one evening when he encountered intruders, in this case a mother skunk and her four offspring. Terry declined to confront the interlopers, retreating from the scene. Attempts to evict the family proved unsuccessful, and the security team appealed to the workforce for ideas on what to do. The skunks were not the only trespassers. A plague of crickets appeared as autumn approached. Attracted by lights, "thousands beat themselves to death on the walls of the factory at night." Some worked their way into the administration building or the factory itself, while others commenced a cacophony of chirping in the shrubs outside. The infestation continued into September, prompting one of the staff photographers to fabricate an illustration showing the flight test unit using a giant cricket to tow an AT-6. The situation was apparently getting on the nerves of some employees, and the plant newspaper suggested having a contest to find a way to deal with the pests. The writer of the piece opined the most effective method would be to take a captured cricket down to the hydro-press, position the insect in the center, and activate the press. The writer conceded that this solution was "Effective, but hardly cricket."[24]

Chapter 11

The Final Months of Peace, October– December 1941

I f crickets are a sign of autumn, then another indication of the season is the annual State Fair of Texas, held at Fair Park east of downtown Dallas. The 1941 State Fair had a substantial military presence associated with it, indicating that citizens were increasingly aware of the program to bolster America's military. North American Aviation (NAA) played a prominent role in the events, and there was even a "North American Day." Chronologically, the first event to occur was the "North American Family Party" held on Sunday, 5 October, the second day of the fair. Planned by NAA for its workers, the gathering included speeches by Army and Navy officers, entertainment by acts from the State Fair, and performances by NAA employees. Among the in-house talent from the aircraft factory was a singing group known as "Three Dots and a Dash," with the three dots being female vocalists, and the dash being their male accompanist. The name was a reference to the "V for Victory" campaign in Great Britain, with three dots and a dash signifying "V" in Morse code. There was also a demonstration of cowboy rope tricks by members of the plant security force. Flying Officer Fred F. Willmot of the Royal Canadian Air Force supplied an international touch. Willmot, who was stationed at the plant as a liaison, performed a comedy monologue. Mrs. Willmot was on the bill as well, singing her rendition of "There'll Always Be an England."[1] All in all, for NAA it provided a great opportunity to demonstrate unity and preparedness during the last few months before the United States entered World War II.

Employees who wished to attend the family party were given passes by the payroll department on Friday, 3 October 1941. Every employee received a ticket good for free entrance into the fair that coming Sunday. Additional tickets entitled the bearer to half-price admission to eleven attractions.[2] With rides, games, and shows aplenty, the State Fair offered patrons a fun-filled excursion. Yet at the same time, observant attendees would have detected ominous reminders of a hostile world. Six hundred soldiers were camped at Fair Park, mostly from the 36th Infantry Division (Texas and Oklahoma National Guard). These men were on hand to maintain and demonstrate equipment, as there were plans to display tanks, airplanes, and antiaircraft artillery. Fair President Harry L. Seay told reporters that "Army authorities seem as anxious as is the fair to have the public see the nation's defense equipment and the trained soldiers." There were members of the Navy present as well. The mariners had their own displays, including depth bombs, naval mines, and a Morse code blinker gun. Naval personal observed that visitors consistently requested a demonstration of the "V" signal.[3] Even local defense forces appeared, with one thousand Texas Defense Guardsmen, accompanied by ROTC units from local high schools, marching in the opening parade on Saturday 4 October. The Defense Guard was a newly established entity, having been authorized by the state legislature on 10 February 1941. Their mission was to replace the Texas National Guard, which had been called to active duty in November 1940.[4]

With so many military displays, it seems likely that many visitors to the 1941 State Fair left with a heightened awareness of the ongoing military buildup. This was probably not the case with the NAA employees who came for the "Family Party." They were living and working in one of the key defense industries and aware of the importance of their work. Nevertheless, those employees who arrived in the morning to walk through the fairgrounds might have taken note of the various military trappings and personnel at the park and paused to reflect on the work they were doing. Some of the NAA workers visited the midway, where a German Messerschmitt Bf-109 fighter was on display.

A twenty-five-cent fee was collected to see the plane, with the proceeds going to the "Bundles for Britain" campaign. The aircraft, described as "battle-scarred [and] riddled by British bullets" had been shot down near London. The plane had been on tour throughout the United States and had been trucked in from its previous stop in Dayton, Ohio. Two NAA employees had reassembled the fighter for display, giving them a firsthand look at German manufacturing. Other NAA workers must have looked at the airplane on display with a sense of professional curiosity, and some might have pondered the nature of their work, and the violent motivations behind it.[5]

In the afternoon on 5 October 1941 the NAA employees, and their guests, gathered at the Fair Park band shell, where the company party was held. It commenced at 4:30 p.m. with an estimated crowd of three thousand in attendance. The master of ceremonies was R. L. Burla, who had been instrumental in arranging the NAA open house in April 1941. He had come from California, bearing greetings from President James H. "Dutch" Kindelberger, who could not attend.[6] The main speaker was Brigadier General Hubert R. Harmon, who commanded the Gulf Coast Air Corps Training Center, headquartered at Randolph Field in San Antonio. He sought to impart to his audience a sense of their importance:

> I would like to say to you gentlemen that, to all intents and purposes, you "North Americans" and all the air corps people whom I represent today—all the personnel of our three huge training centers— are already in the war. If Congress tomorrow were to make a formal declaration, your mission and our mission would remain just as they are today. We would experience, or course, a thrill of excitement, and increased tempo. We would, I believe, feel a sense of relief from the terrors of uncertainty.

The mission, said Harmon, was simple: "Keep 'em flying." This required "three simple steps: Production of aircraft; production of air men; and finally, the union of the two into efficient fighting units." The general explained the numbers to the crowd:

> In our advanced training program, we need one AT-6 for each two student pilots. One AT-6 produces on an average of two pilots every ten

weeks, so roughly ten a year. To produce 1,000 pilots in a year, we need 100 AT-6 airplanes, exclusive of replacements for accidents. You know that our present program calls for 30,000 pilots a year.

Because of this need, Harmon said, "our training centers are literally crying for the product of your great factory," and that the arrival of a new trainer was like "manna from Heaven." He expressed confidence in the workers, stating that "I know there will be no relaxation; that the production rate will continue to increase." Harmon concluded by thanking the audience, and praising the teamwork displayed between the Army and NAA.[7]

While there was entertainment aplenty at the NAA family party, there was a serious tone to it as well. A representative from the Navy also spoke. Lieutenant C. C. McCauley hailed from the Naval Air Station in Corpus Christi, and he, too, stressed the important role of trainers. It is impossible to determine what impact the military speakers had on the workers. But it seems likely the attendees came away with a heightened awareness of the task at hand. The show closed after Captain Garland Seale of the NAA security force led an audience sing-along of "God Bless America." He also sang "The Eyes of Texas." This might have just been a bit of Texas pride, but perhaps there was a message being sent as well—that NAA had a crucial role in the defense preparedness of both nation and state.[8]

As the State Fair faded into memory, the NAA employees continued at their tasks. Rumors circulated that the plant might be expanded, but these were discounted by Dutch Kindelberger and Lee Atwood during a stopover in Dallas during October 1941. The facility was still not operating at full capacity, and Atwood asserted that "there were no even vague plans for such a move." By this time there were over thirty-five hundred employees at the factory. October also brought foreign visitors to the plant, when officers of the Bolivian military came to observe AT-6 production. Colonel Oscar Moscoso expressed his admiration for the speed at which the factory had been constructed and gone into operation. He liked the airplane being produced and commented that his country was in favor of "hemisphere defense," the concept championed by Franklin D. Roosevelt. In support of this, a United States military mission was sent to Bolivia to assist in enlarging and organizing the Bolivian Army Air Force. The country would receive three AT-6 aircraft early in December 1941.[9]

As November began, NAA approached the anniversary of the beginning of operations at the temporary facility on Commerce Street. After a year in Dallas, the economic impact of NAA upon the city had been quite substantial. The company calculated it had either spent, or made commitments to spend, $31,365,000 on the Texas facility. Much of that had been spent locally, either on construction of the factory, locally acquired materials, or payroll for the plant. Certainly, some specialized equipment and materials had been ordered from sources outside of the area, but the company had committed to buy from Texas firms whenever possible. Meanwhile, local employment at the NAA factory continued to grow, with 6,087 workers on the payroll by 19 November 1941.[10]

To mark the occasion of NAA's first anniversary in Dallas, Kindelberger summoned his supervisory personnel to a celebratory dinner on Saturday night, 22 November 1941. More than two hundred executives, foremen, and department heads gathered at the Crystal Ballroom in the Baker Hotel, the seemingly obligatory venue for such events. The NAA president revisited familiar themes, but many in the crowd might have never heard him speak in person. "A lot has happened in the last year," he began, "and it means you've been working hard and well." His only disappointment was that national security regulations prevented disclosing the current production totals, but he said that "he was very proud of the record and would like to tell the public about it." Kindelberger, wearing a large NAA button on his lapel, referred to a large banner that decorated the room, which bore the statement "To Keep 'Em Flying, We Must Get Them Built." Vice President Atwood echoed this sentiment, stating: "That's our job today. We must get 'em built so Uncle Sam's fliers can keep 'em flying. This is a teamwork job, in which our work is vitally important to our United States of America." At some point Atwood demonstrated non-aviation skills by playing an electric guitar at the request of his employees. Some of the transplanted Californians demonstrated their musical talents as well, taking to the microphone for a spirited singing of "The Eyes of Texas."[11]

The next day marked another milestone. In what was the largest single delivery to date in Dallas, fifty trainers were turned over to the military. Ferry pilots from the Navy and Army had arrived the previous day, suggesting the timing was intended to dovetail with the meeting on Saturday night. However,

AT-6 Trainers awaiting delivery to the military. This photograph was
reportedly taken the night before a mass delivery of fifty planes on
November 23, 1941. *North American Aviation. Copyright ©Boeing.
Used by permission.*

inclement weather delayed the departure until Sunday, when the airmen flew
the planes out of Hensley Field. It was one year since the first structural steel
had arrived at the plant site, and less than eight months since the first trainers
had been delivered at the dedication ceremony. The Texas division of NAA
remained "consistently and considerably ahead of contract schedule."[12]

But time was running out. On 26 November 1941, elements of the Japanese Navy sailed for Hawaii. Included in the fleet were six aircraft carriers, which reached their destination on 7 December.[13] At noon on Monday, 8 December, President Roosevelt went to the Capitol, where senators and representatives were gathering for a joint session of Congress. Cabinet members soon arrived and took their seats. Their host was Sam Rayburn, who had represented Texas' 4th Congressional district since 1913. Rayburn had been in this situation before, when Woodrow Wilson had come to Congress in 1917 to ask for a declaration of war against Germany. Now, twenty-four years later, he was the Speaker of the House. As such, it fell on him to gavel the audience into order and introduce the President, who was greeted with a bi-partisan round of applause lasting several minutes. The House chaplain offered a prayer, then all eyes and ears focused on Roosevelt, who began with "Yesterday, December 7, 1941—a date which will live in infamy ..."[14] No one who heard that speech ever forgot it, and Congress gave the President his declaration of war against Japan.

In Dallas, workers at the NAA factory gathered around radios, "listening quietly but with deep intent." The atmosphere in the plant was restrained and subdued, with one observer writing that "Faces simply became a trifle grimmer, more set in determined lines." Some employees had personal stakes in the news from the Pacific theater. Cora Moore from the personnel department had a brother-in-law stationed at Hickam Field in Honolulu, Hawaii. Another worker in personnel, Doris Sandlin, had relatives in the Philippines near Manila, in what was now a war zone. One unnamed employee simply said, "Now we know what we've got to do." By the time the day shift went home the United States was officially at war with Japan, and Dallas was already showing signs of the times. That night, members of the Texas Defense Guardsman were on sentry duty at Bachman Lake to prevent possible sabotage. Carrying rifles with bayonets affixed, the militiamen stood watch over city water utilities. Monday night also found ten suspected Japanese held in custody at the Dallas County jail, as officials rounded up possible foreign nationals, including some Germans.[15]

Female welders at work. *North American Aviation via Aircraft Manufacturer's Collection, History of Aviation Collection, Special Collections and Archives Division, Eugene McDermott Library, The University of Texas at Dallas. Copyright ©Boeing. Used by permission.*

Female employee Flo Burch at work in the template layout department. *North American Aviation via Aircraft Manufacturer's Collection, History of Aviation Collection, Special Collections and Archives Division, Eugene McDermott Library, The University of Texas at Dallas. Copyright ©Boeing. Used by permission.*

The next day the *Dallas Morning News* approached local defense industries to inquire about their status and plans. The Guiberson Diesel engine factory in Garland was still under construction, but there was hope that engines could go into production in February. A few miles away, the Southern Aircraft Company anticipated going to a 24-hour a day, seven days a week schedule, with plans to double the workforce by February. Officials at NAA, however, offered no grand statement or details regarding specific plans. Their answer was short and to the point: "We are going to build more airplanes."[16]

Chapter 12

Expansion, 1942

The declaration of war affected the Dallas operation of North American Aviation (NAA). It is probable that the mood in the factory changed with the dire news of military setbacks in the Pacific. The immediate task was the production of the AT-6 trainer. Dallas production, along with that at Inglewood in California, was meeting War Department expectations in 1941, but the entry of the United States into the war resulted in an expanded and accelerated program. NAA officials worked closely with federal authorities, and as a result the Dallas facility expanded, at a significant cost to the national government, to produce B-24 bombers in addition to the trainers.

Within days of the attack on Pearl Harbor, NAA President James H. "Dutch" Kindelberger was rallying his workers to meet the challenges at hand. In a published statement, he declared "We at North American are in the thick of the toughest fight we have ever faced. Neither I or anyone else need tell you the seriousness of the situation. You all recognize it and I am keenly aware that each of you is determined to do his job better and faster than ever before." He added that the planes being built were "real and tangible things which we can contribute to the war effort. Let's keep 'em rolling out the door."[1] To promote this, NAA adopted a new slogan that started to appear in company publications in December 1941: "To Keep 'Em Flying—Get 'Em Built!" The visual artwork featured the slogan arranged in a circle around the NAA corporate logo. This reminder graced the pages of the plant newspaper as well as the company magazine. It also appeared on signs within the plant, with at least one large example hanging from the overhead rafters above a busy intersection within the factory.[2]

Throughout late 1941 the Dallas plant had been getting aircraft out the door in a timely fashion. Monthly production numbers are elusive, as the information was not released for reasons of security. This practice likely began in September 1941, after Acting Secretary of War Robert P. Patterson wrote a brief memorandum to President Franklin D. Roosevelt. This short note reported that national production in August totaled 1,854 aircraft, an increase of about 400 over the figure for July. Referring to "the practice of O.P.M. to publish monthly production of planes in the United States," Patterson wrote, "I understand that Churchill thinks we would worry the Nazis more if we kept them in ignorance of our output." He concluded, "I suggest that the figure for August be published, it being such a good figure, and that thereafter the publication of monthly figures be discontinued." This apparently became practice sometime before the NAA management meeting on 22 November, at which Kindelberger commented about not being at liberty to disclose production figures.[3]

Confidential company documents do provide information regarding cumulative NAA production figures for both California and Texas. The Inglewood factory manufactured 1,533 trainers during the year 1941, along with spare parts equivalent to an additional 338 aircraft. By comparison, the Dallas plant produced 740 trainers, with equivalent spares totaling 96. If only complete airplanes are taken into consideration, the output of the two plants totaled 2,273 during 1941, with Dallas accounting for 32.5% of the total number.[4]

Since the Inglewood facility also produced trainers for the British, these numbers do not necessarily indicate how many of the aircraft went to the United States military, nor when they were delivered. To answer this question requires government reports. One useful document, classified as "Secret," was the "Weekly Statistical Report" (WSR) compiled by the

War Department. These reports contain information concerning military readiness, especially the production of weapons. For example, the version issued on 20 December 1941 is of interest, as the information spanned the period before and after the Pearl Harbor attack. The report showed that in the first half of December manufacturers produced 949 military planes. Of this total, 498 were combat airplanes, with 451 other aircraft delivered as well during the two-week period. Among this number were three categories of trainers: primary, basic, and advanced. By this time, 35% of the trainers ordered by the US government had been delivered, with the majority still to come.[5] The next WSR, for January 1942, shows that as of 31 December a total of 1,098 advanced trainers had been delivered. This number indicates an increase in production in the last half of December, but it fails to account for the 2,273 planes reported by NAA, leaving at least 1,075 unaccounted for. Part of the difference can be attributed to the fact that the WSR was issued by the War Department, and as such specifically refers to Army procurement programs. Therefore, it might be assumed that its delivery figures for trainers represent only those planes procured for the Army, not those delivered to the Navy or the British.[6]

The Navy also used the NAA trainers, under the designation SNJ. Unfortunately, no information has been located on the number of NAA trainers delivered to the Navy in 1941. Apparently, the Navy was concerned, as a bulletin dated 25 July 1941, states that "the shortage of airplanes of the type required for advanced training is becoming critical." There are documents that provide clues to the number of aircraft manufactured for the Navy. On 8 October, Capt. John R. Beardall (Roosevelt's naval aide) forwarded a confidential report to the President that provided information from the Bureau of Aeronautics. The report showed the state of naval aviation as of 15 September, when there were 399 advanced trainers on hand, with a total planned program of 942. Not all the 942 were to be NAA products, as the Navy also contracted with Curtiss-Wright and Vultee for trainers. The total number of SNJ aircraft on order at the time was 501, of which only 181 had been delivered by 1 September. The document specified the anticipated delivery of SNJ trainers during the last four months of 1941, with twenty scheduled in September, twenty-three in October, twenty-seven in November, and twenty in December, for a total of ninety by the end of the year. Another twenty-four trainers were scheduled to be delivered in January 1942, at which point deliveries would stop until the next November.[7] If all the SNJ aircraft in inventory as of September had been delivered in 1941, and the Navy received ninety more SNJ trainers during the period from September through December, it is possible that the Navy obtained as many as 271 trainers during 1941, many of them from NAA. Given that the War Department WSR shows trainer production program was ahead of schedule, there is no reason to think the delivery of the Navy aircraft was not fulfilled. At the same time, it also appears that the British received a lot of NAA trainers.

The truth is that the lack of records makes it impossible to determine the precise production schedule for NAA Dallas during the 1941 calendar year. The only number that is verified is the figure of 740 found in NAA documents. Of these, the majority apparently went to the Army, with a smaller portion going to the Navy. It is also possible some trainers were destined for Canada, based on the presence of Royal Canadian Air Force officer Fred F. Willmot at the plant. But other than the first three planes delivered on 7 April 1941, the one-hundredth plane around the end of July, and the large delivery of fifty on 23 November, the delivery schedule remains unclear. The only certainty is that the pace of production continued to increase as the employees became more experienced, and processes at the plant became more efficient. Thus, as 1941 closed the Texas division of NAA was well underway in the production of advanced trainers.

As the calendar flipped into 1942, the nation faced a troubling military situation. In the Pacific, the situation was particularly grim. Wake Island and Guam were both occupied by the Japanese in December 1941, and the battle for the Philippines was underway. There, American and Filipino forces were withdrawing into the Bataan Peninsula for a last-ditch defense. With no realistic hope of resupply or reinforcements, the defenders of Bataan appeared doomed. Conditions in the Atlantic were difficult as well. On 11 December, Germany and Italy declared war on the United States. The new year brought German submarines operating near American waters on 12 January 1942, when a British ship was sunk some three hundred miles east of Cape Cod. This was the first of many losses within the area designated as the Eastern Sea Frontier, which ranged from Canada down to the top of Florida. German submarines scored fourteen kills in this area in January alone, with another seventeen in February. Soon Nazi U-Boats plied their trade in the Gulf of Mexico as well, with a favorite target being oil tankers carrying products from Texas refineries. The carnage continued for some time, as the Navy and Army endeavored to develop effective countermeasures.[8]

While American military leaders spent the opening days of the year coping with the harsh realities of war, residents of Dallas were coping with the harsh realities of a cold winter. New Year's Eve featured temperatures in the mid-fifties throughout most of the day, peaking at 62 degrees at 7:00 p.m. But a cold front arrived on New Year's Day, with a noontime low of 25. Rain turning to snow was predicted, but the frozen precipitation appears to have either missed Dallas or been inconsequential. The cold lingered into the next day, with temperatures hovering in the twenties on Friday, 2 January. An inch of snow finally fell on Saturday, causing "innumerable minor accidents," as well as a larger incident involving twenty vehicles. The cold weather continued into the next week, and enough snow accumulated to allow the employees at NAA to engage in snowball fights during their lunch break. It also presented the unusual sight of AT-6 trainers coated with a dusting of snow while parked on the flight line.[9] In spite of this, production continued.

While the citizens of Dallas were slipping and sliding, President Roosevelt was preparing his annual State of the Union address. On 6 January the Chief Executive traveled once again to the Capitol, not quite a month since he had made the journey to call for a declaration of war. In his 1940 and 1941 annual addresses he had commented upon a troubled world filled with military conflict. Now the nation he led was embroiled in that struggle, and his message focused entirely on the war. He admitted the setbacks encountered on the battlefield but spoke optimistically about the steps being taken to meet the coming challenges. He referred to a coalition of nations—twenty-six countries engaged in a coordinated effort to defeat the Axis powers. He stated, "The militarists of Berlin and Tokyo started this war. But the massed, angered forces of common humanity will finish it." To do so would require that United States industrial production "must be raised far above present levels." The President called for increased numbers of tanks, antiaircraft guns, and merchant ships. But the first item on his list was aircraft.[10] The President was very specific about how many aircraft he wanted:

> First, to increase our production rate of airplanes so rapidly that in this year, 1942, we shall produce 60,000 planes, 10,000 more than the goal that we set a year and a half ago. This includes 45,000 combat planes— bombers, dive bombers, pursuit planes. The rate of increase will be maintained and continued so that next year, 1943 we shall produce 125,000 airplanes, including 100,000 combat planes.[11]

Roosevelt was not pulling figures out of thin air. The realities of war had demonstrated the need to expand the defense program and had been the topic of study in December. Evidence is found in a classified report issued by the Office of Production Management (OPM) on the last day of 1941. The first page addressed the need to increase spending:

> It is proposed to step up the present 1942 schedule of munitions production and defense construction $27 Billion to $40 Billion. A $40 Billion program would mean that by the end of 1942 more than half of our national income would be devoted to the war effort. This would make our effort nearly on a par with the British and German effort.[12]

Such funding required legislative approval, prompting Roosevelt to call for the increases. The President had already set the process in motion for the increased numbers, even before his State of the Union address. On 3 January, he sent a directive to Secretary of War Henry L. Stimson, with carbon copies going to Secretary of the Navy William F. "Frank" Knox, as well as William S. Knudsen and Sidney Hillman (Associate Director of the OPM). Knudsen responded to the President on 7 January, assuring him "the schedule you have outlined shall go into effect immediately and the necessary steps taken to ensure the deliveries as specified." Knudsen observed "There will be a large amount of funds required for facilities and which I trust Congress will speedily provide." With five battleships of the Pacific Fleet resting on the bottom of Pearl Harbor, such action by Congress was assured.[13]

If production increased, NAA had to be part of the process. The company was operating plants in Inglewood and Kansas City (Kansas) as well as Dallas. By 1942 the California factory was finishing the building of Harvard trainers under British contracts, delivering the last eight airplanes in January. From this point forward, the Inglewood facility would concentrate on two models: the P-51 fighter and B-25 bomber. The new NAA plant in Kansas City was starting to produce B-25 bombers, delivering two aircraft in February. An additional consideration was that the Kansas City facility was intended to use many components supplied by the Fisher Body division of General Motors, making it more of an assembly plant than a full-scale manufacturing entity. With California already heavily committed to two combat models, and with Kansas just beginning to reach production, Dallas offered the best opportunity for increased output. But adding combat aircraft into its production schedule could also curtail delivery of the much-needed trainers.[14] Whatever decisions were to be made, company leadership was prepared to accept the challenge. Following Roosevelt's address, Kindelberger released a public statement expressing his belief that the aviation industry could meet the 60,000-aircraft goal for 1942, as well as the 125,000 number in 1943. Kindelberger declared "we have confidence in our ability to do any job which we are given, and we believe that the other manufacturers in the industry are equally confident."[15]

The short timeframe between Roosevelt's address and Kindelberger's statement suggests that administration officials had conferred with aviation industry executives about their ability to meet the new goals. Roosevelt publicly called for increased production on 6 January, and Kindelberger's statement was in the 8 January plant newspaper, suggesting it was released no later than 7 January. That meant that Kindelberger only had about 24 hours to consider the 125,000-aircraft request before he declared it to be obtainable. While it is possible that Kindelberger was simply being positive in reacting to the President's remarks, the *modus operandi* of the administration by this point was to consult with the aviation industry about what was possible. OPM director Knudsen had stated in his remarks at the NAA Dallas dedication that he relied heavily on the knowledge of industry leaders, and there is no reason to believe that the new numbers were not discussed prior to Roosevelt's directive of 3 January. It is possible that informal inquiries could have dated back to October 1941, when Kindelberger and Lee Atwood visited Washington to "confer with Army officials." During a stop in Dallas on their way home, the men told reporters that "their trip to the East was purely routine and no subjects of particular public interest were discussed." This may have been true. But it is conceivable the two were withholding sensitive information regarding possible expansion, which might never occur. At that time the prevailing idea was that any increase in industrial capacity would not be brought about by building new facilities. Historian Irving B. Holley Jr. wrote, "From midsummer through 7 December 1941 the official position was that expansion was over. Future increases in capacity would be achieved by conversion." This referred largely to the automobile industry, which could be used for additional output of aircraft components, but the large numbers requested by Roosevelt also required expansion of the aviation industry.[16]

Whatever the case regarding pre-knowledge of expansion, a week after Roosevelt's address there were tangible efforts to get it underway. On 13 January the Air Corps Material Division issued a letter of intent to NAA, stating that the War Department planned on ordering 750 four-engine B-24 bombers from the company. The airplanes, along with spare parts, had an estimated cost of $215,625,000. Such letters were used during the procurement rush in the hectic days after Pearl Harbor. Holley explains their use in place of contracts expedited the procurement process; "It authorized a manufacturer to incur expenses in starting production and obligated the government to reimburse him for expenses whether or not a formal contract could subsequently be agreed upon." The letter authorized NAA to purchase "jigs, dies, tools and fixtures, and such materials as are necessary for the production of the articles referred to," up to a cost of $64,700,000. Negotiations for a formal contract were to follow, with a deadline of 1 April. Kindelberger signed the letter on 15 January, signifying his acceptance of the terms, putting NAA on the path toward producing heavy bombers.[17]

What the letter of intent did not specify is where the bombers would be built. The B-24 "Liberator" was a larger aircraft than anything NAA was then producing, with a wingspan of 110 feet. By comparison the B-25 had a wingspan of slightly less than 68 feet, and the AT-6 came in at a mere 42 feet. While the existing factory buildings might have been able to accommodate the B-24, manufacturing processes were set up around the current models. A massive rearrangement of assembly lines would be required, disrupting production during a critical period. The best solution to the problem was to construct a new facility to produce the B-24. Theoretically, this new factory could have been constructed at any location that fit existing parameters regarding the availability of transportation, labor forces, and power. But with war underway, time was of the essence, and to spend it scouting locations was time ill-spent. Better to build a new plant alongside an existing one, where the infrastructure was already in place. This would also allow the existing factory to support the new one during the startup process.

The exact sequence of events behind the site selection for the new factory is unclear. The decision was almost certainly made before Kindelberger signed the letter of intent on 15 January. This is indicated by a War Department teletype message dated 19 January, which referenced a proposal received from NAA concerning an expansion of the Dallas plant. The teletype stated NAA planned to increase its manufacturing capacity in Dallas, from three hundred trainers a month to four hundred. More significantly, the company sought to "attain additional capacity for the manufacture of seventy-five B-24 airplanes per month." To accomplish this required buildings and other site improvements estimated to cost $9,686,000, and new equipment and machinery valued at $11,550,000. Altogether, the estimated cost for the expansion project was $22,198,500. Financing would be handled through the Defense Plant Corporation (DPC), with the new facility becoming part of the existing Plancor 25 lease agreement. Preliminary figures indicated that the expansion would create 1,300,000 square feet of new production space, as well as an additional 280,000 square feet of nonproductive (i.e., offices) space. An additional twenty-five thousand employees would be needed to handle the workload. Defining details of this nature must have required more time than elapsed between the signing of the letter of intent and the submission of the proposal. Kindelberger and his team almost certainly had prior knowledge of the project to complete the planning as they did.[18]

By 26 January the expansion of the NAA facility at Dallas was the subject of a War Department memorandum. Written by Col. W. F. Volandt of the Army Air Corps, the document was intended for the Under Secretary of War,

Robert P. Patterson. Colonel Volandt referenced the teletype of 19 January concerning NAA and observed that the Plant Site Board of the OPM had formally approved the proposal on 24 January. Volandt recommended that the War Department also approve the project, and he requested the authorization of up to $11,335,109 in Department funds to pay half of the expected expenditures. Patterson endorsed the project on 27 January.[19]

Dallas thus received the assignment to build B-24 bombers in what was essentially a complete second factory, located only a few hundred feet to the west of the existing unit. This new facility was designated as the "B-plant," with the older operation becoming the "A-plant." According to the specifications NAA provided to the DPC, the B-plant was to feature a main building consisting of four separate sections: warehouse, machine shop, manufacturing, and final assembly area. The warehouse was to be eight hundred feet by one hundred feet, and two stories high. The manufacturing section was also two stories high, 350 feet wide, and ran the length of the plant. The final assembly section featured a clear height of thirty feet from floor to ceiling trusses, was two hundred-feet wide, and stretched for twelve hundred feet along an east-west orientation, parallel to Jefferson Avenue. The width allowed for two rows of aircraft on the assembly floor. Bombers would begin the final assembly on the west end of the building, moving toward the east, before turning and coming back down the line heading west. Finished aircraft left the building through a large door on the west side of the plant. The entire main building measured 1,200 feet by 650 feet, with a total floor space of 1,368,700 square feet. This gave the B-plant a rectangular shape, in contrast to the A-plant which was almost a square. Like the existing plant, the new facility was designed to be bomb resistant, and built to blackout standards with no windows.[20]

The cost estimate for the main factory building at B-plant was $4,265,000. Additional support structures included an office building, a paint building, and a garage. Additions were to be made to the existing drop hammer and foundry buildings. There was also a two-hundred-foot-long sky bridge that connected the two plants, allowing personnel to pass from one building to the other. Altogether, the expected cost for the buildings and improvements was $6,183,180. To cover unforeseen circumstances, a 10% contingency fund was added, giving a final estimate of $6,801,498. This did not include equipment and machinery. These estimates were apparently submitted on 2 February 1942. At any rate, the numbers soon changed. A revised document dated 20 July shows the paint building converted to a hangar, with the addition of a less sophisticated "touch up paint building" built at a cost of $45,000. At the same time, the contingency fund was decreased, leaving the final estimated total unchanged.[21]

The estimated construction budget only covered erection of structures, with all other costs listed separately. Electrical power and lighting were anticipated to cost $1,230,000; climate control was budgeted at $690,000, and plumbing and fire protection at $440,000. Water supply would require $30,000, and plant protection requirements needed $100,000. Adding in a 10% contingency fund brought that subtotal to $2,739,000. In addition, there were the costs of improvements to parking and railroads, architect fees, and miscellaneous expenses.[22]

All of the above merely created an empty building. To construct the bombers would require a massive amount of equipment. Estimates ranged up to $464,043 for drill presses, $224,600 for hydraulic presses, $390,530 for welders, and $328,600 for riveters. These were just some of thirty-eight categories listed in documentation provided to the DPC, with the largest single entry being $881,059 for "general." This amount was largely devoted to the transportation and installation of equipment, including making the necessary electrical connections. Altogether, the estimate totaled $8,743,757.47 for equipment, which was more than the projected cost of the actual buildings. The largest expenditure within the machinery and equipment category was for "general plant requirements," a list that encompassed such items as three thousand workbenches at $32.50 apiece, thirty-five hundred stools at $5.00 each, and seventy-five timeclocks to track thousands of employees working in the facility. Standard racks and shelving were a substantial expense, with $175,000 estimated for what must have been thousands of linear feet of storage. Another $300,000 was devoted to specialized storage racks for materials such as sheet metal and tubing. General plant requirements totaled $691,625. This brought the projected amount for machinery and equipment to $1,139,939.80. The inclusion of the eighty cents is somewhat humorous given the large numbers at play, suggesting that NAA officials tried to be precise in dealing with the DPC.[23]

In addition to the apparatus needed to build airplanes, there was a need for office equipment used by support staff to manage the plant. Planners for NAA organized the requirements into twenty different categories, providing detailed listings of what each department required. The accounting department alone needed seventy desks, fifteen file cabinets, two safes, ten manual typewriters, three electric typewriters, fifteen calculators, and six adding machines, totaling $17,944. An itemization for the payroll department shows similar needs, with sixty-five desks, forty file cabinets, ten typewriters, and specialized devices including two check-writing machines, to provide a partial list. The equipment for the payroll department was budgeted at $35,550. Other support departments dealt with nonclerical matters. The medical division had a main hospital and three first aid stations, with a total of twenty beds. An operating table and anesthesia machine allowed for emergency surgeries, and a complete X-Ray unit was included as well. The manufacturing process utilized hundreds of potentially dangerous machines; if a worker were to be injured the medical team was equipped to handle the situation. The budgeted cost for medical gear was $25,000.[24]

The final section in the estimated budget addressed portable tools and automotive equipment. NAA planners called for 3,750 electric drills, 1,012 pneumatic drills, 400 soldering irons, 1,800 vises, and a plethora of other devices too numerous to name. These tools, plus a built-in contingency, were estimated to cost $892,741.30. As to automotive type equipment, the B-plant needed four station wagons at $950 a unit, as well as two semi-rigs at $3,300 each. Safety and protection vehicles included an $8,000 fire truck, an ambulance at $4,500, and a police car worth $950. Gas and oil trucks were needed to service planes on the ramp, and employees could move about the factory by riding on one of twenty motor scooters. These various vehicles were predicted to cost $61,765. All of this was thoroughly explained in the detailed documents created by NAA. Known collectively as "Appendix A," the package was submitted to the Army Air Corps Material Division at Wright Field, with the ultimate recipient being the DPC. In a letter dated 2 February 1942, NAA Vice President Lee Atwood explained that the company was forwarding fourteen copies of Appendix A for approval. At this time the total projected cost of the B-24 program was listed as $23,905,835.42.[25]

According to projections, the B-plant would encompass 1,720,000 total square feet. North American estimated that the facility would employ up to twenty thousand "productive workers" engaged in manufacturing, receiving, storage, shipping, and maintenance, while five thousand "nonproductive" workers would be assigned to administrative and support activities. Plans called for two main production shifts, with a small night shift of five hundred employees. The pay rate for skilled labor would range from $.75 to $1.60 an hour, with semiskilled employees earning from $.60 to $.90 an hour. Supervisory personal and executives could earn salaries ranging from $200 to $1,000 a month.[26] Once construction was authorized, it was anticipated that the facility would be ready in approximately two hundred days, with production beginning fifteen days later. Delivery of the B-24 bombers could begin in early 1943, with peak production reached 580 days after approval of the project. These figures were supplied to the Air Corps within an "Application for Emergency Facilities," signed by Kindelberger and submitted as part of the 2 February documentation package.[27]

The exact timing surrounding the final approval of the B-plant is uncertain. The expenditure of War Department funds was approved on 27 January. The question of additional financing lay in the hands of DPC administrators. The decision-making process apparently lasted throughout February. On the 24th of the month a letter was sent to Frank H. Shaw, who was still the DPC engineer for the Dallas area. This stated that an approved copy of Appendix A was being sent to Shaw separately, suggesting a preliminary decision had been made. The best available documentation is found in a 14 March letter sent from the Army Air Corps to NAA through the DPC. This communication referred to an amended lease, dated 28 February, regarding the expansion of the Dallas facility. This suggests that the DPC decision to fund the B-plant might have been finalized in late February. As to the proposals in Appendix A, the letter specifically states that "Preliminary plans and schedules applicable to the increased expansion, submitted by your company as Appendix 'A' have been studied, analyzed and approved by this office." The documents had also been forwarded to the DPC on 11 March, where they presumably met with

Three types of planes produced in Dallas: P-51 (front left), B-24 (back), and AT-6 (front right). *North American Aviation. Copyright ©Boeing. Used by permission.*

quick approval. At some point all the required authorizations were obtained, and work could begin on the new factory.[28]

As with the original plant, J. Gordon Turnbull served as the project engineer. Unlike the previous construction project, this time there was apparently no media coverage. A search of the *Dallas Morning News* for 1942 yielded no articles concerning the expansion. Whereas the original factory had been the subject of numerous stories and photographs, the construction of the B-plant appears to have been subject to a news blackout. There is no indication of a grand public dedication ceremony, an open house, or any of the celebratory occasions associated with the initial arrival of NAA to Dallas. This might have been partly due to the pressing needs of the war effort, but the main reason was probably concern about security. Even *Take Off*, the NAA plant newspaper, provided no information regarding the erection of B-plant. However, in June the paper did refer to a reorganization of the factory into two administrative units, designated A and B. The executives named as section heads later appeared on the organizational chart as heads of the two respective plants, indicating that B-section was the administrative nucleus of the expansion factory. Obviously, it was impossible to hide the building of a 1200-foot by 650-foot structure from the thousands of employees who worked mere yards from the job site, nor from the nearby residents of Grand Prairie. But publicity about the plant was withheld from print sources that might have spread the news to areas outside the immediate vicinity, and details about the factory were presumably on a need-to-know basis. It was the closing days of 1942 before any information was released to the public.[29]

Chapter 13

Life During Wartime, 1942

While construction crews labored to build the B-plant, the workers at the Dallas facility for North American Aviation (NAA) endeavored to produce urgently needed AT-6 trainers. At the same time, the employees had to adjust to the demands of operating in a wartime environment. Challenges included the effects of rationing, transportation issues, and worrying about loved ones in the military. Many of these problems were featured in the pages of the NAA plant newspaper *Take Off*. This publication provides the clearest picture of life inside an aircraft factory at war.

One of the constant themes found within *Take Off* was the need to purchase defense bonds. In January 1942, a program was initiated by which employees could have money withheld from their paychecks. The amount was determined by the individual, but it had to be at least three dollars. Each employee also chose the value of the bond to be acquired. Once enough money had been withheld to cover the cost, the company arranged to purchase the bond on behalf of the employee. Through this process the purchasing of defense bonds was made simple for workers, who filled out an authorization card and let the personnel department do the rest. The initial response was favorable, and departments within the plant competed to see

which could reach 100% participation first, prodded by factory manager
Harold F. Schwedes. By 12 January employees had committed to monthly
deductions totaling $55,086.13 toward the purchase of bonds. This repre-
sented a maturity value of $73,448, and if deductions continued at that rate
it could account for $881,378 worth of bonds in a year. Company officials
set a goal of purchasing $1,000,000 worth of bonds annually, a realistic
target under the circumstances. Updates on the goal were featured in *Take
Off* as the year progressed, and by 14 May employee participation reached
93.4%. Ten departments were at full participation, and many others had
rates exceeding 90%. The lowest ranked department was purchasing, where
only 64% of the employees authorized withholding.[1]

The publication of these numbers was intended to stimulate participation in the "Bonds for Victory" program, by encouraging departments who
were close to meeting the goal, or by the public shaming of the recalcitrant
departments. To drive home the point, the newspaper published a picture of
John D. Owen, who had signed up to withhold 10% of his paycheck, the first
employee in the plant to reach that threshold. Sales efforts continued; on the
last Friday in May the plant was visited by actress Dorothy Lamour as part
of a bond drive. Lamour "addressed the workers and presented a certificate
from the Treasury Department showing that 95 percent of the employees
have signed up for bond purchases under the pay roll deduction plan."[2]

Buying bonds was easy for employees, but transportation was another
matter, as commuting to the plant became increasingly difficult. A variety
of issues affected this situation. Some were temporary, such as floodwaters
from the Trinity River, which blocked Jefferson Avenue on two different
occasions in April 1942. One NAA employee, R. M. Parker, had to abandon
his car and swim for safety after driving into water that had submerged the
street. Even without the occasional flood there were problems with traffic
into and out of the plant, as Jefferson Avenue became overcrowded during
peak traffic hours. And while car-pooling was common, even this created
issues when drivers stopped in front of the plant to unload passengers
before driving to the parking lots. Attempts were made to deal with traffic problems, including the stationing of officers from the State Highway
Patrol around the plant to help control the flow of vehicles and pedestrians.

There were also plans made to improve Jefferson Avenue, converting it into a military highway, "consisting of two concrete lanes each 22 feet wide, with a four-foot asphalt separation strip and 10-foot asphalt shoulders." This $270,000 project was slated to run from Grand Prairie to the Naval Air Station at Hensley Field. Other improvements were planned for Skyline Road, located south of the plant. A high-water road was also proposed for the river bottoms along Jefferson Avenue. It seems unlikely that these projects provided a quick answer, as building roads took time, and employment at the factory steadily increased.[3]

While valuable, road improvements were of little use without a functioning automobile. Unfortunately for drivers, maintaining a car became difficult. The war was scarcely underway when the government announced plans to ration tires beginning in January 1942. The Japanese offensive in the Far East had effectively blocked the importation of rubber from that area, and officials sought to reduce the consumption of crude rubber by 80%. The military had priority for what was available, and civilian consumption was to be limited to ten thousand tons a month. This severely reduced the number of tires produced for civilian use, and available tires were allotted at the state level. The entire state of Texas was allowed only 36,680 tires for January 1942, with the majority of those designated for use on trucks. Only 12,530 tires were available for use on passenger cars, and these were controlled by local rationing boards. Dallas County was allotted 1,045 car tires in January, and the number fell to 511 for February. With such limited availability it was necessary to tightly control the supply, and priority was given to vehicles such as ambulances and police cars. Medical doctors were also permitted to purchase tires, in order that they could get to sick patients. Most of the public was unable to buy new tires at all, instead having to repair old ones, or obtaining retreaded tires in some cases.[4]

This situation had repercussions at NAA. The classified ads within the plant newspaper were soon filled with employees seeking transportation to work, or from drivers offering rides. For example, the last issue printed before Pearl Harbor featured twenty-five such ads. Two months later the number of transportation ads had increased to seventy-two.[5] One possible solution was the use of mass transit, and efforts to improve bus service were initiated late in January. The Grand Prairie Motor Coach Line purchased additional vehicles to increase service to the plant, operating on a route from downtown Dallas to NAA. These buses departed every thirty minutes from 5:15 a.m. until 8:15 a.m., with additional buses at 8:30, 9:40, 10:45, and 12. Afternoon workers could catch buses at 1:15, 2:15, and 3:15, and then every thirty minutes from 3:45 to 6:30. Nighttime workers were served by six buses running between 8:00 p.m. and 2:20 a.m. The total time for the bus ride was thirty minutes, with stops in Cockrell Hill and the Naval Air Station. While the passenger capacity of the buses is unknown, an average load of forty could have brought a thousand workers a day to the plant. This service utilized Jefferson Avenue, but other companies were also offering service on different routes.[6]

The buses helped, but they could not accommodate everyone, and in July there were still sixty-four ads in *Take Off* from employees wanting to rideshare to the factory. Evidence of the tire shortage is present in the ads as well, with two different employees wishing to trade one size tire for another, and three more employees looking to buy used tires. At this point NAA got involved in the tire situation. On 20 July the company opened a transportation office in the plant to help employees deal with the rationing program. To qualify for replacement tires the applicant had to meet certain parameters. The employee had to reside more than two miles from the plant, with no other practical means of transportation. Bus or streetcar rides of less than an hour were considered practical and would disqualify the application. Drivers were also required to "regularly transport three fellow workers." Exceptions might be made if the worker could demonstrate that his route to work did not pass by any NAA workers in need of rides.[7]

If all qualifications were met, the transportation office would issue a letter of certification. The employee could then take the documentation to have their tires inspected to verify the need for replacement. Tires that were suitable for recapping or retreading would be referred for those processes. If the tires were not salvageable, the employee might be able to obtain recapped or retreaded tires, if available. Authorization for the purchase of new tires was difficult to obtain, leaving drivers in the position of pampering tires for as long as possible. The need to conserve rubber eventually led to the implementation of national gas rationing in November 1942, which forced drivers to limit travel. Federal officials also called for a thirty-five-mile-per-hour speed limit. This was intended to further reduce tire wear, as well as counter the safety issues involved in driving on worn tires. The lower limit was imposed upon Texas drivers in October. With tires and gasoline rationed, finding reliable transportation to the factory must have been a challenge. Furthermore, the low-speed limit increased travel time for employees. Add in the heavy traffic around the area, and it seems likely that the daily commute to North American was a tedious endeavor.[8]

Transportation issues were one thing, but for some workers the most pressing concern was the fate of loved ones in the war zone, especially the Pacific Theater, the main combat arena during most of 1942. Evidence of the troubled situation manifested itself in different ways in the pages of the plant newspaper. One example was Leonard Ellis, an employee whose shirt featured crude artwork depicting an exploding warship, with the battle cry "Remember Pearl Harbor" written across his back. He had a young brother in the Air Corps who was stationed in the Philippines, a decidedly dangerous place to be in January 1942. Ellis's attire contained an additional motivational message. Printed across the bottom of his shirt was the exhortation: "Let's Get 'Em Built." The same sentiment was also expressed in a poster painted by employee George Barlow of the woodshop, which portrayed an angry eagle with talons spread and the words "Remember Pearl Harbor." The eagle was superimposed over an image of an AT-6, with the NAA "Get 'Em Built" logo featured as well. The artistic endeavors of Ellis and Barlow were created mere weeks into the war. Plant employees understood the importance of their work and embraced the responsibility of producing trainers.[9]

Some minds were on China. Richard B. Fielder, aged 20, worried about his father, who had formerly been the pastor of Hillcrest Baptist Church in Dallas. The elder Fielder was a missionary in China and had not been heard from since December 1941. Richard had attempted to join the Naval Air Service but failed to meet the physical requirements. Denied the opportunity to "fly airplanes against the Japs," he opted instead to help build them at NAA. As for his father, he reportedly became a prisoner of the Japanese, presumably until the end of the war.[10] A worker with an even stronger Chinese connection was Chin Wai Yen, a native of that country. The twenty-two-year-old was the first Chinese national to work in the factory, operating a drill press in the machine shop. Chin, nicknamed "Tommy" by his co-workers, had been in China when the Japanese first began military operations there in 1931. Shortly thereafter his father brought him to America, and the two eventually settled in Dallas. The elder Chin became a waiter, while the son attended the Cumberland Hills School on North Akard Street. Plans to reunite the family did not come to pass, and Tommy was concerned for his mother and two younger brothers, who were still in China. He envisioned a day "when there will be no more japs to bomb cities and slaughter innocent people," and he looked forward to the end of the war, when he hoped to bring the rest of his family to the United States.[11]

Perhaps the highest-profile example of a missing family member involved a duo of employees, Bobbie Cherry and her brother-in-law Tom. Bobbie was married to Capt. William Cherry, a former American Airlines pilot who was now in the military. In October 1942, Cherry piloted a B-17 Flying Fortress in route to the South Pacific. On board was the famed aviator Edward "Eddie" Rickenbacker, the most decorated American pilot of World War I. Rickenbacker had entered the aviation industry after that conflict, and in 1942 he was the president of Eastern Airlines. He was working on behalf of the War Department as a civilian and was heading out on an inspection tour of airbases. However, a navigational error caused the aircraft to go off course, and when the fuel ran out Captain Cherry was forced to ditch the plane in the ocean. The passengers and crew were able to get into life rafts, but they were left adrift, their whereabouts unknown. On 23 October the Army announced that Rickenbacker was missing, some two days after the last transmission had been received from the aircraft.[12]

The disappearance of the famed aviator made national news, with both the United Press and the Associated Press wire services picking up the story. But to the citizens of Dallas there was a local angle, as Cherry was identified as the pilot of the missing aircraft in a wire report on 25 October. To Bobbie and her young daughter Paula, it was a personal family event, and the NAA newspaper kept her fellow employees informed. Good news was slow in coming, but it eventually arrived on Friday, 13 November 1942, when plant managers informed Bobbie that her husband had reportedly been rescued. Given the option of taking the rest of the day off, Bobbie chose to stay on the job, stating "I am so happy that I could not think of stopping work right now. I'm so grateful that all I can say is praise the Lord—praise the Lord and smash the Japs and Nazis." The next day, the Navy reported that Rickenbacker and his companions had been rescued. The Rickenbacker connection placed the ordeal of the Cherry family into the realm of the public interest, and Bobbie and Tom were featured in a dramatized recreation of the event broadcast on radio station KRLD on the evening of 18 November. They were joined by E. F. Eastman, a fellow NAA worker who had been a mechanic in Rickenbacker's squadron during World War I. Three more weeks passed before Bobbie was reunited with her husband. The couple briefly met at the airport on 9 December, when William stopped on a layover during a journey to Washington on board an American Airlines flight. During the entire time that Captain Cherry was missing, Bobbie continued working to help "Get 'Em Built."[13]

While some plant employees fretted over the safety of loved ones abroad, other workers had firsthand experience of overseas combat. The first World War II veteran to gain employment at the plant arrived surprisingly early in the conflict, when John Bellamy joined the workforce. Bellamy was serving in the Navy on 7 December 1941, but his ship was at sea and missed the attack on Pearl Harbor, although his brother Jack, a Marine, was one of the antiaircraft gunners who fought against the Japanese onslaught that day. John Bellamy's opportunity for action came at the Battle of the Coral Sea, during the first week of May 1942. His ship was attacked by Japanese aircraft, and a bomb exploded alongside the vessel near Bellamy's station. As a result, he suffered "from increasingly severe headaches resulting from the bomb concussion." These were serious enough to put the young sailor into the hospital, and he was eventually given an honorable discharge. Bellamy, now a veteran at the age of nineteen, returned to his home in Dallas, where his father was a traffic officer. The former Seaman First Class applied for work at NAA, where his sister also worked, and by the end of August he had rejoined the war effort by helping produce the AT-6. Bellamy felt he was still "getting his licks in at the japs," stating that "the more planes we have, the better it will suit me." So, he signed on to the task to "Get 'Em Built.'"[14]

The hiring of John Bellamy signaled the arrival of veterans into the NAA workforce, but it was more common for employees to leave to join the military. The names of those leaving were chronicled within the pages of *Take Off*, and the departure of coworkers served as a poignant reminder of the ongoing war. For example, in October 1942 the paper listed the names of sixty-one employees who had left NAA in recent weeks. Thirty-three more names appeared in print just one week later. Thirty men were listed on November 6, and thirty-nine more were gone by November 13. In one month, the plant newspaper thus listed 163 employees as being "called to colors," and it is possible that others left without recognition. And while men were the majority of those leaving, women also chose to enlist. Jacqueline Mooneyham, a secretary, was the first to go; she joined the Women's Army Auxiliary Corps (WAAC) on 3 October. Eda Dooley followed shortly thereafter, the second known female employee to do so.[15]

Such workforce shrinkage could be problematic. A continuous loss of workers could negatively affect production. Highly skilled specialists might be difficult to replace. Even lower-level workers typically became more efficient with experience, so a high turnover rate could be detrimental in any manufacturing position. The situation was not unique to NAA, and eventually, the national government sought to gain more control over the manpower situation. On 20 November 1942, President Roosevelt revealed that new policies were being developed, including "tighter regulations for exempting necessary war industry workers from the draft." The President sought better cooperation between employers and local draft boards, and for factory management to certify "whether prospective draftees are or are not essential and irreplaceable." The challenge "boiled down to finding a definition for the word essential."[16]

Although Roosevelt specifically addressed issues related to the draft, action was also taken to deter voluntary enlistments by certain workers. Military leadership announced that recruits would no longer be accepted from the ranks of war workers. This new policy was explained by a joint statement issued by Secretary of War Henry L. Stimson and Secretary of the

Navy William F. "Frank" Knox near the end of November. They declared "During the past month a large number of men employed in the aircraft industry, shipyards, and other war plants have resigned their positions in order to enlist in the Army or Navy." They lauded such men for their patriot spirit but stressed that workers might best contribute by staying on the job:

> However, in the present world-wide struggle the task of maintaining an increasing flow of the tools with which we fight is as important as that of effectively using those tools in battle. You men who are engaged in this vital work should remember that you are doing your full duty in staying at your present position, unless and until you are called, or until your service can be spared.[17]

Thus, military leaders found themselves in the position of advocating that less men volunteer for the armed services, at least if a potential recruit was already engaged in war production.

The situation was further clarified on 5 December 1942, when President Roosevelt issued Executive Order 9279. This sought "to promote the most effective mobilization and utilization of the national manpower and to eliminate so far as possible waste of manpower due to disruptive recruitment and undue migration of workers." To pursue this goal, Roosevelt decreed that control of the Selective Service System would be assigned to the War Manpower Commission (WMC), which in turn was under control of the Office for Emergency Management. Going forward, the War and Navy departments would consult with the WMC regarding their needs, which could then be filled by the Selective Service System.[18]

The changes put into place by Roosevelt did not merely concern Selective Service. Voluntary enlistment of males between the ages of 18 and 38 was halted, which prevented men from joining the service of their choice. Civilian jobs were also affected, as the WMC was tasked to ensure that the recruitment of workers for essential industries was handled through the US Employment Service, unless some alternative arrangement was made.[19] This effectively placed the manpower needs of the nation under the control of Paul V. McNutt, the chairman of the WMC. The United Press wire service reported that the arrangement "gave the

WMC virtually unlimited authority to hire, recruit, and transfer labor."
Any job considered vital to the war effort was theoretically subject to
WMC control. This included agriculture as well as industry. James H.
Bond, a WMC regional director, acknowledged that Texas "is predomi-
nately agricultural and we are constantly concerned with the vital problem of producing livestock or harvesting crops of food and fiber." Thus,
the potential reach of the WMC was broad, leading the *Dallas Morning
News* to observe that "The President's man-power order is aimed at more
than superficial reclassification for civil and military effort. It is intended to
effect wide-spread reorganization of our practice of man-power utilization during a machine-age war." As for Commissioner McNutt, he moved
quickly into his enhanced role. On 7 December—the first anniversary of the
Pearl Harbor attack—the Associated Press reported McNutt's "first official
act" as "man-power czar" was to announce a labor shortage in Beaumont,
Texarkana, Houston, and Dallas. The announcement was a harbinger of
things to come.[20]

It is obvious that the year 1942 brought numerous challenges to the
employees of NAA as they adjusted to life during wartime. Despite this,
there seems to have been an effort to maintain some semblance of normal-
ity. As had been the case before Pearl Harbor, the plant newspaper continued to report on the social and recreational activities of employees. Sports
were regularly featured, with workers bowling and playing basketball and
baseball, often on an intramural basis but sometimes in local leagues. Some
male employees competed in Golden Gloves boxing matches held at the
Sportatorium in Dallas, while others participated in a track meet at the Fort
Worth Stock Show. Female workers could swim at weekly splash parties
or sign up for a softball team or tennis. Employees of both sexes could be
found playing volleyball during lunch, using courts installed near the drop
hammer building.[21]

Not all recreational activities involved sports. Employees started many
clubs during 1941, and these continued to be formed in 1942. One new group
was dedicated to the fine arts. They attended a talk at the Dallas Museum of
Art, planned an art show to showcase artwork by NAA workers, and started
a mixed chorus that practiced weekly. Another club was devoted to flying

model airplanes. Given the variety of different teams, clubs, and events, it appears likely that some sort of activity was available to any employee who desired social interaction.[22]

All these social activities could help keep up spirits during a diffi-cult period of the war. The company took other steps as well, outside the realm of recreation. The most notable of these was the opportunity to participate in a comprehensive survey of employees' opinions regard-ing the company. This took the form of a four-page questionnaire that was printed in the plant newspaper, accompanied by a reproduction of a hand-written letter from NAA President James H. "Dutch" Kindelberger. In this, Kindelberger lamented that the demands of the war, as well as a vastly expanded workforce, prevented him from interacting with the employees in the manner he formerly practiced. He wrote, "In spite of that, I still want to know what you think, the bad things as much as the good." He asked employees to fill out the questionnaire and acknowledged that some might "want to call me a few names." He invited the employees to utilize the portion of the form designated as the "gripe corner" to do just that, or to use the space to submit any ideas "that don't fall into the regular suggestion plan. Just let down your hair and tell me the first thing you would do if you were in my shoes." The questionnaire had fourteen general questions regarding the workplace, along with demographic ques-tions regarding the type of work the employee performed and how long he or she had been with NAA. True to his promise, there was a half-page of blank space where the employee could anonymously record any compli-ments or complaints.[23]

The survey appeared in the plant newspaper on Thursday, 15 May 1942. Kindelberger arrived at the plant on Saturday to find over fifteen hundred surveys had already been submitted. A photographer captured the image of a large pile of the questionnaires stacked atop a desk, as Kindelberger and NAA Vice President Lee Atwood looked through the responses. They were joined by Dallas factory manager Harold F. Schwedes and assistant manager K. P. Bowen. The men were amused when Kindelberger came across one survey on which an employee had expressed his belief that "you'll never see this Dutch."[24]

In the end, 1808 questionnaires were submitted, with the responses reported in the plant newspaper. Asked if NAA was the best aircraft plant in Texas to work at, 49.3% of the responses answered yes, with another 29.8% expressing no opinion. This left just 18.8% of the employees answering no, which meant that generally workers were happy with NAA. When comparing their work at NAA against their previous employment, 86% of the responders indicated that they preferred their new jobs. Queried about their reasons for working at NAA, slightly more than half the workers said career potential: 15.9% felt the acquired training could be useful for future work in the aviation industry and 36.7% were interested in job advancement at NAA. A sizable minority of 43.4% replied that their motivation for working at the plant was to help in the war effort. The biggest complaint was about the lunch carts, with which a majority of the employees expressed a level of dissatisfaction. As to the question of morale, 72.7% of the surveys indicated that the general spirit at the plant was good. As to the written "gripes," the most common complaint was with the staggered arrangement of the work shifts, which resulted in employees working on weekends.[25]

While the survey invited general suggestions, there was also a formal program at NAA that allowed workers to make suggestions to improve production. This process had been in place since March 1937, and employees whose ideas were adopted had been given rewards. Now, with the pressures of the war bearing down, the company decided to stage a high-stakes contest. On 12 March 1942, Dutch Kindelberger announced that $10,000 in defense bonds would be awarded to worthy ideas. The top suggestion in each of the three NAA plants was to receive a $500 bond, with smaller prize amounts given to other entrants. The top winners in the Dallas and Kansas City plants would also receive an expense-paid trip to Inglewood, where a final decision would be made regarding the best suggestion from the three facilities. The grand prize was a $1,000 bond, given in addition to the $500 bond awarded at the plant level. This made the grand prize worth a total of $1,500 in bonds, an impressive sum for the time.[26]

Response to the contest in the Dallas factory was significant, with 807 suggestions submitted by the 15 April 1942 deadline. In addition, the contest was back dated to the end of the last suggestion period, to allow

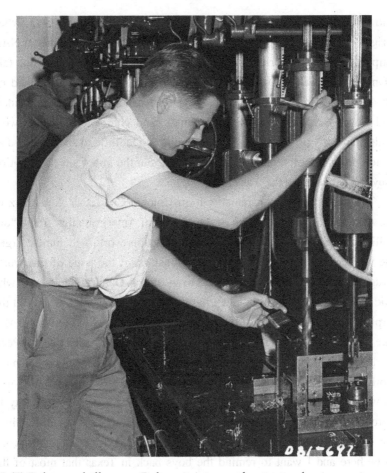

H. T. Baker at drill press. Baker won second prize in the suggestion
contest held in April 1942. *North American Aviation via Aircraft
Manufacturer's Collection, History of Aviation Collection, Special Collections
and Archives Division, Eugene McDermott Library, The University of Texas
at Dallas. Copyright ©Boeing. Used by permission.*

employees who submitted ideas prior to the announcement an opportunity to participate. Furthermore, all those who had won suggestion prizes
anytime since January 1941 were to be considered for the top prize.
The top prize winner for Dallas was James R. Hinds, who suggested a
"ball bearing grease exchanger."[27] As promised, he received a war bond

and traveled to Inglewood. He was there on Monday, 1 June 1942, when Brig. Gen. James H. "Jimmy" Doolittle appeared before thousands of NAA employees. These workers had gathered to hear the famed aviator talk of his bold attack upon the Japanese homeland, which had launched on 18 April 1942 from the aircraft carrier USS *Hornet*. The Doolittle Raiders had flown NAA-produced B-25 bombers, and company managers were understandably proud of this fact. Bringing in Doolittle to speak served as a motivational tool, reminding the employees of the important contribution they were making to the war effort.[28]

The event began with remarks from Colonel Charles W. Steinmetz of the Army Air Force. He spoke of the quality of American aircraft and "our ability to out produce every other country in this world." Steinmetz urged the workers to continue their efforts and act "as if the issue of this world struggle depended on me alone." Next to speak was Dutch Kindelberger, who said that Doolittle was at the plant to tell the men and women who built the airplanes what he thought of their work, as well as to describe what it was like to fly a B-25 on a visit to "the little yellow men who called on us at Pearl Harbor." But before Doolittle spoke, Kindelberger expressed his pride in the work being done at NAA, stating, "our job is production, building airplanes as well and fast as we can get the materials." He took the opportunity to introduce the three winners of the suggestion contest, including Hinds. Given the opportunity to say a few words, Hinds responded, "I'm mighty proud to be here and I want to remind the boys back in Texas that most of the pilots who flew with General Doolittle were trained in the North American combat trainers we build down in Texas." The other winners spoke as well, including Andrew Brown of Inglewood, the winner of the grand prize of the $1,000 war bond. Brown declared that the NAA workers admired Doolittle and the job he had done, and he expressed his desire that the general do it again, "right over Tokyo." Kindelberger finally introduced Doolittle while wondering aloud if the aviator might disclose the location of Shangri-La, the mythical base given by President Roosevelt as the starting point for the attack. Doolittle jokingly spilled the beans, saying "Dutch, don't tell a soul, but Shangri-La is right here at the North American plant—that's where our B-25 bombers came from." Doolittle was restricted in what he could divulge, but he provided some details about his mission in a speech broadcasted over the CBS radio network.[29]

Although the Doolittle event occurred in California, visitors frequently came to the Texas factory. There were celebrities such as Dorothy Lamour, but many were military service members. Some of the latter had no particular status, while others were more noteworthy. Guests such as these were most likely there to encourage the workers. Other individuals came in official capacities to inspect production, or to watch firsthand the efforts being made. Whatever the reason, NAA Dallas hosted many visitors during 1942.

Politicians were among the most frequent visitors of note. On 2 January W. Lee O'Daniel visited the plant. As governor of Texas, he had spoken at the dedication ceremony in April 1941. He had since been elected to the United States Senate. He commented that he was "delighted that the men and women in this plant seem so happy in their work, and so genuinely anxious to do their upmost to further our counties fight for freedom."[30] Early in March Governor Coke Stevenson toured the plant and reported that he was "tremendously impressed." His visit to the facility provided "revitalized confidence in the strength and ultimate complete victory of our country." Congressman Hatton Sumners came in July and lauded "the wonderful record of achievement of the people working in this plant." Congressman Wright Patman showed up as well, visiting the factory some-time around the beginning of August, accompanied by R. Eugene Risser of the War Production Board (WPB). Near the end of the year the operation was visited by Joseph C. Grew, the former United States ambassador to Japan. Grew commented on the great effort he saw at NAA, stating that "It is an inspiration to see these people at their work."[31]

Servicemen who toured the plant ranged across the spectrum of both rank and branch. While Inglewood got Doolittle, Dallas was visited by other partic-ipants of the Tokyo raid. Capt. David M. Jones had served as the pilot and commander of plane number five. He was apparently in town to join a touring group that included combat veterans from the American and British armed forces. Jones' itinerary took him to the Consolidated Aircraft factory in Fort Worth, where he participated in a ceremony accepting two B-24s that had been sponsored as part of a "Bonds for Bombers" campaign. The ceremony was overseen by businessman Ben E. Keith, with the obligatory appearance by Amon G. Carter.[32] In what might have been a mere coincidence, another Doolittle raider came to Dallas at this time: Lt. Ross R. Wilder, the copilot of plane five. Both aviators toured the NAA facility, apparently separately, observing operations and visiting with employees. Jones was photographed chatting with Alice Thornton, possibly about her husband, who was in the Army Air Corps. The plant newspaper identified Jones as a resident of Winters, Texas, and the Captain obligingly provided a quote filled with state pride, observing that "You can really see that good old Texas spirit at work here." Lieutenant Wilder had a Texas connection as well, having been born in Taylor, and posed for pictures with employees. He commented that he had received his advanced training in the AT-6, which he described as a smooth-flying ship. He was also reportedly impressed by the size of the plant, along with cleanliness of the facility, and he predicted that "There is no doubt about the outcome of this war if folks like these NAA workers keep turning 'em out at the rate they're going."[33]

The Navy had an interest in the North American plant as well, due to the production of the SNJ trainer. A notable visitor was Lt. Clarence E. Dickenson, who had an interesting life as a naval aviator. Dickenson was a pilot stationed aboard the USS *Enterprise*, and he had the misfortune to fly his Dauntless dive-bomber into the airspace above Pearl Harbor on 7 December 1941, during the Japanese attack. His plane was shot down by enemy fighters, resulting in the death of his radioman and forcing Dickenson to parachute to safety. He remained with the *Enterprise* during the desperate fighting that occurred in the opening months of 1942. He participated in the bombing attack that destroyed three Japanese aircraft carriers at the Battle of Midway on 4 June 1942 and had ditched his plane at sea when he ran out of fuel. Dickenson had been rotated out of combat and assigned as an instructor at the Naval Air Station at Corpus Christi, Texas. He reportedly smiled when he spotted finished trainers on the flight ramp, and he declared the plane was "a real sweet ship to fly."[34]

Aviators such as Jones, Wilder, and Dickenson clearly had a professional interest in the trainers produced by NAA, and while their praise for the aircraft was probably sincere, there seems little doubt their visits were intended to remind employees of the importance of their work. Yet not every military visitor had an aviation background. One such guest was Lt. Lucy Wilson, a native of Big Sandy, Texas. Wilson was a nurse in the Army Medical Corps and had been on Corregidor Island during the siege of that beleaguered fortress, leaving just forty-eight hours before the island was surrendered on 6 May 1942. She escaped aboard a submarine, and the timing suggests she was among two dozen people evacuated on board the USS *Spearfish*, the last group to be removed from the island before its fall. At one point reported as missing, she was safely back in the United States by the end of June. On 23 July she was honored in her hometown, which declared it to be "Lucy Wilson Day," and the young woman spoke to a crowd of well-wishers. Wilson, "a slender girl in a dark blue uniform, with silver lieutenant's bars on her shoulders," toured NAA in the first part of August. Her story provided a poignant contrast to the triumphant deeds of Jones, Wilder, and Dickenson. She described how "day after day on Corregidor we sat and wondered what they were doing in the States. We would have given a lot to have been sure that planes such as these were being built in plants such as this. For in those last days we had given up all hope and knew that every plane flying over couldn't be anything but a jap zero." But, having witnessed the bravery of the troops on Bataan, and seeing the workers laboring at NAA, she was confident that "the enemy doesn't have a chance."[35]

Upper-level military brass also arrived frequently in 1942. One of the first was William S. Knudsen, who returned to the factory just short of a year since he had delivered his address at the dedication ceremonies. At the time he had been the head of the Office of Production Management (OPM). Now he had a new role, and a new title. Roosevelt had established the WPB through an executive order on 16 January 1942 as part of a restructuring of the nation's war industrial efforts, with Donald M. Nelson named as director. As part of this reorganization, Knudsen had been commissioned into the Army as a lieutenant general and, as Director of Production, assigned to the office of the Under Secretary of War, Robert P. Patterson. In his new role Knudsen became "the War Department's top expeditor and trouble-shooter." As such, he visited war plants, working to solve production problems. He toured the NAA plant at Dallas on 24 March, escorted by Dutch Kindelberger and plant manager Schwedes. Knudsen made a "thorough trip through the shop," asking "a rapid-fire series of questions" during his inspection tour. He believed that the plant was doing a good job but stated "we will all have to do much better than good to win this war." He added, "I'll never be satisfied with production until we win this war."[36]

Other generals also came to check out operations in Dallas. One unexpected guest was Lt. Gen. Henry H. "Hap" Arnold, Chief of the Army Air Forces. Arnold and his entourage toured the factory on Saturday, 11 July. Arnold had been in Fort Worth and apparently decided to make an unscheduled trip to NAA, in what the plant newspaper later reported as a surprise inspection. Evidence of the unplanned nature of the visit is found in a photograph of Arnold being escorted by Ken Bowen, the assistant plant manager, instead of a higher-ranked official.

Arnold was on the ground in Grand Prairie for only ninety minutes before he left for his next stop. During his brief time at the plant he made a point of talking to several female employees. He told them that he appreciated the work that women were doing for the war effort, and he commented that "The job these women are doing is amazing." He stopped at the "B-section" offices, suggesting that one motive for his visit might have been to check on the progress of the B-24 program. In addition to the kind words regarding women workers, Arnold also praised the operation, asking his hosts to "Tell Dutch that he has a wonderful plant here." As he departed, Arnold also told Bowen, "You folks are doing a swell job, Keep it up."[37]

The cavalcade of compliments continued in August, when Brigadier General Kenneth B. Wolfe visited the plant. Wolfe was described as "chief of the production division of the Army Air Forces' material center," located at Wright Field in Dayton, Ohio. He issued a statement to the workers praising them for "the outstanding hum of activity in your plant. It was apparent right from the start of my tour that the employees all know that we are in a war and they are doing their best to help win it." Like Arnold, Wolfe also expressed admiration of the women working in the plant, observing that they "were doing their work exceptionally well and are playing a most vital role in the battle of production."[38]

Given the consistent praise heaped upon the Dallas plant by visitors, it appears that NAA was performing at a high level. More substantial praise came on 5 September 1942, when it was announced that the Dallas operation was to receive the "Army-Navy E" award in recognition of the work performed at the factory. Official word came in the form of a letter from Under Secretary of War Patterson, arriving in an envelope addressed "To the Men and Women of the Texas Division." Patterson wrote: "This is to inform you that the Army and Navy are conferring upon you the Army-Navy production award for high achievement in production of war material." He added, "Your patriotism, as shown by your remarkable production record, is helping our country along the road to victory." Patterson praised them for "accomplishing more than seemed possible a year ago." Indeed, it was just under two years since the ground had been broken for the factory.[39]

News of the "E" award was well received by the employees, management, and the local community. Congratulatory telegrams came from many of the business leaders who had endeavored to bring NAA to Dallas. John W. Carpenter of Texas Power and Light sent his regards, as did Robert L. Thornton of the Mercantile National Bank. Other telegrams arrived from Sanger Brothers, the Dr. Pepper Bottling Company, Lone Star Gas, Titche-Goettinger, and Mrs Baird's Bread. Among the well-wishers was J. Ben Critz of the Dallas Chamber of Commerce. Critz wired that "I have always thought that the North American plant would be the greatest of its kind in the country, and you have proved it by winning the Army-Navy E. We are grateful to you and know that you will do even greater things in the future."[40]

A ceremony to present the award was held on Monday, 21 September, with representatives from the Army and Navy in attendance. A platform was erected for the dignitaries, with an AT-6 parked on each side. Speeches were given by Brig. Gen. Arthur W. Vanaman from the Material Center at Wright Field, who addressed the NAA employees as "fellow soldiers" in the fight against "tyrants who would enslave our world." Also speaking was Capt. Alfred E. Montgomery, commandant of the Naval Air Station in Corpus Christi, as well as NAA Vice President Atwood, who referred to his employees as "soldiers of production." The actual presentation of the award fell to the Army, as it was the primary customer at the plant. The officer to present it was Major General Barton K. Yount, commander of the Army Air Forces Training Command, which relied so heavily on the AT-6 trainer. Yount delivered a speech in which he noted the importance of the aircraft, stating, "They have been the backbone of the single seater advanced training in our service and on the air services of the other United Nations." He went on to quote Lieutenant General George H. Brett, who had said of production workers "Yours is not a glamorous part, sweating along the production lines. You will get no cheers, there will be no parades for you. But without you there will be no victory. On you depends everything we do. You've got to give." Yount proceeded with his own words, addressing the assembled crowd of employees, before concluding "Mr. Kindelberger, it is with great satisfaction that I present to this great institution and to its personnel the E award flag on behalf of the United States."[41]

As he accepted the award, Kindelberger thanked General Yount, saying "it is a source of great pride to us—and it is also one of the greatest challenges we have ever received." He then addressed the now familiar themes; that the plant was staffed primarily with Texans, who had learned the tasks of aircraft production with the guidance of a small group from the parent factory, but that the Dallas plant had been "given the reins and you went ahead on your own." And now, with the facility winning the Army-Navy E, Kindelberger's belief in Dallas had been vindicated. He declared. "When this plant was started, I made some promises in Washington—promises which no one believed we could make good on. You've made good, just as I knew you would, and we all share in your pride over this recognition of your work." Now came the challenge. After six months the Army and Navy would review the work of the Dallas plant, to see if the high standards were being sustained. If they were not, then the factory would lose the honor of flying the E pennant flag. If the plant was still operating at a top level, a star would be added, and the flag could continue to fly. This was the challenge that Kindelberger had referred to earlier. He concluded, "Today we hitch our wagon to a star," pledging that "a glorious constellation will keep company with our Lone Star of Texas and the E of achievement."[42]

Speeches aside, there were the usual rituals that accompanied this type of event. A military band was on hand from Camp Wolters to provide music, and the NAA mixed chorus performed. Since the Army had presented the coveted pennant flag, Captain Montgomery represented the Navy by symbolically giving out E pins to three employees: plant manager Schwedes, David Garland, and Jean Hanna. All workers who had been employed at the plant on 5 September were to receive one of the pins, which could be worn on their clothing. The pins themselves measured about half an inch tall by one inch wide, and featured red, white, and blue stripes, with a blue center containing the letter E (for excellence). As to the pennant flag, it was big. A group photograph shows officers Yount, Vanaman, and Montgomery lined up with Schwedes and Kindelberger, along with Comm. Arthur Laverents from the Naval Reserve base at Hensley Field. The six men are lined up shoulder to shoulder with the flag in front of them, showing it to be several feet in length, suitable for flying from the main flagpole at the plant. The flag was in fact hoisted above the plant, while the band played the now-customary "The Eyes of Texas." At least some portion of the ceremony was broadcast over radio stations WRR and KRLD, which had set aside thirty minutes of programing for the event, with about twenty other Texas radio stations picking up the live feed from WRR. The ceremony was also repeated in the evening for the benefit of the night shift; although Montgomery and Yount were not present, their places were filled by other officers. NAA night superintendent Bill Landers also attended the later ceremony, but whether the other high-ranking executives were present is unclear, as news coverage focused on the daytime event.[43]

The presentation of the E award certainly supported the belief that NAA-Dallas was working efficiently to "Get 'Em Built." The awards were not just passed out casually; the Naval History and Heritage Command reports that 4,283 facilities earned the award during the war. At first glance this appears to be a high number, but it equated to roughly 5% of the eligible war plants. And true to Kindelberger's pledge, the Dallas plant won the desired star the following spring, thus keeping the prized pennant flag flying overhead.[44]

Encouraging words from visitors were welcome, and the E award provided a sense of pride and accomplishment, but in the end the most important indicator of success was the production of aircraft. Certainly,

Lucy Martin inspects a finished AT-6 trainer. *North American Aviation via Aircraft Manufacturer's Collection, History of Aviation Collection, Special Collections and Archives Division, Eugene McDermott Library, The University of Texas at Dallas. Copyright ©Boeing. Used by permission.*

it was a hectic and trying year for the management and employees of NAA. The beginning of 1942 found the country still coming to grips with the reality of war, but work at the Dallas plant continued without serious interruptions. In January the facility delivered 203 trainers, followed by 174 in February. From here the numbers continued to climb; March saw 212 planes accepted, then 250 in April. In July the number reached 311.

Draftswoman Rosalie Stephens at work in the engineering department. *North American Aviation via Aircraft Manufacturer's Collection, History of Aviation Collection, Special Collections and Archives Division, Eugene McDermott Library, The University of Texas at Dallas. Copyright ©Boeing. Used by permission.*

The increasing output corresponded with a decrease in the number of man hours needed per aircraft. Part of this can be attributed to the increasing experience of the workers as time progressed.[45] Another factor was the installation of a conveyor system during the spring. This device used chains installed in the factory floor, which pulled the aircraft down

AT-6 trainers near the hangar building. *North American Aviation via Aircraft Manufacturer's Collection, History of Aviation Collection, Special Collections and Archives Division, Eugene McDermott Library, The University of Texas at Dallas. Copyright ©Boeing. Used by permission.*

the assembly line. As part of this redesign, the assembly sequence underwent modification. In the original process, the fuselage of the trainer had been mated to the center section, then outer wing panels were mounted. Under the new system the entire wing section was assembled into one unit that included both the port and starboard wings. This was in turn mated to the fuselage. This rearrangement must have disrupted work to some degree as the transition was made, but once completed the benefits were obvious. After the assembly line was motorized, more conveyors were installed to move subassemblies through the plant. The completion of the conveyor network was accomplished by mid-summer, becoming "one of the largest applications of the conveyor principle, for mass production, ever made in the aircraft industry." Plant manager Schwedes described it as "the capstone for North American's mass production plan in this factory."[46]

Completion of the entire conveyor system is a likely reason for the increasing production numbers in the second half of 1942. In August, 379 trainers were delivered, followed by 430 in September. The highest monthly figure was in December, when 450 trainers were accepted by the military. In total, the military took delivery of 3,668 completed trainers during 1942, an average of just over ten units per day. This was a great increase over the 740 aircraft produced in Dallas during 1941, even after considering that the plant had not operated the entire year. The reasons for this increase are easy to determine; increased knowledge of the employees, new ideas gained through employee suggestions, and improved efficiency of operations via methods such as the conveyor system. An additional factor was surely the knowledge that the country was at war, giving the workers a sense of mission as they worked to "Get 'Em Built."[47]

Chapter 14

Turbulence Ahead

As 1942 ended the North American Aviation (NAA) plant in Dallas was operating at a high state of efficiency, and bigger things were on the horizon. Late in December there was public announcement of the B-plant, with the news that NAA was to build bombers and fighters in addition to the trainers already in production. Further information was released days later, when James H. "Dutch" Kindelberger revealed the fighter to be built was the P-51 Mustang. This would put Dallas into the business of manufacturing combat aircraft, and expectations were high. Company forecasts anticipated that more than four thousand trainers would be produced in 1943, along with over eight hundred fighters. Projections also called for more than four hundred bombers to be built in the B-plant. It was a substantial goal, with numerous obstacles to overcome.[1]

The decision to build the P-51 fighter in Dallas was in response to the need for large numbers of this aircraft. While a detailed examination of the airplane is outside the scope of this study, a brief explanation is justifiable to provide context. A useful account of the situation can be found within an NAA internal document:

The company first considered the fighter project which later developed into the Mustang in February, 1940, when representatives of the British Air Ministry asked the company to build Curtiss P-40 fighters. After considering this proposal, the company suggested that it be permitted to build a new type of its own design, incorporating all the latest aerodynamic refinements and all knowledge gained in air combat. This proposal was accepted by the British Purchasing Commission late in the spring of 1940, and design drafting on the new fighter began on May 5.[2]

Spurred on by the necessity of war, and facilitated by fast-working engineers, NAA went to work on what was designated the NA-73.

The company managed to finish a prototype aircraft (minus the engine) on 9 September 1940. This was a mere 127 days since the design team started its work, in what an anonymous NAA historian suggested "will probably stand as the greatest single aeronautical engineering feat of the war." Even if this is discounted as corporate propaganda, the rapid development of the NA-73 was an impressive piece of work. Furthermore, despite the fast pace of the process, the finished aircraft proved to be a solid design. It featured a laminar flow wing, taking advantage of recent research conducted by the National Advisory Committee for Aeronautics (NACA). The result was an aerodynamically clean ship with good handling characteristics. This enabled the NA-73 to outperform the Curtiss P-40, even though the North American fighter utilized the same Allison engine. Test flights of the prototype were conducted starting in October 1940, with the delivery of production models in the autumn of the following year. The plane, soon christened the Mustang by the British, entered operational service with the RAF in November 1941, with combat sorties beginning in 1942.[3]

The Mustang had proven to be a useful warplane, and the United States Army Air Force became interested in it as well. However, early models were hindered by their Allison engines, which limited the effectiveness of the P-51 at higher altitudes. The British suggested replacing the Allison with the Rolls Royce Merlin engine, and modified a Mustang to serve as a prototype. The resulting aircraft had significantly improved capabilities at high altitudes. At this point the Army, which had previously ordered small numbers of the plane, began showing great interest in the P-51. The first American Merlin-powered Mustang flew on 30 November 1942, under the designation XP-51B. NAA had already received a letter of intent for four hundred planes in October, presumably based on the projected performance of the XP-51B.[4]

With the P-51 becoming a priority for the Army, NAA needed to increase its production capacity for the aircraft. At the time the Mustang was only built at Inglewood, and the desirability of a second source was obvious. According to NAA records the decision to manufacture the planes in Dallas was made in October 1942, possibly in response to the previously mentioned letter of intent. The exact process by which the decision proceeded is unclear. Since the Texas facility was engaged in war production, and owned by the federal government, official authorization was needed. On 14 December 1942 a government teletype outlined the proposal to initiate P-51 production in the Dallas A-plant. The usual parameters were taken into consideration, including the availability of labor, transportation, and utilities, all of which were considered adequate. There was concern over the availability of housing, which was deemed insufficient for the increased workforce, and it was stated, "several hundred additional housing units will be required." This teletype worked its way through the channels. On 18 December, Army officials at the Headquarters of the Material Command forwarded the proposal to the Facility Clearance Board, which itself was part of the War Production Board.[5]

Information from the teletype proposal was summarized in a memorandum dated 23 December, in which approval was sought for $1,325,216 dollars to start manufacturing of the Mustang. Since factory space was needed, this required a reduction in AT-6 production. The plant was capable of building as many as 500 trainers per month; this would be reduced to 240, thus allowing for the monthly production of up to 270 P-51 fighters. It was anticipated that another 5,400 employees were required, of which 4,320 could be women. Initial manufacturing could begin one hundred days after approval, with maximum production within five hundred days. The memorandum recommended approval, as "the project has been carefully screened and is essential to the war effort." On 5 January 1943 the Facility Clearance Board approved the project, forwarding it to the War Department, which in turn sent it to Under Secretary of War Robert P. Patterson, who issued his approval on 7 January. This was two weeks after Dutch Kindelberger had publicly announced the production of the Mustang in Dallas, suggesting he had prior assurances of the approval of the program.[6]

The formal approval of Mustang production in Dallas was a major development. Another development, albeit of less importance, was also announced early in January 1943. Dutch Kindelberger shared the news in a telegram sent to Governor Coke Stevenson:

> North American Aviation is today able to announce that it has given the name Texan to its AT-6 series of combat trainers. This name has been formally approved by the War Department as the official Air Forces name for the aircraft. This name is in recognition of our Texas plants, manned by Texans, who are building the Texan and other types with a speed and efficiency that does credit to their great heritage.[7]

Kindelberger stated that the name also served as acknowledgement of the large number of training fields in Texas, where a "large percentage of American pilots" received instruction. The telegram closed with an appeal to Texas pride; "We confidently hope, Governor Stevenson, that every Texan will have cause for genuine pride in his state's new winged namesake." Thus, the AT-6 series of trainers acquired the moniker by which they are still known today—the Texan. At the same time the War Department officially adopted the Mustang designation for the P-51, conforming to British practice.[8]

To a citizen of Dallas reading press coverage, it must have appeared that the year was getting off to a good start for NAA. A new plant was coming online to build an unspecified bomber, and Mustangs were to be built in the A-plant. These were important developments. There was also the naming of the AT-6 as the Texan, a not particularly significant event, but one that likely gave residents a boost of pride. But there were difficult times ahead, and although the impending problems were not immediately obvious, there were clues that hinted at things to come.

One issue that continued to be bothersome was a shortage of housing. This had been an issue when the plant was first announced, and it had been partially addressed through the construction of private homes, as well as the government projects such as Avion Village. These efforts had helped the situation, especially

AT-6 crated for shipment. *North American Aviation via Aircraft Manufacturer's Collection, History of Aviation Collection, Special Collections and Archives Division, Eugene McDermott Library, The University of Texas at Dallas. Copyright ©Boeing. Used by permission.*

with the relatively small number of people employed at the factory prior to Pearl Harbor. But with an expanding workforce, the need for housing was once again becoming critical. New hires that were Dallas residents most likely had accommodations, but job seekers from outside the area needed to find housing near NAA. With gasoline and tires rationed, and a thirty-five-mile-per-hour speed limit in place, it was hard for workers to commute long distances.

The problem was twofold; the demands of the war had increased the need for housing in Dallas, while at the same time building materials became scarce. The needs of the military and defense industries took priority over private interests. As a result, homebuilding in Dallas had dropped dramatically. In December 1942, the *Dallas Morning News* reported that "new residential construction virtually has stopped in Dallas, because of governmental freezing orders and limitation of construction." The paper reported that in November there were only 111 single-family homes under construction, as well as 90 duplexes, for a total of 201 units. Most of these were in the Oak Cliff area, due to its proximately to the NAA plant. In fact, 4,428 family units had been constructed during the first eleven months of 1941, compared to only 2,758 during the same period in 1942, representing a decrease of 1,670 units. These figures were compiled by Dallas Power and Light, so it is unclear whether they included construction in Grand Prairie. Either way, it seems reasonable to conclude that the decrease in construction was consistent in the municipalities surrounding the factory. If defense workers wished to move to Dallas for employment, they might have difficulty finding housing. Indeed, a shortage of housing was a concern mentioned in the December teletype that had proposed the building of P-51s in Dallas.[9]

Some steps had been taken to help alleviate the problem. For example, a federally sponsored housing unit had been constructed south of the campus of the North Texas Agricultural College in Arlington. This dormitory-style habitat consisted of three separate two-story buildings and was originally intended to provide space for up to one hundred single male workers at NAA. This small amount of housing was insignificant in comparison to anticipated needs, but it provided an option for some employees. The two-story brick units were ready for occupancy in June 1942, when an announcement of their availability appeared in the NAA plant newspaper. Single occupancy rooms were rented for $3.50 a week, with double occupancy costing $5.00. Each room had a lavatory, but showers were shared. This arrangement was not likely to appeal to everyone, and it certainly was not suitable for families. This may explain why space was still available at the beginning of October 1942, by which time one of the units had been designated for women employees.[10]

The housing issue continued to draw attention as 1943 progressed. One example can be found in the availability of housing at Washington Place, a low-rent development that had been initiated by the Dallas Housing Authority (DHA) in 1941. Located to the southeast of Baylor Hospital in East Dallas, the brick buildings were built to replace substandard housing in that area and were to provide accommodations for 234 families. Washington Place was to be ready for occupancy in October 1942, but its planned use as low-income housing was pushed aside in favor of the military. The Army commandeered the residences for use by personnel assigned to the headquarters of the Eighth Service Command, which relocated to Dallas late in 1942. As it happened, the Army did not need the housing, which was opened to defense workers at the beginning of 1943, along with units at another DHA property known as the Cedar Springs Place Addition. This resulted in over four hundred units being allotted for use by NAA workers. Rent for these unfurnished apartments ranged from $33.50 to $41.00 per month, depending upon the number of bedrooms, and utilities were included. To qualify for the housing, a worker had to earn less than $56 a week.[11]

The chronic need for adequate housing was a concern for NAA management, for the company announced a program to begin on 4 February 1943. This plan provided a daily list of "houses, apartments, and rooms available in the Greater Dallas area." This was available through the Employees Transportation Office, with the list itself compiled by a housing bureau operated by the Dallas Chamber of Commerce in cooperation with the Dallas Real Estate Board. Plant Manager Harold F. Schwedes emphasized that NAA had nothing to do with the operation of the housing bureau, nor its policies. The company was providing the list "as a service to our employees," so that workers could "quickly and easily determine" what accommodations were available in the Dallas area. Officials who maintained the list urged property owners in suburban areas to provide information for the list, especially Grand Prairie because of its proximity to the factory. Indeed, Grand Prairie itself had greatly expanded since the NAA opening, with its population increasing from about fifteen hundred residents to over fifteen thousand in the space of two years.[12]

By early 1943 employees at NAA were living in a variety of housing. There were the private homes built nearby in the early months after announcement of the plant, as well as the defense housing at Avion Village.

Single workers might be living in dormitories in Arlington, and couples and families could be living in the public housing developments operated by the Dallas Housing Authority. Unknown numbers were probably renting homes or rooms from individual property owners. But with employment at the plant still rising due to the opening of the B-plant, and the start of P-51 production, more housing was needed. Adding in the needs of the Eighth Service Command, as well as other Dallas wartime industries, created what the *Dallas Morning News* referred to as "the vexing housing problem," which eventually became a major source of disagreement during 1943.

Another cause of contention in 1943 was the effort to determine which union was to serve as the collective bargaining agency at NAA in Dallas. While there had been union activity at the plant since the earliest days, a single organization had not gained control. The reasons are uncertain, but several factors could have been at play. First, the unsanctioned strike at Inglewood in 1941, followed by the plant seizure by the military, presumably left the Congress of Industrial Organizations (CIO) in a weakened position regarding NAA. There was also the general public annoyance with strikes in defense industries. Not to be forgotten is the common antiunion sentiment in Texas, as demonstrated by the state antistrike violence law of 1941, which had been passed just before the NAA plant opened. Add in a patriotic fervor during the opening years of the war, and it comes as no surprise that formal recognition of a bargaining union was slow to arrive.[13]

Both the CIO and its rival, the American Federation of Labor (AFL) were anxious to become the negotiating union for North American's Dallas factory. The CIO moved first, filing paperwork with the National Labor Relations Board (NLRB) in mid-January 1943, calling for an election at the plant to settle the question. The AFL responded in kind, and the NLRB scheduled a hearing to work out the details. At that time, both unions had members working at NAA, but news reports indicated the CIO was more active, having opened an office in Grand Prairie. Arrangements were made and a vote was scheduled, to be held over three days in February.[14]

Company response to the situation appears to have been restrained. NAA plant management was apparently aware of union attempts to call for a collective bargaining agreement, evidenced by a notice appearing in the plant newspaper on 15 January. The announcement was a reprint of a previously released statement from 1941 and was being reissued to clarify the official policy. To wit:

(1) The management is under no obligation, contractual or legal, to force an employee under penalty of losing his job to join any particular organization. We are prohibited by law from doing so. The management has always taken the position that membership or nonmembership in any organization is not necessary to obtain or hold a job with North American.

(2) We respect the rights of employees granted by the National Labor Relations Act to bargain collectively through representatives of their own choosing. We respect their rights not to be coerced to join or not to join a union.[15]

Other than this announcement, there was no specific coverage of the impending vote in the plant newspaper. Union activities were protected by the National Labor Relations Act, and company officials surely wished to avoid clashing with the government. Management needed to tread carefully on the issue.

The two unions were free to compete for the support of the employees. There was typically no love lost between the two rival organizations. However, it appears that the CIO directed more of its criticism at the company, rather than the AFL. This might have indicated a stronger position of the CIO among the workers at the plant. At a meeting prior to the vote, its representatives "disputed the claim of the plant management that wage rates at the Dallas plant are the same as at Kansas City and Inglewood." The regional director of the CIO, John Livingston, told his audience that "The UAW (United Auto Workers) intends to apply the same program at the Dallas [NAA] plant as prevails at the other aircraft factories." He specifically mentioned "seniority rights, equal pay for equal work and equal pay for women." Livingston also took aim at Sen. W. Lee O'Daniel, stating his "whole labor program is anti-union." Joining the attack, UAW president R. J. Thomas said that "he liked Texas but he couldn't understand how Texans could elect a former Kansas flour salesman as their Senator."[16]

Two days later the AFL held its meeting regarding the impending vote, which was to begin the next day, Tuesday. Wallace Reilly, an AFL leader from Dallas, attacked the rival organization, declaring "I don't believe the CIO has anyplace in Texas whatsoever, and I don't believe Texas will accept it. But I do know that a union organization is needed at North American." Also speaking was L. M. Fagan, a representative of the International Association of Machinists, the specific union seeking to win bargaining rights at NAA. Fagan argued that "the most important thing is not a wage increase, but job protection and seniority rights." Fagan was looking ahead to a period after the war, telling members that "your job is to sell Texas on your union." Fagan had another reason to want the AFL to win the election at NAA: he was leading efforts to have the AFL become the bargaining agent at the Consolidated bomber plant in Fort Worth. That election was to occur the following week, and an AFL win at NAA could provide momentum for the upcoming vote at Consolidated. Fagan also took a shot at O'Daniel, noting that "We've got a Senator who runs from state to state trying to cut labor's throat." He added, "It's shameful that he's a United States Senator, but there he is." Whatever their differences, there was consensus between the two rival unions when it came to O'Daniel.[17]

It was to be, according to reports, "the most important union labor election ever held in this area," because it involved such large numbers of workers. As it happened, the first vote failed to produce a winner. This probably surprised officials from the two unions, both of which anticipated a clean win. The final vote tallies were not released to the public, as the number of employees at the plant was sensitive information. But the percentages told the story. More than 85% of the eligible employees participated in the election, with 46.3% voting for the UAW (CIO). Only 25.3% voted for the International Association of Machinists (AFL). In what might have surprised organizers from the two groups, 27.8% voted against either organization representing the workers, showing a strong antiunion sentiment existed. The lack of a majority made a run-off necessary between the CIO and the "no-union" option. Since 71.6% of the ballots had favored some sort of union, CIO officials anticipated victory in the second balloting.[18]

Workers who opposed the union did not admit defeat. Employee C. B. Hunt of the B-plant authored a circular against unionization, and reportedly bankrolled the printing costs on his own. The *Dallas Morning News* printed the circular in its entirety. Hunt titled his appeal "Our Last Chance to Think," and presented his case against unionization. He argued that workers had been "besieged with an avalanche of vote-getting propaganda in the form of rank misleading statements, claims and promises." He believed the CIO had dominated the debate because they had money, while the nonunion voters had no way to effectively respond with advertising. Therefore, he took it on himself to address the issues. He argued against the costs of joining the union, presumably in respect to dues, which he felt would enslave the workers to the CIO. His biggest concern was that the only real instrument of power for the union was the strike, and he argued that "our government will not allow nor will the public tolerate a strike at North American." Hunt asserted that "Unions are all right in their places, but a war plant is no place for one any more than in the Army or Navy." He wrote that most NAA workers considered it a privilege to help the war effort, believed that working conditions in the plant were fine, and "most of us are drawing better wages than we can get anywhere else. Everything possible has been done for our comfort by the company that I know of and it would likely continue such a policy unless a union disrupts things. Everybody seems happy and friendly. It is often best to let good enough alone."[19]

Obviously, Hunt saw little advantage in the union. Given the governmental reaction at Inglewood in 1941, he may have been right about the risks of unionization. He worried the situation could breed conflict, and he appealed to his coworkers that they should "remain good friends." Hunt claimed to have distributed twenty thousand circulars, but in some cases his efforts were blocked. He arranged for boys to hand out copies of his circular at the Jefferson Hotel and at the corner of Jackson and Lamar, two locations where buses to NAA stopped for passengers. Hunt told police that CIO agents "snatched them from the boys and tore them up, and that a policeman stood by and watched without interfering." Furthermore, he claimed that some of the union men told the boys they were with the Federal Bureau of Investigation, presumably to intimidate them. CIO representative

R. E. Curtis denied that CIO men were involved in the incident, and he added that distributing the flyers while voting was underway was a violation of NLRB regulations. The truth of the matter is unclear, but this sort of conflict went against Hunt's desire for harmony in the workforce.[20]

The runoff was completed by the end of February, and the CIO carried the day. The NLRB released the vote tally, showing 83.6% of the eligible employees had cast ballots, down slightly from the original election. Interestingly, the CIO carried 55.54% of the vote, while the no-union option carried 44.6%. This means the CIO picked up around 9 percentage points, while the no-union contingent gained over 16 points. It appears some workers who endorsed the AFL preferred no union at all rather than supporting the CIO. This could be due to inherent animosity between the two organizations, but another possibility is that some workers held negative feelings toward the CIO due to the union's role in the defense strikes of 1941. Whatever the case, the CIO became the collective bargaining agent for NAA in Dallas. As for the AFL, that group won a victory the following week when it gained the rights to organize at the Consolidated bomber plant in Fort Worth, defeating the no-union option in an election that did not include the CIO at all.[21]

Whether the union fight at NAA had negative consequences to employee morale is uncertain. It might have had little or no effect on some individuals, while others might have reacted with hostility toward proponents of the CIO. It seems unlikely that the union struggle had positive effects at the plant. For every employee who was happy about the outcome, there was probably one that was embittered by it, and it is possible the whole process caused a degree of animosity among many workers. Add in the natural state of antagonism between workers and management, and it seems reasonable to speculate the spirit of teamwork in the plant suffered. This could have been a factor in the discontent that hit NAA in the latter half of 1943.

Tensions surrounding the union election, along with the ongoing housing question, were two issues that concerned NAA managers during the opening months of 1943. But there was another development that could negatively affect what was to come, and that was a continued demand for more aircraft. Evidence can be found barely two weeks into the new year, when an inspection of the plant was undertaken by members of the Aircraft Production Board (APB). This body had been formed on 9 December 1942, due to "the overriding importance attached to the aircraft program." It consisted of civilians from the government and aviation industry, as well as military representatives from the Army and Navy. The chair of the APB was Charles E. Wilson, who also served as vice-chair of the War Production Board. Among the members was Lt. Gen. William S. Knudsen. This board "assumed central direction of aircraft production, including scheduling."[22]

The APB had existed for just over a month when it visited Dallas on 12 January on a tour of aircraft factories. As was normal, the visitors praised the operation, with Knudsen observing "This is a swell bunch you have here, and that comes right from the heart." Rear Admiral Ralph Davison was impressed by the plant, commenting, "There is a fine tempo here. Everyone is working. The spirit is excellent." But board members offered warnings of what lay ahead. Maj. Gen. Oliver Echols commented, "We must more than double what we are already doing in 1943." Chairman Wilson also alluded to an increased tempo ahead, stating, "You have two very fine plants here. They are being well manned. I think it only fair to warn you that we are expecting an awful lot from you and I see no reason why we shouldn't get it."[23]

The implication was that production numbers assigned to NAA would increase, especially in the case of the B-24 Liberator. At this time the Army Air Force was ramping up its forces in Europe in order to pursue its strategic bombing campaign against Germany, which required large numbers of heavy bombers. With the B-plant coming online, it seems natural that Dallas was viewed as a source of additional planes. It is known that NAA delivered substantially more B-24 Liberators than the 750 specified in the original letter of intent from January 1942, and that additional numbers of aircraft were cancelled in 1944. Given the timing of events, it appears that the increased numbers arrived in 1943. This probably occurred with the adoption of production schedule W-6 on 12 August, which has been cited as "the original production schedule," for Liberators manufactured in the B-plant. If this is the case, it could help explain subsequent events.[24]

As far as production of the B-24 went, Dallas reached a milestone when the first completed bomber rolled out for its maiden flight on 16 March 1943.

This was 319 days since the production contract was signed. The olive-drab aircraft featured the phrase "More To Come" painted on the side of its nose, where crews typically painted the name of their plane. Company pilots that took the ship on its first flight reported a routine shake-down, in which the ship performed excellently. The aircraft still had to be flown by Army pilots before it was formally accepted. The exact date this happened is uncertain, but on 9 April the plant newspaper printed a statement from Col. Frank Cook of the engineering section at Wright Field. Cook complimented the workers on their fine efforts, stating that "the airplane was flown on a complete shake-down flight and the characteristics indicated that the contractor's tooling and manufacturing procedures resulted in an excellent B-24 airplane." The same issue included warm congratulations from Brig. Gen. K. B. Wolfe, who had visited NAA the previous August. Wolfe was chairman of the B-24 Liaison Committee, tasked with coordinating efforts between the various manufacturers of the Liberator.[25]

With the first plane completed, it was publicly announced that the B-plant was engaged in B-24 production. Up to that time the exact model of bomber had been unreleased, but with the large plane outside the hangar and taking off from Hensley Field, it would have been difficult to keep it under wraps. And so, Dallas openly joined Fort Worth in the production of the Liberator. The problem was there was no rush of Liberators rolling out of the door of the plant. The first ship promised "More To Come," but the reality was that the plant was not ready to enter full-scale production. There had been a series of delays, beginning with a failure of structural materials to arrive as scheduled. Equipment also arrived late, including hydraulic presses, and machine shop fixtures. Contractors had difficulty hiring enough skilled labor, and there was a shortage of electrical power in the plant until additional transformers arrived. All these factors caused the B-plant to be completed about four months later than scheduled. In the meantime, the first B-24 had been largely built in subassemblies in the hangar building of the A-plant, which was no longer used for storing AT-6s due to the large number of trainers being produced. There B-24 components were gathered and fabricated into subassemblies, which later were moved into the unfinished B-plant for final assembly. This process produced the first ships, and an internal company document reported, "The first five B-24s are being built in temporary quarters in the hangar, since the factory buildings were not sufficiently complete to permit work to begin as scheduled." The equipment delays were partially addressed by using parts supplied by Consolidated and Ford, which allowed NAA workers to start gaining experience while awaiting the arrival of needed machinery.[26]

The situation was summed up by Maj. Frank C. Merrill, the Army Air Force liaison at the NAA plant. When an investigator asked when the first B-24 came off the assembly line, Merrill responded "I think back in February; you can hardly say it came off the line, it was built mostly by hand; some of the parts we made and some were shipped in." It would be some time before planes were being completed as intended. The delays in reaching large-scale production were reflected in a company document that provided a forecast of acceptances, which projected only twenty-five bombers would be completed by the end of June 1943. From there the numbers were to increase, until reaching a monthly output of 75 bombers during the last four months of 1943, totaling 408 aircraft by the end of the year. In the end, these numbers were overly optimistic. The failure to meet these goals was a significant factor in a major controversy centering on the city of Dallas, as well as the operation of the NAA factory.[27]

Chapter 15

Crisis, 1943

While delays in the B-24 program were a concern in the spring of 1943, there was another issue causing unrest. Housing had been a recurring problem since the plant began construction in 1940. Since then, various approaches had been tried, including federally financed projects, private developments, dormitories, and public housing. But the issue continued to arise as employment at North American Aviation (NAA) increased. Early in July, the *Dallas Morning News* described the plight of newly arriving workers:

GRAND PRAIRIE, Texas, July 3.—The story of the growth of a town to a city overnight, of a flat blanket of prairie land grown into territory overrun with government housing units, is Grand Prairie, where the song of the factory worker has struck a new note.

Where shall I live and what shall I do with my family? is the question put to Grand Prairie citizens daily.

The boom of factory workers has pushed up population to more than 16,000 from a mere 1,600 in 1940. During the last three weeks fifty-eight more families arrived.

"That's not unusual," say old and permanent residents of the city with a sad shake of the head.

One family who arrived about three weeks ago paid its moving van
to drive up and down main street at a dollar an hour while the man of
the family raced wildly about the countryside in search of a house, cash
or rent. The moving van was moving long into the night.[1]

This was the situation in the community closest to the airplane factory.
If prospective workers were willing to live farther away, then their options
were presumably greater, but this brought up the issue of transportation.
The shortage of housing made it harder for qualified applicants to move
to the area to work in defense industries. If all the available jobs could
have been filled by current Dallas residents, then the issue of housing
would not have been as critical. The problem was that an in-migration of
workers was needed. The stage was set for an impending crisis as lack of
housing threatened efforts to secure sufficient manpower to operate the
NAA plant.

Growing concern continued in the spring of 1943. On 22 April, Clyde
Wallis of the Dallas Chamber of Commerce sent a letter to the office of
the War Manpower Commission (WMC), located in the Mercantile Bank
building in Dallas. In this letter Wallis argued for reclassifying Dallas
from a Group Two labor market to a Group Three, a less critical designation. In a detailed reply to Wallis, WMC regional director James H. Bond
responded with employment projections for the Dallas area. The WMC
anticipated "that demand on the Dallas labor force will total approximately 21,000 workers to the end of six months and 35,000 to the end of
the next twelve-month period." To meet these needs, Bond wrote, meant
that "approximately 8,000 workers will have to be in-migrated into the
Dallas area during the next six months and approximately 21,400 will
have to be brought in during the next twelve-month period." If these
estimates proved accurate, the housing situation was going to get worse.
Wallis was persistent and answered Bond two days later with counter-
arguments. In the process of doing so he revealed his interest in the
matter. The Chamber of Commerce understood that the War Production
Board was contemplating the establishment of "three additional aluminum extrusion mills to supply the aircraft industry." Wallis maintained
that Dallas was a logical choice for one of these facilities, as it could

service aircraft factories in Dallas, Fort Worth, and Tulsa. But for this to happen required approval of the WMC, which is why Wallis had written. But Wallis was to be disappointed, for in May a letter arrived from the WMC in Washington, stating that the Group Two classification was to stay in effect. Dallas was not likely to get an aluminum mill.[2]

Indeed, while the Chamber of Commerce was lobbying to have Dallas upgraded to Group Three status, the real worry should have been the possibility that the city could be downgraded to Group One, designating it as a critical labor area. Public awareness of this possibility was starting to rise early in July, when the *Dallas Morning News* reported that two governmental agencies had differing ideas over how to address the ongoing housing issue. The newspaper stated, "The disagreement is between the War Manpower Commission, which has demanded immediate provision of temporary housing, and the National Housing Agency, which holds out for construction of permanent housing only." The dispute had come to the attention of the Dallas War Housing Committee, which had met with Orville W. Erringer, a banker who served as area director for the WMC. The agency was looking at the situation from its own priorities, seeing an immediate need for housing based on projected manpower needs in Dallas. Erringer believed the situation could only be resolved by using temporary housing, and failure to do so would leave the WMC with no alternative other than designating Dallas as Group One. The atmosphere at the meeting was apparently tense, with one observer describing the situation as "loaded with dynamite."[3]

The National Housing Administration (NHA), for its part, was looking at the issue from the aspects of the long-term housing needs of the area, with area director Harold G. Reynolds saying that the agency "was pretty well settled in favor of permanent housing. The matter of temporary housing was explored and found not to be feasible." Reynolds opined that "No builders seem willing to go into temporary building, such as the erection of prefabricated houses. They cannot get federal loan insurance on such housing and it is hard to borrow money for building now unless loans are insured." As a result, the NHA had asked Washington to allow three thousand permanent housing units to be built, including twenty-three hundred by private enterprise. But news reports indicated there was uncertainty whether this would happen:[4]

> Authorization by the NHA of housing is no guarantee that houses will be built, or built in time to solve the critical needs. After authorization by NHA, builders willing to construct the house must come forward. They must then obtain War Production Board priorities, then go through the formalities of Federal Housing Administration approval if the building is to be financed under FHA. All that takes time. Then there is the battle to get scarce materials.[5]

But Washington did approve the housing program, allowing work to start on 2,296 homes. This quantity was insufficient to solve the problem, but it was a beginning. Officials with the NHA thought that some of the houses could be completed within sixty days.[6]

In the meantime, the public continued to learn about the problem. On 13 July 1943, Erringer appeared before the Dallas Kiwanis Club during a luncheon at the Hotel Adolphus. His briefing provided a summary of the manpower situation, and the consequences to come if it did not improve:

> The available labor supply is scraping bottom. There is a complete absence of skilled mechanics available. There still is a small floating supply of white-collar workers, but they are untrained to work with their hands. An unknown quality is the number of home women—wives and mothers—who can be induced to enter the war production program. That just about cleans up the possibilities of white workers. There is a large potential group represented by negroes, but most of them are unskilled and would have to be trained.

Erringer went on to explain the consequences of being designated as a Group One area:

> When demand exceeds supply, then you enter the critical stage. When a city becomes a No.1 critical area it means the War Manpower Commission not only supervises the manpower but administers the whole civil economy. Its stops issuance of new war contracts and means business and industry must go on the forty-eight-hour week. It becomes necessary then for the WMC to channel labor away from lesser industries into the war industry.[7]

It was not reported how the members of the Kiwanis Club reacted to this information. Given the typical membership of fraternal service organizations at the time, it probably came as a shock. In a city where local businessmen wielded much influence, having the WMC oversee the "whole civil economy" must have seemed like a monstrous mutation of the New Deal.

Erringer reiterated that the housing supply was a critical part of the problem. At one point there had been anywhere from twenty-five hundred to three thousand workers moving to Dallas each month in search of work in war industries, but that the number had "dropped to a mere trickle because word went out that Dallas was unable to house the migrants." With the pool of labor dwindling in Dallas, and with the city unable to provide accommodations for new workers, the problem was acute. Erringer encouraged civic leaders to work on a solution to the housing situation.[8]

As it happened, there were individuals seeking to do just that. After being briefed by Erringer, the Dallas Chamber of Commerce formed a committee to look for solutions to the problem. Among the members were Robert L. Thornton and Nathan Adams. A primary concern for the committee was housing, but other ideas were considered to improve the manpower situation as well such as "bringing more women into industry" and "encouraging Dallasites to share homes with war worker families."[9]

Meanwhile, there was still talk of temporary housing. One possibility was to utilize prefabricated barracks that were built in Dallas by the National Housing Company for the Army. There were reports that several thousand units of prefabricated temporary housing were in storage. Proof of this appeared on the front page of the *Dallas Morning News*, which published a picture of a long line of houses packed in crates that might be used to alleviate the problem. Where this photograph was taken was unfortunately not specified, but it was credited to a staff photographer, suggesting it was a Dallas-area location. It is unknown whether the crated dwellings were the barracks produced by National Housing, or some other type of temporary structure. There was also talk of bringing in government-supplied trailer homes.[10]

The proposed use of temporary buildings continued to stir controversy. The Dallas Real Estate Board passed a resolution "that only permanent housing conforming to neighborhood standards be built in Dallas." The board advocated

that any temporary housing be built in the vicinity of war plants. This aggra-
vated officials in Grand Prairie, who accused Dallas of trying to monopolize
new permanent housing while saddling their community with temporary units.
Mayor G. H. Turner declared that prefabricated homes "would create a fire
hazard, insanitary conditions, and have a denigrating effect on the permanent
homes of residents of Grand Prairie." The city would be burdened with providing sanitation, water utilities, public safety, and educational services to the residents of the temporary housing, then be left with nothing after the buildings
were removed at the end of the war. An unnamed official stipulated that "Grand
Prairie will be willing to take its share of any necessary temporary construction
if Dallas will take its share, but we won't bear the whole burden." This was
not yet resolved when NHA officials requested the building of one thousand
temporary units within walking distance of NAA. The request was approved,
with the task to be handled by the Federal Public Housing Authority.[11]

Residents of Grand Prairie were concerned that their community might
become the site for all one thousand homes. Municipal services were already
strained by the rapid growth of the city. Another concern was that one thousand
new families could bring an estimated 750 school-age children, overwhelming
a school system which had 1,800 students. Concerned citizens signed a petition
against the project. Whether these had any effect on the decision is unknown,
but when the final plans were announced only two hundred units were to be in
Grand Prairie, just north of Avion Village. Most of the units were to be built just
outside the city limits of Dallas, at the edge of Oak Cliff. Initial plans called for
eight hundred homes, and construction began in the latter part of September.
The first units were ready by 2 December 1943, when ten families moved into
the housing units. One of the first residents was R. S. Crofoot, a machinist at
NAA. Crofoot, with his wife and two children, rented a two-bedroom furnished
apartment for $44 a month. It was his second time in Dallas. "We came here
last January," he said, "but we had to go back to South Bend [Indiana] when we
couldn't find a place to stay."[12]

All of this kerfuffle assumed that the projected manpower needs were
accurate and justified. But some individuals were starting to question whether
NAA actually required so many workers. One such person was T. Frank
Timmins, 58 years old and a resident of Waxahachie. He had been a roofing
contractor prior to the war, but in 1943 he was an NAA employee in the heat

treatment department of the B-plant. He had gone to work there because he wanted to help the war effort. But he was distressed by what he saw, and on 27 July 1943 he typed a letter to Congressman Hatton Sumners:

> I am employed in what is known as the "B" plant of the North American Aircraft at Grand Prairie, Texas, and, as such have been observant and listening. At the outset, what I state is facts, and, without any desire for personal advancement. I went to work as a father of one in the service, with a desire to do a full man's work in the interest of our country's great needs in supplies and armament. I have been observant and listening, and, it is my frank opinion and solid judgement that at least one-fourth (1/4) of the entire man hour at this place is being willfully wasted. I have heard the young men state frankly that they are there doing time to keep out of the war and active enlistment.[13]

Timmins provided more information about the situation and how he believed the deferment lists should be examined to see which workers were undeserving of protection against the draft. He ended his letter by expressing his desire that "I hope you will personally read this letter, and, then will not throw it into the waste-basket, but DO SOMETHING ABOUT IT."[14]

These were serious allegations. If 25% of the man hours were being wasted, then there was no justification for hiring more employees for NAA. Maybe what was needed was better utilization of the existing workforce. If that were done it might alleviate the need to recruit workers from outside the area and negate the housing shortage. Timmins felt strongly enough about the matter that he also sent letters to Senators W. Lee O'Daniel and Thomas Connally, as well as to Representative Lyndon B. Johnson.[15]

With letters such as these appearing in Washington, it was natural for questions to be asked. Connally was a member of the Senate Special Committee to Investigate the National Defense Program, also known as the Truman Committee after its chairman, Harry S. Truman of Missouri. The committee was established to oversee the massive amounts of money spent on America's war production. Members of the committee were scheduled to visit North Texas in August as part of a tour of aviation plants. They were particularly interested in learning more about the modification centers, such as the one at Love Field in Dallas operated by Lockheed. Members of the committee anticipated to make the trip were Senators

Homer Ferguson (Michigan) and Harley Kilgore (West Virginia). They were to be joined in Dallas by Truman. On 6 August, Senator Connally announced that he intended to join the others during their visit.[16]

Unlike some other high-profile visits, this one was under-reported in both the Dallas press and the NAA plant newspaper. What is known is that Senator Truman toured the B-plant with Factory Manager Harold F. Schwedes, while other members of the group were escorted through the A-plant by Maj. Frank C. Merrill, the Army Air Force on-site representative. Truman reportedly told his hosts that "the visit to NAA was not an investigation," and that committee members "wanted to see production at the Dallas Division just to get a better overall picture of the war effort in the southwest." The members later were guests of the Chamber of Commerce during a dinner at the Petroleum Club, where Truman said, "I think North American will be able to come out of its difficulties. It is just getting started on bomber production. The trouble there has been changes in bombers."[17]

As August progressed it was the third anniversary of the public announcement that NAA was coming to Dallas. The Chamber of Commerce celebrated the anniversary with a luncheon at the Baker Hotel on 24 August 1943, with NAA represented by James H. "Dutch" Kindelberger, John L. "Lee" Atwood, and Schwedes. As usual Kindelberger did the talking, consistent with his character as an "affable plane producer of international reputation." He spent some time praising the P-51 Mustang, which he called "The world's best fighter plane at any altitude." The first Dallas-built versions, designated the P-51C, were preparing to roll off the assembly lines at this time, some three months later than forecast. But the kinks were being worked out of the process, and large numbers of planes were scheduled for production. Kindelberger informed his audience that an additional nineteen thousand workers would be needed by 1 January 1944. Furthermore, to retain that number the company needed to hire twenty-four thousand men to offset turnover. These new workers would need accommodations, and even with the recently approved units there remained concerns about inadequate housing.[18]

The housing issue eventually brought repercussions. On 7 September 1943 a communication was sent to the headquarters of the WMC in Washington, from Lt. Col. Orville S. Carpenter, executive officer of the Dallas office of the WMC.

First P-51C off the Dallas assembly line, photo dated 17 July 1943.
North American Aviation. Copyright ©Boeing. Used by permission.

The message recommended that Dallas be reclassified from Group Two to Group One. Louis Levine of the WMC responded on 9 September that the headquarters agreed. A follow-up teletype on 16 September stipulated that the 1 October list would move Dallas into the Group One category. Meanwhile, business leaders in Dallas sought a thirty-day extension so that the city could develop a plan for coping with the situation. Chamber of Commerce president B. F. McLain stated, "We won't stop fighting for a delay to give Dallas an opportunity to work out a solution of the problem." Arguments were reportedly presented to the WMC by "members of the Texas delegation in Washington," as well as Chamber of Commerce representatives. These apparently fell on deaf ears, and Dallas was declared to be a Group One Critical Labor Area, effective 1 October 1943.[19]

Chapter 16

Dustup in Dallas

O n 28 October 1943, Julius H. Amberg answered a phone call from Dallas. A lawyer by training, he had served in a variety of political jobs since 1910, when he began his legal career with the Federal Trade Commission. In 1941 he became a special assistant to Under Secretary of War Robert P. Patterson, his former classmate at Harvard Law School, and served in this role until 1945.[1] On the other end of the call was Maj. Gen. Charles E. Branshaw, Chief of the Material Center at Wright Field. He had been in Dallas for three days, along with Brig. Gen. Ray G. Harris, a procurement supervisor stationed in Wichita, Kansas. The two officers were part of a team investigating conditions at the North American (NAA) plant. Leading the group was Charles E. Wilson, vice-chairman of the War Production Board (WPB), who doubled as head of the Aircraft Production Board. Two additional officials from the WPB were also in the group.[2]

Branshaw told Amberg the team had crafted a telegram to Paul McNutt, the chairman of the War Manpower Commission. The telegram concerned NAA manpower needs. The labor situation was one of the primary reasons that the WPB team had traveled to Dallas. "This whole situation," Branshaw said, "involves the Company's labor policy, which is none too good." The conversation addressed other matters as well, including apprehensions concerning Maj. Frank C. Merrill, the Army liaison officer at the NAA plant. But the discussion inevitably returned to the topic of manpower. Branshaw explained that although the plant had a management-labor committee, it was not large enough to handle the size of the operation. There was a need for a "better relationship between management and labor," so that "they would learn about all these things which were reported to the Truman Committee which were largely true. Loitering, loafing, playing with the girls, favoritism in giving jobs."[3]

Amberg queried Branshaw about another concern: "How about what either Ferguson or Kilgore told us that they were teaching their people to disregard Government Inspectors." The General replied, "There is absolutely nothing to that. We could find nothing on that at all." By now the conversation was moving toward a conclusion. Amberg offered encouragement and guidance to Branshaw, saying:

> Now, what you're doing is just exactly what should be done, and when you're through and if you make any changes in personnel or anything of that sort, if you'll let me know, then I'll draft something up to send to the Committee, you see. And you tell me what you think I should send.

Branshaw in turn replied:

> I think it's been very constructive. Mr. Wilson does not intend to make any exhaustive, detailed investigation of the specific charges in this long Truman report because they all wind up to about the same thing. Inefficient management, over-employment, people becoming dissatisfied and disgruntled. And I think some rather broad recommendations will amply fill the bill.

The entire phone call was probably less than ten minutes in length, but it did not need to be a long discussion. Both men understood the problem. The question was how to remedy it.[4]

The reason the two men were aware of the problem was because there had already been an intensive inquiry into conditions in Dallas. Hours of testimony by dozens of witnesses had produced hundreds of pages of transcripts detailing labor and housing problems related to NAA. This investigation was conducted by the Truman Committee, the group of senators overseeing the defense program. Some of them had been in North Texas in August, when they visited Lockheed, Consolidated, and NAA. With the declaration of Dallas as a Group One Critical Labor Area, members of the subcommittee on aviation returned to examine the labor situation in the city, with an emphasis on NAA. The delegation included Senators M. Charles Wallgren and Homer Ferguson, who arrived in Dallas by train on Saturday morning, 9 October. Rudolph Halley, the Assistant to the Chief Counsel of the committee, preceded them, arriving on Friday to start lining up witnesses.[5]

Meanwhile, reclassification of Dallas as a Group One Critical Area triggered a flurry of activity as businesses and politicians sought ways to address the situation. One suggestion was endorsed by Charles L. Henry, chief engineer of the Smaller War Plants Corporation. This entity was established in 1942 in order to promote the awarding of production contracts to smaller firms and to assist them with the costs associated with war production. Henry suggested that NAA should make more use of subcontractors, who could build parts and subassemblies. This could spread the work out into areas where labor was available. The main NAA facility could then be used for final assembly. Henry believed that "With only the final assembly being performed at the Dallas plant, the labor demand could be met with housing now under construction and the crisis would be over."[6]

As it happened, NAA was pursuing the idea of moving some operations out of the main plant in Dallas, although not by using subcontractors. Instead, the company chose to retain administrative control. On 1 October 1943 Plant Manager Henry F. Schwedes announced that the company was opening a branch factory in Waco, Texas. Four buildings had been leased in the downtown section of that city, and it was anticipated that the facility could open within a few weeks. Registration for employment began the next day at the United States Employment Office in Waco. Details were not immediately released, but it was to be a feeder plant that supplied components to

Dallas. Schwedes suggested that other satellite factories in other cities might be forthcoming as well, although there is no indication that this occurred. However, the Waco unit did open, with training classes starting in mid-December. According to Schwedes, establishing the NAA branch in Waco was "due to an effort to take production to available labor and housing." It would not reduce labor needs in Dallas, he said, "but will avoid increasing the Dallas demand."[7]

Regarding the demand for labor, NAA officials were not backing down. On 2 October a one-page advertisement appeared in the *Dallas Morning News*. Appearing under the banner "Manpower—How we have used it and why we need more," the text offered a defense of NAA and their use of labor. More accurately described as an open letter than an advertisement, it expressed concern that negative rumors surrounding the plant could hamper the ability to recruit workers. These were needed to produce the aircraft that were "critically needed." The company proudly pointed to winning the Army-Navy "E" for production excellence, as well as the renewal of the award six months later. The company went on to counter charges that had been made, arguing that productivity in the trainer plant had increased since 1942, and that manpower requirements were based on production schedules. As it neared its conclusion, the letter stated "North American is proud of its production record in Dallas. We feel that this record reflects with credit upon the city and upon the state." The message ended with an appeal for any available persons to consider applying for work at NAA, promising that the firm "will vigorously oppose any actions which may be detrimental to our production effort."[8]

The same day that the open letter appeared in the morning paper, NAA ran a classified advertisement declaring "BOYS WANTED TO HELP BUILD WARPLANES." This noted that boys between 16 and 17 could work at the factory. The only stipulation was that the applicant had to have been out of school for at least one full semester. This might have been to avoid providing an incentive for students to drop out of school. The next day, Sunday, the paper contained a NAA advertisement proclaiming, "THIS IS A CALL FOR RED-BLOODED MEN" to "get in the fight!" by helping to build planes "that will help bring defeat to the Nazis and Japs."

Monday's advertisement sought trainees of both sexes, who would be paid while attending the Dallas War School at 2222 Ross Avenue to learn skills needed in the factory. On 5 October the classified section called for "WOMAN-POWER TO HELP BUILD AIRPLANES," stating jobs were available "for literally hundreds of women who want to work for victory." Advertisements seeking help for NAA were not new, but there was a certain urgency to these.[9]

NAA did not just employ classified ads during this period. On 3 October 1943, the company purchased a large advertisement that covered a third of a page in the first section of the newspaper. The ad featured artwork of a clock surrounded by crosses, with the statement "time costs lives." The text informed potential workers that "The hour of victory depends on you. And now you can have your share in bringing victory sooner by helping to build planes at the Dallas plants of North American Aviation, Inc. Thousands more men and women are needed to build the bombers, fighters and trainers vital to victory." NAA was determined to pursue large numbers of workers.[10]

While NAA defended its record and sought more employees, other voices decried the labeling of Dallas as Group One. Editorialists at the *Dallas Morning News* argued that there should be no shortage of labor "if the manpower available were utilized efficiently." The newspaper admitted that "the uneven flow of materials makes necessary overemployment at times," but "the cost-plus system of contracting encourages inefficient production." These comments were directed toward "the aviation plant here." But there was plenty of blame for all. The paper criticized government actions as well, particularly regarding housing, which "could have been provided but for underestimates of need by housing authorities and other official bungling, confusion and shortsightedness." The proposed imposition of a 48-hour week was disparaged, as it would drive up overtime costs for companies who might not be able to afford it. Instead, the editorial suggested moving the threshold for overtime from the normal 40 hours up to 48. This would allow for more utilization of existing manpower while holding down costs at smaller firms and would solve "the national manpower problem without the complicated machinery and un-American methods of coercion of both management and labor."[11]

If the *Morning News* editorial provided an accurate reflection of the mood in Dallas, then the city must have been getting tense. NAA was demanding large numbers of workers and showed no signs of reducing their projected needs. At the same time, the WMC maintained there were not enough workers available, and insufficient housing available to bring them from other areas. Meanwhile, NAA employees such as T. Frank Timmins complained that the factory was not making effective use of the manpower already there, and that production was harmed by this inefficiency. And finally, the business community in Dallas had worked itself into a tizzy over the yet unknown repercussions of the city being classified as a Group One Critical Labor Area. This was the atmosphere hanging over the city when the members of the Truman Committee arrived on 9 October.

The committee wasted little time. By 2:15 that afternoon they convened a hearing in the courtroom of Judge T. Whitfield Davidson, United States District Judge for the Northern District of Texas. Present were Senators Wallgren and Ferguson, Assistant Counsel Halley, Judge Davidson, and Representative Hatton Sumners. The latter had arrived in Dallas on Thursday to pursue his own inquiries into the manpower crisis. He told newsmen that his trip "was not in connection with the Truman investigation, but coincidental." Sumners added that he had "received hundreds of telegrams and telephone calls from Dallas citizens about the critical situation," which led him to return home to investigate. Senator Wallgren, acting as the chair, invited Sumners to sit with the committee and ask questions of the witnesses.[12]

The first witness was Judge Davidson, in whose courtroom the hearings were held. Davidson revealed that he had been approached by numerous people with worries about what was happening at NAA. These individuals, said Davidson, sought him because of his "position and interest in public affairs." He had practiced law in Dallas and had served in the Texas Senate for two years. He was also lieutenant governor of Texas for one term, beginning in 1923. His Texas pedigree, combined with his status as a federal official, apparently led citizens to view him as a suitable recipient for their concerns, which he conveyed to the committee:[13]

My Information, gentlemen, is very much like that you will undoubtedly gather from the general public here. It is hearsay. I have never been out to the plant, but if you accept even to a small degree, the reports from the streets and from the conversations in the homes of Dallas, the situation, so far as production at the North American plant is concerned, is in a bad way.[14]

Davidson continued with a litany of accusations, based on information he had received from NAA employees. One of the first individuals who approached him was Henry Fagin, a mechanic who had been in the railroad industry before working at NAA. He told Davidson that "his experience qualified him to do blueprint work and planning and building a locomotive, and that he could take blueprints and build those planes." But the informant was distressed, saying that the lack of productivity worried him. Davidson continued, "He stated in effect, that there was a want of authoritative supervision." There was also a lack of urgency, that productive employees were told to slow down, "that we are in no hurry here." The informant placed part of the blame on the fact that the plant operated on a cost-plus basis, thus removing much of the incentive to work efficiently. Finally, it was said that "a man capable of doing work and who actually did work was not only discouraged, but never promoted, but that men would be placed over him who would be frequently a man without experience and wholly unable to direct his activities."[15]

This was quite a laundry list of complaints, but Davidson observed that he had heard similar remarks from a "number of people." After a short discussion of the veracity of what he had said, which was in fact hearsay, the members of the Committee agreed with Davidson that there was enough public concern to continue exploring allegations concerning the manpower situation. Chairman Wallgren then invited Judge Davidson to sit with the committee during the inquiry, while expressing his belief that "While we are here, I am sure the story will gradually unfold." Davidson therefore became a fifth member of the panel, joining Senators Wallgren and Ferguson, Assistant Counsel Halley, and Representative Sumners. Together the group would learn about conditions at NAA.[16]

For the rest of the day a string of witnesses testified before the committee, and while hard facts were sometimes lacking, accusations were plentiful. The second person to appear was Charles H. Alexander, a "real estate man and

member of a pioneer Dallas family." He asserted "there seems to be some
collusion between the North American Aviation Plant and the War Manpower
Commission," and believed both should be investigated. He criticized the
cost-plus nature of the NAA plant and accused Kindelberger of understating
the contract percentage.[17] Next was Jack Wolf, who was secretary to Dallas
County Judge Al Templeton. Wolf had come on behalf of Templeton, who
had been called out of town unexpectedly. Wolf said that he had the names
of thirty to forty workers who were potential witnesses, as well as a number
of letters about the situation. His observation was that "conditions out there
are common knowledge and general talk among the people here." There were
also rumors that some workers were "on the job out there half drunk."[18]

The witness who was most prominent that Saturday was Orville Erringer
of the WMC. The committee grilled him thoroughly, resulting in forty pages
of testimony. The foremost topic concerned the labor requirements in the
Dallas area; the committee wanted to know how much of this was due to the
demands at NAA. By way of explanation, Erringer offered that the current
employment at the Lockheed modification center at Love Field was approximately seven hundred, although the number fluctuated. By comparison, the
NAA plant was expected to demand 48,900 by November due to increased
production quotas assigned to NAA. Asked by Senator Ferguson whether the
WMC had investigated the NAA demand for that many workers, Erringer
said no, there had not been time since the approval of his appointment by the
Senate in May.[19]

The committee also sought to understand how workers were hired for war
industries in the area. This was a somewhat convoluted process, which had
started to be developed at the end of the previous year, when the WMC gained
control over the manpower pool. Anybody interested in working at NAA had
to apply at the United States Employment Service (USES), which sent applicants to the various industries as needed. A "certificate of availability" was
also needed in order to switch between certain jobs. If a worker in a critical
industry wanted to leave, then the employer had to provide the employee with
this certificate, allowing the worker to seek a job elsewhere. The issuing of
such certificates had begun with the imposition of a labor stabilization plan
for Dallas in June 1943. The fact that the employer had to issue a certifi-

cate theoretically deterred critical workers from leaving over trivial issues. A worker could not be prevented from quitting, but those without a certificate could not immediately reenter the workforce, leading to thirty days of unemployment. Problems arose when an employer and employee disagreed over a separation. Employees who were not granted a certificate could appeal to the USES, which then investigated the matter. One unintended consequence was that employees needed to justify departures, which likely encouraged them to complain.[20]

This process was implemented to discourage job hopping between different companies, which could leave war plants in the lurch when employees went in search of greener pastures. Turnover was a problem, as it meant the loss of trained workers. Erringer revealed that the NAA turnover rate had grown from 3.8% in May to 5.4% in August. This shrinkage meant that new employees had to constantly be training, and a less experienced workforce lowered the efficiency of the plant. Reasons for turnover varied by the individual, but housing and transportation issues were often a consideration. Sometimes the individual was new to industrial work and found themselves to be physically incapable of the job. Women might leave because of pregnancy. Of course, disagreements with management, or dissatisfaction on the job, were always present in companies, either in war or peace.[21]

All this related to the overriding issue of manpower, and how much was needed, or perhaps wasted. Chairman Wallgren asked Erringer for his opinion regarding the situation at NAA, and the rumors regarding idleness. Erringer replied "I have felt, gentlemen, going into the vernacular, that where there is so much smoke, there is bound to be some fire." He revealed that he had discussed the issue with NAA management and had "come to the conclusion that a certain amount of it is unavoidable." He realized, "they must over hire to offset absenteeism," which could lead to an "overload on labor at that plant when the labor suddenly turns up and they have good attendance." When Wallgren inquired whether NAA was "asking for too many in reserve," Erringer replied that a lack of supplies further complicated the situation. Wallgren said he understood that problem had been solved, to which Erringer responded "Much of this comment has been smoldering and it takes time for it to come out—and each person on the street is a booster station."[22] He added that training and moving workers between the two plants at the NAA factory had led to idleness in the past, but no longer. Erringer's responses, while reasonable, reveal potential bias in his understanding of the situation. Having only been on the job since May, he was not present when many issues started to arise. His statements suggest that his opinions had been influenced by exposure to company management.[23]

The committee shifted to the matter of Dallas being declared a Group One Critical Labor Area. Senator Ferguson asked Erringer if he had anything to do with the decision. Erringer replied that "I endeavored to join my citizens here in seeking a 30-day deferment." When Ferguson pushed the issue, the resulting discussion was held off the record. Erringer did say that the housing shortage was a key factor, and another lengthy exchange was held concerning this, with Erringer explaining how the Mayor's Committee on Housing had attempted to get the National Housing Agency (NHA) to approve the erection of temporary buildings. Preston Wright, regional director of the NHA, agreed and sent his recommendation to Washington in July 1943. The houses, Erringer understood, would be ready for occupancy on September 1. When this did not happen, he discovered on 8 September that the contract had not yet been signed. This led Chairman Wallgren to ask a series of questions about the six thousand prefabricated houses available in the Dallas area, forcing Erringer to admit that most of them had been sent elsewhere while he waited for a response from Washington, which never came. An opportunity to use them slipped away, apparently due to bureaucratic inefficiency and differing objectives. And now construction of temporary housing was "bogging down for want of labor." Erringer also mentioned another agency involved in providing temporary housing: the Federal Public Housing Administration. This agency had its own ideas that required lumber to be shipped in from the outside. Erringer's words imply a sense of frustration on his part; "With the situation so critical, you get to the point where you don't care—you want to get the houses, for housing is one of the major reasons for separation at that plant."[24]

Senator Ferguson next raised the issue of transportation. Erringer had opinions on that as well, asserting "It is growing more involved and more desperate; there is only one arterial highway that feeds that plant."

He lamented, "there are so many accidents on that highway on account of the traffic." Chairman Wallgren inquired about the availability of gasoline and tires, and Erringer stated that these resources were available, "but people find going to and from that plant is more of a nervous ordeal than the work itself; it is something to try to look down the road ahead, we had no idea that plant would be as large as it is now."[25]

Erringer remained in the hot seat, fielding questions from the committee. As the session neared its end, attention returned to the label of Group One Critical Labor Area. Halley wanted to know more about how the designation was made, asking "In calculating the available labor supply for Dallas, what labor supply did you take into consideration?" Erringer replied, "The supply that was available; there were three sources; one was the floater supply, always present; it is indeterminable, some of those never work; many were visitors to the city; the second is your housewife, and third your minority groups." Halley asked, "What geographical area did you take into consideration in determining this supply?" "We had to take the county itself," replied Erringer, "we cannot use in-migrant workers, we had to take the people here in this county." Halley observed that the county line was very close to the NAA plant, and when the committee inquired whether the potential manpower in Tarrant County had been taken into consideration, Erringer said yes. This led Ferguson to ask why Fort Worth had not been named as a critical area. "Because the future demand here is so much greater," said Erringer. "They only need 7,000 in this plant to do away with the Critical Area designation," observed Ferguson, "why should you not treat all counties within the radius that the workers come from, consider all those counties to determine whether or not it is a Critical Area?" Erringer sighed, "Well, it gets down to this; you have the pattern of bureaucracy." It is difficult to determine whether Ferguson was annoyed, incredulous, or frustrated when he asked, "In other words, bureaucracy won't let this be done?" His mood probably did not improve when a few more questions elicited the information from Erringer that Fort Worth got two thousand temporary homes.[26]

While Erringer was the witness that spent the most time in testimony, another spent a prolonged period before the committee. This was Maj. Frank

C. Merrill, the Army Air Forces representative at the NAA plant. But if the committee gained valuable insights from Erringer, they appear to have been frustrated by what they heard from Merrill. He explained he supervised different departments at the plant, and his assignment was to "help and assist the contractor in any way he can to get his production; to help him secure material and do everything possible to aid him." He had four officers and a team of civil service workers, including between eighty and ninety inspectors. A pilot since 1924, he was not a trained engineer, but he did have some technical knowledge from his civilian employment.[27]

The committee was interested in conditions inside the plant, as Merrill had firsthand knowledge the senators were lacking. Ferguson asked how many employees were in the A-plant, but Merrill was unsure. He knew the two plants employed in excess of thirty-three thousand workers, a figure that meshed with what Erringer had reported. When asked about the quality of inspections at the plant, Merrill admitted they could be better. Then the situation deteriorated. Senator Ferguson asked if Merrill was "satisfied with the labor situation" at the two plants. "As far as I know," was the reply. Ferguson rephrased the query, "I mean the whole labor set up." When Merrill asked for the question to be repeated. Ferguson responded: "Are you satisfied with the entire labor set-up at the A and B plant of the North American Aviation Company, are the men doing a good job or are they idle?" Merrill admitted there was some idleness. This prompted tense sparring between the Senator and the Major over the meaning of terms such as "some" and "idleness."[28] Wallgren joined in the exchange, prompting Merrill to declare that production had improved. Wallgren then cut to the chase:

> Major, we are here as an investigating committee of the United States Senate, we have with us Representative Sumners and Judge Davidson; we are holding these sessions to get to the bottom of this because there have been so many complaints about the labor conditions in this plant, so many people not doing the job. We know that you, as the chief inspector in that plant, being there in and around it, probably see something and we would like to know if you could be helpful and tell us whether that plant is doing an efficient job, and the men being employed in the right way."[29]

Merrill admitted he had seen idleness, but he could not say anyone walking around was necessarily idle. Some of them might be carrying messages to other parts of the plant.

At this point, Sumners joined the fray:

> Major these men are senators, and they are interested in Texas getting for the American people as nearly as possible, one hundred cents on the dollar. I know, like you, these common reports, and I also know it is a difficult job to operate a plant like that and keep it going and being in that plant—I have only been in there once myself, and I saw what the senators saw. You are there every day and you are bound to see a lot, and you have had a lot to do with everything about a plane. I know you have a pretty good horse-sense notion about how those fellows are working and what can be done to get that plant up; what's your idea?[30]

Merrill answered, "there is a considerable lag in the work at this time." He attributed it to the startup of production of two new types of aircraft, stating "It will take some time to get around the curve and level off." Ferguson wanted to know "Why should they hire those men and put them in there and make this a Critical Area?" "I don't know," replied Merrill.[31]

As the hearings became more intense, an officer accompanying Merrill clashed with Ferguson over the Major's testimony. The officer stated, "Major Merrill is in a position where I don't believe you can expect him to give an opinion." Ferguson was adamant that the committee wanted exactly that, and questioned why the Army officers were reluctant to provide information.[32] Wallgren intervened, asking Merrill to "say what you think might be wrong with the plant—you spoke of changing over to this Mustang?" "That is your problem," replied Merrill. He added that "around 18,000" workers were needed to make the AT-6 trainers, but now the two plants had closer to 33,000 employees. Merrill explained that taking on the manufacture of two additional models required new "jigs, dies, and all the other factors, plus an airplane they did not know anything about." Wallgren reiterated the situation to verify his interpretation: "While they were setting up and transferring from the manufacture of the trainer to the Mustang, they had airplane frame workers who were idle, but were kept there because they were waiting for the jigs to be set up for the Mustang?" Merrill responded, "That's what I was trying to say." Wallgren continued, "Yet, if the company were to have let those men go, awaiting the time when the jigs were available on the new job, then the men would not have been available? "Yes," replied Merrill, "I think that is your greatest trouble now, in trying to keep these men available." Ferguson interjected, "In other words, they are hoarding labor, and we might as well be frank about it." Merrill replied that all were working in some department, qualified or not, until the plants reached full production, when the workers could be put to proper use, as they had been. Ferguson then questioned the delay in starting, asking, "How do you explain that when this same company made this P-51 for 32 months?" "The one we build is the P-51C," replied Merrill, "the airplane is now equipped with the Rolls Royce engine, which requires fifty odd changes."[33]

The discussion turned to the B-24 bomber. Merrill testified that thirty-two aircraft had been produced to that point. He was unaware of how many man hours had been expended building the planes, but it was anticipated that at peak production the airplanes should require around twenty-four-hundred-man hours each. Wallgren returned to the question at hand, on whether workers in the plant were being underutilized, to which Merrill responded in the affirmative. Wallgren asked if better management could lead to higher efficiency, but Merrill doubted that it would, maintaining "I can't find any fault with the management of it."[34] Ferguson returned to the question of the cost-plus contract on the B-24, asking if the Army had anyone at the plant to keep watch on expenditures. Merrill replied that there was a contracting officer assigned to monitor costs, but he had no direct enforcement authority over the contractor, he could only notify plant management of any concerns. After a few more questions, Merrill was excused for the night, with Ferguson requesting his return on Monday.[35]

The next witness sworn in was Henry D. Fagin, an NAA employee who had been mentioned by Judge Davidson as a source of his information regarding problems at the plant. It was the first time the committee would hear from someone who worked for NAA, and as an experienced machinist his insights could be helpful. Fagin, age 47, was apparently a Native American, as he had graduated from Carlisle Indian University during the Jim Thorpe era, sometime around 1908–1912. He had served as an apprentice with the Missouri–Kansas–Texas Railroad, where he worked on locomotives. He was in the military during World War I, reached the rank of captain, and was wounded in the stomach, which apparently caused lingering health problems. He mentioned having a son who was serving overseas as a major, as well as a nine-year-old boy. Fagin thus had a wide range of experiences. He also had a wide range of complaints concerning NAA.[36]

Chairman Wallgren swore Fagin in and had him explain who he was. Fagin had been at NAA for just over a year and was assigned to the B-plant, apparently part of the team building parts in the hangar prior to the completion of the new factory. Wallgren invited him to "Go ahead and tell the Committee what your opinion is of this entire plant's situation out there, as you see it, through a mechanic's eyes, labor and management, the whole set up." Fagin replied, "There is no such thing as a labor shortage out there; the only thing they need to do is to get rid of about one-half of the employees and put the other half to work." Wallgren asked if half the employees could do the same job, to which Fagin responded, "Much better and more of it if they would enforce discipline and put them to work; they walk around, hours at a time with not a thing on their mind except the idea of staying out of Uncle Sam's Army." Wallgren asked if they were young men, and Fagin said yes "and most of them single; they will draft men out of there with three and four children, hard working men and leave loafers, young fellow that have not done anything for a week." But not all were dead weight. Fagin said, "They have as good mechanics and machinists out there as I have ever known and men with real ability, but they won't give them a chance; they take up these little boys that have never had a day's experience in their life and put them over experienced men as supervisors and foreman and some of them are drawing $5600 a year, boys that never worked a day in their life, or only the last year or so with no dependents."[37]

The committee may have enjoyed the colorful Fagin. Ferguson asked about employees walking back and forth through the plant. Fagin suspected they were "Going to get a drink or to smoke a cigarette, or going to meet their best girl or best boyfriend." Ferguson asked if there were love affairs at the plant. Fagin's response might have been profane or risqué, as it was stricken from the record at the request of Wallgren. Another topic was the large amount of overtime being worked at the plant, even while many complained of idleness and lack of work. Fagin estimated "that one-fourth of all the departments are working overtime at one time or another, each night." "Why?" asked Ferguson. Fagin replied, "There is a 10 percent cost plus, you know, at North American." The senator corrected Fagin, "I think you are a little high on the figure." Fagin responded, "That's what I heard." At the same time, Fagin maintained that he kept busy, except when he had been slowed down by a hemorrhage in his stomach. He was now working on a power saw, an apparent underutilization of a trained machinist. This was conceivably intended as a form of lighter duty while he recovered from his illness; Fagin did not really explain the switch. He did say that he had been told to "take his time," however, it is unclear whether this was in reference to his recovery, or to the speed of his work. But other employees were not busy, and Fagin reported that he had heard foremen say, "Get something and walk around, make it appear to the superintendent that you are busy when he was around."[38]

Senator Ferguson asked Fagin if he knew anything about the A-plant. Fagin thought conditions there were equally bad, in fact the employees there did less. He observed, "They don't have time to work; there are so many other things to do, all of the girls have to be entertained; they have a Coca-Cola machine and candy machine and they have to make these honky-tonks at night; they just don't get enough rest in 10 hours out there." Ferguson asked if there was anything else to tell, and Fagin went back to the draft issue, "I believe those boys out there are staying out of the Army by paying their way. Does this look reasonable to you—would you take a man that never had a day's experience in anything and make a lead-man or foreman out of him—would you?" "Usually, I don't answer questions," said the senator, "but I would not do that." "Anything else?" asked Ferguson. "I can't prove this," said Fagin, "but I have heard that a man could get a foreman's job out there for $100." When Ferguson asked who told Fagin that, the mechanic responded, "That is generally known out there, that you can get a foreman's

job for $100 or stay out of the army for seventy-five to two hundred dollars."
Pressed for details, Fagin admitted he had not actually confirmed this as
fact.[39] If this accusation was true, it suggested that a man could buy a draft
deferment as an essential war worker.

As the testimony neared its end, the committee asked if Fagin had
anything he wished to report. He declared that the food in the plant was "not
fit to eat," adding that "I don't know what could be done about it; you can
get ptomaine poison and you could not get a lawyer in town to bring a suit
against Earl Wyatt or North American." He also mentioned transportation
issues, saying the bus service was awful. Judge Davidson agreed, "I know
that is right. I have seen it myself." Changing topics, seemingly out of the
blue, Chairman Wallgren asked if there was any drinking while on the job.
Fagin responded that he did not think so, but that they come in "full up."
It was not a dry county, and sometimes workers arrived "in pretty bad condition." With that, the witness was excused.[40]

With Fagin gone, the committee called the last witness of the day, B. H.
Maddin, formerly of the United States Employment Service. He had resigned
in early October to return to the private sector and make more money. "I saw
this Critical Area coming on," he said, "and now is the time for me to get with
private employment that are in need of my services to help solve the labor
problem." He had several roles in his time at the agency, including "placement work in the negro division and the placement work in the skilled division with North American, Lockheed, and so forth, and other war industries."
He often issued certificates of availability. Ferguson asked what reasons
people had for wanting to change jobs. Maddin said that workers switched
plants to get extra pay, such as when Lockheed had more overtime available.
Later he had NAA employees saying, "We don't have enough work to do
out there." "I did not believe it," he said, "I thought they were just telling me
this as an excuse to get a certificate of availability." Queried by the panel, he
estimated about a third of the male NAA workers seeking certificates stated
that to be the case. "I passed it off," he said. But another employee at the
agency told Maddin that he received similar reports. There were also NAA
employees who claimed "they were leaving because they could not make
enough to live on and pay rent on the number of hours they were working.

Consequently, they raised the hours at North American to nine or ten, which alleviated that."[41]

Maddin testified he asked some workers why they were not busy. One, Alfred Long, reported that sometimes they did not have the needed materials. Once materials arrived, they would work until the supply was depleted, "Then we had to polish machinery or do something until we could get in new materials." In response to Senator Ferguson, Maddin admitted this was all second-hand information. Ferguson then asked if he could "give us any personal knowledge on the manpower situation and at the Employment Service in connection with this plant." Maddin said that NAA needed to expand its hiring to include "older men and handicapped persons and young women." He testified that a NAA representative had said "We have reached the bottom of the barrel" but was still "turning away older men, handicapped persons, and young men," as well as "negroes and Mexicans of American descent." He thought this was a mistake, as he knew there were many such workers available in Dallas. He observed that "we referred 1100 negroes for farm work." Halley asked if blacks were considered when "placing an area in a critical designation?" Maddin believed they should be, but he was unsure what the WMC did. He also thought that some of the young men at the plant could be drafted and replaced by women. Finally, he said that many employees were unhappy with the night shift. This led to turnover, especially among women. With that the committee called it a night, adjourning at 6:55 p.m. They had been in session for almost five hours, heard from seven witnesses, and generated 106 pages of testimony.[42]

The committee members had plenty to ponder. Two prominent citizens of Dallas, including a federal judge, had related rumors that were endemic through the city concerning NAA. This concerned wastage of manpower, inadequate supervision, draft dodging, and an accusation the company showed little financial responsibility due to the cost-plus contract at the B-plant. These witnesses clearly were concerned citizens, but they repeated second-hand information. Was it unsubstantiated hearsay, or was something terribly wrong at NAA? Then there was the information provided by Erringer of the WMC. He had explained how anticipated manpower needs at NAA had thrown Dallas into being a Group One Critical Labor Area, largely because of the housing issue. Erringer's testimony pointed to government deficiencies in dealing with problems. Was the situation in Dallas mostly due to bureaucratic inefficiency? The committee had also heard from the military, though Merrill appeared at times to be defending the company, which had suffered setbacks due to mitigating factors such as material shortages and design changes. Was Army oversight weak, or was the military simply letting the experts do their jobs? Finally, there was Fagin, the only actual NAA employee to testify that day. He brought a long list of complaints, including untrained workers, lackadaisical and unqualified supervisors, unwarranted overtime, unappetizing and unhealthy food, and a general lack of urgency. He made serious accusations that unqualified men were buying their way into essential jobs in order to avoid the draft. Was Fagin a patriotic citizen wanting to improve the situation at the NAA plant, an embittered curmudgeon with health issues, or a combination of both? There was a lot of information to absorb, and apparently no simple answers.

Chapter 17

Grouse Hunt

The committee hearings reconvened on Sunday morning, 9 October 1943, and the first witness was Dallas Mayor Woodall Rogers. After admitting he had no firsthand information, Rogers asked to introduce into the record a *Dallas Morning News* editorial that had appeared that morning, which he said, "expresses the sentiment of this community." The editorial, titled "Let's have the Facts," lauded the Truman Committee and called for "the co-operation of our entire community" in the investigation. The editorialist did not profess to know the facts about the manpower or housing issues. What he did know was "that rumors and gossip are rife on the streets of the city, especially with respect to alleged hoarding and otherwise mishandling of the manpower situation at the big aviation plant. And the *News* is convinced that this kind of talk now threatens to become a very damaging influence against the high morale and eager and consistent war effort that has hitherto been maintained in this community." If the problems were real, they needed to be fixed. If the rumors were untrue, then they needed to stop.[1]

Rogers explained that the Chamber of Commerce had appointed a committee to oversee the housing problem even before the United States was at war. The group was chaired by Holmes Green, a "fine man; one of our leading merchants." Unfortunately, he was out of town, thus unable to appear. Rogers therefore requested that Green be able to submit an affidavit upon his return. The mayor insisted, "We knew we were in for difficult times and anticipated the needs. At the same time, the record will show that had our request for houses been complied with during the last two years, we would have been spared this critical designation." Rogers complained about the abruptness of the declaration of Dallas as a Group One Critical Labor Area. Although there had been much talk about the possibility, Rogers said that when the actual decision was made there was no advance notice, and city leaders thought there should be a hearing to allow the city to make proposals to deal with the issue.[2]

One issue that resurfaced was the process of determining Group One status. Rogers agreed with the committee that the populations of surrounding counties should have been considered, and he suggested that Green could provide further information about this. Rogers remained on hand as Bernard F. McLain was sworn in. McLain was the president of the Dallas Chamber of Commerce, and he opened by declaring "The position of the Chamber of Commerce is that this No. 1 Critical classification is arbitrary, unfair, and unjustified." His complaints echoed those of Rogers regarding housing. The Dallas housing committee had worked to get authorization for additional units but had run into bureaucratic entanglements from different Federal agencies.[3]

McLain expressed frustration with the War Manpower Commission (WMC) over a lack of communication. McLain had wired the WMC prior to the declaration of the Critical Labor Area but received no response. He repeated that the Chamber of Commerce "was never officially notified," of the decision. As far as McLain was concerned, his city had a problem, and the business community was interested in solving it and was willing to work with the WMC. But higher-level administrators at the WMC were seemingly not receptive to outreach from the chamber. While Orville Erringer, the local WMC official, seemed willing to interact with local leaders seeking solutions, he could not get support from his superiors. McLain was similarly frustrated with North American Aviation (NAA), and he concluded sharply, "it is unfair to this community to place us under the Critical Area designation."[4]

Rogers then rejoined the conversation. He and McLain, as well as committee members, returned to the issue of the boundary between Dallas and Tarrant counties. There was the B-24 bomber plant in Fort Worth, and the committee asked if that facility absorbed significant labor resources in the area. Rogers could not provide a definite number, but he pointed out the factory was on the west side of Fort Worth. People living in the eastern part of Tarrant County were more likely to seek work at NAA because it was an easier commute for them. It was possible that thousands of workers at NAA did not live in Dallas County at all. With the NAA plant located almost astride the county line, it seemed incongruous that the entire labor force was being counted against the available manpower of Dallas County.[5]

The investigation into manpower continued with the questioning of Lt. Col. Orville S. Carpenter of the WMC as a witness. McLain had mentioned Carpenter as the administrator who turned down the request that Dallas get a thirty-day reprieve from becoming a Group One Critical Labor Area. He was, by his own description, a certified public accountant and a lawyer, having practiced in Wichita Falls and Dallas. In 1935 he had become involved in relief efforts, serving in various capacities, including as director of the State Unemployment Commission. He had held this post until 1940, when reserve and National Guard officers were called into active duty. Carpenter informed the senators that he was with the Selective Service System, but that he was on loan to the WMC. He had been named executive officer for the region in June 1943. When asked if he knew why Tarrant County was not considered in determining the labor supply for the NAA plant, Carpenter replied, "Yes, sir, I know exactly why." He explained the creation of the National Re-employment Service in 1933. Texas had been organized into twelve districts, and these had remained in use by the State Employment Service and then by the WMC. He added that he set the figures for NAA labor needs in accordance with what he was told about contracts by James H. "Dutch" Kindelberger, concluding "After all, I have no reason to say Mr. Kindelberger is a damn liar."[6]

Over the rest of the day, the committee heard testimony from another twenty-seven witnesses. Included were union representatives from the AFL and the CIO, clerks from local draft boards, and homebuilders who had been frustrated in their desire to build near the plant. Another WMC member was interviewed, as well as a civil service employee who worked at the plant. Over a dozen witnesses were current or former NAA workers, and they provided the committee with inside information. The first of these was William Humphrey, who had resigned the day before "because I wanted to be a free agent in this investigation." He had been a bookkeeping clerk in the material control department on the night shift. He said he had little actual work to do, and that some members of his department just flipped pages to look busy. Despite this lack of work, he had been working overtime, and he saw no reason this was needed. Other employees told similar tales, including S. G. Fagan, a machinist in the B-plant. He believed that the plant had "about ten thousand hands they don't need." There were also problems with male employees flirting with the female workers. Fagan felt that "Some of the women would make good hands if they [the men] would leave them alone, but they can't get their minds above the women's belts." He observed that many workers were "young men, just schoolboys," with "four or five months training." They could be useful if experienced machinists were supervising them, but this was not done. W. C. Robinson, a former employee who had resigned because he "felt he wasn't doing much good at the plant," recalled again how lack of materials led to work stoppages. At least three women testified; all of them recounted the crude conduct of men toward women, and two declared they spent a lot of time correcting mistakes made by others in producing wiring harnesses for the B-24 Liberator.[7]

Most of the witnesses corroborated each other. Fred W. Estes, vice-president of Local 645 of the CIO and a worker in the A-plant, said that promotions to supervisory positions were often awarded based on favoritism rather than technical or leadership ability.[8] Jack Cowart of the WMC regional office, located in Dallas, admitted he knew nothing about NAA, but he did talk about chaos in his agency. A veteran administrator, he described a tangled bureaucracy that could take ten days to deliver a communication from Washington to Dallas. He also made it clear that he had little use for Carpenter, who had testified earlier. Asked what Carpenter did, Cowart responded, "Frankly, he doesn't do anything but sign mail if he is there, and when he isn't there somebody else signs his name." Cowart then slightly contradicted himself when he declared that Carpenter had decided that Dallas would not get a delay in being designated as Group One. After that testimony, Cowart was dismissed moments later.[9]

While Cowart was a critical witness regarding the WMC, the most significant testimony arguably came from Herbert C. Durham, who identified himself as "the principal investigator for the Army Air Corps, Intelligence Section." A previous member of the Arkansas State Police, he had been at the NAA plant since 3 November 1942. His official responsibilities involved plant protection. He also described himself as a "kind of trouble shooter for the Army Air Forces."

His superior was Maj. Frank C. Merrill, but he had contacted the committee directly, which made him uneasy. After some discussion of this, he testified. The members may have been shocked to learn that he was investigating labor waste at the NAA plant because of a letter that had been sent to President Roosevelt. The unnamed author was a woman whose husband worked at NAA, and she complained that he did not have enough work to do at a vital war plant. Durham had observed many idle workers and said the problem was a lack of training.

He added, "I found considerable loafing," and, when asked about management, replied, "There is discord in the office of the company." Allegations of timecard fraud were also in a report he submitted to the Army and NAA, with Merrill's signature on it. But the only response Durham had observed was the production of a much shorter summary of his investigation results by a higher-level supervisor. Durham regaled the committee with stories of a man who bought war bonds at a discount from black workers and sold jobs at the plant, as well as subpar inspections of planes and other troublesome matters. All this could be found in reports which he claimed to keep locked in a safe. The committee spent a lot of time with Durham, whose testimony filled forty-nine pages. They also questioned him off the record on at least three occasions. As the session moved toward a close, a final topic was examined briefly. Asked if Kindelberger's friendships with people in Washington made it hard for the Army to challenge NAA, Durham agreed.[10]

Other witnesses appeared as the hearings continued into the evening, but very little was revealed that had not been touched upon earlier. Employees and ex-employees told similar tales of wasted labor and unqualified workers; repeating charges that had been explored the previous day. Some witnesses were critical of the cost-plus contract at the B-plant, saying it allowed the company to disregard costs. Indeed, some witnesses appeared to believe that the cost-plus contract encouraged the manufacturer to drive up the costs, so that the profit percentage would result in a higher dollar figure. But Sunday's hearings did bring out additional concerns, especially regarding the inefficiency of government. Federal agencies had struggled to supply adequate housing, while the WMC appeared to be run by largely absent administrators who had little interest in cooperating with local government. Finally, the Army had been criticized for being unwilling or unable to exercise effective control over operations at NAA, seemingly due to the political connections of Kindelberger. Two days of witness testimony had produced a veritable laundry list of complaints and accusations. Even if these were exaggerated, the sheer volume indicated serious problems at the plant. At the very least, there was a public perception of the problems. On Monday morning the committee planned to visit the NAA facility to examine conditions, to be followed by another round of hearings that afternoon. The facts of the matter seemed to be emerging. Answers and solutions, however, remained distant.

Chapter 18

Double Dutch

While there had been concerns over efficiency at North American Aviation (NAA) in Dallas for some time, the tipping point came with the increased projections announced in August 1943, when the company called for 48,900 workers by November. This was the catalyst for the declaration of Dallas as a Group One Critical Labor Area, which caused so much turmoil. As civic leaders and government agencies struggled to make sense of the situation, NAA was forced to deal with the problem. As discussed earlier, one strategy NAA pursued was the opening of the satellite facility in Waco, where subassemblies could be made for shipment to Dallas. Although the announcement was made on 1 October, it seems likely that the planning for the Waco operation began in response to the manpower needs articulated in August, if not earlier. With accusations of inefficiency and idleness circulating, productivity needed to be increased not only to build airplanes, but to improve public perception of the company.

It is unclear exactly how or when allegations reached James H. "Dutch" Kindelberger. Certainly, he became aware of the situation before the arrival of the Truman Committee. Direct evidence of this appeared in the plant newspaper on 8 October, the day before the hearings began in Dallas. Conspicuously placed on the front page of *Take Off* was an acknowledgement that

255

"Newspaper reports state that a sub-committee of the Truman Committee is coming to Dallas to investigate manpower utilization at North American Aviation's plants." NAA welcomed "the opportunity of furnishing information to any properly authorized agency of government." because there was "a great deal of confusion and misinformation" about conditions at the plant. The message stated, "It is difficult for outsiders to grasp the scope of our operations, or the problems involved in rapid expansion, the training of tens of thousands of new workers, and the maintenance of a flexible production system to accommodate design changes in military aircraft." Attributed to Kindelberger, the statement shows that corporate leadership was aware of the ongoing controversy. In an interesting juxtaposition, the headline of the paper proclaimed "Texas Division of NAA Wins Third Army-Navy E," along with a reprint of a letter from Under Secretary of War Robert P. Patterson, who wrote, "In maintaining the fine record which first brought you distinction, you have set an inspiring example for your fellow Americans on the production front." The company could now add a second white star to the "E" pennant flag that flew on the flagpole in front of the factory, "as a symbol of your great and continuing contribution to the cause of freedom."[1]

The dichotomy here is striking. On one hand the War Department awarded NAA an Army-Navy E for excellence, while on the other a committee of the United States Senate was in Dallas to investigate the company for wasting manpower. It is easy to imagine company officials being befuddled by the contradiction. Nevertheless, it was evident that something was wrong at the factory. The problems might have been real, or they could be faulty perceptions. Given the dynamics of an operation as large as NAA, it was likely some combination of both. In any case, the situation needed to be addressed.

Kindelberger had sent another communication to his employees on 5 October 1943, coincidentally the same day that Patterson wrote his note announcing the renewal of NAA's Army-Navy E award. *Our Job* was a twelve-page booklet that addressed the concerns that had arisen about the plant. The message was mix of commendations, explanations, and exhortations.[2] Kindelberger began with the observation that the specialized nature of each job could make it difficult to "grasp the entire picture." He stated that his intent was to "give you such a picture in this letter—straight from the shoulder and just as completely as military security will permit." He related the now-familiar tale of how Texans had quickly learned the art of building aircraft. Through "hard work, a spirit of teamwork, and a little industrial magic," the employees had created a functioning factory where none had existed previously, while working "under the compelling pressure of war." Kindelberger offered "this diversified collection of individuals has been fused into a production team which is making one of the most vital contributions in the nation to ultimate victory." All of this was standard rhetoric for Kindelberger, who made similar comments at many luncheons and events in Dallas. He then raised an issue of interest to all employees: the pay structure. He observed that many employees "do not fully grasp the extent of the present War Labor Board and Treasury Department controls over wages and salaries." A wage stabilization program was in effect to help control inflation, but this made it impossible to offer pay raises in most cases.[3]

Wages, while of interest to the employees, had little to do with the problems of getting new assembly lines started for the B-24 and the P-51. A serious problem in that regard, Kindelberger declared, was a shortage of materials. He cited supply issues in "aluminum alloy sheet stock, castings, forgings, and extrusions." At times inventories of some items were "down to practically nothing." The situation was improving however, and he wrote that "North American will get all the material it can efficiently use." That left NAA with another challenge: finding more workers to increase productivity. The company, Kindelberger wrote, was working to "bring new employees to North American by every means at our disposal, including extensive advertising, special plans for boys of 16 and 17, and appeals to partially disabled veterans." There was also room for more women; they already were "approximately 33 percent" of the workforce, but Kindelberger declared, "we will need many more women to meet our production schedules." He addressed the matter of untrained workers, writing, "As we have expanded and made replacements, the experience and general qualification level of incoming employees has slowly but steadily decreased." In response, NAA had "made a systematic effort to simplify jobs, so as to reduce the amount of experience and training necessary for a new employee to perform his or her job well."[4]

Apart from labor and materials, an additional factor in delaying production was that design changes had been made in both the Liberator and Mustang. In the case of the fighter, there was the engine switch from the Allison to the Merlin. Since Dallas had never built the earlier version of the aircraft, no changes were needed on the assembly line. But production in Dallas had to wait for the revised design to be finalized. There had also been delays in receiving the Merlin engines, which were manufactured by Packard in Detroit, Michigan. Another major change involved the Liberator. As originally designed the aircraft featured a "greenhouse" style glass nose, with manually operated machine guns, and the first twenty-five Liberators produced in Dallas had been built to this specification. But experience in the war zone had proven this armament to be inadequate in dealing with head-on attacks. This resulted in the front of the aircraft being redesigned to incorporate a power-driven gun turret. This was a major change that required revised components and some retooling, further delaying the start of quantity production of the Liberator.[5]

Problems with manpower, materials, and modifications had all combined to disrupt the flow of aircraft out of Dallas. These were the most pressing issues, but others were present as well. Kindelberger's pamphlet reviewed many of the concerns contained in news reports and rumors. He addressed the housing shortage, transportation issues, and even the food in the plant cafeteria. He explained what some of the problems were, and he highlighted attempts to correct them. He also discussed efforts the company had made to support employees.

One example was the transportation section, which was created to help arrange carpools, but which had expanded to help workers navigate the rationing system. Kindelberger pointed toward "things like a liberal group insurance plan, systematic provisions for your personal safety when you are on the premises, and a complete industrial hospital service right in the plant." He stated, "every single one of these services is good for the company because it's good for you." It was all part of maintaining a "happy organization," with the only motive being "to make it possible for each employee to do his best on the job, and thus help get out the planes which already have shown they can be the difference between defeat and victory."[6]

Having commended the employees on their efforts and offering explanations why production was lagging, Kindelberger focused on motivating his workers. He asked them to stay with the company, as the departure of experienced employees led to the loss of valuable training and skills. He wanted them to reduce absenteeism, to buy war bonds, and to recruit friends and family to work at NAA. Most importantly, he appealed to the patriotism of the men and women who labored at the factory, reminding them that "yours is a heavy responsibility." Industrial workers were contributing to the war effort in a critical way, and he wanted them to recognize the importance of their work. *"We must get these airplanes built,"* he emphasized, "because the Army and Navy are depending on North American planes to a degree greater than I can tell you."[7] As the letter closed, Kindelberger pulled no punches:

> Unlike the men and women in the armed forces, we have made relatively few personal sacrifices, endured almost no personal hardship and risks. We are not called upon to give our lives; therefore it is reasonable and right that we should voluntarily dedicate ourselves to the successful completion of our nation's war effort. There is no death penalty for desertion here at home. But there is your conscience.[8]

The content of the *Our Job* booklet indicates that Kindelberger was aware of the controversy surrounding the plant and wanted to defend his company against the charges directed toward it. It can be viewed as a somewhat self-serving piece of corporate propaganda, a proactive response to what might emerge in the Truman Committee hearings. Yet at the same time the letter offers NAA's side of the story, presenting plausible reasons for inefficiency and delays. It is possible that Kindelberger's main motive in creating the letter was to correct misconceptions and dispel rumors. This could improve employee morale and encourage workers to increase their efforts. As written, the letter was probably intended to fulfill multiple roles, defending the company while calling upon workers to rededicate themselves to the task at hand. Whatever the case, Kindelberger had made his case to his employees. On Monday, 11 October, he would present his case to the members of the Truman Committee. Whether they would be receptive remained to be seen.

The committee members spent their third morning in Dallas touring the NAA factory. The group was met by Kindelberger and other NAA executives, who had arranged a tour of the facility. But news reports stated "the Senators admitted with grins, that the place was just too big to follow the guides. The investigators kept getting lost. And, to find their way back they had to do a lot of talking to employees." The inspection tour ended shortly after twelve o'clock, and the committee asked Kindelberger to gather certain records and appear that afternoon.[9]

When the proceedings reconvened, the first witness to appear was County Judge Al Templeton, who had missed the earlier hearings. Templeton wanted to talk about the Group One Critical Labor Area designation, and mostly reiterated the testimony of earlier witnesses. He criticized War Manpower Commission (WMC) regional director James H. Bond, repeating the allegation that he spent hardly any time in Dallas. Monday's hearings thus began as more of the same, and much of what would be heard fell into the now familiar pattern. More NAA employees appeared in the early afternoon, complaining of a lack of work and overall inefficiency. It was reported that they were told to look busy when a government official came. One former employee, Warren Earl, suggested that this also occurred whenever Kindelberger arrived. "When he comes out to the plant," said Earl, "you don't see this, because the grapevine works and everything is fixed up." But, he added, "I think Mr. Kindelberger is innocent of the whole thing." A more interesting tale was told by James Hereford, the son-in-law of Bernard F. McLain, president of the Dallas Chamber of Commerce. He recounted he was part of a group at the Baker Hotel the previous Friday night that had included Kindelberger, Orville Erringer of the WMC, prominent business and political leaders, and a "fellow named Merrill," who might have been Maj. Frank C. Merrill.[10] This testimony indicated Kindelberger, Erringer, and Merrill had the opportunity to discuss their testimony and possibly coordinate their answers. The committee did not ask any follow-up questions, indicating that they already knew the answers or were not interested in pursuing the matter.

Although new witnesses did appear before the committee on Monday, there were also some who returned for a second round of questions. One was Merrill, the Army representative at the NAA plant, who was again accompanied by Capt. Paul Eggleston. When asked why he was present, Eggleston replied he was to see that confidential information was not released, where-upon he was sent out of the room. Merrill clearly faced a hostile committee. He had presented them with a letter based on instructions from Col. Earl Patterson, Assistant Air Judge Advocate at the War Department. The document authorized Kindelberger, as well as his associates, to disclose classified information regarding "production costs, employment, and manpower figures." The problem, for the committee, was that the letter put stipulations upon the testimony. The Army wanted any such information to be treated as classified and marked accordingly and specified the committee should provide the Judge Advocate's office with two copies of any hearing transcripts involving NAA officials or Army representatives. Counsel Rudolph Halley offered his legal opinion that the letter had "no binding effect on this committee," suggesting that they could ask anything they want. Merrill was informed, "The committee does not acquiesce in any of the restrictions in your letter made by the Army." Merrill replied, "That is all right, I have cleared myself." He had been told to deliver the letter, and he had followed his instructions. He declared his intention to answer any questions to "the best of my ability."[11]

The committee wanted to revisit some of the issues addressed during Merrill's earlier testimony. They had been to the factory that morning and saw many men standing around apparently doing nothing. Pressed, Merrill proceeded to give examples of loitering and other idle activities. After some bantering about semantics, Sen. M. Charles Wallgren sharply asked "Major, in your opinion, do you think the men are being properly employed and utilized at this plant?" Merrill replied, "Giving you a definite answer, gentlemen, some of them are and some of them are not." Wallgren tried to get the officer to express it as a percentage of efficiency, but Merrill felt it could not be broken down that way. He admitted some workers were "not up to par," and that problems "might be caused by improper supervision." After more discussion, Merrill referred to the letter that had been mentioned by Herbert C. Durham, from the wife of a NAA worker to Roosevelt. This led committee members to question Merrill extensively about Durham's testimony on Sunday, especially the case of a Liberator assembled with a defective longeron, a load-bearing member. The longeron had excessive holes in

it, and Merrill wanted it replaced. The company wanted to solve the problem
by riveting a patch onto it. Kindelberger offered his assurance that the repair
technique was sound according to company engineers, and Merrill was asked
to accept the repair. Kindelberger declared that if Merrill could not make the
decision, then "we will take the decision to Wichita, and if they can't do it,
we will take it to Wright Field or Washington." In the end, Merrill accepted
the company's recommendation, and the committee was concerned that NAA
might have pressured him by threatening to appeal to a higher authority. After
a long interview, Merrill promised full access to any documents the committee desired and was allowed to depart.[12]

Kindelberger appeared next. He did not immediately delve into the issues of
manpower and production because of discussion about the disclosure of information the War Department considered restricted. This focused on the letter that
Merrill had presented earlier. Kindelberger was in somewhat of a bind. "Well,"
he said, "I can't go beyond that letter because I am sworn in on restrictions by the
Army and this letter applies to me." But he added, "I'm willing to tell you any
damn thing you want to know." Eventually the committee went off the record
at least twice to discuss matters before deciding to proceed. With all the maneu-
vering, it apparently took time before the hearing got down to the business at
hand. After briefly recounting the history of NAA, Kindelberger asked that Vice-
President Lee Atwood join the hearing in order to assist with the reports on hand.
What followed was a detailed discussion of how airplanes were produced, and
how much work was involved.[13]

Wallgren wanted specific information about NAA's Dallas operations.
Was the plant built by a defense corporation? How much government
money had been spent on the facility? Did NAA have any of its own money
in the plant? Eventually the subject turned to Liberators. "The fee on the
B-24 was based upon cost, which was determined by negotiation," declared
Kindelberger. The cost was estimated at $250,000 per aircraft, with NAA
earning a 5% fee on top of that. Wallgren asked if NAA was the only
contractor with this agreement and was told that both Ford and Douglas
operated under similar provisions. NAA's first contract was for 750 bombers, with a second contract for 650 aircraft estimated at $175,000 each and
a fee of 4%. The lowered numbers clearly indicate the efficiencies of larger

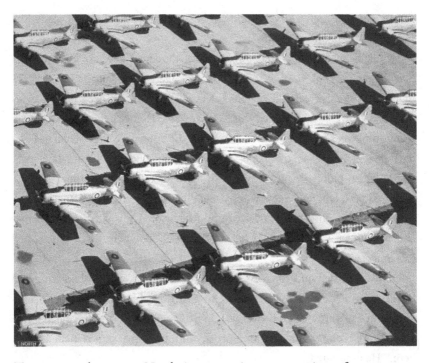

Trainers on the ramp. *North American Aviation via Aircraft Manufacturer's Collection, History of Aviation Collection, Special Collections and Archives Division, Eugene McDermott Library, The University of Texas at Dallas. Copyright ©Boeing. Used by permission.*

production runs, as the economies of scale would result in more efficient manufacturing. Another example of the economy of scale could be seen in the AT-6 trainer. Kindelberger explained that the Dallas-built trainers were originally contracted at a fixed price of $18,000 each, $1,300 higher than the version built at Inglewood. This presumably reflected start-up costs associated with bringing the new plant into operation. Kindelberger explained that the price was reduced later, at his instigation. "In January, 1942," he said, "nine months after we delivered our first airplane, why, I went to Hiram Jones, General Jones, who is the contracting officer, with our figures and I said, "We get too much money for these airplanes." Kindelberger continued, "I voluntarily cut the price to $12,900 in January, 1942. By that time we had built up a large volume of business and had the tools going, the people training, and whatnot."[14]

Kindelberger offered further information to the committee, providing production figures for Dallas. As of 9 October 1943, the NAA plants had built 7,923 trainers, 34 bombers, and 32 fighters. Not all of these had been delivered, as some planes were still awaiting flight checks. Sen. Homer Ferguson asked how many employees were involved in producing the trainer. "We reached a peak on the trainer in the A-plant of 16,000," responded Kindelberger, "before the pursuit [P-51] began pulling them away." With three aircraft now in production, the projected peak employment was forty-eight thousand workers in January 1944. Full production should be underway by March or April, when Kindelberger anticipated "we will be turning out, in March, 93 bombers, 254 fighters, and 233 trainers."[15]

It was the demand for forty-eight thousand workers that had triggered the declaration of Dallas as a Group One Critical Labor Area, and the discussion turned toward that controversy. Kindelberger stated, "we have had a fine community feeling in this community up until the threat of a critical area hit here." He continued:

That threat caused a number of people to talk loud and long. They did not know what it was. They were visibly perturbed about a 48-hour week which has been put into effect on some businesses. They did not know that the War Manpower Commission grants exceptions in many cases and that in Los Angeles, has granted exceptions to thousands of firms. They thought that all their contracts would be cancelled and that no other contracts will be brought into the district.[16]

"What benefit does it give you to have this area a critical area?" inquired Wallgren. "It does not particularly benefit us," replied Kindelberger, "Usually, there is a little more action on housing." Ferguson joined in at this point, asking "Didn't it benefit you in this way, that no employees go to any other plant than yours?" Kindelberger responded in the negative, stating "That is not in effect here." Ferguson queried, "Isn't that a critical area rule?" Kindelberger observed that such a rule was in effect near one west coast plant, but that did not apply to

Dallas. When Wallgren asked if the "community" was "unduly exercised over the designation," Kindelberger replied, "I think they yelped before they knew what it was."[17]

Kindelberger spent a lot of time schooling the committee on corporate management to convince them that his labor estimates were valid for the increased productivity the Army needed. He had to review his employment statistics month-by-month for the summer of 1943. The committee found it difficult to accept that some months there were no planes produced, yet thousands of workers remained employed. Kindelberger's explanation that time was needed to produce everything from parts to production systems elicited little sympathy from them. They remained focused on the fact that the Army was not getting any airplanes when employees were being paid to build them. And Kindelberger's argument that some delays were due to the Army's requests for design modifications, apparently failed to impress the committee.[18]

The committee returned time and again to the calculations of how many workers were required. Kindelberger and Lee Atwood fielded their questions, trying to explain the rationale behind the labor requirements. But the two sides were not connecting. "You have heard the accusation that your plant is hoarding labor?" asked Ferguson. "We are not hoarding labor —" began Kindelberger, only to be interrupted by the Senator: "Wait a minute. Inefficiency and people loafing on the job. What is your answer to these charges?" The NAA boss continued, "There are some people in there every day that are loafing, there are some people that challenge you to keep them busy, there are other people that would like to work but can't because of a thousand reasons." Sometimes workers were idled by a lack of parts. And even in the most efficiently run plant, three and a half percent of the workers "are going to the toilet or washing their hands or getting a drink." Ferguson continued to insist that he had seen idle workers during his tour of the factory, until Kindelberger responded to yet another demand for a solution by saying, "The remedy is to talk to them, beg them. You have no discipline in any plant in the United States today. You lay a man off today and you lose him, he never comes back if you lay him off; if you fire a man you have to get another one and maybe he isn't any better. As a result, they defy you and everything." Rudolph Halley commented that witnesses testified "the factor was not in the discipline, but in the inefficiency of the lead men and the foremen." Kindelberger admitted that some foremen did not know their jobs. Finally, Ferguson brought up the topic of corruption among the employment department, mentioning accusations that one of the managers was selling jobs and trafficking in war bonds. He asked if the company had investigated this case, and asked Kindelberger to check into it.[19]

By this point the hearing had moved through several different topics, prompting several committee members to offer a summary of the proceedings. Wallgren said:

> We have heard during the past few days some approximately seventy-five witnesses. A great many of them have been employed at the plant. They have told us over and over again that they have seen just one case after another of loafing on the job and, what you might term, very, very poor management as far as the personnel is concerned. Women and men, working there, anxious to do a job, we have had men who told us they have been trained to do one job, at the government's expense, and were taken into the plant and put on another job ... and that they are patriotic, they are sincere, they are anxious to do a job, and found things out there are just in a miserable mess. They just can't understand it.[20]

"I don't agree with them that it is a miserable mess," said Kindelberger, but Wallgren declared that there was "considerable trouble" and it needed to be corrected. When Kindelberger took out a written report on efforts at the plant to improve management, Wallgren asked to see it, and Kindelberger allowed him to keep it. Halley then offered his own summary. The matter was tied up in two things he said. First, the situation at the NAA plant "became common talk in town, resulting in what we might call a scandal in this city." Second, the plant was behind in production. Wallgren joined in, declaring that there had "Never been a case like this." Ferguson added, "Where lead men say, where lead men come up to men who are working and tell them to slow down. There is no discipline. A man might make twenty things on a machine while a woman opposite him makes a hundred; one is criticized and one is praised. The lead man will signal when big shots are coming through."

Kindelberger pointed out that the latter occurred in every plant. Wallgren stated that the plant needed stronger supervision. Kindelberger responded by submitting a loose-leaf binder that contained documentation about hiring, training, releases, and turnover in the workforce, showing how the company "studied and checked over" its employment practices. He pointed out that NAA had devoted 717,000 hours to training in just one month.[21]

Wallgren then recalled Warren Earl, who had appeared as a witness earlier in the day. He had been critical of conditions at the NAA plant, especially improperly fabricated parts and tooling. He had experience running a factory in Houston and had described numerous problems to the committee. Ferguson told Kindelberger that Earl "is going to tell you some things about your plant." Earl delivered a lengthy explanation of problems in the plant, including an incident where he had written a report concerning $68,000 worth of improper tooling that became waste. He believed the report had been repressed, and he expressed frustration at his inability to bring attention to the issues he encountered. He cited cases where imperfect parts were corrected by hand at great expense. Kindelberger acknowledged that such things did occur, as mistakes were discovered and improperly fabricated parts had to be modified. "Don't you inspect in the line?" asked Ferguson. "God, yes," replied Kindelberger. Halley then remarked that toolmakers had complained of thousands of junked parts. Kindelberger admitted that was "possible," but again explained that mistakes were bound to occur, especially in new manufacturing processes. When he repeated that there were not enough qualified supervisors to reduce miscues, Earl declared that he would rather be directing an assembly line than working as a recruiter. In response, Kindelberger asked for and got his name and telephone number.[22]

After dismissing Earl, the committee returned to grilling Kindelberger. They asked about the personnel department, and about "trainee" armbands that had recently been distributed in the plant. Some witnesses believed that the armbands were passed out haphazardly, in order to hide inactivity when the committee toured the plant. Kindelberger explained the reasoning behind the armbands, an idea he had gotten from Walter Beech (founder of Beech Aircraft). The committee also inquired whether some of the foremen were "without ability" and using their jobs to avoid the draft. Kindelberger said he had no personal knowledge of this occurring. Asked about turnover at the plant, which was 5.92% in August, Kindelberger observed that the turnover was similar to other aircraft manufacturers. Halley asked if Kindelberger ever discussed the manpower situation with local authorities and was told that he had talked with Erringer of the WMC. There was extended discussion of fees and how the company profited from building airplanes, during which Kindelberger's responses seemed to convince committee members that it was in his best interest to produce planes as quickly and efficiently as possible. Further questions focused on an issue raised by Earl: how often did Kindelberger visit any of his plants? Told that he usually spent only a few days per month at each one, the committee later suggested that he should be spending more time in Dallas.[23]

Kindelberger might have been relieved when the focus returned to the subject of manpower. When he related the difficulties encountered in obtaining workers at Inglewood, a conversation ensued about the WMC, with opinions exchanged about the problems that had been encountered. Both sides agreed that the current system was not working well, and there was criticism of the certificate of availability process, which had done little to reduce job turnover. The Group One Critical Labor Area designation also was discussed, and Kindelberger related how the city of Dayton, Ohio had come up with a community plan for dealing with their own designation as a critical area. Ferguson wondered why Dallas had not been given the opportunity to work out a solution before the designation was made, echoing the concerns of earlier witnesses. Kindelberger observed that on 1 October 1943 there were seventy-two such areas in the United States. "That being true,' Ferguson wondered, "What good are critical areas? If you have it all critical areas, what good is it?" Kindelberger replied, "That, again, is beyond me." He said that NAA had been working to alleviate it. Ferguson commented "If you could get some real help, I am satisfied with the evidence here on that plant, you could go in that plant and really do a job. I am talking about really doing a job, you could do a lot." Wallgren added, "And with fewer people." Kindelberger responded by asking where he could get such workers, prompting Ferguson to reply, "I don't know where you are going to get them, that is your job." Kindelberger agreed, answering, "That's right." Despite such moments of apparent agreement, the questions continued, returning to the same subjects again and again: wasted labor, cost overruns, and lack of proper management did not give the Army the full value for the money it had spent.[24]

Up to this point there may or may not have been tension in the room. Certainly, it must have been irritating to Kindelberger to hear that NAA was not getting the job done. From his viewpoint the situation probably looked quite different. It had been just over three years since ground had been broken for the A-plant, and about the same amount of time since the starter plant had gone into operation on Commerce Street. Since then, NAA had brought the factory into operation, created an industrial workforce from scratch, and produced 7,923 advanced trainers. These were significant accomplishments, for which NAA had twice won the Army-Navy "E" award. Admittedly, producing the P-51 and B-24 had been more complicated. In the case of the fighter, it had been necessary to reconfigure the A-plant, integrating a second assembly line while continuing to manufacture the AT-6. Design changes to the P-51 to accommodate the Merlin engine had caused delays. But fighters were starting to roll out of the A-plant in August 1943, and as Kindelberger told the committee, thirty-two had been completed at the time of the hearings. Given the normal production curve, there was every reason to expect increasing output in the months ahead.

The most serious problems surrounded the B-plant. Here things had not gone smoothly, with construction of the factory hindered by wartime shortages. There was also the fact that the B-24 was considerably larger than the single-engine trainers and fighters built in the A-plant. It was therefore a more complicated aircraft to manufacture, and NAA had no previous experience with the design, which originated at Consolidated Aircraft. Furthermore, the B-24 was subject to continuous modifications. Early versions of the bomber went through several design changes, including various configurations of armaments. Many of these had occurred before NAA went into production, but these changes still required updated drawings and redesigned components. A more serious issue was the decision to equip the airplane with a power-operated nose turret. This was done after production began in Dallas, causing further delays and the scrapping of outdated parts. Yet these problems were being overcome, and the plant was starting to manufacture

P-51C Mustang. *North American Aviation. Copyright ©Boeing. Used by permission.*

B-24s in quantity. If the Truman Committee had come to town three months later, they would have probably found a much different situation.

It is likely that Kindelberger took offense at the accusations surrounding the "cost-plus" contract for the B-24. Multiple witnesses complained that NAA had no reason to try to control costs under the arrangement, and it seems reasonable to assume that Kindelberger had heard these grumbles. Worse, many individuals apparently believed that NAA deliberately ran up the costs of aircraft in order to increase profits. Such misconceptions were probably due to misunderstanding how "Cost-Plus-Fixed-Fee" (CPFF) contracts actually worked. Many critics apparently envisioned an arrangement where manufacturers could increase their profits by increasing the costs of production. To use a hypothetical example, if a company incurred costs of $100,000 in manufacturing an aircraft, then a 5% "fixed fee" equated to $5,000. However, if the company could increase costs to $150,000, then the same fee would yield $7,500. Naturally, such a system could be exploited by unscrupulous business leaders, and contracts of this type "had been generally discredited by the abuses perpetrated under this name during World War I." In fact, this type of contract had been outlawed in 1934 by the Vinson-Trammell Act, which limited the amount of profit that could be earned when manufacturing armaments. In 1940 Congress authorized the use of CPFF contracts during the defense buildup. Historian Irving Holley Jr. opines that officials "displayed a certain lack of semantic sensitivity when they continued to use the phrase *cost plus* in spite of all its obnoxious connotations." It is not difficult to imagine that the general public, including aviation workers, might misunderstand CPFF contracts. Numerous witnesses commented that the B-plant was operating on a cost-plus basis, insinuating that NAA had no incentive to maintain fiscal responsibility.[25] Kindelberger had to spend a considerable amount of time explaining to the committee that while the CPFF contract theoretically allowed the company to bill the government for all costs, there were limits to what could be charged and all charges were subject to review by the Army.

At times the hearings became acrimonious. One clash came when Halley brought up the open letter that NAA published in local newspapers on 2 October 1943. He seemed hostile:

> You were talking about man power. Now, as to this profit and these rumors about loafing. Here is a self-serving statement in the form of a full-page newspaper ad, headed "Man Power—How we have used it and why we need more." Has that ad done any good for the morale at the plant or corrected conditions out there, and don't you think some other method might?"

"Maybe," replied Kindelberger, adding, "This seemed reasonable." Halley asked again if the witness had other ways to approach the problem, "other than the viewpoint of public morale?" Kindelberger pointed again to the experience of Dayton, Ohio, suggesting that Dallas should look for guidance from that community. He also mentioned efforts to simplify work in the NAA factory, and he reiterated the various educational programs devoted to employee training.[26]

Ferguson joined the exchange, badgering Kindelberger about the published letter until the NAA executive exploded, "I think the Dallas Division has done a hell of a good job; anytime anyone wants this they can –" Kindelberger had reached his limit, he expressed his frustration and irritation with the continued besmirching of his company. Exactly what he said, or how long he vented his anger, is unknown because his comments were purged from the transcript. When the record resumes, Ferguson asks, "Do you mean that you don't care if you produce for the United States Government?" Kindelberger's response, "I think a lot of this criticism is unfair," led Ferguson to retort, "And I think that statement is unfair, and we are at war."[27]

After more bickering between Ferguson and Kindelberger, and a failed effort by Wallgren to intervene, Judge Davidson, who had been relatively quiet throughout the hearings, spoke up. He noted that Kindelberger's outburst bordered on contempt. Kindelberger apologized for his transgression and requested that his remarks be stricken from the official record, and Ferguson agreed. Wallgren mercifully changed the subject away from NAA, asking, "Do you think we are trying to do too much in this aviation program?" Kindelberger responded with his customary observation that the Dallas community was doing a good job. Wallgren clarified his question, "I mean our program of making planes, do you think we are trying to build more planes than we can with the supervision, machinists, mechanics and materials available?" When Kindelberger said that production was generally efficient and on schedule, Ferguson asked if it might not be necessary to concentrate on certain aircraft and eliminate others. Kindelberger agreed with that in principal but added that aircraft moved up and down in levels of importance. He cited the Lockheed P-38 as an example. There was also the question of design modifications, which could slow down production but also improve the model in question. Asked by Wallgren if he thought the "situation" at the Dallas plant would improve "shortly," Kindelberger responded, "It will be improved; it will not be spectacular," and he assured Wallgren that "after we get over the hump on the curve there will be a lot of improvement."[28]

Kindelberger's time before the committee was drawing to a close. The members related some of the observations they had made during their tour of the plant and asked final questions regarding efforts to solve the labor problems. The answers were largely a recap of previously discussed issues. Kindelberger explained he had acquired one hundred thousand square feet in Waco, in order to relieve some of the load in Dallas. By that time he had endured three-and-a-half hours of questioning in a sometimes-contentious environment, chronicled in eighty-seven pages of transcripts. The committee broke for dinner, then reconvened and continued past midnight. Kindelberger was asked to be available for additional testimony but was not recalled.[29] He had done his best to defend his company, now the committee would have to decide its fate.

Chapter 19

Aftermath

The testimony of James H. "Dutch" Kindelberger before the Truman Committee did not bring an end to the hearings, although his appearance was certainly a highlight. The committee continued its investigation throughout Monday evening, beginning with a visit from fourteen North American Aviation (NAA) workers who met with the members in their suite at the Hotel Adolphus after dinner. The workers and politicians engaged in a group discussion concerning conditions at the NAA plant. The witnesses complained about improper tooling, favoritism in assignments, and poor management.[1] These complaints were by now familiar, and probably added little to the story, other than to reinforce the opinions of the investigators.[2] But there was more to come.

Formal hearings resumed at 9:50 p.m., as the committee worked into the night.

The next witnesses to appear were members of the NAA management team in Dallas: Charles E. Kelley, director of employment, followed by Nate Molinarro, the personnel director. Kelley had joined the firm early in 1941, while Molinarro had been with the company since 1939 and had transferred from Inglewood. Both men were quizzed about the infamous employee accused of selling jobs and trafficking in war bonds. Molinarro also explained he was not related to Kindelberger, dispelling rumors raised in earlier testimony. The committee members were unimpressed with at least one man's qualifications. Rudolph Halley grilled Molinarro about his training, asking "Did you ever in the entire course of your entire life take any course or training in employment and personnel work?" "No, sir," replied Molinarro. When Molinarro added he had worked at Inglewood in the employment office, interviewing prospective employees, Halley bluntly asked, "Do you think that qualifies you for the position of industrial relations, over 35,000 men?" In reply, Molinarro said, "I am in no position to judge my own qualifications."[3]

The last witness of the night was Walter L. Smeton, the General Superintendent of the B-plant. After some routine questions, Wallgren asked directly, "What is the matter with this plant out here?" Smeton responded that there was "nothing radical" wrong, and that things were improving as the workforce gained experience. Ferguson inquired, "Is there any hoarding of labor in that plant?" Smeton hesitated for "about 45 seconds" before answering "Yes." The committee sought to discover exactly how much of the workforce was actually needed, asking about inactivity and loafing, while Smeton responded with the now-familiar answers regarding inexperienced workers. There was little said that had not come up already with Kindelberger. The committee appeared to be unimpressed by his answers; eventually one of them asked, "Are you really running that plant?" When Smeton replied in the affirmative, he was met with "Why don't you do a better job?" Questioning continued along these lines until the witness was excused and the hearings concluded for the night.[4]

On Tuesday the hearings continued for a fourth and final day. A multitude of issues had brought the committee to Dallas, and there was still information to be obtained. A major concern was housing. On Tuesday morning the committee "changed tactics and called in all witnesses together for a free-for-all session." Included were administrators from the National Housing Agency, the Federal Housing Administration, and the Federal Public Housing Authority. Also on hand were representatives from the Dallas Real Estate Board and Dallas War Housing Center, as well as Winfield Morten, the executive manager of the Texas Pre-Fabricated House and Tent Company. Sen. Homer Ferguson declared that part of the problem was "a failure to see the picture as it is today, and just what can be done today." He said that the committee had heard a lot of "meaningless figures" that did not solve this, adding, "Figures and idealism won't do the job. It is going to take realism." The housing officials were directed to investigate the situation and submit reports about what was being done.[5]

Having addressed housing in the morning, the committee devoted the afternoon to one last session regarding NAA. This started with Matthew P. Crow, an NAA worker who had quit on Saturday in order to appear before the committee without being disloyal to his employer. He had only been at the factory for two months as a flight mechanic on the B-24. During his limited time at the company he had observed numerous problems, and he repeated the same charges as many of the earlier witnesses. He at least had thoughtful suggestions, a list of which he had typed, and which was introduced into the record.[6]

After Crow finished his testimony, the focus shifted to the War Manpower Commission (WMC). The committee wanted to further explore the role played by that agency in supplying workers to the industry, as well as the classification of Dallas as a Group One Critical Labor Area. This led to the recall of two members of the WMC who had testified previously. First to appear was Orville Erringer. He had been asked to bring data and correspondence with him for his second appearance and was presumably better prepared for this round of questioning. Erringer was accompanied by James T. Black, the assistant area director for the WMC. When asked how the WMC assessed NAA labor needs, Black stated, "We know, or have reason to believe, that 48,900 would be too many; we have taken that up with them." He was basing this partly on the floor space in the plant, which seemed inadequate to handle that number of workers. Ferguson queried the witness, "You would not seriously attempt to estimate their needs, would you?" "No Sir," replied Black, "I know nothing about airplane production from an efficiency basis."[7]

The second issue the committee wanted to revisit was the process by which Dallas was declared a critical labor area. All Erringer could produce was one memorandum, and he claimed the WMC local office was not

informed of the decision beforehand. Ferguson examined the memorandum and asked, "Even in this report you don't find a shortage of labor?"
Erringer replied "No, Sir," leading Ferguson to inquire, "Then why were
we put here in a critical area?" Erringer did not have an answer to that; he
apparently did not consider the shortage severe enough to warrant the critical
labor designation. He believed that the exact supply of labor was "indeterminable and you cannot reach out and verify it." A discussion ensued
concerning how the existing labor pool was calculated, which proved to be
an inexact process.[8]

Another potential source of labor was discussed at this time. In response
to a question from Rudolph Halley, Erringer verified that he had met
Kindelberger at the Baker Hotel, where Erringer had been invited to meet
with Robert L. Thornton. According to Erringer, Thornton was working to
establish a committee to investigate the manpower situation, believing that
"the citizens had been relaxed in getting their own house in order." One of
the ideas being considered was "trying to get a plant located in this city to
house the negroes." Halley asked for clarification, and Erringer explained
that the proposal was to lease a building where work could be performed
for NAA. This obviously would be a segregated plant, where Black workers
could take part in manufacturing airplanes. The most likely role of such a
facility would have been to create parts or subassemblies, which could then
be transported to the main factory. Halley followed up, "Is there resentment
and dissatisfaction at the North American Plant over the few negroes in that
place?" "Yes," replied Erringer, "at this time they have 2500 negroes in that
plant and several times in recent weeks, they have had flare-ups." Erringer
supplied no details about these incidents, but he suggested Thornton was
concerned about the situation. Building a satellite factory could defuse racial
tensions and allow the hiring of more Blacks to ease the manpower shortage.
Erringer said, "They contemplate employing six to seven thousand." This was
not the first time Erringer had discussed the use of minority workers. He had
mentioned it in a speech before the Kiwanis Club in July 1943, when he
discussed the labor shortage.[9]

As the discussion of labor continued, Erringer was asked if Kindelberger
was "personally conversant with the manpower situation in his plant?"

Erringer answered "I don't think he is." He blamed the size of the operation for part of the problem, commenting that "in large war plants of
this kind, they lose the human contact." Ferguson pondered whether the
problem could be mitigated by better leadership, asking "Have you found
any inspirational forces in that organization?" "None," replied Erringer.
"Have you found any human dynamos inspiring the output of airplanes?"
asked Ferguson. "None," answered Erringer, but he observed that the rapid
expansion of the plant had left the company with a lack of experienced
administrators. Ferguson mused, "There is surely in America executives
that could inspire men?" Erringer agreed, but the problem was finding
them. Many inspirational leaders had joined the military, and Ferguson
opined that maybe they could be of more use in the factories, rather than
"sitting around in swivel chairs with stars and leaves and bars on them."
Erringer again agreed with this assertion, but the ability to influence such
actions was beyond his authority.[10]

The committee recalled Lt. Col. Orville S. Carpenter of the WMC to
serve as the final witness. He had first appeared on Saturday, when he had
been extensively questioned about the designation of Dallas as a critical labor
area. He was expected to bring documentation regarding the decision, but
apparently brought nothing, stating that Erringer was supposed to have it.
He was unable to answer questions about how the decision was made, claiming that it came from Washington. Carpenter was asked about a letter he had
sent to Erringer in which he complained that NAA had not been cooperative.
He responded that he did not know of such a letter, but "I sign a lot of letters
that many others write." Halley asked that the letter be found, then inquired
if Carpenter had been able "to keep in close touch with this North American
labor situation?" "I would not say I have," Carpenter replied, adding, "in the
nature of the War Manpower Commission's organization, it is not intended
that I should." Halley, perhaps annoyed, retorted, "Just what is the nature of
that organization with regard to you?" Ferguson quickly changed the topic,
asking if Carpenter was paid by the Army, which he confirmed.

A discussion ensued in which the particulars of Carpenter's assignment
were explored. He had been with the WMC only since 9 June 1943, indicating he had inadequate time to become accustomed to his role. Ferguson

speculated that an Army officer had been placed in the position to avoid having to seek senatorial confirmation for the appointment, a possibility that Carpenter acknowledged. Further questioning revealed that Carpenter was with the WMC because regional director James H. Bond had asked him to join the organization. Carpenter was perfectly fit for active duty and had asked three times for a transfer, only to be ignored by the often-absent Bond.[11]

Carpenter was the last witness to appear before the Truman Committee. Ferguson and Halley departed for Washington on Tuesday night. Newspaper reports stated the committee had interviewed over one hundred witnesses, and that about one hundred more individuals gave statements to committee assistants. The question remained as to what to make of all this information. Some time was needed to process the data, but before the investigators left Dallas, they offered some general statements. The *Dallas Morning News* reported that, reading between the lines, it was possible to make three main deductions. First, "an inefficient use of personnel" existed at NAA. Second, the "housing problem has been mismanaged." Finally, the paper concluded that "Dallas was treated unfairly in its designation as a No. 1 critical labor area because of a lack of sufficient investigation." Whether the Truman Committee would agree with these deductions remained to be seen.[12]

Upon his return to Washington, Ferguson apparently met informally with WMC officials regarding the declaration of Dallas as a critical labor area. The next day a formal hearing was held in the Senate Office Building. Ferguson, as well as Hugh Fulton, Chief Counsel for the Truman Committee, spoke for almost two hours with five WMC administrators, who brought documentation with them in response to requests made the previous night. What the committee discovered was that there was apparently no specific study of the situation in Dallas. There were statistics and projections concerning labor demands that had influenced the decision, but no documentation regarding the decision. Likewise, there was apparently no study of the probable effect on the community, nor was there a list of actions to be taken to deal with the manpower shortage. There were guidelines as to what sorts of actions could be taken to address the problem, but the system was apparently designed to allow flexibility at the local level. The downside to this approach was that it caused uncertainty. Ferguson worked to pin things down, declaring "I want to know what a critical area is, so that the people in the area know, so that each company knows what it is up against. I want to know what the regulations are and the rules are. Where is that in writing?" Louis Levine of the WMC replied, "Senator, you are assuming that the classification of an area is the basis for a whole series of actions. A classification of an area is an objective appraisal of the labor market conditions prevailing in that area, the supply and the demand, the community facilities as they affect the supply and demand." When Fulton asked if anything specific could be sent to Dallas leaders to explain the designation and its effect, Levin said no.[13]

Another item that came up at this time was the assessment of manpower needs. The WMC officials confirmed that the required labor force was determined by the manufacturer, and that they were largely unable to substantiate the information. There were Army figures based on airframe weight output per man, and the WMC was not really in a strong position to question the guidelines. Nor were they qualified to assess the efficiency of a manufacturer. This information supported what the committee had heard in Dallas. If NAA forecast a need for a certain number of workers, it was difficult to contradict the numbers. All of this had factored into the classification of Dallas as a Group One Critical Labor Area.[14]

Further clarification of these issues came on 28 October 1943, when WMC director Paul McNutt appeared at a hearing conducted by the Senate committee tasked with investigating the defense program. Six senators were present, including Tom Connally of Texas and Chairman Harry S. Truman. Senators Wallgren and Ferguson also attended, as did Rep. Hatton Sumners; all three had been involved in the Dallas hearings. The themes covered at this meeting were by now familiar ones, but McNutt represented the ultimate authority within the WMC, and his reiteration of the procedures provided the senators with the final word regarding the process by which Dallas was declared a Group One Critical Labor Area. McNutt's answers supported those offered by his subordinates in previous testimony. He did offer some insight into why the WMC had not monitored efficiency at the NAA plant more closely, stating "We certainly have not been given a sufficient staff to make an examination of all these war plants." Truman said he believed that NAA was hoarding labor, but that the problem was widespread. He stated that members of the committee had "visited nearly every plane plant and every ship construction yard in this country, and we have seen this very situation developing."[15] The circumstances were summed up concisely by Sen. Joseph Ball of Minnesota, who observed:

> It seems to me your big difficulty in this whole picture is that you get an employer with a contract and you get a representative of the procurement agency who is given the responsibility of seeing insofar as he can that that particular contract is fulfilled; the whole tendency of those two men us to see they get everything they need. They are concentrating on their own little sector.

McNutt agreed, adding, "I know it has happened, too, but I doubt very much if even the Truman committee can change human nature."[16]

Sen. Scott Lucas of Illinois was apparently determined to find a specific culprit for the NAA situation in Dallas. The reason for his attendance is unknown, as he was apparently not a member of the committee. Referring to Kindelberger, Lucas declared, "there is something fundamentally and basically wrong with the fellow who will make that kind of request, when we are all out in this war effort to do whatever each individual can do to win it at the earliest possible time." Chairman Truman, however, was more understanding. He observed "I think he was just doing what we all do; if we find there is a shortage of shirts we order 10 dozen when we can get along with 10, and I think he ordered 48,000 people when he knew he needed 38,000 and he would only get that many." Lucas was unconvinced. He argued that Congress should enact a penalty against companies that hoarded labor. Wallgren responded with a defense of the aviation industry:

> The Government found it necessary to have to go out and get these men to do the job for them; they are the only men that know how to build these planes; a lot of these men don't want to take on another plant; a lot of them haven't wanted to see the industry blown up to the proportions it is, but the Government and Army comes along and says, "We have to have 10,000 of this and 50,000 of that."[17]

By this point the hearing was moving toward its end. Some residual discussion continued, including questions regarding draft deferments for war workers. But aside from Lucas there appeared to be little interest in taking a vindictive attitude against NAA. There was inefficiency within the organization to be sure, but government agencies had also failed to provide effective oversight. The goal was to move forward with solutions to these problems, in order to get production back on track.

Kindelberger wanted answers as well. He had invited the WMC to send an official to conduct a manpower utilization study. McNutt told the committee that he was sending George C. Chesney, who had done a "grand job" with a similar study at Bell Aircraft in Buffalo, New York. McNutt pointedly told Ferguson that he had sent Chesney "at the invitation of North American." Chesney arrived in Dallas on Saturday, 23 October 1943, by which time there had been a change in the situation there.[18] Records of the October hearings led by Wallgren and Ferguson had been given to Charles E. Wilson, Vice-Chairman of the War Production Board (WPB), who Truman described as "one of the Nation's foremost production experts." Wilson was scheduled to arrive in Dallas on Monday, 25 October, accompanied by two other WPB officials. They were not the only officials coming to examine conditions at NAA. Two Army Air Force officers came to Dallas at Wilson's request, Maj. Gen. Charles E. Branshaw and Brig. Gen. Ray G. Harris. The five men visited the NAA plant, and conferred with company officials, including Kindelberger. It had been just two weeks since the Truman Committee had left town; things were moving quickly compared to the normal pace of government action.[19]

Exactly what the atmosphere was like during these meetings cannot be determined, but it appears that a constructive dialogue took place. On 27 October 1943 Wilson sent a telegram to Truman in which he reported his findings. He announced, "the estimated manpower requirements of North American Aviation's Dallas plants have been reduced by approximately 10,000 workers from the previously announced peak load." This was made possible by a new set of production schedules that had been released by the Aircraft Production Board. Wilson explained that this "Realistic rescheduling of future production" considered "actual requirements of the air services, the over-all availability of and flow of war materials, and the ability to supply engines and other items to the aircraft manufacturer." These revised schedules allowed for "a reduction of 4,000 workers from the anticipated peak requirements for the Dallas plants. Wilson also declared that more efficiency in production would be achieved faster than anticipated. This reduced anticipated peak labor needs for the plant by "approximately 6,000 workers." Wilson's telegram offered this summary:

> As a result of these two reductions in requirements North American will need to hire only a minimum of new employees until January 1944, principally for replacements, and after that time the build-up to the ultimate stabilized manpower load in the Dallas plants will be on a gradual scale based upon the new schedules.

The most important point was that Dallas no longer needed to be designated as a Group One Critical Labor Area. A slightly condensed version of Wilson's telegram was sent to McNutt, who discussed it when he met with the Truman Committee on 28 October. Given the reductions, McNutt said the "labor demand and supply relationship in Dallas is substantially in balance and a reclassification from group 1 to 2 is thus permissible." This happened on 1 November, which resolved the main local issue that had brought contention to the city.[20]

The federal government remained concerned about production and cost inefficiencies. One directive issued by Wilson was for NAA to improve cooperation between management and the workers. Wilson stated, "This job of producing warplanes calls for complete cooperation by management and labor and we intend to see that an efficient, functioning labor-management committee is placed in operation." In a printed message to his workers, Kindelberger admitted that the existing structure had been inadequate. "We have not made the most effective use of our production drive committee, and we readily admit our shortcomings in that respect." He announced that the previous committee was to be replaced by two new groups, one for each of the production plants. All employees were encouraged to "transmit ideas and constructive criticism" to members of the committees.[21]

Other changes followed. Plant manager Harold F. Schwedes announced the creation of a board to oversee promotions to supervisory positions. This board was intended to "eliminate the possibility of favoritisms" by evaluating every candidate for "mechanical ability, technical knowledge, intelligence, and leadership." Other important attributes to be considered were "temperament, attitude and personality, ability to instruct, and job ability." Steps were also taken to increase the number of supervisors, with about two dozen appointments announced near the end of November. Some of these individuals transferred from Inglewood, bringing with them experience in producing fighters and bombers. Kindelberger, in yet another message to his workers, announced a change in the operating schedule for the plant, moving away from a staggered seven-day schedule to a six-day schedule in which the shop workers had Sundays off. Schwedes explained that the change would create "a smoother over-all operation," as "full crews will be on the job every working day." It also allowed more supervisors to be on hand as they needed to cover fewer shifts.[22]

Efforts such as these were intended to increase both efficiency in labor and production of aircraft. However, there was yet another item that caused suspicion among portions of the general public, and even within the ranks of the NAA workforce. The item in question was the "cost plus fixed fee contract" (CPFF) on the B-24, which had caused some uniformed observers to suspect the company was deliberately inflating expenses in order to increase their profits.

The CPFF was also unpopular with some officials, including WMC director McNutt, who told the Truman Committee, "I don't believe in them."[23] Kindelberger expended much effort during the October hearings trying to explain to the committee why CPFF contracts were a sound business idea, even if the initial agreements provided more federal dollars for NAA than the organization appeared to be worth, according to its asset reports. When Kindelberger signed the letter of intent for the B-24 he was agreeing to a contract that exceeded the value of his entire company. The high costs of evolving airplane production, coupled with a lack of existing facilities and properly trained personnel, made it imperative that federal funds be provided in a manner that shifted to match company needs.

In order to expedite production, the government essentially told contractors to get the job done and bill for whatever was needed.[24] This of course raised the possibility of fraud, so numerous regulations had been imposed and officials had been assigned, including inside the plants, to monitor salaries and material costs. The tangled web of regulations and the exploding number of military contracts overwhelmed the regulators, however, convincing critics of CPFF contracts that they were right about inefficiency and possibly government-sanctioned corporate theft.[25]

The inherent difficulties associated with the CPFF were magnified in Dallas because the A-plant operated on a fixed price basis, while the B-plant was on a cost-plus basis. This meant that the two operated as separate entities, making it complicated to interchange personnel and materials. This eventually led NAA management to examine the possibility of converting the B-24 program into a fixed-price contract. Kindelberger announced in early November 1943 that the company was working to make the change, claiming the process had begun "some time ago" and that NAA had taken the step on its own initiative. He wrote that the intention was to "make this change as soon as production on the B-24 had reached sufficient quantity to enable North American and the Army to determine a fixed price which would be fair to both parties."[26]

By the end of December Kindelberger announced that the Undersecretary of War had signed the new contract, and that all planes built by the Texas division were now on a fixed price basis. The plant newspaper claimed that negotiations for the change "were begun by the company several months ago." If this is accurate, negotiations for the conversion predated the Truman Committee hearings in October. If so, then the change was not due to the accusations made against NAA during those proceedings. Whatever the motives behind the conversion, it was a noteworthy change. NAA officials believed their firm was "the first major aircraft company to have voluntarily requested conversion" of a CPFF contract.[27] Historian Irving Holley supports that claim, and he observes that NAA "was able to lay off as many as 1,800 employees who had been engaged in property accounting and inventory work." The reduction yielded a savings in payroll, as well as a leaner workforce.[28]

The announcement of the new B-24 contract appeared in the plant newspaper on 31 December 1943, a significant piece of news to close out a contentious year for NAA. There had been a series of issues that had brought conditions in Dallas to a state of crisis, but by the end of the year these had been brought under control. The most newsworthy item to the citizens of Dallas was the declaration of the city as a Group One Critical Labor Area, which had resulted entirely from NAA labor demands, magnified by the accompanying housing shortage. This problem had been alleviated through efforts led by Wilson of the WPB, who worked with NAA, the WMC, and the Army Air Force to revamp the projected labor needs at the plant. The reduction of the anticipated peak workforce by ten thousand workers allowed for the removal of Dallas from the Group One category, in turn reducing the housing crisis. Further efforts to improve the housing shortage were also underway. On 14 October the WPB announced that more than one million board feet had been set aside for temporary housing in Dallas. Other projects were pursued as well, including two hundred temporary houses near the aircraft factory, and two hundred FHA houses that were to be finished by the end of the year.[29]

Another issue that had been addressed was alleged managerial inefficiency at the two plants, particularly B-plant, which did not have two years of production accomplishments to its credit. The solution to this problem represented a multitude of steps, including the efficiency study undertaken by Chesney, a revamping of the selection process for supervisors, and an increased number of supervisors. Additionally, there was the creation of a committee that brought management and labor together to address problems. The company also continued to invest in training, offering classes in subjects as diverse as Trigonometry and Blueprint Reading. Finally, conversion of the B-24 program to a fixed price contract allowed for consolidating some administrative functions as well as simplification of inventory accounting regarding government property. The revamping of the contract yielded added benefits in the area of public relations, as it effectively removed accusations that NAA had no incentives to control costs.[30]

Perhaps the greatest contribution to increased efficiency might have been a heightened awareness on the part of Kindelberger that his Dallas operation had problems. In public statements he had typically extolled the accomplishments of the Texas Division, especially in the early days of operation when only the AT-6 trainer was being built. During that period, he consistently praised employees regarding the way in which they became adept at producing aircraft. Yet in his appearance before the Truman Committee he admitted that his plant had "a mass of people brought in whose efficiency is low." His opinions do not necessarily contradict; it is probable that the rapid buildup of employees during 1943 outpaced the ability of NAA to provide adequate training.[31]

Regardless of Kindelberger's earlier opinions concerning the NAA plant in Dallas, he did implement improvements in response to the Truman Committee and Wilson's subsequent visit. Evidence of his attitude toward the investigation can be found in the records of the National Aircraft War Production Council. This council consisted of representatives from eight aircraft manufacturers located on the west coast, who organized in April 1942 to facilitate cooperation within the industry.[32] On 18 March 1944, John C. Lee sent a letter to Kindelberger in which he offered his memories of a meeting he attended the previous November. Lee wrote, "I have the distinct recollection of the meeting you called at the Inglewood Plant of North American, after your return from Dallas last November." During this meeting, Kindelberger had related his experiences with the committee and Wilson, referring to them as "my recent education in Dallas." As Lee remembered it, Kindelberger believed that the probes had proven constructive, as they alerted upper management to issues that had escaped their attention. Kindelberger admitted to "weaknesses of supervision and foremanship," which he attributed to the rapid growth of NAA. Having called the meeting to brief his peers on his experience, he suggested that "top management should do some hard-boiled self-examination in every plant." Lee closed his letter by recalling Kindelberger's mindset; he had not enjoyed hearing the criticism of his firm, but he admitted the inquiries were "the best thing that ever happened to the North American Company."[33] What Kindelberger might have felt in private cannot be determined, but in public he implemented the investigators' recommendations and urged others to do so as well. In the end

B-24 production line, Dallas B-Plant. *North American Aviation.*
Copyright ©Boeing. Used by permission.

Mustangs on the ramp near the hangar. *North American Aviation via*
Aircraft Manufacturer's Collection, History of Aviation Collection, Special
Collections and Archives Division, Eugene McDermott Library,
The University of Texas at Dallas. Copyright ©Boeing. Used by permission.

Vice-President Henry Wallace (left) with Brig. Gen. Ray G. Harris (right) visiting the B-Plant in October 1943. The worker is sixteen-year-old Reese Broyles. *Acme Newspictures, copyright © Getty Images. Used by permission.*

the goal was to "Get 'Em Built," which was the real solution to reducing political and public disapproval of NAA.

On 20 November 1943 the morning newspaper in Dallas printed a photograph on the first page of the second section, five columns wide and dominating the area above the fold. It showed, for the first time, the final assembly area inside the B-plant. The production line for the B-24 Liberators could be clearly seen, with a bomber in the foreground nearing completion and about a dozen more stretching back into the eastern end of the twelve-hundred-foot-long building. Some of these might have been completed in time to be among the deliveries in November, when thirteen aircraft were accepted by the government. In December the deliveries were up to twenty-one, and by the end of 1943 the plant had produced sixty-one B-24 Liberators. It had been a difficult beginning, but the airplanes were finally starting to move out the door and onto the flight line.[34] Perhaps more important, NAA had survived a serious challenge from federal investigators who could have made recommendations to curtail airplane production in Dallas.

Chapter 20

A Well-Oiled Machine, January–August 1944

A s Dallas began its third year at war, the North American Aviation (NAA) factory in Dallas moved beyond the chaos and controversy that accompanied the federal manpower investigations. The cost-plus fixed fee contract had been converted into a fixed price contract, retroactive to the beginning of the B-24 Liberator program.[1] The projected manpower needs had been lowered, and the city was no longer classified as a Group One Critical Labor Area. Most importantly, the production of Liberators was accelerating.

Some repercussions of the 1943 crisis still lingered, but NAA officials worked hard to resolve these. One frequent accusation during the Truman Committee investigation was there was inadequate supervision in the plant. It is human nature that some individuals are not self-motivated and require close supervision to keep them on task. Because NAA did not have enough effective leaders, some workers wasted time on the job. It is also a sad fact that some individuals lack a strong moral compass. In an organization employing thousands of people, it is inevitable that some workers fell into this category, taking advantage of the confused and chaotic atmosphere of the developing plant. A handful were prosecuted for indiscretions.

One example involved theft of property, a common occurrence in large businesses. The difference in this case is that the government owned much of the tooling and material in the two factories. This made theft a federal issue, leading to the involvement of the Federal Bureau of Investigation. In November 1943 two employees were charged with stealing tools from the plant, and both men admitted their guilt. Somewhat surprisingly, their names were published in the plant newspaper, along with details of the case. NAA Security Chief R. E. Smith indicated that other cases were under investigation as well. This was presumably done to send a message to any workers tempted to pilfer items.[2]

Other criminal prosecutions followed, presumably based on information supplied by Herbert Durham, an investigator for the Army Air Force. He had appeared before the Truman Committee during the October 1943 hearings, at which time he stated he could document at least a dozen cases of timecard fraud. Durham apparently was correct, for in January several cases were presented to a federal grand jury. This led to thirteen indictments for fraud, and several former employees found themselves in Judge T. Whitfield Davidson's courtroom. They were possibly surprised to find that falsified timecards could be a federal case because of the cost-plus contract that had been in existence at the time of the infractions. Action was swift in most of the cases; within days of the indictments seven of the defendants pled guilty to defrauding the government. Four of the offenders were women, each of whom were sentenced to sixty days in jail. Two men were given harsher penalties, each receiving six-month prison sentences. The lighter sentences given to the women might have been due to their gender, but a more likely explanation is that the two men were held to higher standards because they held supervisory positions. The seventh offender received a suspended sentence and a three-hundred dollar fine due to his cooperation with investigators, as well as the fact that he was working at another war plant, where his skills were needed.[3]

Two other defendants fought timecard-related charges in a trial that featured testimony from NAA personnel director Nate Molinarro, and Capt. Donald E. Eggleston of the Army Air Force. Dale J. Bowen and Margaret Adamson were charged with falsifying Adamson's timecards. Adamson, described by news reports as a "striking blonde," was Bowen's secretary. Defense lawyers for Bowen maintained that company policy allowed him to authorize pay for her when she was absent. The defense argued that any perceived violations of policy were a matter between the company and its employees, and not within the purview of the government. This trial ended with an undecided jury, necessitating a second proceeding in February, at which the two were acquitted. Similar timecard cases continued to be heard in the early months of 1944, while other individuals were prosecuted for theft of tools from the plant.[4]

A particularly sordid case involved Orville Raymond Jr., a former night foreman in the B-plant tool crib. Raymond, age 27, had a wife and children, but he was arrested in Nevada along with his former secretary, Capitola McDonald, age 23. The two were among those charged with timecard fraud. Judge Davidson was particularly angry with Raymond. He assigned him a two-year sentence and recommended that the District Attorney consider charging Raymond with violations of the Mann Act. McDonald, described as "a little country girl under the domination of her former boss," was fined one hundred dollars.[5]

While federal prosecutors targeted assorted miscreants, NAA management pressed forward with two projects that had been stimulated by the manpower crisis. The first and more substantial of these was the satellite factory in Waco, which had been announced in October 1943. The company acquired four buildings in downtown Waco, including one that had previously served as a National Guard armory. News coverage of the satellite operation was sparse in Dallas, coming as it did so soon after the city was declared a Group One Critical Labor Area. The Waco press understandably paid more attention. The official announcement was made by NAA on Friday, 1 October 1943, with the news appearing in the Waco Sunday paper two days later. Officials of the Waco Chamber of Commerce envisioned that "hundreds of central Texas men and women will step directly into the firing line on the production battlefront." A follow up article in November confirmed that the leases had been signed, and that the Waco facility would "be staffed almost entirely with residents of this area, with a small nucleus of supervisory personnel being transferred from the Dallas plants."[6]

Preparations progressed quickly, and by 13 December 1943 the first training class began at the employment office at the old armory in Waco. New
hires attended an orientation about the types of aircraft produced by NAA,
received information regarding rules and practices, and heard a briefing on
the fundamentals of riveting. This was all in one day, but Nate Molinarro
hoped "that some of the new employees can be placed on actual production jobs within two weeks." News about this class appeared in the Dallas
plant newspaper, with a picture of some of the trainees. Some of the men
were former National Guardsman who had been given honorable discharges
because of age or disabilities and were now back in their former armory
learning new skills. Initial wages for the Waco employees were set at fifty
cents an hour for untrained production workers, while those who stayed on
the job would receive monthly raises until their pay reached sixty-five cents
an hour. Beginning office workers got 85 dollars a month, with increases up
to 115 a month. Trained or experienced workers could earn higher starting
rates. These numbers were only temporary. NAA intended to put the Waco
operation on the same pay structure as its other plants, but this had to be
approved through the national offices of the War Labor Board. In the meantime, the temporary wage scale allowed for staffing to begin.[7]

By the middle of January 1944 the training program started to yield
results, and the NAA plant newspaper featured a photo of a female
employee stacking some of the first aircraft parts fabricated in Waco.
In March James H. "Dutch" Kindelberger visited the Waco factory, where
he had his picture taken with workers as they ate lunch. By April the Waco
operation was furnishing AT-6 wings to the Dallas plant. Starting with the
7 April 1944 edition, the masthead of the plant newspaper was changed to
read "Dallas and Waco," and several articles were included on the satellite
facility, as well as two dozen photographs of the Waco plant and its employees. As it happened, it was the third anniversary of the formal dedication
of the A-plant, when the first three Dallas-built trainers had been delivered. Things had progressed exponentially since then, for the paper proudly
declared that the Texas division of NAA had delivered 1,310 aircraft during
the first three months of 1944. This figure was announced by Col. Frank W.
Cawthon, the acting supervisor for the Midwestern District of the Army

Air Force Material Command. Cawthon added that it was "an achievement equaled in few plants during a similar period."[8]

The opening of the Waco satellite plant served two purposes. First, it tapped into a source of manpower located outside the Dallas area. But the Waco facility had the additional purpose of moving some operations out of the A-plant, which had originally been set up just to build trainers. By 1944, with fighters and trainers being constructed in the same building, floor space was likely becoming cramped. The relocation of wing manufacturing to Waco surely eased congestion within the Dallas factory. Sometime later the center section of AT-6 trainers also began to be assembled in Waco, where the plant became a small but useful component of NAA.

While the Waco satellite factory received a degree of recognition by the Dallas plant newspaper, there was an additional support factory that received little acknowledgment. Indeed, even clues to its existence are slight, although a short news article in mid-January 1944 provided some basic facts:

A downtown Dallas production unit of North American Aviation, Inc., consisting of several assembly departments, which have been moved intact from the main plants, has been opened in the building at Harwood and McKinney formerly occupied by the General Motors Buick division, Factory Manager H. F. Schwedes announced Wednesday.

A nucleus of employees, including a number of skilled Negro workers drawn from the main plants, is now at work at the downtown unit, where it is planned eventually to develop a production force composed principally of Negroes.[9]

The downtown unit, it was explained, "will operate both as a training and a production center," where trainees could learn operations and then move into production. Otherwise, very little information was released, with the entire article consisting of only three paragraphs found on the first page of the local section of the Dallas morning newspaper. Surprisingly, the NAA plant newspaper provided scarcely more information, with the announcement of the downtown unit relegated to page two. In this case the article contained five paragraphs, three of which were identical to the version printed in the *Dallas Morning News* the previous day. One of the extra paragraphs stipulated that that the opening of the downtown facility "does not mean that the number of Negroes working in the main plants will necessarily be reduced."[10]

The plan to open a satellite plant for African American workers had been mentioned by Orville Erringer during his appearance before the Truman Committee the previous October. At the time Erringer had initially said that some twenty-five hundred African American employees were at NAA, but in a second reference he placed the number at thirty-five hundred. Whichever figure was accurate, it established the presence of a substantial number of African American workers in the NAA factory at Dallas. It is uncertain what roles they performed but given the realities of the era it seems probable most were employed in physical work such as warehouse and custodial duties. Nevertheless, the news release announcing the downtown unit referred to the existence of "skilled Negro workers," suggesting that some of the African American employees were involved in manufacturing. Unfortunately, further evidence concerning their numbers and roles is elusive.[11]

The contrast between coverage of the Waco unit and the downtown Dallas unit is striking evidence of the racial divide that existed at the time. During its existence the plant newspaper published a multitude of human-interest articles about employees, along with thousands of photographs portraying life at NAA. These invariably show an overwhelmingly white workforce. This is probably an accurate portrayal, but the lack of African American employees is striking when viewed against modern day societal norms. Whatever work was being done at the downtown unit apparently received little publicity or acclaim. One exception was during a meeting of the Labor-Management Committees in March. Dutch Kindelberger was in attendance, and he complimented the members on the work they were doing to help improve production in the two plants. Kindelberger stated "Not only are Plants A and B looking better, but both the Downtown Production Unit and the Waco Unit are doing outstanding jobs."[12]

While favorable comments from the president of the company are nice to hear, the tired phrase is that actions speak louder than words. In the case of NAA at Dallas, the grandest gesture was a massive open house held at the factory during March 1944. For this event, employees could invite family members to visit the factory. This was a significant relaxation of secrecy at the plant, which had been closed to the public since the dedication ceremony in April 1941.

The exact process surrounding the decision to hold the open house is unknown, but the idea was likely influenced by the controversy surrounding the factory the previous year. Many NAA workers were concerned about production at the plant, and these doubts spread to citizens in the street. None of this could have been good for morale inside the factory. This was recognized by Maj. Gen. Charles E. Branshaw, who had come to Dallas as a participant in the investigation conducted by Charles E. Wilson of the War Production Board (WPB). In a telephone conversation on 28 October 1943, Branshaw discussed his thoughts with Julius Amberg, and recommended posting a picture of a big thermometer in each plant, showing the number of planes produced each month. He declared that officials had been "very secretive about our production," and it might be time to stop doing that. After all, he added, "we have nothing to be ashamed of." Amberg indicated that he understood the idea. Branshaw concluded, "I think our schedule is so good now and our production so good that we might as well let the people know."[13]

Given that Branshaw was a high-ranking officer, it may be assumed that Amberg passed along his recommendation to his superior, Under Secretary of War Robert P. Patterson. As it was, the federal government had been releasing information about total aircraft production to the general public. For example, in March 1943 Patterson had reported that approximately 5,500 airplanes had been delivered during February. These figures continued to increase, and in early August the WPB disclosed that a new record had been set in July when 7,373 airplanes were produced. If information such as this could be passed along to the general public, it was reasonable to share specific numbers with the workers who were responsible for construction of the aircraft. Evidence of the changed policy started to appear in December 1943, when Dutch Kindelberger authored another of his communiques in the plant newspaper. He disclosed that the factory had failed to meet its schedules on both the B-24 bomber and P-51 fighter. While Kindelberger did not disclose the specific number of aircraft involved, he revealed that production of the B-24 was only 70% of the goal, with the acceptance rate at thirty-three percent of the scheduled level. The situation on the P-51 was somewhat better, with production at 65% of the schedule. He declared, "We've got to do a lot better that that."[14]

The increased openness about production presumably played a role in the decision to hold an open house at the factory. An announcement of the event appeared in the Dallas plant newspaper on 25 February 1944. It was intended to be a "family day" for the relatives of workers, to be held on two consecutive Sundays, when most employees were not working. Office employees from both plants, and production workers in the A-plant, were offered tickets for 5 March. Production workers in the B-plant, along with employees from the downtown unit, were to visit on 12 March. Workers could invite up to five relatives to tour the factory, but the host was to accompany the guests, and no children under six were to be admitted. The open house was scheduled to run from 9:00 a.m. to 6:00 p.m., with day shift workers attending up until two o'clock in the afternoon. Night shift employees received passes for the afternoon session. Both main plants would be open during the event, allowing A-plant workers to visit the B-plant, and vice-versa. Employees were informed that "These open houses are in line with the policy recently adopted by the U.S. Army to let employees' families become acquainted with the operations of war plants." Plant manager Harold F. Schwedes encouraged all NAA employees to participate by inviting guests, "Because we are anxious for the families of North American workers to see for themselves the accomplishments of our employees."[15]

When 5 March arrived, the scenes were reminiscent of the open house held before the dedication of the first plant in April 1941. A news account described "long lanes of traffic" as motorists worked their way to the factory, directed by members of the Texas Highway Patrol. Others came in buses, which ran special schedules that day to accommodate the visitors. Security at the event was provided by the NAA security force, reinforced by Dallas police and an estimated four hundred members of the Texas State Guard.[16]

Crowds gathered at the turnstiles long before the nine o'clock opening, with one of the first through the gate being employee Samuel George,
who wheeled his handicapped son during the tour. The route entailed a
one-and-a-quarter mile hike, starting at the A-plant, where visitors could
see assembly lines for the P-51 and the AT-6. Upon exiting the building,
guests were directed to the east flight ramp, where Mustangs and Texans
were on display. Some of the aircraft had platforms erected over the wings,
so that curious onlookers could see down into the cockpits. Upon entering
the B-plant, guests were ushered onto the second-floor level. From here
they could look out over the B-24 production line, where the big four-
engine bombers were being assembled. Outside on the west flight ramp
there were at least six B-24 bombers on display, some with mirrors under-
neath so the visitors could see the bomb bay without having to stoop down
under the aircraft. Three major sections of a Liberator were also on exhibit,
including a nose and a tail. This allowed guests to see how the airplane was
fabricated in sections prior to its final assembly. Attendees were also given
a fourteen-page souvenir booklet titled *"Plants People Planes,"* which
contained information about NAA, the three models of aircraft manufactured in Dallas, photos of employees at work, and statistical information
about the factory.[17]

Interviews with employees suggested that they were grateful for the
chance to see the full plant. Many workers with clerical jobs had possibly
never seen the production areas, and employees of the A-plant had likely not
been inside the bomber facility. A typical response was that of Julia Sanner,
who brought her father, brother, and aunt as guests. She was enthusiastic
about their experience, saying "I just can't tell you how much we enjoyed it.
The final assembly line in Plant B simply takes your breath. We were able
to see the planes so well, something I hadn't been able to do before and it
was thrilling." Other employees voiced similar sentiments. Carl M. Innfeldt
brought his wife and two daughters and declared, "It was grand to be able to
bring my family in and show them not only what I do but how these planes
are made. I think all of us in our plant were anxious to see Plant B." Young
children were impressed as well, with one child heard to say, "Gee Daddy,
I didn't know you made all these."[18]

The excitement continued the following Sunday, when the second day of the open house welcomed employees of the B-plant and their invited guests. Hours were extended for the second day, with the event running until seven o'clock. Once more the two plants hosted teeming crowds as guests journeyed through the vast complex. Music and announcements were played over the public address system, which photographs indicate was operated by female employees. Visitors on the second day could also view a German Messerschmitt 109 fighter, which had arrived too late for the first family day celebration. The intact German aircraft was displayed alongside a pile of wreckage from a destroyed German bomber, with the Nazi swastika conspicuous on the debris. Turnout for the second day of open house was reported as ninety thousand, an increase over the estimated sixty-five thousand to seventy thousand people who had come on the first Sunday. In the final tally, company sources claimed 160,000 people had visited the factory during the two days. This roundness of the figure indicates it is imprecise, but there is little doubt that a massive number of people came to see the NAA plant firsthand.[19]

The estimate of 160,000, even allowing for inexactness, represents a sizable percentage of local residents. The 1940 census reported the total population of Dallas County as 398,564. This number had increased during the war as individuals moved into the county, and obviously not every attendee lived in Dallas County. But attendance for family day proves there was a great deal of public interest about the plant. This dated back to the beginning, when it was first announced that an aircraft factory was to be constructed on the outskirts of the city. The entrance of the United States into the war had added significantly to the importance of the factory, and the controversies of 1943 likely shook the confidence of some individuals about the work performed at NAA. Any visitors with doubts should have found reassurance at the sight of finished aircraft lined up on the flight ramps.[20]

NAA managers must have viewed the open house as an opportunity to address official concerns as well. Their souvenir booklet highlighted not just the production of planes, but the partnership between the city and the factory. This relationship had begun with a promise that NAA would minimalize the disruptions to the community that could arise with the arrival of a new industrial facility, and "to train, and make efficient aircraft builders of, thousands of non-industrial workers." In return, the city was to provide manpower and support new housing and transportation. The problem, explained the booklet, was that the plant became "four times as big as originally contemplated in 1941." The "stress of wartime working and living" affected the relationship between the community and NAA, but the partnership continued:

> Today, the welfare and even the reputations of Dallas and North American are inseparably linked. A production job well done reflects credit on the entire community; a failure becomes a black mark against Dallas itself. And likewise, a misunderstanding on the part of the community can actually affect aircraft production, for there is not a neighborhood in Dallas County without its share of North American employees, susceptible to encouragement or criticism from their friends and neighbors.

Further explanations followed in the form of statistics about the factory. In three years of operation the Texas Division of NAA had manufactured products worth $193,000,000. While doing so NAA had paid $144,000 in state and county taxes, and $2,500,000 in unemployment insurance contributions. The factory used subcontractors in the Dallas metropolitan area, and in 1943 their contracts amounted to $3,819,000. The biggest impact of all was in wages; since the start of operations in Dallas the company had paid a total gross payroll of $120,000,000. This represented a huge influx of cash into the local economy. To provide context, the total amount of deposits in Dallas banks in December 1939 was $305,668,000. By the end of 1944 this figure had jumped to $809,538,000, an increase of 165% in five years. Clearly there were many factors accounting for this, but NAA was a major contributor in this growth.[21]

With some 160,000 attendees, it appears the open house was a rousing success in terms of public outreach. Determining its effect upon the workforce is difficult, but it seems reasonable to assume it had positive results. The opportunity to show the fruits of their labor to relatives must have given the typical worker a sense of pride and accomplishment. Additional morale boosting events continued after the open house, including a variety of visitors who toured the plant offering praise and encouragement. These guests were typically either dignitaries or common military men, following a pattern that been established in the earliest days of operations in Dallas. On 21 March 1944 the famed aviator Alexander P. de Seversky toured the factory, guided by Dutch Kindelberger. Seversky was the founder of a company that eventually became Republic Aviation, the manufacturer of the P-47 fighter. He was also a noted advocate for air power, publishing a book about the subject in 1942. During his visit Seversky complimented Kindelberger for "a smooth, well-thought-out production scheme." He also observed that "Everyone seemed to be on his job and doing it. There were no waste motions, no one running around aimlessly." If Seversky's remarks were genuine, then conditions in the plant were much improved from those found the previous year.[22]

Other visitors followed. On 28 March 1944 the B-24 bomber *Blue Streak* was slated to appear. The aircraft had completed 110 missions in the Mediterranean theater and had been sent back to the United States for a war bond tour. As it happened, the *Blue Streak* failed to arrive, sidelined by mechanical repairs. But her crew dutifully made the trip to Dallas, where they toured the two NAA plants during both the day and night shifts, as well as speaking to the workers over the public address system. Dallas Mayor Woodall Rogers visited in April, taking advantage of the opportunity to be photographed sitting in the cockpit of a B-24. The first week of May featured a visit from Rear Admiral Percy Wright Foote, who served as Inspector of Naval Material for Texas and three neighboring states. He was photographed sitting in the cockpit of an SNJ trainer, reaching out to shake hands with employee Mildred Lux. While at the plant Foote lauded the efforts of NAA employees in Dallas, commenting that "their work and attitude are two of the reasons why we are winning this war."[23]

The real evidence that NAA operations in Dallas were succeeding can only be found in production results. Unfortunately, research has failed to produce a definitive record of monthly figures in 1944. However, by comparing different sources of information it is possible to extrapolate some numbers on each of the three aircraft types built at Dallas during the first half of the year. The aircraft that had caused the most controversy was the B-24. A document kept by the National Aircraft War Production Council indicates that B-plant delivered 55 bombers in January, with another 66 in February. This compares to the 61 manufactured in all of 1943. The Liberator program was accelerating as the factory moved deeper into the production curve. Given the total number of 966 Liberators produced by NAA, it is certain that the monthly deliveries increased further as the year progressed, reaching a peak of about 100 per month. This estimate is consistent with testimony provided to the Truman Committee by Dutch Kindelberger, who predicted that the B-plant production would reach 93 bombers per month by March or April of 1944.[24]

There is a similar lack of precise data available concerning the output of the P-51 during 1944. The initial version of the Mustang built in Dallas was the P-51C, a designation specific to the Dallas plant. Production of this type totaled 1,750 aircraft, before the plant shifted to the P-51D, which sources indicate was done around July 1944. This is an imprecise date, but when combined with other information it provides a basis for computation. During his testimony before the Truman Committee, Kindelberger stated that the A-plant had produced 32 fighters as of 9 October 1943. At this time, the P-51 program had barely gotten underway, and the number of planes manufactured should have increased each month during the rest of 1943. An NAA internal document states that "Dallas reached 83 acceptances" in December of that year. Acceptances by the military inevitably lagged behind production, as the planes had to be inspected and test flown before the Army took delivery, but it does provide some idea of the production pace at that time, which seems to have been no less than 25 units per month.[25]

The production of P-51 planes must have greatly accelerated in 1944. Given that the quantity of P-51C models is known to be 1,750, and that only 32 had been built through the first week of October, that leaves 1,718 aircraft to be accounted for. If Dallas switched to producing the P-51D in July 1944, it means that the remainder of the "C" models had to be manufactured during a period of from nine to ten months. Using the longer period as a guide results in a monthly average of around 170 aircraft. Given that the production curve increases over time, the numbers in late 1943 should have been lower than the hypothetical average, steadily increasing as 1944

progressed. Dutch Kindelberger anticipated that the A-plant should be turning out 254 fighters a month by the spring of 1944. Considering the total
number of P-51C models built, it is reasonable to accept his prediction as
accurate. There is no way to produce 1,718 aircraft in ten months without
building 200 units a month or more at some point in the process.[26]

All that remains to be considered is the Texan trainer. The introduction of
fighter production into the A-plant required a decrease in number of trainers
being built, but the AT-6 continued to be manufactured in large numbers.
During the October 1943 hearings, Dutch Kindelberger reported that Dallas
had built 7,923 trainers. Documents indicate that by the end of 1943 the
A-plant had produced a total of 8,609 aircraft, almost all of which were trainers.
Production in the A-plant was at a high pace during the early months of 1944,
with 328 aircraft reportedly produced in January, with the same number
repeated in February. Since the P-51C was still on the low end of the curve at
that point, the majority of these planes must have been trainers. Kindelberger
envisioned the A-plant producing 233 trainers a month in March 1944. By all
indications, this level was reached, as trainer production in Dallas reached
the ten-thousand-unit milestone in July 1944. This represents 2,077 aircraft
between October and July, equating to an average of over 200 a month.
This is consistent with Kindelberger's prediction.[27]

The estimates of monthly production rates for the Dallas plant in the
first half of 1944 do involve some informed speculation, but the numbers
seem reasonable when compared to figures reported by NAA for the entire
calendar year of 1944. According to a company report, the acceptance
rate for the Dallas plant that year averaged 275 trainers, 218 fighters, and
82 bombers per month. Thus, the figures for the twelve-month period of
1944 are consistent with the trends established earlier in the year. It appears
that Dutch Kindelberger's explanation of the production curve was on
target, and that the two factories had emerged from the chaos of 1943 and
were now running like the proverbial well-oiled machine. In the first five
months of 1944 the factory delivered more than 2,400 aircraft, with 646 in
the month of May alone—a new record for the Texas operation.[28]

But even as the B-plant was reaching a high degree of production, there
were rumors in the air that change was coming. On 2 June 1944 a United Press

wire report appeared that cited Mead L. Bricker, the superintendent of the massive Willow Run aircraft factory operated by the Ford Motor Company. Bricker said that Ford was poised to take sole responsibility for building the B-24 bomber. Willow Run was expected to achieve a monthly production of four hundred aircraft by September, which should meet the demand for the airplane. Bricker named two factories that were currently building the B-24: the Consolidated plant in Fort Worth and the Douglas factory in Tulsa, Oklahoma. Both these plants were to shift to other programs. There was a glaring omission here in that the spokesman made no mention of the other two manufacturers in the B-24 pool, which were Consolidated in San Diego and NAA in Dallas. Contacted for comment, NAA plant manager Schwedes explained that the current B-24 contract called for production to continue in Dallas well into 1945.[29]

The possibility of drastic changes in the B-24 program caused immediate turmoil. The initial report appeared on the front page of the 3 June 1944 edition of the *Dallas Morning News*, a Saturday morning paper. The next day the same newspaper published an article that claimed there were "reports of hundreds of workers resigning at North American" following the previous day's publication. Concern about these developments prompted a quick response from authorities. Brig. Gen. Ray G. Harris of the Army Air Force Material Command issued a statement from his office in Wichita, Kansas. He declared that current manufacturing schedules for the B-24 called for continued production at NAA in Dallas, as well as Consolidated in Fort Worth. He announced, "The need for the present working forces of men and women at both plants will continue and no layoffs are in prospect as far as the B-24 program is concerned this year at the two Texas plants." Harris stressed that both plants needed to maintain their current employment levels. He was certainly familiar with conditions in Dallas, having been part of the manpower investigation the previous October.[30]

Charles E. Wilson of the WPB also weighed in on the matter. As part of his duties, he chaired the Aircraft Production Board, which allowed him to speak with a level of authority. Wilson talked with reporters on 5 June, when he stated that any cutbacks contemplated for aircraft production in 1944 had already been announced. He discounted reports that Ford would assume all responsibility for manufacturing the B-24 and anticipated that NAA in Dallas "would continue production of the Liberator at the present rate indefinitely." This information was prominently featured on the front page of the Dallas plant newspaper, probably to reassure employees that no job cuts were imminent.[31]

It is unclear just what exactly happened in June 1944, but it was definitely a case of conflicting information. Ford spokesman Bricker announced that Willow Run was to be the sole source for the B-24, and an Army officer at that plant indicated that release of this information had been cleared by Washington. Yet the report was discredited by General Harris the next day, and by Wilson after that. Obviously, someone was wrong somewhere. Given the timing of the announcement, it is tempting to point the finger at Ford and accuse the company of either prematurely disclosing future plans or misunderstanding the certainty of a proposed course of action. Given the date, the latter seems to be the more likely scenario. At the time the report about Willow Run was released, the invasion of Europe had yet to occur. A failure of the Normandy landings could have prolonged the war for an indefinite period. Were this to happen the strategic bombing campaign against Germany might have continued for a very long time, requiring a steady supply of the B-24. While it is possible that Willow Run may have been able to satisfy the demand on its own, it seems improbable that such a decision would have been finalized prior to knowing the outcome of the invasion. It is logical to assume that discussions had been held concerning the future of B-24 production, and that plans were formulated on what steps were to be taken in the case of a successful European campaign. A plausible explanation for the Willow Run report is that some unknown official looked at what could happen and reported it as though the decision had already been made, leaving Harris and Wilson scrambling to issue corrections.

As it happened, the day after Wilson issued his rebuttal, Allied forces landed in France. Many Dallas residents learned of the invasion at 2:47 a.m., when sirens blared around the city. Those working the night shift at the NAA plant heard the news over the public address system, which later broadcast a prayer. Many employees had friends and family members who were in the service in Europe, potentially involved in the great attack. D. D. Coughran had a cousin in an airborne division who was likely in the fight. Violet Rogers in the A-plant tool crib was anxious about her brother, who was in England with the Army Air Force, "but I just have faith that he will be all right," she said, "that's what I'm going to believe." Maurice Callaway had a husband in England, or perhaps he was in France now. Jacob Big Soldier, Native American from Oklahoma, had both a brother and a nephew in England and wished he could be there with them. Since that was impossible, he said "I'll continue to do the next best thing and that is doing my job at North American." Daisy Walters expressed similar sentiments. When her husband had left for England, she had come to work at NAA. She declared "I know our boys won't let us down—and we at home can't let them down. This is the time for us all to do our utmost." Against the backdrop of D-Day, it is likely that worries about potential layoffs faded, as thoughts turned toward the safety of loved ones.[32]

With the long-anticipated second front underway at last, life at the NAA factory in Dallas continued as it had done since the start. Workers played intramural sports and engaged in social activities. Employees submitted suggestions to improve efficiency, and the company continued a safety campaign that had been launched in May 1944 to reduce injuries. Another ongoing campaign was the ever-present drive to have workers purchase war bonds. The factory at one time had been able to fly the Minute Man flag issued by the Treasury Department because there had been greater than 90% employee participation in buying war bonds. This honorific had been rescinded the previous August, just before the manpower crisis exploded, when participation dropped below the required level. June 1944 brought the start of a new bond campaign, and employees responded by taking the plant back above the threshold, probably influenced by the invasion of France that month. Once more the Minute Man flag was hoisted on the flagpole in front of the administration building.[33]

July 1944 began on an unusual note, with production halted for three days in order to conduct a plant wide inventory, starting on Saturday, 1 July. By this point the NAA plants were closed on Sundays, so only two days of production were lost. Most of the employees were off, other than those required for inventory, maintenance, and plant protection. Tuesday was the

Fourth of July, and all workers were to be off except for protection and maintenance personnel. It was the longest pause in operations since the plant opened in 1941. Employees were encouraged to take advantage of the shutdown to donate blood to the Red Cross. But lurking in the background there were still concerns about layoffs. One worker, Mrs. A. N. Boggs, decided to address the matter in a letter to plant manager Schwedes. She wrote, "I never pay any attention to rumors out here." In her mind, if some contracts were cut back, then it meant that those planes were in less demand, and that the plant "will get to build something that is needed more." She believed there was still critical work to be done and wanted her coworkers to focus on the job at hand. But the subject of layoffs still troubled some of her colleagues, and she hoped that Schwedes could do something to help alleviate the situation.[34]

Schwedes took the time to respond to Boggs, and the correspondence between the two was published in the NAA plant newspaper to "answer some of the questions raised by current rumors." Schwedes stated that the company was not engaged in mass layoffs. Some workers had been let go for inefficiency, chronic absenteeism, or an unwillingness to work. There had been 567 employees released for cause in the four weeks prior to 18 June 1944. Others left for a variety of personal reasons. This sort of attrition was normal in an operation the size of NAA, and while Schwedes did not discuss it in his letter, the need to account for departing employees had been one of the factors driving the massive labor demands of 1943.[35]

What was different for NAA by July 1944 was that the remaining employees were more experienced at their jobs than in the previous year. "We have passed the critical point on the learning curve," Schwedes wrote, "and the average employee today is doing his or her job both better and faster." This improvement meant that the company could maintain its production schedules with less workers, and there was not always a need to hire a replacement for a departed employee. Therefore, the number of workers in the plant was decreasing even though there had been no layoffs. Left unstated was that Dutch Kindelberger had forecast this during his testimony before the Truman Committee, when he anticipated that employment at the plant would decrease over the course of 1944. This is what was happening, without any need to lay people off. Schwedes admitted that the situation could change if the federal government cancelled contracts, as "the demand for our products depends entirely on the course of the war." But for now, both General Harris and Wilson had said that NAA was to remain as part of the B-24 production pool. Assertions to that effect continued to appear. On 18 July a wire report contained a statement from Maj. Gen. Bennett E. Meyers of the Army Air Force Material Command. Meyers, speaking at Wright Field, denied reports that Ford's Willow Run plant would be the sole producer for the Liberator bomber. He declared "There is no plan for immediate cessation of B-24 production" at either Consolidated or NAA.[36]

Just over three weeks later, the situation changed dramatically. On the afternoon of 10 August 1944, Schwedes got a phone call. On the other end of the line was General Harris, who had called to give verbal notice of an impending cutback in the B-24 program. Harris informed Schwedes that the Office of War Information (OWI) was preparing an official announcement to be released within hours. Schwedes immediately prepared a press statement on the situation:

> The Government's production program made public today came as a complete surprise.
> Since we received preliminary notice only a few hours ago concerning the decision of Government officials to cut back on aircraft production, which includes a cutback on B-24s, we are unable to accurately forecast at the moment what effect this unexpected readjustment will have on our operations in Dallas.
> Our plans have been based on B-24 output continuing at least another eight months. Changes in these plans made necessary by the Government's action will be announced as soon as we are more fully advised of the Government's new program and have had an opportunity to study it.[37]

This statement was supplied to the media on the night of 10 August, after the announcement was released by the OWI. A slightly longer statement intended for employees was read over the loudspeaker system to workers on the night shift. Workers in the print shop stopped the presses on the next issue of the plant newspaper and added the announcement to the front page.

The announcement was also blown up into 30-by-40-inch sheets that were posted at the plant exits, so that it could be seen by workers as they left the job. Company documents state that the intent was to quickly release as much information as possible, with the purpose of softening the blow to the community and the employees. Another goal was to prevent large numbers of workers from quitting their jobs and leaving the factory short of personnel.[38]

As for the announcement from the OWI, a preliminary wire from the Associated Press (AP) provided the public with some details, specifying three aircraft that were affected. These were the C-46 cargo plane, P-47 fighter, and B-24 bomber. The AP reported that production of the Liberator was being deemphasized partially "to clear the way for the huge new B-29 and B-32 superbombers" that were wanted for use in the Pacific theater. It was anticipated that some work might be transferred to Dallas from California because of labor shortages in that area, but it was too early to know specific information.[39]

While this was unfolding, NAA management reacted to the information by initiating several steps. Another announcement was prepared and broadcast over the public address system at noon on 11 August 1944. Employees were reassured that B-24 production "will continue for the time being," and that "the closing down of our B-24 production will be achieved gradually, over a period of several months." Nevertheless, the phase out of the B-24 program meant immediate reductions in the Dallas workforce "of several thousand within the next ten days." This update was printed and distributed to employees, as well as supplied to local press outlets. The company halted advertising in the employment section of the Dallas newspapers, and several hundred new hires were notified by telegram to not report to work as scheduled. Notification by telegram started on the night of 10 August, as some of the individuals had been slated to begin work the next day. These telegrams were followed by apologetic letters sent by mail.[40]

By Saturday, 12 August 1944, NAA leaders were able to determine how many workers faced immediate layoff. A meeting was held that afternoon with representatives of the War Manpower Commission and other federal agencies to establish a method by which affected employees were to be

Mustangs, Liberators, and Texans. *North American Aviation.*
Copyright ©Boeing. Used by permission.

referred to the United States Employment Service (USES). Company officials prepared another press release, in time for publication in the Sunday
papers. Layoffs were to begin Monday, with 3,689 employees to be released
over a period of three days. All the affected workers had been hired since
10 May and were involved in manufacturing departments. Since the P-51
and AT-6 were to remain in production, there were no layoffs scheduled for
the Waco or downtown Dallas units. However, some newer employees at the
A-plant were to be let go and their jobs given to B-plant workers with higher
seniority. One attendee at the Saturday meeting was Orville Erringer from
the local WMC office. He told reporters that there were plenty of other jobs
available to accommodate the displaced workers.[41]

On Monday 15 August 1944 the first of the laid off employees started to
report at the office of the USES. Some of them had been conveyed in buses
directly from the NAA plant. At the USES office there were forty clerks

on hand to assist those workers who wanted placement in other positions. The *Dallas Morning News* reported there were no signs of anger among the terminated workers, and that some of them "accepted the high priority jobs in shipbuilding and aircraft plants on the West Coast." Among them were an unspecified number of "recently employed Negros."[42] The limited number of people laid off in the initial round was small enough that the USES was apparently able to place most of them. Yet they represented only 10% of the total workers at NAA, which reportedly employed 38,132 in June 1944. Concerns started to reappear about what might happen when the war eventually ended, when the entire NAA operation could be shut down. In the earliest days of the plant there had been recognition that the factory was largely an emergency enterprise, but such thoughts seem to have been largely set aside during the critical years of 1942 and 1943. Now talk again turned to the future, with the *Dallas Morning News* noting, "The cutoff brought to the attention of Dallasites the fact that the time is approaching when the big North American plant will be making few or no planes." Chamber of Commerce officials expressed hope that the plant could be used to manufacture consumer goods such as automobiles, refrigerators, or air conditioners. In the meantime, the war was not over, and there were still Liberators, Mustangs, and Texans to be built. Production at the factory had reached a new peak in July 1944, and in August 653 new planes flew out of Hensley Field for delivery. This brought deliveries to 4,370 aircraft for the first eight months of the year, and the company proudly announced that the Texas division of NAA "has produced one out of every 15 airplanes built in the nation this year."[43]

Chapter 21

The Sky's the Limit, August 1944–August 1945

What a difference four years made for North American Aviation (NAA) and its plant at Dallas. On 17 August 1940 the *Daily Times Herald* had announced NAA intended to open a factory in Dallas, bringing thousands of jobs to the city. Four years later, on 17 August 1944, the *Dallas Morning News* declared the cessation of the B-24 program could eliminate seventeen thousand jobs by the middle of November. Whatever the news, the month of August was consistently noteworthy in the NAA timeline.[1] By August 1945, their operation in Dallas was closing entirely.

In the days immediately after the government announcement in August 1944, the cutbacks in the B-24 program were assessed and absorbed. Originally NAA was slated to build up to fourteen hundred Liberators, with production lasting into March 1945. This number had been reduced by 434 aircraft, cutting the total number to 966, with the final units scheduled for completion in November 1944. Other manufacturers in the B-24 pool were affected as well: the Douglas plant in Tulsa had already delivered its last Liberator, Consolidated had its numbers reduced by 1,032 and Ford saw cutbacks of 683 from the Willow Run factory. Decreasing losses in Europe, combined with the increasing use of the B-29 in the Pacific, had reduced demand for the B-24. The great industrial mobilization of the aircraft builders, combined with the efforts of the automotive industry, had put the United States into the desirable position of having an excess aircraft manufacturing capacity. This led William S. Knudsen to remark, "We have airplanes running out of our ears." And while he was not specifically referring to the B-24, that aircraft was being scaled back. These lowered requirements made the North American B-24 program redundant.[2]

What happened to the workers at NAA was not unique, as other manu-facturers also experienced cutbacks. For example, the Higgins plant in New Orleans lost its entire production contract for the C-46 cargo plane. Nonetheless, the situation in Dallas was viewed as a case study for some of the challenges arising from the cancelation of wartime contracts. Evidence is found in a briefing report generated by the War Production Board (WPB) and sent to the White House. Published in a magazine-style format, these reports came out about every two weeks. The issue for 16 September 1944 took a specific look at NAA in Dallas, classifying it as a "Preview of Postwar Problems." The three-page article offers a useful summary of the effects of the B-24 shutdown.

According to the WPB, the reduced orders for aircraft from NAA in Dallas had a massive financial impact, with more than $120,000,000 in contracts being canceled. The article does not specify whether these were all associated with the B-plant. There were also 1,324 trainers canceled, and while that aircraft was to remain in production, it could have accounted for some of the 120 million figure. Either way, these reduc-tions were certain to affect the community. Unless some other contract was assigned to the B-plant, "more than 20,000 workers will be laid off." This involved "more workers than all Dallas factories employed in 1939." The cutbacks also had a ripple effect on subcontractors. According to the report, "North American had 48 subcontractors in the Dallas-Fort Worth region, and 7,000 purchase orders aggregating $21,000,000 outstanding among 501 vendors." In response to the federal cutbacks, NAA had imme-diately issued stop-work notices, pending further information. This hit subcontractors hard, with twenty-three firms losing about 50% of their NAA business. Eight more firms lost all their business from NAA but had other orders on which they could work. Two of the subcontractors lost all the work they had, with no other projects underway, presumably placing them into a precarious position.[3]

The article implies the WPB was impressed by the way in which the Dallas layoffs were handled by NAA and the War Manpower Commission. The latter "moved rapidly to set up re-employment machinery." One step was to send representatives of "fifteen high priority projects" to Dallas to recruit workers. This effort yielded results, as some 15% of the laid off workers accepted jobs "as far away as Alaska, Hawaii, and the West Coast." At this point they still had opportunities in other industries, and it was expected that "The WMC will continue to tap this surplus labor supply until North American, Dallas, is down to its expected 12,000 employees at the end of January." By then the employment at the B-plant was expected to be approximately three thousand workers engaged in subcontracting work and supporting the P-51 program in the A-plant.[4]

One problem was that these projects were not taking full advantage of the capabilities of the B-plant, which was described as "no mere assembly plant, but a complete, integrated airplane factory where 95% of the plane is built." The WPB observed it had been proposed to shift manufacture of the P-51 from Inglewood to Dallas, but that NAA managers did not think that was practical. While the report does not give a reason for this, one likely explanation is that any relocation almost certainly entailed a slowdown in production to transfer equipment, at a time when P-51 production was a priority. This left the future use of the B-plant uncertain, unless some new contract was awarded to it. This possibility was under consideration, but a final decision had yet to be made:

In line with recent [Army Air Force] policy, vigorous attempts will be made to move other airplane work (probably on the B-29) to this specialized plant, thus freeing automotive and other less specialized plants about the country for reconversion activity. However, if these plans do not materialize, and if manufacture of the P-51 cannot be shifted from labor-starved California ... it looks as if the plant and its labor staff as now constituted are virtually out of war production.[5]

The good news for NAA employees and Dallas was that the B-24 cancellations came while there were still jobs available in other war industries, providing that workers were willing to move. Meanwhile, the WPB and the WMC were studying "the lessons of Dallas" regarding future reductions in other cities, especially those with only one aircraft plant. The agencies involved agreed that future cutbacks "must not be made without preliminary consultation with the contractor" and notification of relevant government agencies. And so, it transpired that NAA in Dallas once again served as an example. At the beginning of the defense build-up the plant had been one of the first facilities built by the government. Now Dallas was one of the first plants dealing with the difficulties of an uncertain future.[6]

In the meantime, efforts continued to find uses for the B-plant and the trained workers available in Dallas. One of the first projects was announced in mid-September 1944, when it was disclosed that the B-plant was to manufacture nose units for the B-25 Mitchell, the twin-engine bomber produced at NAA's Kansas City facility. There were two variations of the B-25; one featured a glass-nosed bombardier position for medium level bombing, while the other utilized a solid-nose with machine guns for low level strafing attacks. Dallas was to produce the solid nose unit, which mounted an array of eight Browning .50 weapons. By January 1945 production of these units was in full swing, with completed noses having their guns test fired prior to shipping.[7]

Another discussion focused on the possibility of manufacturing subassemblies for the B-29 Superfortress. This idea proceeded far enough along that Harold F. Schwedes, manager of the NAA plant in Dallas, made an announcement to that effect after a luncheon attended by Dallas business and civic leaders on 27 September 1944. This information was then featured prominently in the *Daily Times Herald*, which reported that the B-plant was to build aileron flaps and tail empennages for the B-29. This work "will not result in the need for additional hiring," said Schwedes, but it meant that "the plant will be able to keep some of the workers it would otherwise have to release." Unfortunately for NAA and its workers, these plans were canceled by early November, and the B-plant did not participate in the B-29 program, as other schemes were underway that could make better utilization of the factory.[8]

While NAA management and government officials sought new uses for the B-plant, the workers in the different NAA factories continued to produce aircraft. NAA reached a milestone on 6 October 1944, when its Kansas City plant delivered the 30,000th aircraft produced by the company since the outbreak of World War II. The B-25 bomber was turned over to Brig. Gen. Ray G. Harris by James H. "Dutch" Kindelberger as part of a special program which included the award of the Army-Navy "E" for excellence to the Kansas City plant. The Dallas factory had made a substantial contribution to this effort, as the twin plants had produced 13,802 flyaway airplanes as of the end of September, along with spare parts equivalent to another 1,500 aircraft. The Texas Division had become a major component in the Arsenal of Democracy.[9]

These numbers included B-24s, but the production of these aircraft was nearing the end. On 31 October 1944 the last NAA Liberator rolled off the assembly line and joined the queue of aircraft awaiting flight testing. The bomber was emblazoned with the names of the workers who built it, many of whom signed their handiwork and left other messages on the outer surfaces of the shiny aluminum skin. It was also marked with the number 966, signifying the number of B-24s manufactured in Dallas. Painted in large letters below the cockpit windows was the name of the ship: *Sky's The Limit*, the moniker assigned by Maj. John Van Ness, who was acting as the resident representative of the Army Air Force. It had been nineteen months since the first B-24 had been largely hand-built in Dallas, and just over a year since the B-plant had started toward mass production. Most of the Liberators—approximately nine hundred—had been built during a ten-month period in 1944. Large scale production yielded financial benefits, with the company calculating that the last units produced "were delivered at a cost of 26.2 percent less than the first Liberators." Dallas had indeed achieved the efficiency that had been predicted by Dutch Kindelberger in his testimony before the Truman Committee. But now the machine was being turned off.[10]

As anticipated, the shutdown of the B-24 program continued to decrease the number of workers at NAA. Peak 1944 employment had been in April, when there were 38,658 workers. By November employment was down to

The last B-24 produced in Dallas. *North American Aviation. Copyright ©Boeing. Used by permission.*

15,465 men and 6,935 women, for a total of 22,400. This was a substantial reduction in eight months, and further cuts were imminent. Less than a week after the last B-24 was assembled, the company announced the workforce at the Waco satellite factory was to be reduced by two hundred employees. With the B-plant largely vacant there was room available to move the manufacture of AT-6 center sections back to the main factory, thus simplifying logistics.[11]

With an abundance of floor space and employees available in Dallas, the days of the Waco branch were numbered. In December 1944 it was announced that the production of wings for the AT-6 was also moving back to Dallas, and that the entire Waco operation was to be closed by 29 December. It was just over a year since the first training classes had been held in Waco. Manager Schwedes issued a statement about the impending demise, pointing out that "Our operations in Waco were established on an emergency basis late in 1943," and that civic and business leaders were aware the satellite plant in Waco was intended as a temporary establishment. He offered his appreciation to the local community:

> Waco people have done an excellent job in our plant here—a job which was very necessary to North American's uninterrupted production of war planes. We are deeply grateful for the assistance we have received in Waco.[12]

This is perhaps a fitting eulogy for the Waco operation. By the end of the year the satellite factory was closed, and the name Waco no longer appeared on the masthead of the NAA plant newspaper.

While the news for Waco employees was grim, some workers in Dallas suffered the same fate. During late November 1944 another six hundred layoffs were scheduled. Still the Dallas workforce continued to produce aircraft, as Texans and Mustangs rolled off the assembly lines. Their day-to-day life remained much as before, chronicled in the weekly pages of the NAA plant newspaper. One piece of news in November involved a promotion in support of the latest war bond drive. Employees who purchased more than five hundred dollars with of bonds would be rewarded with a picture of them-selves posing next to a P-51 Mustang. Workers who participated received a standard print suitable for framing, as well as the original negative so that reprints could be done. The number of employees who took advantage of this offer is unknown, but evidence of it remains in photographs found in the North Texas area today. These pictures are typically the same, other than the worker posed alongside the aircraft.[13]

As the calendar rolled into December 1944, news arrived concerning the B-plant. On 7 December the United States began its fourth year at war, and that same day Dutch Kindelberger announced that NAA had completed negotiations to build cargo planes for the military. Work on the aircraft was to be split between Kansas City and Dallas, but the final assembly was to be done in the B-plant. At this moment there was no requirement for additional manpower, as it would take some time to prepare for production. But the awarding of the new contract offered the possibility of future hiring. Details were yet to be worked out, and the release of more information awaited approval by the War Department.[14] By the middle of December 1944 NAA was able to tell employees what was in the works. Kindelberger revealed that the firm was to produce a new aircraft known as the C-82 Packet. This was noteworthy as "the first competitive bidding held by the Army Air Forces since 1940." NAA had submitted its bid on 2 December and been awarded a fixed-price contract to build one thousand of the aircraft. Kindelberger pointed out that "Considerable preliminary work is necessary before quantity production of an airplane of this type can be undertaken." It was anticipated that the first aircraft should be finished in September 1945.[15]

As for the C-82 itself, the aircraft had been designed by the Fairchild Engine and Airplane Corporation, which was also scheduled to build the plane at a plant in Hagerstown, Maryland. The aircraft was a twin-engine model with twin tail booms and a large center fuselage section. This layout was intended to facilitate loading and unloading cargo. The tail booms were high enough off the ground to allow trucks to pull up behind the aircraft, and the fuselage was the height of a truck platform to expedite moving materials on and off the airplane. The C-82 also featured a tricycle landing gear so that the fuselage was level when on the ground. In comparison, the earlier C-46 and C-47 cargo ships had tail wheels causing them to sit at an angle when parked.[16]

The awarding of the C-82 contract solved the problem of what to do with the B-plant. While the manufacture of B-25 noses and AT-6 parts provided some work, the new project was a far better use of an expensive and fully equipped aircraft factory. It also offered the prospect of additional jobs in the future. All of this was contingent on the fortunes of war, and a sudden change in the military situation could alter plans, as had happened with the B-24. But the war was not yet over. The day after the plant newspaper announced the details on the C-82, the German army launched a massive offensive through the Ardennes Forest of Belgium, thus beginning the Battle of the Bulge. Clearly the war in Europe was to last into 1945, and the war against Japan continued as well. It appeared that Dallas would be manufacturing aircraft for the foreseeable future. And so, the workers of NAA prepared for their fourth Christmas at war, having built more than sixty-eight hundred airplanes during 1944.[17]

The new year brought with it a change in management, when it was announced that Schwedes was taking a new position at NAA corporate headquarters in Inglewood. Schwedes had been in command in Dallas since May 1941, shortly after the factory began production. Before his departure he crafted an open letter that appeared in the plant newspaper, in which he complimented the workers on their hard work and accomplishments. He boasted, "We have delivered to our government more airplanes, on a unit basis, than any other plant ever has." While doing so, the factory was the only one in the country that was simultaneously building three different models of airplanes, and it had been "one the few plants which ever had to tool up for two new airplanes at the same time." The employees had done excellent work, and Schwedes declared, "I am proud of you, and shall always be proud of you." He asked that the teamwork continue under Robert McCulloch, who was to become the new Division Manager in Texas. McCulloch, age 41, was well acquainted with the NAA factory, having served as interim manager in Dallas prior to Schwedes' arrival.[18]

With a new manager on hand and a new project underway, the NAA workers in Dallas unknowingly moved into the last calendar year of the war. While the conflict in Europe was going well for the Allies, there was no certainty as to when Germany might collapse. Indeed, the ongoing Battle of the Bulge demonstrated the fighting was not over. Meanwhile, American forces continued to advance across the Pacific Ocean, with invasion of the Japanese home islands looming as a likely scenario. If this occurred, the new C-82 Packet would be a valuable instrument. And so NAA set about preparing to manufacture the aircraft.

One of the early steps in this process was to determine any new equipment needed to build the cargo plane. While the B-plant was a complete manufacturing facility, it had been set up and equipped to manufacture the B-24, and it was inevitable that additional machinery was needed. NAA provided the Army Air Force with a preliminary assessment of these needs in a memorandum endorsed by NAA Vice President Lee Atwood on 11 January 1945. This document explained that "approximately $1,853,748.84 of uncommitted Defense Plant Corporation funds" were still available for the Dallas complex. NAA requested "$825,910.00 for acquisition of additional machinery and equipment" to produce the C-82. Per standard procedure, the company provided an itemized list of the required expenditures. Included among the items were two spar milling machines at $55,000 each, a three-hundred-ton stretching press at $21,500, four furnaces totaling $30,000, and other assorted devices. The largest single outlay involved no technology at all, with plans for five transfer bridges and thirty-four hundred feet of bridge railing. The total cost of these was estimated at $100,000, but the structures would permit the utilization of preexisting monorail and hoisting equipment within the B-plant. These requests were based on information obtained from Fairchild, and the memorandum stipulated that a more detailed study could discover further needs.[19] In the meantime, the procurement process could begin. The request had to clear the usual bureaucratic hurdles, but by 12 February it had been authorized. Officials at Wright Field in Dayton notified the Washington headquarters of the Defense Plant Corporation [DPC] on 14 February. Notice of the approval was also forwarded to Frank H. Shaw at the Cotton Exchange Building in Dallas. Shaw had overseen the original construction of the A-plant in 1940 and continued to serve the DPC as a division engineer. The release of these funds was another step toward the production of the C-82.[20]

The acquisition of new equipment was but one of the many issues that had to be resolved in order to set up an assembly line. Another task was to determine how to arrange the flow of parts and subassemblies through the factory. Using a template of the building and cutouts representing the C-82, planners mapped the process. There were clearance issues to be resolved due to the size of the Packet, as the airplane was larger in some respects than the B-24. NAA explained some of the difficulties involved in the production of the new aircraft:

> While the wing spread of the C-82 is four feet smaller than the B-24, the main components of the ship, with the exception of the center wing section, are larger than the comparable components on the B-24, and the handling difficulties involved in the final assembly area have consequently been multiplied. We have found it necessary to place in the final assembly area, certain sub-assembly work which normally

would be done elsewhere in the plant, but can only be handled in final assembly because of the lack of sufficient vertical clearance between the floor and the trusses in other manufacturing areas.[21]

This was the sort of challenge faced by the engineers as they worked to determine the most efficient way to organize the manufacturing. A seemingly mundane matter such the distance between a floor and ceiling could affect the way in which major components moved through the building. Other steps involved organizing drawings provided by Fairchild, which needed to be assigned NAA control numbers and distributed for study. The print shop had to reproduce detailed templates received from Fairchild, while other groups worked on production scheduling "from fabrication of the first detail parts to the delivery of the last C-82." McCulloch, the newly appointed division manager, compared the process to forming a snowball, observing "A good job—and a fast one—has been done thus far. Now we are in the position of starting the snowball rolling." He continued the metaphor, predicting it would roll "slowly at first, and then faster, it will get bigger and pick up speed."[22]

While the NAA engineers laid the groundwork for building the cargo plane, January 1945 brought another ceremonial event at the factory. In this case, it involved the awarding of newly created service pins to some 17,500 eligible employees. This prompted a massive assembly during the afternoon of 24 January, with employees of both shifts gathered outside on the west flight ramp. It was the first time since 1942 that the entire NAA workforce had been called together. Dutch Kindelberger appeared, congratulating his workers on their many accomplishments. He presented as evidence that "this plant, in one month, turned out more airplanes than were delivered to the Army and Navy by all aircraft companies during the entire year of 1936." He made ceremonial presentations of new service pins to five employees as representatives of the plant's complement. Five-year pins were awarded to James Bryant Miller and Silvio John Orler, who had both transferred to Dallas to help establish the factory. Three-year pins went to Andrew A. Parham and Mary E. Brockway, with Parham being among the earliest employees hired for the Texas Division, and Brockway one of the first women. A one-year anniversary pin was given to Lewis Earl Thompson, who had just reached that milestone. The five employees symbolized the thousands of workers attending the proceedings, who were to receive their own pins a couple of days later. Additional ceremonies continued that evening, at a dinner attended by the upper managers. At this event Kindelberger awarded ten-year pins to seven employees, some of whom had been with the predecessor companies since 1927, before the firm was even known as North American Aviation. These men had been with the company through the fiscal depths of the Great Depression and the astronomical growth of wartime mobilization. Along the way most of them had risen to management positions in the greatly expanded operation, including McCulloch, whose hiring date was listed as 28 June 1927.[23]

The awarding of the service pins offers a momentary glance into the world of the seldom-mentioned Downtown Production Unit, the satellite facility where components were fabricated for the AT-6. On 26 January 1945 the facility was visited by McCulloch, who spoke to the workers while presenting service pins to selected employees. He lauded the work done by the unit, telling the gathered workers that they were "vital cogs in producing the famed Texan trainer." He offered encouraging words:

> Because you are not working at the Texas Division main plant you may have a feeling that you aren't so important. That's wrong. You've been doing a splendid job down here, and you are contributing your part in building the planes that go out our doors. You should feel just as much a part of North American as though you were working on a final assembly line at the Grand Prairie plant.

McCulloch informed the group that plans called for continued operations at the facility, and he briefed the workers on the C-82. With three aircraft in production there was plenty to do, and there was a possibility that additional subassembly work would be sent to the satellite unit. These types of compliments and updates were routine utterances at NAA meetings. What differentiates this gathering was the composition of the audience. McCulloch was speaking to African American workers, and he had his picture taken with them, rare proof that the NAA downtown unit employed minority workers.

The exact number of employees cannot be ascertained from the photograph, but the crowd may be as many as a hundred individuals. Additional workers might have been present outside the boundaries of the image.[24]

Also present at the gathering, but photographed separately, were a similar number of white employees who worked at the NAA Downtown Production Unit. The two groups appear separately in the pictures, and it is unclear whether they are even in the same room together. If they are, then the two races were obviously divided into separate sections, indicative of the Jim Crow segregation that was existent in the city. The separation of the races poses additional questions that are impossible to answer with the information on hand. The white employees could have been supervisors and clerical staff who oversaw African Americans, or there might have been segregated departments within the production areas. It is possible more racially tolerant whites were assigned to the satellite plant to help prevent interracial strife, but that is conjecture. Information about the NAA Downtown Production Unit is regrettably absent from most available documents, leaving the role of African American workers largely unknown. Their absence from the pages of the plant newspaper is conspicuous, with the photograph of the service pin ceremony being a rare exception.[25]

Although African American employees received little attention within the pages of the NAA plant newspaper, the start-up of the C-82 project garnered extensive coverage. This contrasted with the beginnings of the P-51 and B-24 programs, which had been launched amid the secrecy practiced earlier in the war. Employees were kept abreast of the progress of the C-82 as various production milestones were achieved. As January 1945 ended, jigs were starting to emerge from the tooling departments. Production jigs were designed to hold parts in place during assembly to provide uniformity in finished subassemblies, such as a pickup jig designed to guide workers building the center section. There were also master tooling jigs, used as templates for fabricating additional tools. One example was a large cartwheel-shaped structure as tall as a human, which was associated with the production of the tail boom. These jigs were among the first pieces manufactured of an estimated twenty-five thousand tools required to produce the cargo ship.[26]

Updates on the C-82 continued throughout the following months of 1945, keeping employees informed of progress on the project. As February progressed a massive twelve-ton milling jig was under construction for use in producing the center section of the aircraft. The base of the structure was fabricated out of eighteen-inch steel pipe, and the assembly dwarfed two workers photographed doing welding on the unit. As fabrication of the jigs was underway the company announced that a ten-hour class was being organized to familiarize workers with the cargo plane. By 23 March it was reported that the program had reached "the last pre-production phase," with the tool planning "70 percent complete." Meanwhile, the engineering department had completed most of the drawings needed to begin manufacturing the first aircraft, and purchase orders were being placed for necessary materials. The process was moving steadily forward as the final winter of the war transitioned into a hopeful spring.[27]

As the engineers and toolmakers prepared to build the Packet in the B-plant, the men and women of the A-plant continued at the task of building Texans and Mustangs. Production of the trainers had been reduced, but the workhorse AT-6 was still rolling off the assembly line. And while the strategic bombing campaign in Europe was nearing its end, there were still plenty of uses for the Mustang as the Allied forces made their final push against Germany. In the Pacific theater there were opportunities for the use of the P-51 as well. In February 1945 the United States Marines landed on Iwo Jima, securing the island in a difficult and costly battle lasting into March. The capture of Iwo Jima provided airfields from which P-51 fighters could reach Japan, and on 7 April they went into action when they accompanied B-29 Superfortress bombers in a strike against the Japanese home island of Honshu. The P-51 had emerged as a preeminent fighter and was still in demand. The Dallas factory was doing its part; 286 Mustangs were delivered in January 1945, exceeding the production schedule by ten units.[28]

As the employees at NAA labored to build airplanes, the citizens in Dallas were being asked to contribute to the war effort by offering financial support. Campaigns to encourage the purchasing of war bonds had been common throughout the war, and these efforts continued in 1945. One such exercise was an exhibit called "Shot from the Sky." The event was held at Fair Park, near the Cotton Bowl, and featured "approximately 10,000 pieces of captured Axis warplanes." Also included were intact examples of a Japanese fighter plane and a German Messerschmitt 109. The display was free to the public, and the theme of the event was "Get a War Job and Stay on Your Job to Finish the Job." The stated goal was to "discourage absenteeism and encourage the sale of War Bonds."[29]

This exhibition provided an opportunity for NAA to showcase itself to the community, and the firm responded by erecting a large display at the event. This resulted in an unusual sight during the post-midnight darkness, when two aircraft were towed through downtown Dallas. The planes were making the sixteen-mile journey from the NAA plant to the Fair Park to be placed on display. Towed by flight-ramp tractors, the two warbirds made their way from the factory with a P-51 Mustang in the lead, followed by an AT-6. A challenging moment came when the strange procession passed through the landmark triple underpass near Dealey Plaza as the convoy traveled eastward down Main Street. With spotters sitting on the wingtips, the Mustang cleared the underpass with little room to spare. The Texan must have been the more difficult of the two, as the wingspan of the trainer was five feet greater than that of the fighter, and it was reported that the clearance was measured in inches. Having successfully navigated through the obstacle, the unusual caravan continued to its destination.[30]

Once the aircraft arrived at Fair Park they were placed outside of a large tent as part of NAA's "Wings for Victory" exhibit. Wooden ramps were constructed over the wings so visitors could look down into the cockpits, and employee Margaret Carter gave talks about the fighter. Curious spectators grilled the NAA personnel for information. One puzzled woman asked how the pilot of the Mustang could get out onto the wing to fire the machine guns, only to learn that they were fired from inside the cockpit by a trigger on the control stick. Some male visitors were equally befuddled; one inquired how the wire strung outside the AT-6 was strong enough to move the rudder. It was explained to him that the wire in question was the radio antenna. Not all the questioners were uninformed. It was noted that "small boys in particular showed an amazing knowledge of aircraft," sometimes asking "difficult technical questions for the NAA representatives to answer."[31]

Inside the exhibit tent were additional items related to NAA's operations in Dallas. Visitors could examine the Pratt & Whitney Wasp engine used in the AT-6, as well as the Packard-built Merlin engine from the P-51. Also available for viewing were subassemblies from the AT-6 and the new C-82, and an example of the eight-gun nose for the B-25 produced in the B-plant. NAA was also represented in other ways unrelated to aviation. Employee Locille White was scheduled to sing in a stage show being held as part of the larger event, and members of the NAA fencing team were to give demonstrations of their sport. Turnout by the public was strong, with a reported 179,000 attendees during the three-day event. How many of these individuals visited the NAA exhibit is uncertain, but it was estimated that 150,000 people passed over the ramp built across the Mustang. Clearly there was still a great deal of interest in the machinery of war, even after three years of conflict.[32]

What no one could be certain of was how much longer the war would continue. Germany appeared to be on the brink of defeat but fighting in the Pacific was anticipated to continue. Thus, preparations continued for manufacturing the C-82. On 7 April the NAA plant reached its fourth anniversary, prompting a congratulatory message from Dutch Kindelberger, who wrote that the cargo plane represented "the start of an entirely new chapter in what I like to call The Dallas Story." However, as April progressed there were developments that pointed toward a changing plotline.[33]

On 12 April 1945 President Franklin D. Roosevelt died at his presidential retreat in Warm Springs, Georgia. The news arrived at the NAA plant via an Associated Press wire at 4:53 in the afternoon, as the day shift neared its end. Announcements went out over the public address system as the shift change was underway, notifying arriving and departing employees of the loss. The plant newspaper observed that "It was a solemn, silent procession which filed through the turnstiles for the evening trip homeward." Night shift personnel participated in a brief memorial service during the 7:30 p.m. rest period, and a similar service was held during the next day shift. News accounts are silent about production during the first few hours after the death of the President. Surely the assembly line continued to move, but it seems likely that the atmosphere in the plant was somber. For those employees in their mid-thirties or younger, Roosevelt was the only president they had known during their adult lives. And while his passing did not lessen the need for warplanes, the alteration of their familiar world might have struck some workers as an omen of changes to come.[34]

Changes were indeed coming. The week after Roosevelt's death, advance notice was given of new production schedules that were to be implemented at some unknown future date. This preliminary notice was apparently in response to the reaction to the sudden reduction of the B-24 contract the previous year. After the disruption caused by that incident, the WPB had determined that contractors should have advance warning of cutbacks. With the war in Europe coming to a close, the Army Air Force notified NAA of reductions that could be implemented based on developments in the military situation. A notable reduction was to be in the P-51 fighter, with production to be cut by 50% within sixty days of the activation of the new schedule. The delivery schedule for the C-82 was to remain unchanged, presumably in order to provide enough aircraft to support operations against Japan. The one definite cutback was the AT-6, which was to remain in gradually declining production until the end of 1945.[35]

Given these projections, the A-plant should have had work for about another year, with P-51 production running through June 1946. By that same month the B-plant was scheduled to have delivered 235 cargo planes. With the contract calling for one thousand aircraft, it was likely that C-82 production could continue into 1947. It appeared the Dallas plant might be churning out airplanes for another two years. At the same time, the proposed reductions did eliminate the possibility of an increased workforce at the factory. When the C-82 contract had been announced the previous December, it was thought employment levels at the factory could reach twenty thousand workers by November 1945. New calculations had decreased that number, and a maximum number of sixteen thousand employees was anticipated. This meant no new hiring was needed, and in fact it was estimated that about two thousand personnel might lose their jobs in the interim period before the Packet reached full production.[36]

Additional layoffs were forthcoming in early May 1945, when the B-plant completed its production run of the eight-gun nose kits for the B-25 bomber.

Dallas had produced twice as many kits as originally planned, adequate to meet the demand. This reduction was considered a "small-scale layoff," and those affected were notified on the last day of April. Employees being dismissed were told that the future manpower needs of the plant could result in them being rehired later. It is doubtful that this happened, as on 7 May representatives of the defeated German military signed a surrender document at Gen. Dwight D. Eisenhower's headquarters at Reims, France. A formal surrender was signed the next day in Berlin, officially ending the European war. Employees reportedly reacted with mixed emotions, happy to hear the news, but reflective of the cost that had been paid to achieve that victory. A typical reaction was voiced by Mrs. E. M. Connell, part of a husband-and-wife team working at NAA. "How would any mother feel," she said, "whose son has already given his life in that war and who still has a son in Europe and one in the Pacific?" Workers were also conscious of the work that remained to be done. "I was mighty glad to hear the news," stated G. A. Presswood, who declared "I'm sticking to my rivet gun until the last Jap sniper lays down his rifle."[37]

The arrival of VE-Day assured that production cutbacks were looming. In the meantime, the factory was an operational unit with ongoing programs. On 5 May 1945 a letter from Under Secretary of War Robert Patterson notified NAA that the Dallas plant had once again been awarded the Army-Navy E Award. It was the fourth time that the operation had won the coveted award. Meanwhile, in the B-plant the first C-82 fuselage was beginning to take shape, aided in part by subassemblies provided by the Fairchild company. Thousands of smaller parts had already been completed, and necessary equipment was being set up and arranged for production. Other steps were also underway to support the project. On 13 June a C-82 flew into Hensley Field and moved to the factory so engineers and assembly workers could examine the aircraft firsthand. Local press reporters were given the opportunity to inspect the plane, as well as tour the B-plant to see work that was underway. The aircraft did a flight exhibition on 15 June, when a Fairchild test pilot demonstrated the short take off run and steep rate of climb it was capable of, as well as flying the craft on one engine. At about the same time the center wing section was being installed on the first C-82 being assembled in the

B-plant, and by the end of June the twin tail booms and wing panels had been installed, and the vehicle was starting to resemble a finished aircraft.[38]

But even as the C-82 was taking shape, the production cutbacks announced earlier were becoming reality, and employees were notified on 25 May 1945 that new schedules were going into effect. The reductions were significant, with contracts for 1,450 trainers and 1,371 fighters being canceled. Even the C-82 was affected, with the original order for 1,000 aircraft lowered to 792. Counting all three models together, there had been 7,127 aircraft on order from the Dallas factory on 1 May. Cancelations subtracted 3,029 planes, resulting in a total decrease of 42.5% during the month of May. There were still thousands of planes slated to be built, but it was clear that the plant would never again reach the employment levels of late 1943.[39]

July would be the last full month of the war, although this was unknown to the workers at NAA. They continued to build airplanes as they had been doing since 1941. The Dallas plant reportedly delivered 450 airplanes in June 1945, bringing the total since Pearl Harbor to 17,681. Life continued at the plant much as it always had, with employees building aircraft and pursuing other interests as well. The security department pistol team won the NAA tri-plant shooting competition, defeating their counterparts from Inglewood and Kansas City. Employees played sports, purchased war bonds, and gathered at "Shangri-La," a recreation area the company had opened near the B-plant. The park included "ample facilities for picnicking, softball, volleyball and other sports, as well as dancing in an open-air pavilion." There was also an ongoing contest to find a female employee to serve as the pin-up girl for the 77th Fighter Squadron, a P-51 unit based in England. An officer in the squadron had written a letter to the factory in April, asking if NAA workers could assist in the selection of a suitable model. Since the pilots flew Mustangs, they felt it would be appropriate to have an NAA employee as their pin-up. Response was apparently favorable as more than fifty female workers entered photographs in the contest. Many of these entrees were printed in the plant newspaper, with the last appearing on 6 July 1945, before the pictures were forwarded to the squadron for the selection of the winner.[40]

Chapter 21

But the biggest news in July 1945 was the completion of the first C-82 manufactured in Dallas. Near the end of the month the massive cargo ship rolled out of the B-plant. It had been eight months and eleven days since NAA had been awarded the contract to build the Packet, and the first plane was delivered ahead of schedule. The aircraft undertook its maiden flight on 2 August, a month earlier than expected. This was "particularly noteworthy," according to Division Manager Robert McCulloch, "in view of the fact that this plant originally was scheduled to handle seventy percent of the C-82 project." Instead, Dallas was managing the entire process. McCulloch opined this was only possible due to "the existence of this plant and the trained personnel available to tackle the job." After a series of test flights, the first Packet was moved back into the assembly area of the B-plant to be inspected by Army Air Force personnel from Wright Field prior to acceptance of the aircraft. Nearby stood aircraft number two, which was well along the way to completion, with the major airframe components all in place. Further down the production line, additional subassemblies were taking shape, and the plant newspaper cheerfully reported that "It's beginning to look like old times again in Unit B."[41]

It might have looked like old times, but it was a glimpse of an alternative future that was never to be. On 6 August 1945 a B-29 Superfortress dropped the "Little Boy" atomic bomb on the Japanese city of Hiroshima, inflicting massive destruction upon buildings and inhabitants. This attack was followed three days later by a second nuclear bombing against the city of Nagasaki. The situation for Japan was further complicated by a declaration of war from the Soviet Union on 8 August. The atomic attacks and the Soviet intervention were enough to convince many Japanese leaders of the futility of continued resistance. Emperor Hirohito himself settled the issue by supporting capitulation, and on 14 August Japan notified the Allied powers of its desire to surrender. The news was announced by President Harry S. Truman at 6:00 p.m. Dallas time, and a festive air filled the city. Buses and streetcars were jammed with citizens making their way downtown, where crowds gathered to celebrate. Car horns honked and bells were rung in jubilation. Night shift workers at NAA "heard the news, cheered, sang the National Anthem and went home." The employees were given 15 August off as a holiday.[42]

As it happened, the majority would never return to work at the NAA plant. On 15 August 1945 the company announced that the government had terminated all aircraft contracts for Dallas. Workers were told not to come to work on 16 August, except for those working in administrative departments charged with processing payroll and activities related to the shutdown. A handful of other employees were specifically notified to report for duty; these probably included members of the plant security force, selected maintenance personnel, and other individuals whose skills were needed to prepare the facility for closure. Approximately fifteen thousand people had lost their jobs, either immediately or in the near future.[43]

The narrative had come full circle. The news that NAA was coming to Dallas had been officially announced on 17 August 1940. The notification of the plant shutdown occurred on 15 August, just two days short of five years later. What Dutch Kindelberger referred to as "The Dallas Story" had effectively ended. Left behind were two eerily quiet manufacturing facilities, thousands of people trained in industrial skills, and a production legacy calculated as 18,784 aircraft. This number represented the greatest output achieved by a single United States plant during the war years, achieved by personnel who were typically inexperienced in such work prior to the conflict. The successful transition from plains to planes was a substantial accomplishment.[44]

But the NAA plant was more than just a Dallas story, it was a national one as well. As the first factory constructed and financed by the Defense Plant Corporation, it represents a working partnership between the national government and private enterprise. This cooperation facilitated the prewar enlargement of the American aviation industry into a manufacturing juggernaut that produced 295,959 aircraft during the period from July 1940 through August 1945. NAA played a significant role in this accomplishment, operating factories in California, Texas, and Kansas, which together produced 41,839 aircraft. Measured in units, this made the company the largest airframe producer in the United States, with the Dallas operation being the most prolific of the three plants.[45]

In the end, any historical evaluation of the Dallas NAA plant must recognize these facts: the factory was the first of the emergency expansion

An SNJ trainer on the ramp. The person in the cockpit is wearing
a flight helmet, suggesting a pilot is running tests on the aircraft.
North American Aviation. Copyright ©Boeing. Used by permission.

facilities financed by the United States government, making it the prototype example of such a facility; it produced more aircraft than any other
wartime factory; and it played a significant part in transforming the city of
Dallas into an industrial center. Considering these facts together, it becomes
clear that the story of NAA in Dallas is more than just a matter of state or
local history. It is arguably the premier example of industrial mobilization
for the famed Arsenal of Democracy, and as such it is a story worthy of
remembrance.

Chapter 22

Epilogue:
The Phoenix

lthough NAA received a shutdown order for its Dallas plant on 15 August 1945, a great deal of work was required to prepare for deactivation. There was also the question of what would become of the facility. The process of closing the plant, and decisions about its future, ensured that the factory remained on the minds of Dallasites during the immediate postwar period.

The most urgent task was to pay those employees who had lost their jobs upon the shutdown order. A schedule was established for those affected to return to the plant to collect their final pay and retrieve personal belongings, and special bus service was arranged to transport workers to the site. The process began at 7:00 a.m. on Monday, 20 August, when employees from Departments 1, 2, and 3 walked through the turnstiles into the plant and reported to their normal work areas. There they were to turn in their badges and identification cards to collect their pay, in what would be their last actions as NAA employees. At 8:00 a.m. departments 4 through 14 went through the procedure. This continued hourly until the last batch of departments entered at four o'clock in the afternoon. The proceedings restarted on Tuesday morning, as the last groups of workers arrived to gather their earnings. The entire process was scheduled to be over by midday, and as the employees left the NAA plant for the last time it signaled the effective end of what had been the largest single industrial workforce in Dallas.[1]

Some twelve hundred workers were to remain on the payroll, to prepare for closing the factory. One major task was to take a physical inventory of tools and machinery in the plant, much of which belonged to the Defense Plant Corporation (DPC). Aircraft under construction also had to be accounted for, as the company was entitled to compensation for work that had been performed. Unused aircraft components such as engines and other items had potential value to the military as spare parts and were presumably set aside for future use. Another task must have been to secure any weapons on hand. Each P-51 Mustang was armed with six .50 machine guns, meaning there should have been many on the premises. These weapons needed to be kept secure, pending shipment to a storage facility. All these assorted tasks required manpower and time, so the total shutdown of the plant was not immediate. A limited amount of production continued as well, as the military had authorized the completion of three C-82 Packets. The first of these had already been test flown and just needed final touches and adjustments. Aircraft number two was calculated to be 85% complete, with the third ship presumably somewhat less, but far enough along to justify being finished. This apparently required more employees than originally anticipated, and in mid-September 1945 approximately twenty-five hundred workers were still employed.[2]

Work on the cargo planes was anticipated to last into November. Another issue to be resolved was what to do with 104 Mustangs that "were completed or within a few hours of completion" when the contracts had been canceled. The military officer overseeing the process was Maj. Edwin S. Mayer, and he notified his superiors at Wright Field about the situation. One possibility was to complete the aircraft and deliver them to the military, while another option was to scrap them entirely. The fate of the planes remained unclear for six weeks while the matter was taken under consideration. Orders were eventually received to "salvage all usable parts for return to [Army Air Force] depots," by the quickest and least expensive method. The remaining carcasses were to be turned over to the Reconstruction Finance Corporation (RFC) as scrap metal. This negated any need to disassemble the aircraft carefully, and in some cases hatchets were used to cut into fuselages to access the desired components. Mayer admitted that "it really was as though we were committing atrocities when we had to have the planes chopped open." Acetylene torches were used to cut wings apart to remove equipment for salvage, then again to reduce the size of the wings for shipment. The broken wings were moved by forklifts and stacked into piles to await shipment by rail car to Camp Howze in Gainesville, where scrap metals were being gathered for reclamation. There was a time in the war when 104 Mustangs might have made a substantial contribution at the combat front. Now they were merely leftover dross from the crucible of war.[3]

The truth was that the P-51 Mustangs were already being eclipsed by jet fighters in development, including the Lockheed P-80, which was undergoing service testing at the end of the war. With thousands of propeller-driven fighters already on hand, the military had an adequate supply of aircraft to bridge the gap until jet fighters were available in quantity. This was explained by NAA President James H. "Dutch" Kindelberger to an admiring audience in Dallas on 1 October 1945, when he declared that "Every existing warplane is already obsolete." He was speaking at a luncheon held in his honor at the Hotel Adolphus, where about 150 civic leaders and businessmen had gathered to recognize the contributions of NAA to Dallas and the war effort. Kindelberger praised the community and his workers for "a magnificent job of war production," pointing to the accomplishments that had been achieved. It was reported that 12,967 Texan trainers, 4,790 Mustangs, and 966 Liberator bombers had rolled off the assembly lines. In the process the company had spent more than 630 million dollars in Dallas, including nearly a quarter billion in wages. Kindelberger anticipated long term benefits for the city from the presence of NAA. He estimated that seventy-five thousand people had worked at the factory during its existence, providing a pool of trained industrial workers that "may be used for other industry which is sure to come to Dallas." Chamber of Commerce president B. F. McLain offered warm accolades in return, stating that NAA had been "the finest industry Dallas had ever had." This was likely the last time that Kindelberger met with the Chamber of Commerce at an official event, bringing to end a relationship that had begun just over five years previously.[4]

In fact, even as NAA was shutting down its operations in Dallas, there were plans afoot to take advantage of the available workforce. NAA division manager Robert McCulloch had partnered with plant comptroller H. L. Howard to pursue a new business venture to tap into the pool of experienced personnel. Their endeavor was known as the Texas Engineering and Manufacturing Company, often referred to by the acronym TEMCO. McCulloch announced the venture on 27 October 1945, intending to go into operation on the first of November. The firm was negotiating with the RFC to lease a portion of the A-plant, and McCulloch anticipated employing about four hundred people by the beginning of the next year.[5]

The availability of trained workers played a significant role in the decision to start TEMCO. One manager opined that it was an opportunity that might not come again for a century. "I needed twenty-five men for maintenance, and I could choose from 1,200 expert maintenance men from North American," he recalled, "We had the privilege of hand-picking three hundred expert workers from 25,000." With these workers, McCulloch intended to engage in various types of metal fabrication. One early prospect was subcontracting for Fairchild Aircraft to support the C-82, which was still in production at that company. Since Dallas had prepared to manufacture the plane, everything was in place to build subassemblies for it. A contract with Fairchild was negotiated in November 1945, giving TEMCO its first big customer. Another client was the Globe Aircraft Corporation of Fort Worth, which awarded TEMCO a contract to build a personal aircraft known as the Swift. The firm also modified aircraft for Trans-World Airlines, and even built coin-operated popcorn vending machines. The company expanded its workforce to twenty-five hundred workers during 1946 as it pursued its various projects.[6]

The year ended on a rough note, when Globe Aircraft declared bankruptcy and left TEMCO with hundreds of aircraft in various stages of assembly. As 1947 dawned, McCulloch was short of funds to pay the company's expenses. He successfully arranged funding to get through the crisis, and TEMCO was able to sustain itself with a variety of endeavors.

By the end of February, the firm had approximately four million dollars in orders to fulfill, many of which involved aircraft work. In April the stockholders were told that the company had been selected to recondition sixty-five B-25 bombers for the military. There were also contracts for converting former military cargo planes into passenger ships. For examples, TEMCO was selected to convert C-47 aircraft for a Colombian airline, and an Asian carrier in Manila had ordered the conversion of two C-54 aircraft. And the contract for popcorn vending machines was still in effect. With work coming in, the company was able to retire most of its debt, and the first two months of 1947 brought sales of almost 1.5 million dollars, with a net profit of 128,144 dollars before taxes. The company scored another success in June when it bought the patents and manufacturing rights to the Swift during the bankruptcy sale of Globe Aircraft. This allowed TEMCO to continue producing the model, and once again airplanes began to roll out of the A-plant.[7]

While McCulloch and his company employed the readily available workforce, there remained the question of what to do with the gigantic factory itself. NAA had an option to buy the complex, but with no large contracts pending the company had no use for the facility. The RFC tried to sell the plant, producing an informational pamphlet that provided a breakdown of the eighty-five buildings located on the 272-acre site. Also listed were the giant drop hammer forges, hydraulic presses, and other large pieces of equipment. Smaller items were available as well, such as some fifteen hundred machine tools, various laboratory and testing equipment, and approximately thirteen thousand pieces of office equipment. Plumbing facilities included 916 toilets, adequate to handle 19,000 male and 10,000 female employees. But no company stepped forward to acquire the complete factory complex; its sheer size limited the possibilities of a single tenant or purchaser taking over the massive property.[8]

Local business leaders hoped that some sort of large manufacturing company might move into the plant, providing jobs in the process. This had happened with the NAA plant in Kansas City, which was rented in its entirety by General Motors for producing automobiles. There were rumors and false starts in this regard. One report suggested that a group of "eastern industrialists" was interested in renting the Dallas plant to build automobiles, appliances, and prefabricated housing. The planned entity was to be known as North American Motors, and it was anticipated that the operation could generate an annual payroll of 140 million dollars. This proposal apparently collapsed, and other than the original announcement there appears to have been no further news of it.[9]

Despite the lack of a purchaser or lessee for the entire factory, there was still a great deal of activity at the complex. In February of 1947 the War Assets Administration opened offices in the plant, which offered plentiful space for the accumulation of surplus government property. These items were offered for sale to qualified purchasers, with one event on 2 May 1947 listing $300,000 worth of materials. And while TEMCO remained the largest commercial tenant, other businesses also sought accommodations at the site. By November 1947 about two-thirds of the floor space was under lease to twenty-five different businesses. Some used the plant for manufacturing, such as a book binding company located in the former A-plant hospital, while other firms rented offices. Other companies acquired space to use for storage, including Montgomery Ward and the *Dallas Morning News*. These various businesses all together paid $75,000 a month in rent to the RFC. This was enough to cover the $55,000 a month cost of security, maintenance, and upkeep at the factory, allowing $20,000 monthly profit to flow into the RFC coffers. But control of the complex by the RFC was coming to an end, as the decision had been made to place the plant under control of the military. It was to remain government property and held as a reserve facility for any future industrial mobilization.[10]

The option of retaining some of the government-owned plants had been discussed previously. In early 1944 a Truman Committee report on the postwar fate of surplus plants mentioned facilities "required by the War and Navy Departments for standby plants." Enabling legislation had been passed in August 1947 that allowed for transfer of DPC assets to the military "for the maintenance of an adequate Military or Naval Establishment including industrial reserve." The former NAA factory at Dallas had been chosen as one of the facilities to be retained and overseen by the military, and the Navy had been assigned control of the property.[11]

Naval officials moved quickly in their new responsibility. In the middle of October Rear Admiral Alfred M. Pride of the Bureau of Aeronautics stated that "We have been fishing around in the aircraft industry looking for a tenant and we have had a couple of nibbles." The Admiral declared a preference for having the Dallas plant in operation rather than simply held in stand-by. Further information was forthcoming. In November the general manager of Chance Vought Aircraft revealed that the firm was considering a relocation to Dallas. Navy officials confirmed that Vought had submitted an "exploratory proposal" concerning the factory, and that the Glenn L. Martin Company was also interested. In the meantime, TEMCO continued to pursue a long-term lease to stay in the A-plant.[12]

While the Navy prepared to assume control of the factory, another entity was also poised to protect its interests in the massive complex. This was the Dallas City Council, which was moving to annex the property, placing it within the city limits. This move was opposed by a group of businessmen from Grand Prairie, who requested that Dallas not annex the plant. The spokesman for the group was B. A. Stufflebeme, president of the First National Bank of Grand Prairie. He explained to the Dallas Council that the size of his city had grown dramatically since 1940, when the town had 1,591 residents. The population now stood at over fifteen thousand, with most of the growth attributed to the presence of NAA. Stufflebeme explained that the small town had been forced to provide needed infrastructure such as streets and utilities. Much of this had been constructed by the housing developers, and the town was obligated to reimburse them from property taxes, leaving no funds for maintenance and other services. The businessmen hoped that Grand Prairie could eventually annex the plant property in order to gain needed tax revenue. Threats of a possible lawsuit followed, but this course of action was not pursued by Grand Prairie Mayor G. H. Turner. On 14 October the city of Dallas annexed the Dallas Power and Light generating station on Mountain Creek Lake, Hensley Field, and the NAA complex. Potential tax earnings were limited because the NAA factory was property of the national government, but lessees of the plant could be subject to taxes in some cases.[13]

As the year neared its end there were changes underway at the NAA factory, as the Navy officially assumed control on 1 December 1947.

In addition to a new landlord, the property acquired a new moniker as well. It was officially designated as the Naval Industrial Reserve Plant Dallas. The Navy also signed a five-year lease with TEMCO for the A-plant and allowed the firm to occupy additional space in the B-plant for one year. The latter lease was subject to a thirty-day cancellation clause if the Navy found an aircraft manufacturer to operate the factory.[14]

The possibility of obtaining such a tenant was increasing rapidly. On 17 December a visit was paid to Dallas by H. M. Horner, president of United Aircraft Corporation, the parent company of Chance Vought. Accompanying him was Rex B. Beisel, general manager at Vought, along with other executives from the firm. The visitors traveled to the popular Baker Hotel, where Horner spoke of his trip as "a goodwill junket to become acquainted with Dallas business and financial leaders." Among these leaders were Ben Critz of the Chamber of Commerce, who had been involved in bringing NAA to Dallas back in 1940. Another participant was Andrew DeShong, who had been part of the Chamber of Commerce team prior to the arrival of NAA, after which he had gone to work as a public relations director for the firm. The Chamber was once again trying to bring an airplane manufacturer to the city, but this time they had the advantage of a preexisting facility to lure prospects. Horner and his team planned to visit the factory on 18 December. For his part, Beisel gave every indication that his company desired to relocate to Dallas, as he presented the advantages of doing so. The official decision, he said, "awaits only the Navy's signal." The Navy was holding back on final approval, pending a proposal submitted by the Glenn L. Martin firm. Sources indicated this was a formality, and that Vought "had the inside track in its bid for the Dallas plant." Martin later withdrew its bid, clearing the way for Vought to take control of the B-plant. All that was left was to work out the details.[15]

Negotiations between the Navy and Vought continued into 1948. The Navy announced on 20 March that the conditions of the lease had been finalized and submitted to both parties for approval. Among the details to be resolved were questions regarding TEMCO, as that firm had a lease on the B-plant. It was expected that Vought would sublease the facilities from TEMCO until their lease expired, after which Vought could deal directly with the Navy. Actual relocation of the Vought company from Connecticut was expected to take between twelve to eighteen months to complete, bringing with it an estimated $17,000,000 in annual payroll.[16]

Moving Vought to Dallas was to begin on 1 May 1948, when advance echelons of the company were scheduled to start arriving. The *Dallas Morning News* whimsically reported that a sign reading G.T.T.—Gone to Texas— would soon be posted at Vought's headquarters in Stratford, Connecticut. Since not all employees were making the move, Vought announced the anticipated hiring of fourteen hundred workers in Texas by the end of the year. The firm stipulated that no jobs were immediately available, but despite this caveat there was a flood of applicants. On Monday 19 April an estimated one thousand job seekers appeared at the Texas Employment Commission in Dallas to inquire about employment at Vought, to learn that the only current opening at the company was for a stenographer. Nevertheless, some 150 experienced aircraft workers submitted applications. Other groups were mobilizing as well; developers in Grand Prairie prepared for an increased demand for housing to accommodate employees transferring from the east coast. One builder was planning on constructing two hundred new homes, and the morning paper opined that the small town was getting set for "its biggest building spree since 1942."[17]

As 1948 progressed the relocation of Vought to Dallas proceeded slowly, as one report explained it, it was "piece by piece and family by family." Historian E. C. Barksdale described the magnitude of the move, writing "More than 1,300 employees and 27,077,078 pounds of machinery had to be moved the 1,687 miles from Stratford to Grand Prairie." The process eventually required 1,006 railroad freight cars and took slightly over a year to complete. While the transplanted workers settled into homes, transplanted equipment was being installed into the B-plant in preparation for production. Organized labor was on the move as well, as unions competed to represent the workers at the plant. The United Auto Workers represented Vought workers in Connecticut, and its leaders hoped to become their bargaining agents in Dallas as well, although an independent machinist's union also aspired to achieve recognition. However, no election could be called until the hiring process was complete, when all workers were on the job to vote. Months passed, and the B-plant was steadily working back up into a functional aircraft factory. By the end of 1948 the factory had started production of the venerable F4U Corsair, a propeller-driven holdover from World War II that was still in demand as a ground attack aircraft.[18]

While Vought was setting up shop in the B-plant, on the other side of the property TEMCO continued operations in the A-plant. The firm had steady business in converting former cargo planes into passenger liners, but military work was also underway. In May the company was awarded a $2,500,000 contract to overhaul forty-five C-54 transports for the United States Air Force. The company anticipated increasing its workforce by five hundred persons to handle the task, adding to the fifteen hundred normally employed at its facility. Other military contracts were arriving, including one to overhaul ninety-five fighters for the Chinese government. These aircraft had been purchased from older United States stockpiles, including fifty-three P-51 fighters. Once again Mustangs appeared on the flight ramp outside the A-plant, harkening back to when P-51s were built at the facility.[19]

The C-54 overhaul program took on additional importance after the awarding of the original contract, for in June 1948 the Berlin Airlift began. The C-54 transport played a substantial role in the ongoing effort to fly supplies into the blockaded German city. Military officials notified TEMCO to put a rush on the work and revised the contract to cover as many aircraft as needed. Although TEMCO was not actually manufacturing military aircraft, the company was becoming a defense contractor, modifying and refurbishing airplanes for the United States and its allies. The A-plant had originally been constructed to support American airpower, and eight years after the groundbreaking ceremony this work continued. By the end of November there were rows of P-51s and C-54s lined up outside the plant awaiting their turn in the process, and some three thousand employees at work within. This is comparable to the workforce hired at the A-plant during its first months in 1941, so TEMCO can be considered a significant employer in Dallas during the postwar period.[20]

As for Chance Vought, by the spring of 1949 the company was advertising in Dallas for toolmakers, jig builders, and template makers, as well as for aircraft assemblers with two or more years of experience. These were skills

The Texas flag hangs proudly above the production line. *North American Aviation via Aircraft Manufacturer's Collection, History of Aviation Collection, Special Collections and Archives Division, Eugene McDermott Library, The University of Texas at Dallas. Copyright ©Boeing. Used by permission.*

that had been scarce in Dallas prior to World War II, but with thousands of former NAA workers in the area Vought had a pool of experienced applicants. By now the company had largely completed its move to Texas, and on 17 April 1949 the morning paper declared that Vought was now a Dallas entity. The company celebrated the occasion three days later, when the first Texas built F4U Corsair was dedicated. The ceremony included the use of a branding iron, which was used to mark the aircraft with the company logo. Dallas was back in the business of manufacturing warplanes, just over eight years since the first AT-6 trainers had been delivered by NAA.[21]

Beisel, the general manager at Vought, was present for the symbolic branding of the Corsair. He spoke of great things to come, proclaiming "I hope this brand will take its place in company with other famous brands

which have figured in Lone Star history, and of which Texas is justly proud."
His hopes came true, as Vought began a decades-long residence in the former
NAA factory. Gone were the days of propeller-driven Texans, Mustangs and
Liberators, all constructed under the pressing needs of wartime. Vought was
operating in a different kind of atmosphere as the chess game known as the
Cold War played out over the latter half of the twentieth century. Vought
jets rolled out of the B-plant in Dallas and into the hands of Navy pilots
during the 1950s and into the Vietnam era. These aircraft were far advanced
beyond the models that had previously been constructed in Dallas. They were
a different type of warplane, for a different type of war.[22] But they came from
the same facility that began as an experiment in cooperation between private
enterprise and government, and succeeded in providing many of the essential
aircraft that won the air war during World War II.

Appendix

Employment by Major War Plants Erected in Dallas during the War

(Peak Employment in 1944)

Plant	Month	Total	Men	Women	Percentage Men	Percentage Women
North American Aviation	April	38,658	25,309	13,349	65.4	34.6
Continental Motors	Oct.	1,263	1,025	238	81.6	18.4
Southern Aircraft	Nov.	2,696	1,712	984	63.5	36.5
Lockheed Modification	Jan.	2,623	2,037	586	77.6	22.4
Firestone Industrial Products	May	1,773	514	1,259	29	71.0
Austin Bridge Co.	April	977	662	315	67.8	32.2
Texas Pre-Fab Co.	March	1,111	1,085	26	97.6	2.4
National Housing Co.	March	449	437	12	97.3	2.7
Aircraft Foundry Co.	Sept.	267	221	46	82.7	17.3
Totals		49,817	33,002	16,815	66.2	33.8

Source: War Manpower Commission, United States Employment Service, Dallas Office.[23]

Endnotes

Notes for Chapter 1

1. "Airplane Plant Ready to Entertain Crowd," *Dallas Morning News*, April 6, 1941; "Plane Plant Expects 25,000 at Its Party, Then 60,000 Show Up," *Dallas Morning News*, April 7, 1941.
2. "Plane Plant Expects 25,000 at Its Party." To put the attendance figure in perspective, the population of Dallas County in 1940 was just under 400,000 residents.
3. "Airplane Plant Ready to Entertain Crowd."
4. This phrase was used by President Franklin D. Roosevelt in a radio address on Sunday, December 29, 1940, when he stated, "We must be the great arsenal of democracy." The phrase became widely associated with the industrial mobilization of the United States during World War II. Franklin D. Roosevelt, "Fireside Chat, December 29, 1940," The American Presidency Project, accessed August 8, 2022, https://www.presidency.ucsb.edu/node/209416.
5. Irving B. Holley Jr., *Buying Aircraft: Material Procurement for the Army Air Forces* (Washington, DC: Office of the Chief of Military History, Department of the Army, 1964), 574, 578.
6. John Fredrickson, *Warbird Factory: North American Aviation in World War II* (Minneapolis, MN: Zenith Press, 2015), 223.
7. *Texas State Historical Association: The Handbook of Texas Online*, accessed August 8, 2022, https://tshaonline.org/handbook/online.

Notes for Chapter 2

1. Many historical monographs examine President Franklin D. Roosevelt's preparations for war. Two works consulted for this study were Justus D. Doenecke and John E. Wilz, *From Isolation to War, 1931–1941* (Arlington Heights, IL: Harlan Davidson, 1991), and James MacGregor Burns, *Roosevelt: The Soldier of Freedom, 1940–1945* (New York: Harcourt Brace, 1970).
2. Franklin D. Roosevelt, "Annual Message to Congress, January 3, 1938," The American Presidency Project, accessed August 8, 2022, https://www.presidency.ucsb.edu/node/209087.
3. Franklin D. Roosevelt, "Message to Congress Recommending Increased Defense Appropriations, January 28, 1938," The American Presidency Project, accessed August 8, 2022, https://www.presidency.ucsb.edu/node/209359.
4. Bernard Baruch to Franklin D. Roosevelt, April 29, 1938, President's Secretary File, Series 2, Box 10—War Department, 1933–1941 Franklin D. Roosevelt Presidential Library [online; hereafter cited as PSF, with series and box numbers].

5. Robert F. Sherwood, *Roosevelt and Hopkins: An Intimate History* (New York: Grosset & Dunlap, 1950), 100.
6. There are many historical monographs that examine the Munich Crisis. A beginner to the topic would be well-served by examining Winston Churchill's account of the prewar years. Although biased toward Churchill's own opinions, the readability of his narrative makes it attractive to a nonacademic audience. See Winston S. Churchill, *The Second World War, Volume 1: The Gathering Storm* (Boston, MA: Houghton Mifflin, 1948).
7. Mark Skinner Watson, *Chief of Staff: Prewar Plans and Preparations* (Washington, DC: Department of the Army, 1985), 132.
8. Ray Wagner, *American Combat Planes*, 3rd ed. (Garden City, NY: Doubleday, 1982), 245.
9. Irving Brinton Holley Jr., *Buying Aircraft: Material Procurement for the Army Air Forces* (Washington, DC: Office of the Chief of Military History, Department of the Army, 1964), 169.
10. J. H. Burns to the Assistant Secretary of War, June 23, 1938, PSF, Series 4—Departmental Correspondence, Box 83—Louis Johnson file, 1937–1940. James H. Kindelberger might have put his observations into writing as well, but if he did, they have not been located.
11. Lawrence Bell, "Report on Military Aircraft, Plants, and Production in Germany, Italy, France, and England," Sept. 12, 1938, PSF, Series 4, Box 81—War Department 1938 (part 2) [hereafter cited as Bell, "Report." For information regarding the aviation committee, and subsequent actions by Roosevelt, see Watson, *Chief of Staff: Prewar Plans and Preparations*, 134–139.
12. Bell, "Report," 12.
13. Ibid., 5, 13, 18.
14. Ibid., 19.
15. Ibid., 21.
16. Ibid., 4, 5.
17. Ibid., 22–23.
18. Ibid., 23–24.
19. Ibid., 26.
20. Ibid., 4–5.
21. Ibid., 27.
22. Alfred J. Lyon to Harry L. Hopkins, November 3, 1938, PSF, Series 4; Box 81—War Dept 1938 (part 2).
23. Ibid.
24. Ibid.
25. Ibid.
26. Ibid.
27. The government did operate one manufacturing facility known as the Naval Aircraft Factory (NAF). Located in Philadelphia, the factory dated to 1918. While hardly a major manufacturer, the NAF did produce several hundred

aircraft before ceasing operations in 1945. See William F. Trimble, *Wings for the Navy: A History of the Naval Aircraft Factory, 1917–1956* (Annapolis, MD: Naval Institute Press, 1990).

28. Lyon to Hopkins, November 3, 1938.
29. Ibid.
30. Watson, *Chief of Staff: Prewar Plans and Preparations*, 136; Louis Johnson and Charles Edison to Roosevelt, November 2, 1938, PSF, Series 2, Box 10 – War Department, 1933–1941.
31. Watson, *Chief of Staff: Prewar Plans and Preparations*, 137; Holley Jr., *Buying Aircraft*, 169.
32. Watson, *Chief of Staff: Prewar Plans and Preparations*, 137.
33. Ibid., 138.
34. Holley Jr., *Buying Aircraft*, 170.
35. Frank M. Andrews, "Lecture before The Army War College, October 1, 1938," PSF, Series 5, Box 92—Aviation, 1938–1939.
36. Holley Jr., *Buying Aircraft*, 175–178.
37. Ibid., 177.
38. Johnson to Roosevelt, December 1, 1938, PSF, Series 5; Box 92-Aviation, Report – Expansion of the Air Corps and Related National Defense Needs, 1938.
39. Franklin D. Roosevelt, "Annual Message to Congress, January 4, 1939," The American Presidency Project, accessed August 8, 2022, https://www.presidency.ucsb.edu/node/209128.
40. Franklin D. Roosevelt, "Message to Congress on Appropriations for National Defense, January 12, 1939," accessed August 8, 2022, The American Presidency Project, http://www.presidency.ucsb.edu/node/209118.
41. Ibid.
42. Ibid.
43. Ibid.
44. Wagner, *American Combat Planes*, 180, 179, 173, 352.
45. Henry H. Arnold, *Global Mission* (New York: Harper, 1949), 182 (first quote); Holley Jr., *Buying Aircraft*, 174 (second quote), 179.
46. Watson, *Chief of Staff: Prewar Plans and Preparations*, 141, 143.
47. Holley Jr., *Buying Aircraft*, 174.
48. Ibid., 173.
49. Ibid., 174.
50. Ibid., 180.

Notes for Chapter 3

1. Franklin D. Roosevelt, "Proclamation 2349 – Prohibiting the Export of Arms and Munitions to Belligerent Powers, September 5, 1939," The American Presidency Project, accessed August 8, 2022, http://www.presidency.ucsb.edu/node/209996.

2. Franklin D. Roosevelt, "Message to Congress Urging Repeal of the Embargo Provisions of the Neutrality Law, September 21, 1939," The American Presidency Project, accessed August 8, 2022, https://www.presidency.ucsb.edu/node/210082.
3. Ibid.
4. Ibid.
5. Justus D. Doenecke and John E. Wilz, *From Isolation to War: 1931–1941* (Arlington Heights, IL: Harlan Davidson, 1991), 86–87.
6. Doenecke and Wilz, *From Isolation to War*, 86; Robert A. Divine, *The Reluctant Belligerent: American Entry into World War II* (New York: John Wiley, 1979) 72–77; Irving B. Holley Jr., *Buying Aircraft: Material Procurement for the Army Air Forces* (Washington, DC: Office of the Chief of Military History, Department of the Army, 1964), 202.
7. Ray Wagner, *American Combat Planes*, 3rd ed. (Garden City, NY: Doubleday, 1982), 253, 268, 255, 261, 247, 380, 246, 250.
8. For the list of possible expansion locations, see Louis Johnson and Charles Edison to Franklin D. Roosevelt, November 2, 1938, President's Secretary File, Series 2, Box 10 – War Department, 1933–1941 Franklin D. Roosevelt Presidential Library [online; hereafter cited as PSF, with series and box numbers]. For the locations of existing factories, see Alfred J. Lyon to Harry L. Hopkins, November 3, 1938, PSF, Series 4, Box 81—War Dept 1938 (part 2).
9. Edward Jablonski, *Flying Fortress: The Illustrated Biography of the B-17s and the Men Who Flew Them* (Garden City, NY: Doubleday, 1965), 18.
10. Johnson and Edison to Roosevelt, November 2, 1938.
11. Holley Jr., *Buying Aircraft*, 308.
12. "Problems for Post-War Dallas Relating to Employment and the Labor Force: A Report for the Dallas Chamber of Commerce and the Committee for Economic Development," February 1945, 2, DeGolyer Library, Southern Methodist University, Dallas, TX.
13. Darwin Payne, *Dallas, An Illustrated History* (Eugene, OR: Windsor Publications, 1982), 190; Darwin Payne, *Big D: Triumphs and Troubles of an American Supercity in the 20th Century* (Dallas, TX: Three Forks Press, 1994), 144.
14. Payne, *Big D*, 144.
15. Payne, *Dallas, An Illustrated History*, 145, 195, 196.
16. "Financing Two Plane Plants, Second Port and Aggressive Policy Indorsed by Chamber," *Dallas Morning News*, June 30, 1928 (quote); Robert B. Fairbanks, *For the City as a Whole: Planning, Politics, and the Public Interest in Dallas, Texas, 1900–1965* (Columbus: Ohio State University Press, 1998), 138.
17. "Europe's War to Set Pace of U.S. Arming," *Dallas Morning News*, November 14, 1939.
18. "Plane Factory Official Here for Dedication," *Dallas Morning News*, April 2, 1941; "Deeds Taken on Land for Airplane Plant," *Dallas Morning News*, September 6, 1940.

19. Fairbanks, *For the City as a Whole*, 138. An unpublished document obtained from the Dallas Chamber of Commerce states that Robert L. Thornton and J. Ben Critz traveled to California to resolve the problem of two companies wanting the same site. This cannot be substantiated and contradicts other sources.

20. "$7,000,000 Dallas Plane Factory to Be Started Within 20 Days," *Dallas Morning News*, August 18, 1940.

21. "North American Comes to Dallas," *Southwest Business* (magazine), October 1940, 38.

22. Ibid., 39.

23. "$8,000,000 Plane Factory, Employing 5,000, to Be Built Here," *Dallas Morning News*, July 5, 1940; "$7,000,000 Dallas Plane Factory to Be Started Within 20 Days."

24. Winston S. Churchill, *The Second World War, Volume 2: Their Finest Hour* (Boston, MA: Houghton Mifflin, 1949), 42 (quote).

25. Churchill, *Their Finest Hour*, 42 (first and second quotes); Warren F. Kimball, ed., *Churchill and Roosevelt: The Complete Correspondence, Volume I: Alliance Emerging* (Princeton: Princeton University Press, 1984), 37 (third and fourth quotes).

26. For a detailed account of the French failure, see Allister Horne, *To Lose a Battle: France 1940* (Boston, MA: Little, Brown, 1969).

27. Franklin D. Roosevelt, "Message to Congress on Appropriations for National Defense, May 16, 1940," The American Presidency Project, accessed August 8, 2022, https://www.presidency.ucsb.edu/node/209636.

28. Roosevelt, "Message to Congress on Appropriations for National Defense, May 16, 1940."

29. Eugene E. Wilson, *Slipstream: The Autobiography of an Air Craftsman* (New York: McGraw-Hill, 1950), 233.

30. Cordell Hull, *The Memoirs of Cordell Hull* (New York: Macmillan, 1948), 767. It has been suggested that Hull sometimes had a faulty memory, and that "he often exaggerated his own influence." See Doenecke and Wilz, *From Isolation to War*, 182.

31. Holley Jr., *Buying Aircraft*, 209.

32. Ibid., 228.

33. Donald M. Nelson, *Arsenal of Democracy: The Story of American War Production* (New York: Harcourt, Brace, 1946), 85.

Notes for Chapter 4

1. Minutes of Special Board Meeting, Dallas Chamber of Commerce, June 18, 1940, John W. Carpenter Papers, Special Collections, University of Texas at Arlington.

2. Ibid.

3. Ibid.
4. *Handbook of Texas Online*, Joan Jenkins Perez, "Thornton, Robert Lee," accessed August 8, 2022, TSHAonline.org
5. Minutes of Special Board Meeting, June 18, 1940.
6. Ibid.
7. Ibid.
8. In contrast, the Dallas City Council minutes for this period contain no mention of the proposed Consolidated plant. If the council members discussed the issue, it was apparently off the record. References to North American Aviation appear in the Council minutes for August 14, 1940, and January 29, 1941. See Minute Book 52, Municipal Archives, Dallas, TX.
9. "$8,000,000 Plane Factory, Employing 5,000, to Be Built Here," *Dallas Morning News*, July 5, 1940.
10. "$8,000,000 Plane Factory, Employing 5,000, to Be Built Here" (quote); "Council Is Willing to Spend $75,000 on Plane Factory," *Dallas Morning News*, July 6, 1940.
11. Irving B. Holley Jr., *Buying Aircraft: Material Procurement for the Army Air Forces* (Washington, DC: Office of the Chief of Military History, Department of the Army, 1964), 209, 299.
12. Gerald T. White, "Financing Industrial Expansion for War: The Origin of the Defense Plant Corporation Leases," *The Journal of Economic History*, 9, no. 2 (1949), 160.
13. J. L. Atwood to H. H. Arnold, July 11, 1940, Correspondence and Reports Relating to the Expansion of Facilities, Records of the War Department General and Special Staffs (Record Group 165, National Archives and Records Administration, College Park, MD [Box 194]).
14. Ibid.
15. J. H. Kindelberger to Secretary of War, July 20, 1940, Kindelberger to Louis Johnson, July 23, 1940, Records of the War Department Relating to the Expansion of Facilities [Box 194].
16. Ibid.
17. Ibid.
18. Leland R. Taylor to George H. Brett, July 26, 1940, Records of the War Department Relating to the Expansion of Facilities [Box 194].
19. Ibid.
20. Robert P. Patterson to William S. Knudsen, July 31, 1940, Records of the War Department Relating to the Expansion of Facilities [Box 194].
21. Brett to H. K. Rutherford, July 31, 1940, Records of the War Department Relating to the Expansion of Facilities [Box 194].
22. H. H. Arnold to the Assistant Secretary of War, August 1, 1940 Records of the War Department Relating to the Expansion of Facilities [Box 194].
23. Donald M. Nelson, *Arsenal of Democracy: The Story of American War Production* (New York: Harcourt, Brace, 1946), 81; U.S. Civilian Production Administration,

Industrial Mobilization for War: History of the War Production Board and Predecessor Agencies, 1940–1945, Vol. 1, Program and Administration (Washington: Government Printing Office, 1947), 23–24.

24. Paul A. C. Koistinen, *Arsenal of World War II: The Political Economy of American Warfare, 1940–1945* (Lawrence: University Press of Kansas, 2004), 21.

25. Koistinen, *Arsenal of World War II*, 21; Civilian Production Administration, *Industrial Mobilization*, 24 (quote); Knudsen to Patterson, August 1, 1940, Records of the War Department Relating to the Expansion of Facilities [Box 194].

26. Brett, "Aircraft Expansion Program, August 21, 1940," Brett to Assistant Secretary of War, September 25, 1940, Roosevelt to Secretary of War, October 3, 1940, Records of the War Department Relating to the Expansion of Facilities [Box 194].

27. "Dallas Gets Big Plane Factory," *Daily Times Herald*, August 17, 1940; "$7,000,000 Dallas Plane Factory to Be Started Within 20 Days," *Dallas Morning News*, August 18, 1940 (quote).

28. "$7,000,000 Dallas Plane Factory to Be Started Within 20 Days" (quote); "Two More Plane Plants Dallas Bound," *Dallas Morning News*, August 20, 1941.

29. Ray Wagner, *American Combat Planes*, 3rd ed. (Garden City, NY: Doubleday, 1982), 310, 213.

Notes for Chapter 5

1. Gerald T. White, *Billions for Defense: Government Financing by the Defense Plant Corporation during World War II* (Tuscaloosa: University of Alabama Press, 1980), 18. "Loan to Build Dallas Plane Plant Assured," *Dallas Morning News*, September 13, 1940.

2. "Grand Prairie, Hensley Field to Be Hosts Today to Crowds of Aviation-Minded Visitors," *Dallas Morning News*, August 25, 1940 (quote); "Grand Prairie Ready for New Plane Factory," *Dallas Morning News*, July 8, 1940.

3. "Excavators Dig Earth for New Plane Factory," *Dallas Morning News*, August 29, 1940.

4. "Grand Prairie Phone Service to Be Doubled," *Dallas Morning News*, August 22, 1940; "Power Ready for Use of Plane Factory," *Dallas Morning News*, August 19, 1940.

5. "Plane Plant Leaders Due Here Friday," *Dallas Morning News*, September 27, 1940; "Firm Perfects Airplane to Be Built in Dallas," *Dallas Morning News*, September 28, 1940; Nathan Adams to John W. Carpenter, September 24, 1940, John Carpenter Papers, Special Collections, University of Texas at Arlington.

6. "North American Comes to Dallas," *Southwest Business* (magazine), October 1940, 9; "Plane Plant Dedicated to Future Dallas," *Dallas Morning News*, September 29, 1940 (quote).

7. "Plane Plant Dedicated to Future Dallas."

8. Ibid.

9. "North American Comes to Dallas," 14; "Flivver Planes' Future Boundless, Says Breech," *Dallas Morning News*, September 29, 1940.

10. Ibid.

11. Ibid.

12. Ibid. (quote).

13. "Plane Plant Construction to Start Soon," *Dallas Morning News*, October 6, 1940.

14. "Airplane Mechanics' Training to Begin," *Dallas Morning News*, October 19, 1940.

15. "Hiring of Airplane Factory Workers Slated to Begin in Dallas on Oct. 15," *Dallas Morning News*, September 28, 1940.

16. Ibid.

17. "To Direct Remodeling of Plane Plant Office," *Dallas Morning News*, October 8, 1940; "Aviation Plant to Begin Its Training Nov. 1," *Dallas Morning News*, October 22, 1940.

18. White, *Billions for Defense*, 18.

19. Minutes of the Board of Directors of Defense Plant Corporation, November 14, 1940, in Minutes Book, Volume I, August 22–December 31, 1940, 247–261, Entry 143, Defense Plant Corporation Files, Records of the Reconstruction Finance Corporation (Record Group 234, National Archives and Record Administration, College Park, MD).

20. Ibid.

21. Ibid.

22. Patterson to Knudsen, July 31, 1940; Arnold to Assistant Secretary of War, August 1, 1940, Correspondence and Reports Relating to the Expansion of Facilities, Records of the War Department General and Special Staffs (Record Group 165, National Archives and Records Administration, College Park, MD [Box 194]).

23. War Department to the Assistant Secretary of War, January 2, 1941, Records of the War Department Relating to the Expansion of Facilities [Box 194].

24. "Plane Factory Contract Goes to New Yorker," *Dallas Morning News*, November 2, 1940; North American Aviation, "A Brief History of Operations Immediately Prior to and During World War II," 22, General Aviation Collection, History of Aviation Archives, Special Collections, University of Texas at Dallas.

25. Engineers' Reports and Appendices for Plancor 25 [Box 20].

26. Ibid.

27. Information Brochure: Aircraft Manufacturing Plant (Plancor 25), Pamphlets Relating to Manufacturing Facilities, 1940–1945, Defense Plant Corporation Files, Records of the Reconstruction Finance Corporation (Record Group 234, National Archives [Entry A1-E76]).
28. Engineers' Reports and Appendices for Plancor 25 [Box 20].
29. "Building Accident Takes 2d Life at New Plane Plant," *Dallas Morning News*, March 20, 1941; "Double Shifts Looming on 2 Plane Plant Jobs as Weather Halts Work," *Dallas Morning News*, December 29, 1940.

Notes for Chapter 6

1. "Oak Cliff Due to Start 500 New Houses," *Dallas Morning News*, December 29, 1940.
2. "162 Homes to Be Built Near Factory," *Dallas Morning News*, April 11, 1941.
3. Ibid.; "Houses for Plane Workers," *Dallas Morning News*, April 12, 1941.
4. Advertisements in *Dallas Morning News*, January 18, June 8, 1942.
5. Advertisements in *Dallas Morning News*, February 8 (first quote), March 8, June 28 (second quote); July 17, 1942.
6. "Airplane Plant Housing Site to Be Chosen," *Dallas Morning News*, February 7, 1941; "Defense Housing Bill Amended," *Dallas Morning News*, September 17, 1940 (quote); Kristin M. Szylvian, "Avion Village: Texas' World War II Housing Laboratory," *Legacies: A History Journal for Dallas and North Central Texas*, vol. 4 (Fall 1992): 30.
7. "Airplane Plant Housing Site to Be Chosen."
8. Ibid.
9. "Site Staked for Defense Housing Job," *Dallas Morning News*, March 2, 1941; "Lawrence Westbrook Seeks Seat in House," *Dallas Morning News*, May 5, 1928; "Westbrook Asks Loans for Texas for Two Months," *Dallas Morning News*, March 1, 1933; "R.F.C. Relief Fund for Texas Is Gone, Director Declares," *Dallas Morning News*, May 7, 1933; "Relief Works Slash Causes Protest Flood," *Dallas Morning News*, January 20, 1934; "Mrs. Collings Wed to Col. Westbrook," *New York Times*, March 23, 1937.
10. Willis Winters, "Avion Village: Enduring Values of Community," *Texas Architect* (magazine), May-June 1988, 26; Szylvian, "Avion Village," 30–31.
11. Szylvian, "Avion Village," 33.
12. Ibid.
13. "Avion Village to Be Started by Wednesday," *Dallas Morning News*, March 15, 1941 (quote); Winters, "Avion Village,"28; "Site Staked for Defense Housing Job."
14. "Avion Requests U.S. Aid For $319,117 Utilities Job," *Dallas Morning News*, March 21, 1941.

15. "First Unit Takes Form at Avion Village," *Dallas Morning News*, April 1, 1941.

16. "Work Begins on Housing for Big Plant," *Dallas Morning News*, April 22, 1941.

17. "Builder Teams Finish 2 Homes," *Dallas Morning News*, May 17, 1941; "Texas Workmen Build Finished Home in 58 Minutes," *Life* (magazine), June 9, 1941, 59–63.

18. "Rains Bring 9-Foot Rise to Trinity River," *Dallas Morning News*, June 8, 1941.

19. "Avion Village Strike Results in Open Shop," *Dallas Morning News*," July 24, 1941.

20. Ibid. (quote); "Construction Begins on Second Avion Village," *Daily Times Herald*, July 2, 1941.

21. "Completion Date Nears for Avion Village," *Dallas Morning News*, August 1, 1941; "Wedding Occupies Spotlight as Grand Prairie Dedicates Its Avion Village Project," *Dallas Morning News*, August 17, 1941 (quote).

22. "Avion Village WPA Projects Authorized," *Dallas Morning News*, August 28, 1941; "Avion Village Job Finished," *Dallas Morning News*, September 24, 1941 (quote); "Avion Staff Likes NAA Personnel," *Take Off*, September 18, 1941.

23. "Wage Hike Given All at Plane Plant," *Dallas Morning News*, July 25, 1941; "Fifth Housing Project for Workers Planned," *Dallas Morning News*, May 27, 1941.

24. "Realty Men Seek Local Housing Plan," *Dallas Morning News*, April 26, 1941 (quotes); "Capital Awaits Government Advice Whether to Launch Defense Housing," *Dallas Morning News*, May 5, 1941; "End to U.S. Housing in Dallas Is Sought," *Dallas Morning News*, May 16, 1941.

25. "Capital Awaits Government Advice Whether to Launch Defense Housing" (first quote); "End to U.S. Housing in Dallas Is Sought," *Dallas Morning News*, May 16, 1941 (second quote).

26. "Leagues Join Opposition to Second Village," *Dallas Morning News*, May 30, 1941 (first quote); "Air Corps Orders $100,000 Improvements at Plane Plant," *Dallas Morning News*, July 16, 1941 (second quote).

27. "Construction Begins on Second Avion Village;" "Cockrell Hill Soon to Finish Housing Plans," *Dallas Morning News*, November 15, 1941 (quote).

28. Edmund N. Bacon, "Wartime Housing," *The Annals of the American Academy of Political and Social Science* 229 (1943): 136.

29. "Realtor Plans 350 Houses at Grand Prairie," *Dallas Morning News*, January 14, 1942.

Notes for Chapter 7

1. "From Blueprints to Production," *Dallas* (magazine), April 1941, 23; "Double Shifts Looming On 2 Plane Plants as Weather Halts Work," *Dallas Morning News*, December 29, 1940.

2. "Blue Shack, NAA Landmark, Vanishes," *Take Off*, September 11, 1941.

3. "Hiring of Airplane Factory Workers Slated to Begin in Dallas on Oct. 15,"
   Dallas Morning News September 28, 1940; "Plane Plant to Hire Men through
   State," *Dallas Morning News*, October 14, 1940.

4. "Airplane Mechanics Training to Begin," *Dallas Morning News*, October 19,
   1940 (quote); "Aviation Plant to Begin Its Training Nov. 1," *Dallas Morning
   News*, October 22, 1940.

5. "Plane Plant Manager Turns Cowboys into Skilled Mechanics," *Daily Times
   Herald*, February 2, 1941; "Texans Make 'Good Hands' for Aircraft Industry,"
   Dallas (magazine), April 1941, 13.

6. "Rivers to Head Dallas Plane Plant,' *Dallas* (magazine) March 1941, 16.

7. "Plane Plant Manager Turns Cowboys into Skilled Mechanics."

8. "Plane Factory Head Pleased with Progress," *Dallas Morning News*, March 11,
   1941.

9. Plane Plant Manager Turns Cowboys into Skilled Mechanics;" "New Texas
   Workers Build Plane Parts," *Daily Times Herald*, February 3, 1941.

10. "North American Aviation Plant Construction 3 Days Ahead of Schedule, With
    800 on Job," *Dallas Morning News*, February 20, 1941.

11. N.A.A. Plant Turning Out Shop Supplies," *Daily Times Herald*, March 20,
    1941.

12. North American Aviation, "A Brief History of Operations Immedi-
    ately Prior to and during World War II," 22, General Aviation Collec-
    tion, History of Aviation Archives, Special Collections, University of
    Texas at Dallas. "First Dallas-Made Plane Nearing Completion; to Make
    Flight April 7," *Daily Times Herald*, March 20, 1941; "First Dallas-Made
    Plane Is Declared Perfect Specimen," *Daily Times Herald*, March 31, 1941
    (quote).

13. "North American Aviation Special Section," *Daily Times Herald*, April 6,
    1941.

14. "North American Aviation Special Section," *Dallas Morning News*, April 6,
    1941.

15. Ibid.

16. Ibid.

17. Ibid.

18. "Dallas Community Spirit Aided in Decision to Locate Plane Plant," *Dallas
    Morning News*, April 6, 1941.

19. "Dallas Community Spirit Aided in Decision to Locate Plane Plant." This
    article also appeared in the *Daily Times Herald* as "Kindelberger Lauds
    Choice of Plant Site," April 6, 1941.

20. "Open House at Plane Factory Slated Sunday," *Daily Times Herald*, April 6,
    1941; "Public Gets Chance to See N.A.A. Sunday," *Dallas Morning News*,
    April 3, 1941.

21. "Rigidly Defined Areas for North American Plane Plant Visit," *Dallas Morning News*, April 5, 1941; "Airplane Plant Ready to Entertain Throng," *Dallas Morning News*, April 6, 1941.
22. "Public Gets Chance to See N.A.A. Sunday;" "Plane Plant Expects 25,000 at Its Party, Then 60,000 Show Up," *Dallas Morning News*, April 7, 1941.
23. "Plane Plant Expects 25,000 at Its Party."
24. "North American Aviation Opening Ceremony," KGKO radio broadcast, April 6, 1941, Original Archival Recording held by Dallas Historical Society, File 16-1010a (Electronic conversion in author's possession).
25. Ibid.
26. Ibid.; "Texans Make Good Hands for Aircraft Industry," 15–16.
27. "North American Aviation Opening Ceremony," File 16-1010a.
28. Ibid.
29. Ibid.
30. "Texas Unit Starts Independent Trainer Production," *North American Skyline*, October 1941, 2.
31. "North American Aviation Opening Ceremony," File 16-1010a.
32. "Plane Plant Expects 25,000 at Its Party."

Notes for Chapter 8

1. Byron Fairchild and Jonathan Grossman, *The Army and Industrial Manpower* (Washington, DC: Office of the Chief of Military History, Department of the Army, 1959), 57–58.
2. Fairchild and Grossman, *The Army and Industrial Manpower*, 57–62 (first quote); "Huge Defense Plant Stilled by CIO Strike," *Dallas Morning News*, January 23, 1941 (second quote); "Allis-Chalmers Men and Officials Told to Produce Needs," *Dallas Morning News*, March 27, 1941.
3. "Strikes Halt Work on Vast Defense Jobs," *Dallas Morning News*, March 10, 1941; "Allis-Chalmers Men and Officials Told to Produce Needs;" "Police Rout Strikers with Armored Car," *Dallas Morning News*, April 1, 1941; "Defense Shipments Resumed by Allis," *New York Times*, April 9, 1941.
4. Fairchild and Grossman, *The Army and Industrial Manpower*, 62–63.
5. "Antiviolence Strike Bill Voted Out," *Dallas Morning News*, April 2, 1941 (quote).
6. "North American Aviation Special Section," *Dallas Morning News*, April 6, 1941 (quote); "Public Asks More Speed in Defense," *Dallas Morning News*, March 23, 1941; "Labor Leaders Regarded Hampering U.S. Defense," *Dallas Morning News*, March 26, 1941; "U.S. Steps to Avert Strikes Strongly Approved in Poll," *Dallas Morning News*, March 28, 1941.
7. "The Weather," *Dallas Morning News*, April 7, 1941.

8. "Plant Dedication," *Dallas Morning News*, April 7, 1941; "Huge Airplane Plant Dedicated by Knudsen." *Dallas Morning News*, April 8, 1941.

9. "Plane Plant Dedicated," *Edwardsville Intelligencer*, April 6, 1941; "Aviation Firm Dedicates New Plane Factory," *Jefferson City Post Tribune*, April 7, 1941; "Texas in Pledge," *Neosho Daily Democrat*, April 8, 1941; "Dedicate North American Aviation Factory," *Camden News*, April 9, 1941; "Plane Plant Dedicated," *Stanford Daily*, April 8, 1941; "Knudsen Hails Planes," *New York Times*, April 8, 1941.

10. "Radio Programs by the Clock," *Dallas Morning News*, April 7, 1941.

11. "Huge Airplane Plant Dedicated by Knudsen."

12. "Distinguished Guests on Speakers' Stand," *Dallas Morning News*, April 8, 1941.

13. "Museum Gets Record of Plant Opening," *Take Off*, July 24, 1941. These recordings were preserved on sixteen-inch electronic transcription discs and presented by James H. Kindelberger to George B. Dealey of the Dallas Historical Society. They were stored at the Hall of State at Fair Park in the Society archives, where they apparently lay forgotten for decades, with the audio preserved in an obsolete format. Rediscovered during research for this project, the recordings were converted to digital files by the University of North Texas Library.

14. "North American Aviation Opening Ceremony," KGKO and WRR Radio Broadcasts, April 7, 1941, Original Archival Recording held by Dallas Historical Society, File 16-1011a (Electronic conversion of all files in author's possession).

15. Ibid.

16. Ibid.

17. Ibid., File 16-1012a.

18. Ibid.

19. Ibid.

20. Ibid.

21. Ibid.

22. Ibid., File 16-1011b.

23. Ibid.

24. Ibid.

25. Ibid.

26. Ibid., File 16-1012b.

27. Ibid.

28. Ibid.

29. Ibid.

30. Ibid.

31. "Highlights on the Radio," *The Portsmouth Times* (Ohio), April 6, 1941; "RADIO," *Portsmouth Herald* (New Hampshire), April 7, 1941; "KWOS Programs," *The Sunday News and Tribune* (Jefferson City, Missouri), April 6,

1941; "Radio Today," *New York Times*, April 7, 1941; Monday Evening Programs," *Altoona Mirror* (Pennsylvania), April 7, 1941; WRR Radio Broadcast, April 7, 1941, "North American Aviation Opening Ceremony," File 16-1009a.
32. "North American Aviation Opening Ceremony," File 16-1008b.
33. Ibid.
34. Ibid.
35. Ibid., File 16-1007b.
36. Ibid.
37. Ibid.
38. Ibid.
39. Ibid.
40. Ibid., File 16-1008a.
41. Ibid.
42. Ibid.; "Huge Airplane Plant Dedicated by Knudsen," *Dallas Morning News*, April 8, 1941.

Notes for Chapter 9

1. "Plane Plants' Union Drive Slated to Begin Next Week," *Dallas Morning News*, May 10, 1941 (quotes). Potential union activity at the Ford plant in Dallas had been strongly resisted by the management of the company, often by harsh methods. For a focused study of labor relations in Dallas during this period see Courtney Welch, "Evolution, Not Revolution: The Effect of New Deal Legislation on Industrial Growth and Union Development in Dallas, Texas" (Ph.D. Diss., University of North Texas, Denton, 2010).
2. "Texas Unions Formed into Federation," *Dallas Morning News*, April 28, 1941 (first quote); "New Labor Union Asks N.A.A. Join," *Dallas Morning News*, May 23, 1941 (second and third quotes).
3. "New Labor Union Asks N.A.A. Join," *Dallas Morning News*, May 23, 1941 (first and second quotes); "Secretary Explains New Texas Unions' Purposes, Principle," *Dallas Morning News*, May 30, 1941 (third and fourth quotes).
4. "Workers at NAA Issued Charter for Local Union," *Dallas Morning News*, June 25, 1941; "New Union Signs 100th Member," *Dallas Morning News*, June 30, 1941; "Dallasite Head of Federated Texas Unions," *Dallas Morning News*, July 21, 1941 (first quote); "FITU Ouster Called Illegal," *Dallas Morning News*, July 22, 1941 (second quote).
5. North American Aviation, "A Brief History of Operations Immediately Prior to and During World War II," 33, General Aviation Collection, History of Aviation Archives, Special Collections, University of Texas at Dallas.
6. Franklin D. Roosevelt, "Proclamation 2487, May 27, 1941," The American Presidency Project, accessed August 8, 2022, https://www.presidency.ucsb.edu/node/209608.

7. "A New Mark in Radio," *New York Times*, June 1, 1941 (first and second quotes); Franklin D. Roosevelt, "Radio Address Announcing an Unlimited National Emergency, May 27, 1941," The American Presidency Project, accessed August 8, 2022, https://www.presidency.ucsb.edu/node/209607.
8. Roosevelt, "Radio Address Announcing an Unlimited National Emergency, May 27, 1941."
9. North American Aviation, "Brief History of Operations," 33.
10. James MacGregor Burns, *Roosevelt: The Soldier of Freedom, 1940–1945* (New York: Harcourt Brace, 1970) 117 (first quote); John Fredrickson, *Warbird Factory: North American Aviation in World War II* (Minneapolis: Zenith Press, 2015), 97 (second quote); North American Aviation, "Brief History of Operations," 33 (third and fourth quotes).
11. "A New Mark in Radio," *New York Times*, June 1, 1941 (first and second quotes); "Message Torrent Backs Roosevelt," *New York Times*, June 1, 1941 (third and fourth quotes).
12. "U.S. to Take Over Strike-Bound Plane Plant," *Dallas Morning News*, June 7, 1941 (first and second quotes); "Roosevelt to Order Army to Take Over Factory on Monday," *Dallas Morning News*, June 8, 1941; "CIO Aviation Chief Condemns Plane Strike," *Dallas Morning News*, June 8, 1941 (third quote).
13. "Not Beyond the Law," *New York Times*, March 30, 1941; "CIO Aviation Chief Condemns Plane Strike," *Dallas Morning News*, June 8, 1941 (quotes).
14. Franklin D. Roosevelt, "Executive Order 8773, June 9, 1941," The American Presidency Project, accessed August 8, 2022, https://www.presidency.ucsb.edu/node/209639.
15. Fredrickson, *Warbird Factory*, 101.
16. Fredrickson, *Warbird Factory*, 102; "Bayonets End Brief Resistance from Pickets," *Dallas Morning News*, June 10, 1941 (quote).
17. "Aviation Workers Call Off Strike at Army-Held Plant," *Dallas Morning News*, June 11, 1941.
18. "N.A.A, Plant Operating," *Dallas Morning News*, June 12, 1941 (quote); North American Aviation, "Brief History of Operations," 34; Fredrickson, *Warbird Factory*, 103.
19. North American Aviation, "Brief History of Operations," 35 (quote), 88.
20. "Wage Hike Given All at Plane Plant," *Dallas Morning News*, June 25, 1941. The information was repeated in the plant newspaper on July 31.

Notes for Chapter 10

1. Wesley Frank Craven and James Lea Cate, *The Army Air Forces in World War II, Volume 6: Men and Planes* (Chicago, IL: University of Chicago Press, 1955), 566–567.

2. John Fredrickson, *Warbird Factory: North American Aviation in World War II* (Minneapolis: Zenith Press, 2015) 23, 59; North American Aviation, "A Brief History of Operations Immediately Prior to and during World War II," 1, General Aviation Collection, History of Aviation Archives, Special Collections, University of Texas at Dallas.

3. Frederickson, *Warbird Factory*, 62–63. North American Aviation, "Brief History of Operations," gives the number of planes as 82 (p. 7). The reason for the discrepancy is unclear. One possibility is that follow-up orders increased the original quantity.

4. Ray Wagner, *American Combat Planes*, 3rd ed. (Garden City, NY: Doubleday, 1982), 157–158; North American Aviation, "Brief History of Operations," 7.

5. North American Aviation, "Brief History of Operations," 9.

6. Ibid., 4; "North American's Success Story," *Southwest Business* (magazine), October 1940, 22–23.

7. Frederickson, *Warbird Factory*, 79; "Boeing History – Products Through Boeing History – Defense Products - T-6 Texan Trainer" (quote), accessed August 8, 2022, https://www.boeing.com/history/products/t-6-texan-trainer. page.

8. "Rivers to Head Dallas Plane Plant," *Dallas* (magazine), March 1941, 16; "N.A.A. Group Likes Dallas Hospitality," *Daily Times Herald*, April 6, 1941.

9. "Factory Manager," *Take Off*, May 15, 1941.

10. "Former Plant Manager Sues NAA for $182,000," *Dallas Morning News*, July 2, 1941; "Former Employee Seeks $182,000 Of Plane Concern," *Dallas Morning News*, August 28, 1941 (quote).

11. "NAA's Biggest Machine Assembled," *Take Off*, June 15, 1941; "Smithson Praises Dallas Plant's Work; Predicts Rapid Personal Expansion," *Take Off*, June 1, 1941 (quote).

12. "Building Progress," *Take Off*, June 15, 1941; "Administration Building in Service," *Take Off*, August 21, 1941.

13. "North American's Pay Roll Now 2,173 At Grand Prairie," *Dallas Morning News*, June 29, 1941.

14. "NAA Aviators Lose First Softball Game, 8–6, to T. & P. Crew," *Take Off*, May 15, 1941.

15. "Employees Propose NAA Flying Club," *Take Off*, May 15, 1941; "Texans Organize Own Flying Horsemen's Club," *Take Off*, June 1, 1941; "Girl Riders Organize," *Take Off*, June 1, 1941; "Swing Band Meets," *Take Off*, August 28, 1941; "Swing Band Wants More Talent," *Take Off*, September 5, 1941.

16. "Dance Is Big Success," *Take Off*, June 1, 1941; "100 Persons Attend Department Picnic," *Take Off*, June 1, 1941.

17. "Scenes from Texas Factory Shot For 'March of Time' Production," *North American Skyline*, October 1941, 36; "March of Time Visits NAA Factory,"

Take Off, July 15, 1941; "Thumbs Up Texas Shows State as March of Time Sees Us," *Dallas Morning News,* August 16, 1941.

18. "Wage Hike Given All at Plane Plant," *Dallas Morning News,* July 25, 1941; "Hundredth Plane Is Turned Out as NAA Directors Meet," *Dallas Morning News,* July 25, 1941.

19. "Take It Away, Texas!" *Take Off,* August 21, 1941.

20. "F.D.R. Lands Today Following Historic Conference at Sea," *Dallas Morning News,* August 16, 1941.

21. "All NAA Advanced Trainers Will Be Built at Dallas," *Dallas Morning News,* August 16, 1941.

22. "Texas Unit Starts Independent Trainer Production," *North American Skyline,* October 1941, 2.

23. "NAA Guards to Play Professional Football," *Take Off,* August 14, 1941.

24. "Mother and Four Offspring Defy NAA Guards—Trouble in the Air," *Take Off,* August 21, 1941; "Crickets Foretell Texas Autumn," *Take Off,* August 28, 1941 (first quote); "Cricket Plague Inspires Tall Tales," *Take Off,* September 25, 1941 (second quote).

Notes for Chapter 11

1. "NAA Family Party Planned as Special Feature at Fair," *Take Off,* September 25, 1941; "Amateurs and Stars to Join in NAA Show at Fair Sunday," *Take Off,* October 2, 1941.

2. "Fun Aplenty Is Scheduled at State Fair," *Dallas Morning News,* September 14, 1941.

3. Army to Send Men, Planes, Tanks to Fair," *Dallas Morning News,* September 18, 1941 (quote); "Big Parade Will Open Best Fair of Nation," *Dallas Morning News,* October 3, 1941; "V for Victory Holds Center of Interest in Navy Exhibit at Fair," *Dallas Morning News,* October 7, 1941.

4. *Handbook of Texas Online,* William C. Wilkes and Mary M. Standifer, "Texas State Guard," accessed August 8, 2022, http://www.tshaonline.org/handbook/online/articles/qqt01; "Texas Guard, ROTC Ignore Bad Weather," *Dallas Morning News,* October 5, 1941.

5. "Nazi Warplane to Be on Exhibit at State Fair," *Dallas Morning News,* September 26, 1941 (quote); "Messerschmitt to Be Fair Exhibit," *Take Off,* October 2, 1941.

6. "State Fair Day Is Termed Success," *Take Off,* October 9, 1941.

7. "Each AT-6 Is Manna from Heaven, Gen. Harmon Declares," *Take Off,* October 9, 1941.

8. "U.S. Practically at War Already, Air Corps Officer Tells NAA Party," *Dallas Morning News,* October 6, 1941; "State Fair Day Is Termed Success," *Take Off,* October 9, 1941; "Weather Was Fair, Girls Were Fair Plus, The Fair ..." *Take Off,* October 9, 1941.

9. "NAA Heads Deny Rumors of Expansion," *Dallas Morning News*, October 26, 1941 (quote); "Dallas Accomplishment," *Dallas Morning News*, October 26, 1941; Dan Hagedorn, *North American's T-6: A Definitive History of the World's Most Famous Trainer* (North Branch, MN: Specialty Press, 2009), 90.

10. "North American Aviation's First Year Purchases in Dallas Territory Total $31,356,000," *Take Off*, November 6, 1941; "Plant Population Passes 6,000," *Take Off*, November 21, 1941.

11. "Kindelberger Congratulates Plant on Production Record at First Meeting of Texas Supervisory Personnel," *Take Off*, November 27, 1941.

12. "Mass Plane Delivery Establishes Record," *Take Off*, November 27, 1941; "New Planes Delivered," *Dallas Morning News*, November 24, 1941; "Plant Population Passes 6,000" (quote).

13. Gordon W. Prange, *At Dawn We Slept: The Untold Story of Pearl Harbor*, (New York: McGraw Hill, 1981), 390.

14. Justus D. Doenecke and John E. Wilz, *From Isolation to War: 1931–1941* (Arlington Heights, IL: Harlan Davidson, 1991), 2.

15. "Photo Caption," *Take Off*, December 11, 1941 (first quote); "North American Workers Face War Determined to Re-double Efforts," *Take Off*, December 11, 1941 (second and third quotes); "Guarding Dallas Water," *Dallas Morning News*, December 9, 1941; "Suspected Germans Held in Dallas Roundup of Aliens; Total of Jap Prisoners Rises to 10," *Dallas Morning News*, December 9, 1941.

16. "Dallas Defense Firms Rush War Projects," *Dallas Morning News*, December 10, 1941.

Notes for Chapter 12

1. "To the North American Family," *Take Off*, December 11, 1941.

2. See artwork in *Take Off*, December 18, 1941, and photograph of sign in *Take Off*, August 21, 1942.

3. Robert P. Patterson to Franklin D. Roosevelt, September 4, 1941, President's Secretary File, Series 4 – Departmental Correspondence, Box 82 – War, September–December 1941 (part 1), Franklin D. Roosevelt Presidential Library [online; hereafter cited as PSF, with series and box numbers].

4. NAA, "Annual Report of Manufacturing Activities – 1942," 18, North American Aviation Collection, Boeing Archives, Bellevue, WA. The number of spares produced by Inglewood is untypical, suggesting the number might include parts supplied to Dallas during the startup period.

5. Weekly Statistical Report Number 25, December 20, 1941, 22–23, PSF Series 4 – Departmental Correspondence, Box 88 – War Reports, Weekly Statistical December 6 – December 20, 1941.

6. Weekly Statistical Report Number 9, August 30, 1941, 23, PSF, Series 4 – Departmental Correspondence; Box 88 – War Reports, Weekly Statistical,

August 23–September 6, 1941; Weekly Statistical Report Number 28, January 10, 1942, 22, PSF, Series 4 – Departmental Correspondence; Box 89 – War Reports, Weekly Statistical, December 27–January 10, 1942.

7. "Confidential Bulletin, July 25, 1941 (quote)," Aeronautics Statistical Summary of Progress, 15 September 1941, 1–4, PSF, Series 4 – Departmental Correspondence, Box 59 - Navy, July–December 1941 (part 1).

8. Samuel E. Morison, *History of United States Naval Operations in World War II, Volume 1: The Battle of the Atlantic* (Boston: Little, Brown, 1984), 127, 137, 413.

9. "Cold Wave, Snow," *The Dallas Morning News*, January 1, 1942; "Snow Possible," *Dallas Morning News*, January 3, 1942; "Inch of Snow Sends City Traffic Skidding," *Dallas Morning News*, January 4, 1942 (quote); "W-H-A-T-T? Snow in Texas?" *Take Off*, January 8, 1942.

10. Franklin D. Roosevelt, "State of the Union Address, January 6, 1942," The American Presidency Project, accessed August 8, 2022, https://www.presidency.ucsb.edu/node/210559.

11. Roosevelt, "State of the Union Address, January 6, 1942."

12. Office of Production Management, Defense Progress Number 68, December 31, 1941, 1, PSF, Series 5 – Subject File, Box 147 – Office of Production Management, Defense Progress, November-December 1941 (part 2).

13. Roosevelt to Frank Knox, January 3, 1942, William S. Knudsen to Roosevelt, January 7, 1942, PSF, Series 2 – Confidential File, Box 10 – War Department, January–August 1942 (part 1).

14. NAA, "Annual Report of Manufacturing Activities – 1942," 20.

15. "We'll Do Our Share Kindelberger Tells Roosevelt," *Take Off*, January 8, 1942.

16. "NAA Heads Deny Rumors of Expansion," *Dallas Morning News*, October 26, 1941 (first and second quotes); Irving B. Holley Jr., *Buying Aircraft: Material Procurement for the Army Air Forces* (Washington, DC: Office of the Chief of Military History, Department of the Army, 1964) 320 (third quote).

17. War Department Army Air Corps Material Division to North American Aviation, January 13, 1942, Engineers' Reports and Appendices for Plancor 25, Defense Plant Corporation Files, Records of the Reconstruction Finance Corporation (Record Group 234, National Archives, College Park, MD [Box 20]); Holley Jr., *Buying Aircraft*, 336.

18. Teletype Ind-T-234, January 19, 1942, Correspondence and Reports Relating to the Expansion of Facilities, Records of the War Department General and Special Staffs (Record Group 165, National Archives and Records Administration, College Park, MD [Box 194]).

19. W. F. Volandt to Under Secretary of War, January 26, 1942, Memorandum of Approval – No. 74, January 27, 1942, Correspondence and Reports Relating to the Expansion of Facilities [Box 194].

20. Appendix A: Defense Plant Corporation Emergency Facilities, Engineers' Reports and Appendices for Plancor 25 [Box 20].
21. Ibid.
22. Ibid.
23. Ibid.
24. Ibid.
25. Ibid.
26. In comparison, a statistical study of fifty-seven firms in the Dallas area produced for the Chamber of Commerce shows average hourly earnings of 63.9 cents in June 1939. Five years later the average had risen to 84.5 cents an hour, an increase of 32.2% at these firms. These averages do not include NAA as the factory did not exist in 1939. Adding war industries into the survey shows an average hourly salary of $1.042, a 63% increase over the prewar figure. Some of this increase can be attributed to overtime pay in the war plants. "Problems for Post-War Dallas Relating to Employment and the Labor Force: A Report for the Dallas Chamber of Commerce and the Committee for Economic Development," February 1945, 28–29, DeGolyer Library, Southern Methodist University, Dallas, TX.
27. Application for Emergency Facilities, February 2, 1942, Engineers' Reports and Appendices for Plancor 25 [Box 20].
28. Willcox to Frank H. Shaw, February 24, 1942, Army Air Corps to NAA, March 14, 1942, Engineers' Reports and Appendices for Plancor 25 [Box 20].
29. "Promotions Announced; Scope of Texas Staff is Enlarged," *Take Off,* June 5, 1942; "Bomber Line of NAA in Production," *Dallas Morning News,* December 20, 1942.

Notes for Chapter 13

1. "Defense Bond Salary Deduction Plan Inaugurated," *Take Off,* January 8, 1942; "Plant Nears 100% Goal in Defense Bond Drive," *Take Off,* January 15, 1942 (quote); "Employees to Buy $73,448 in Defense Bonds Monthly," *Take Off,* January 23, 1942; "Bonds Purchased Percentage Climbs to 93.4% at Dallas," *Take Off,* May 14, 1942.
2. "Photo Caption," *Take Off,* May 14, 1942; "Dorothy Lamour Sells $175,000 in War Bonds," *Dallas Morning News,* May 30, 1942 (quote).
3. "Flood Waters from the Trinity," *Take Off,* April 17, 1942; "Rising River Covering Bottomlands," *Dallas Morning News,* April 9, 1942; "Traffic Problem Is Under Study," *Take Off,* May 29, 1942; "State Highway Patrol to Regulate NAA Traffic," *Take Off,* June 12, 1942; "Construction on Roads to Aid NAA Traffic to Begin Soon," *Take Off,* June 26, 1942.
4. "Auto Tire Rationing to Start Jan. 4," *Dallas Morning News,* December 18, 1941; "36,680 Tires Allotted to Texas for Trucks and Cars in January," *Dallas*

Morning News, January 1, 1942; "Tire Buyers Have Hard Row to Hoe," *Dallas Morning News*, December 27, 1941.

5. "Classifieds," *Take Off*, December 4, 1941, February 6, 1942.
6. "Bus Service Improved," *Dallas Morning News*, January 25, 1942; "New Bus Schedules," *Take Off*, February 6, 1942.
7. "Classified Ads," *Take Off*, July 10, 1942; "New Office Will Help Workers on Tire Problems," *Take Off*, July 17, 1942 (quote).
8. "New Office Will Help Workers on Tire Problems," *Take Off*, July 17, 1942; "Gas Rations Ordered for Entire U.S.," *Dallas Morning News*, September 26, 1942; "35-Mile Speed Ordered for Texas Roads," *Dallas Morning News*, October 7, 1942.
9. "Photo Caption," *Take Off*, January 23, 30, 1942.
10. "Son Helps Build Airplanes to Fight Jap Captors of His Missionary Father," *Take Off*, January 30, 1942; "Local Church Auxiliaries," *Dallas Morning News*, February 28, 1943.
11. "No Live Japs on China's Soil in Five Years, Predicts Texas Plant's First Chinese Worker," *Take Off*, October 23, 1942.
12. "Rickenbacker Missing on Pacific Flight," *Dallas Morning News*, October 24, 1942.
13. "Texan Pilots Lost Plane of Rickenbacker," *Dallas Morning News*, October 26, 1942; "Missing Pilot's Wife and Brother Working at NAA," *Take Off*, October 30, 1942; "Rickenbacker's Pilot Rescued; Wife Keeps on Building Planes," *Dallas Morning News*, November 14, 1942 (quote); "Eddie Rickenbacker Safe, All of Party Alive but One," *Dallas Morning News*, November 15, 1942; "Three NAA Workers On Radio Broadcast," *Take Off*, November 20, 1942; "NAA Worker Has Joyous Reunion With Husband, Rescued From Raft," *Take Off*, December 11, 1942.
14. "Family All Out for War," *Dallas Morning News*, August 15, 1942. "Coral Sea Battle Veteran, 19, Now Is Worker at NAA," *Take Off*, August 28, 1942 (quotes).
15. "Called to Colors," *Take Off*, October 23, 30, November 6, 13, 1942; "NAA Secretary Will Leave to Join WAACs." *Take Off*, October 9, 1942; "Day Chatter," *Take Off*, October 30, 1942.
16. "War Workers' Release from Draft Impends," *Dallas Morning News*, November 21, 1942 (quote).
17. "Army, Navy Ban Enlistment of Essential War Workers," *Take Off*, November 27, 1942.
18. Franklin D. Roosevelt, "Executive Order 9279, December 5, 1942," The American Presidency Project, accessed August 8, 2022, https://www.presidency.ucsb.edu/node/209831.
19. Roosevelt, "Executive Order 9279, December 5, 1942."
20. "Military, Industry Man-Power Rule Given to McNutt," *Dallas Morning News*, December 6, 1942 (first quote); "WMC to Keep Rural Labor on the

Farm," *Dallas Morning News*, December 20, 1942, (second quote); "Nation's Man Power," *Dallas Morning News*, December 7, 1942, (third quote); "Help Reported Short in Four Texas Areas," *Dallas Morning News*, December 8, 1942 (fourth quote).

21. "Department 16 Wins Basketball Championship in Playoff Tilt," *Take Off*, March 6, 1942; "Foundry Leads, but Bottlenecks Gain as NAA Bowlers Finish 18ᵗʰ Week," *Take Off*, February 13, 1942; "Plant Baseball Team Begins Daily Workouts," *Take Off*, March 27, 1942; "Golden Gloves to Fight Friday Night," *Take Off*, January 23, 1942; "Track Men Ready for NAA Exposition Meet," *Take Off*, March 20, 1942; "Photo Caption," *Take Off*, May 29, 1942; "Fem Softball Game Is Set." *Take Off*, June 26, 1942; "Tennis Matches for NAA Women Planned," *Take Off*, July 3, 1942; "Photo Caption," *Take Off*, March 27, 1942.

22. "Plant's Fine Arts Club Will Have Meeting Tuesday Night," *Take Off*, July 10, 1942; "Art Section Sets Meeting Sept. 9," *Take Off*, August 21, 1942; "Plans Announced for NAA Art Show," *Take Off*, August 28, 1942; "Photo Caption," *Take Off*, August 21, 1942; "Plane Model Enthusiasts Seek to Form North American Club," *Take Off*, July 17, 1942. One member of the model airplane club was Ed Kindelberger Jr., who appears to have been the nephew of James H. Kindelberger.

23. "'Get It Off Your Chest' Invites Kindelberger with Questionnaire," *Take Off*, May 14, 1942.

24. "Workers Let Fly with Flood of Suggestions," *Take Off*, May 22, 1942.

25. "Questionnaire Big Success as 1808 Replies Received at Dallas," *Take Off*, May 29, 1942; "Staggered Shifts Just Prelude to All Out Rush," *Take Off*, May 29, 1942.

26. "$10,000 Production Idea Contest Announced," *Take Off*, March 13, 1942.

27. "Contest Draws 807 Ideas Here," *Take Off*, April 17, 1942; "Scores Enter Ideas Contest," *Take Off*, March 20, 1942; "Hinds, Adams, Baker Top Winners in $10,000 Contest at Dallas NAA Plant," *Take Off*, May 29, 1942.

28. "Shangri-La Is NAA Plant, Declares Gen. Doolittle," *Take Off*, June 5, 1942.

29. Ibid.; "Photo Caption," Take Off, June 5, 1942; James H. Doolittle, "Speech at North American Aviation Inglewood, June 1, 1942," Original Archival Recording held by Dallas Historical Society, File RR-8102 (electronic conversion in author's possession).

30. "Photo Caption," *Take Off*, January 8, 1942.

31. "Governor Praises North American Way," *Take Off*, March 6, 1942 (first quote); "Hatton Sumners Praises Work of NAA Employees," *Take Off*, July 10, 1942 (second quote); "Photo Caption," *Take Off*, August 7, 1942; "Former U.S. Envoy to Japan Visits Texas Plant," *Take Off*, December 4, 1942 (third and fourth quotes).

32. "Ovation Given Visiting Heroes by Throngs Lining City Streets," *Dallas Morning News*, July 3, 1942; "2 Bombers Christened," *Dallas Morning News*, July 3, 1942.

372   Endnotes

33. "Tokyo Bombers, Native Texans, Tour NAA Plant," *Take Off*, July 10, 1942.
34. Edward P. Stafford, *The Big E: The Story of the U.S.S. Enterprise* (New York: Random House, 1962), 14–15, 85; "Three-time Navy Cross Winner Terms SNJ Sweet Ship to Fly," *Take Off*, October 30, 1942.
35. Samuel E. Morison, *History of United States Naval Operations in World War II, Volume 3: The Rising Sun in the Pacific*, (Boston: Little, Brown and Co. 1984), 206; "Nurse Reported Missing," *Dallas Morning News*, May 31, 1942; "Bataan Nurse Gets Heroine's Welcome Home," *Dallas Morning News*, July 24, 1942; "Bataan Nurse Will Speak." *Dallas Morning News*, November 16, 1942; "Nurse Who Was on Corregidor Praises Plant," *Take Off*, August 14, 1942 (quotes).
36. "Knudsen Named to Speed Army's War Supply Production," *Dallas Morning News*, January 17, 1942; R. Elberton Smith, *The Army and Economic Mobilization* (Washington, DC: United States Army, 1991), 507 (first quote); "General Knudsen Visits Plant," *Take Off*, March 27, 1942 (remaining quotes).
37. "Chief of U.S. Army Air Forces Praises Production in Texas," *Take Off*, July 17, 1942 (first and second quotes); "Work Done by Women in Aircraft Making Is Amazing, Says Chief," *Dallas Morning News*, July 12, 1942 (third quote).
38. "Gen. Wolfe Praises Spirit of NAA Workers," *Take Off*, August 7, 1942.
39. "What the Army-Navy E Means to Men and Women of NAA," *Take Off*, September 11, 1942; "Impressive Ceremony to Mark Presentation of E," *Take Off*, September 11, 1942 (quotes).
40. "Scores of Telegrams Congratulate NAA Workers on Receiving E Award," *Take Off*, September 11, 1942.
41. "Superior Job Wins E Flag for Air Plant," *Dallas Morning News*, September 22, 1942; "NAA Workers Win Praise for Getting 'Em Built," *Take Off*, September 25, 1942 (quotes).
42. "NAA Workers Win Praise for Getting 'Em Built," *Take Off*, September 25, 1942.
43. "Photo Captions," *Take Off*, September 25, 1942; "What the Army-Navy E Means to Men and Women of NAA," *Take Off*, September 11, 1942; "Superior Job Wins E Flag for Air Plant," *Dallas Morning News*, September 22, 1942; "Radio Programs by the Clock," *Dallas Morning News*, September 21, 1942: "Photo Caption," *Take Off*, October 2, 1942.
44. "NAA Plant Wins Its Second E," *Dallas Morning News*, April 7, 1943; "Army-Navy E Award," Naval History and Heritage Command, accessed December 28, 2018, https://www.history.navy.mil/research/library/online-reading-room/title-list-alphabetically/a/army-navy-e-award.html.
45. North American Aviation, "Annual Report of Manufacturing Activities – 1942," 20, 22, North American Aviation Collection, Boeing Archives, Bellevue, WA.
46. "Conveyor System Proves Valuable Asset ay NAA," *Take Off*, June 19, 1942.
47. North American Aviation, "Annual Report of Manufacturing Activities – 1942," 18, 20.

Notes for Chapter 14

1. "Bomber Line of NAA in Production,' *Dallas Morning News*, December 20, 1942; "Local Plant Builds Mustang Fighters," *Dallas Morning News*, December 23, 1942; North American Aviation, "Annual Report of Manufacturing Activities – 1942," 25, North American Aviation Collection, Boeing Archives, Bellevue, WA.

2. North American Aviation, "A Brief History of Operations Immediately Prior to and During World War II," 17–18, General Aviation Collection, History of Aviation Archives, Special Collections, University of Texas at Dallas.

3. North American Aviation, "Brief History of Operations," 17–18.

4. Ray Wagner, *American Combat Planes*, 3rd ed. (Garden City, NY: Doubleday, 1982), 282; North American Aviation, "Brief History of Operations," 55.

5. Teletype PRS-128063, December 14, 1942, Army Air Forces Material Command to War Production Board, December 18, 1942, Correspondence and Reports Relating to the Expansion of Facilities, Records of the War Department General and Special Staffs (Record Group 165, National Archives and Records Administration, College Park, MD [Box 194]).

6. S. E. Skinner to War Production Board, December 23, 1942 (quote), Gordon E. Textor to Frederick M. Hopkins, January 5, 1943, Hopkins to Under Secretary of War Robert Patterson, January 6, 1943, Memorandum of Approval No. 1075, January 7, 1943, Correspondence and Reports Relating to the Expansion of Facilities.

7. "Dallas-Made Plane Renamed the Texan," *Dallas Morning News*, January 4, 1943.

8. "Texas Plant Builds Texans, Trainer Officially Named," *Take Off*, January 8, 1943.

9. "Home Building Virtually Ends for Dallas," *Dallas Morning News*, December 10, 1942.

10. Second Housing Unit Set for Arlington," *Dallas Morning News*, March 21, 1942; "Dormitories for Workers Ready," *Take Off*, June 26, 1942; "Rooms Still Available in Housing Project," *Take Off*, October 2, 1942.

11. "Work Starts Soon on Low Cost Homes," *Dallas Morning News*, July 18, 1941; "Army Takes Government Housing Units," *Dallas Morning News*, October 3, 1942; "Army Hands Back Some Rental Units," *Dallas Morning News*, January 1, 1943; "400 New Rental Units Available to NAA Workers," *Take Off*, January 15, 1943.

12. "Housing Service for NAA Workers to Start Feb. 4," *Take Off*, January 29, 1943; "Grand Prairie Will Get City Mail Service," "*Dallas Morning News*, March 1, 1943.

13. An examination of antiunion sentiment during 1941 may be found in Chapter 9.

14. "Unions Gird to Grab Big Texas Plum," *Dallas Morning News*, January 17, 1943; "Union Election Conference Set for North American," *Dallas Morning*

News, January 20, 1943; "Day Is Added for Union Vote at Air Plant," *Dallas Morning News*, February 3, 1943.

15. "A Statement of Policy," *Take Off*, January 15, 1943.
16. "CIO Union Head Scores O'Daniel," *Dallas Morning News*, February 14, 1943.
17. "CIO Played by Dallas Union Man," *Dallas Morning News*, February 16, 1943.
18. "Union Ballot Being Held at NAA Plant," *Dallas Morning News*, February 17, 1943 (quote); "CIO Leads in NAA Ballot; Run-Off Election Ordered," *Dallas Morning News*, February 20, 1943.
19. Union Called Out of Place in War Plant," *Dallas Morning News*, February 26, 1943.
20. "No-Union Plea Seized by CIO Men, Is Claim," *Dallas Morning News*, February 27, 1943.
21. "CIO Union Wins Election at NAA," *Dallas Morning News*, March 1, 1943; "Consolidated Employees Favor A.F. of L. Union," *Dallas Morning News*, February 25, 1943.
22. Wesley Frank Craven and James Lea Cate, *The Army Air Forces in World War II, Volume 6: Men and Planes* (Chicago, IL: University of Chicago Press, 1955) 293.
23. "We Must All Double Our Output during 1943, Aircraft Production Board Tells NAA Workers," *Take Off*, January 15, 1943.
24. Patrick W. Timberlake to Julius H. Amberg, June 28, 1944, Investigation Files: Julius H. Amberg, Records of the Office of the Secretary of War (Record Group 107, National Archives and Records Administration, College Park, MD [Box 863]).
25. "First NAA-Built B-24 Flown 319 Days after Contract Made," *Take Off*, March 19, 1943; "Excellent Job, Col. Cook Says of First B-24," *Take Off*, April 9, 1943 (quote); "Gen. Wolfe Hails B-24's Flight as Aide to Air Power," *Take Off*, April 9, 1943.
26. "First Dallas Bomber," *Dallas Morning News*, March 17, 1943; NAA, "Annual Report of Manufacturing Activities – 1942," (quote) 34–35; "First NAA-Built B-24 Flown 319 Days after Contract Made," *Take Off*, March 19, 1943.
27. U.S. Senate Special Committee to Investigate the National Defense Program, "Investigation of the National Defense at Dallas, Texas, Transcripts of Hearing Taken at Dallas, Texas, Beginning October 9, 1943," 88 [quote; 78th Congress, 1st Session]; North American Aviation, "Annual Report of Manufacturing Activities – 1942," 25, North American Aviation Collection, Boeing Archives, Bellevue, WA.

Notes for Chapter 15

1. "Housing Still Main NAA Worry," *Dallas Morning News*, July 4, 1943.
2. Clyde Wallis to War Manpower Commission, April 22, 1943, J.H. Bond to Wallis, April 28, 1943, Wallis to Bond, April 30, 1943, William Haber to

Wallis, May 6, 1943, Central Subject Files, War Manpower Commission (Record Group 211, National Archives and Records Administration, Ft. Worth, TX [Box 1]).

3. "Housing Row Imperils Dallas' Position as War Industry Center," *Dallas Morning News*, July 8, 1943 (quotes); "Banker Heads New Office of WMC Opened in Dallas," *Dallas Morning News*, May 9, 1943.

4. "Housing Row Imperils Dallas' Position as War Industry Center," *Dallas Morning News*, July 8, 1943, (first quote); "Group Named to Study Housing Plan," *Dallas Morning News*, July 13, 1943 (second quote); "War Bureaus Agree on Housing Plan," *Dallas Morning News*, July 9, 1943.

5. "City Shakes Head at Big Housing Gap," *Dallas Morning News*, July 11, 1943.

6. "NHA Chief Back from Capitol Talks," *Dallas Morning News*, July 17, 1943.

7. "Grand Prairie's Chiefs Say Dallas Would Hog New Housing Benefits," *Dallas Morning News*, July 14, 1943.

8. Ibid.

9. "Group Named to Study Housing Plan," *Dallas Morning News*, July 13, 1943.

10. "Heroes Relax in Barracks Built in Dallas," *Dallas Morning News*, September 8, 1942; "City Shakes Head at Big Housing Gap."

11. "Grand Prairie's Chiefs Say Dallas Would Hog New Housing Benefits" (quotes); "Housing Official Requests 1,000 Temporary Units," *Dallas Morning News*, July 27, 1943; "1,000 Stop-Gap Family Houses Win Approval for NAA Section," *Dallas Morning News*, August 7, 1943.

12. "Grand Prairie Upset at Government's Order for 1,000 New Homes," *Dallas Morning News*, August 11, 1943; "800 Workers' Homes to Go Up at City Edge," *Dallas Morning News*, August 22, 1943; "La Reunion Opens 884 New Units, *Dallas Morning News*, March 18, 1944; "Work Starts Wednesday on Houses at La Reunion," *Dallas Morning News*, September 21, 1943; "First Families Move To La Reunion Homes," *Dallas Morning News*, December 3, 1943 (quote).

13. Senate Special Committee, "Hearing at Dallas, Beginning October 9, 1943," 223.

14. Ibid., 224.

15. Ibid.

16. "Truman Group to Investigate Plan Plants," *Dallas Morning News*, August 4, 1943; "Saving Free Competition Called Truman Group Goal," *Dallas Morning News*, August 11, 1943 (quote); "Truman Group, Connally Plan to Meet Here," *Dallas Morning News*, August 7, 1943.

17. "Sen. Truman And Committee Visit Dallas Division," *Take Off*, August 13, 1943 (first quote); "Saving Free Competition Called Truman Group Goal," *Dallas Morning News*, August 11, 1943 (second quote).

18. "Mass Output of Mustang Announced," *Dallas Morning News*, August 25, 1943; Ray Wagner, *American Combat Planes*, 3rd ed. (Garden City, NY: Doubleday, 1982), 282–3; North American Aviation, "Annual Report of

Manufacturing Activities – 1942," 25, North American Aviation Collection, Boeing Archives, Bellevue, WA.

19. Teletype messages between Dallas WMC and Washington WMC Headquarters, Central Subject Files, Records of the War Manpower Commission [Box 1]; "Dallas Gets New Hope for Chance to Plan Its Own Labor Destiny," *Dallas Morning News*, September 29, 1943; "Dallas Made No.1 Critical Labor Area; Plants Can't Get New War Contracts," *Dallas Morning News*, October 1, 1943.

Notes for Chapter 16

1. "Obituary - Julius H. Amberg" *New York Times*, January 25, 1951.
2. "Army Men, WPB Inspect NAA Factory," *Dallas Morning News*, October 27, 1943. This was not the first time Major General Charles E. Branshaw was involved with North American Aviation. In 1941 he commanded the Army troops that ended the strike at the Inglewood plant.
3. Phone call, Charles E. Branshaw to Julius H. Amberg, October 28, 1943 (Transcript), Investigation Files: Julius H. Amberg, Records of the Office of the Secretary of War (Record Group 107, National Archives and Records Administration, College Park, MD [Box 863]).
4. Phone call, Branshaw to Amberg, October 28, 1943.
5. "Truman Committee Seeks Cause of Manpower Crisis; Will Study Waste Charges," *Dallas Morning News*, October 9, 1943.
6. U.S. Bureau of Demobilization, *Industrial Mobilization for War: History of the War Production Board and Predecessor Agencies, 1940–1945, Volume 1, Program and Administration* (Washington, DC: Government Printing Office, 1947), 527–28; "NAA Asked to Sublet to Small Plants," *Dallas Morning News*, October 3, 1943.
7. "Adroit Use of Manpower Claimed by Airplane Plant's Officials," (quote) *Dallas Morning News*, October 2, 1943; "NAA Seeks Workers for Waco Branch," *Dallas Morning News*, October 3, 1943.
8. "Manpower" (advertisement), *Dallas Morning News*, October 2, 1943. The records of the U.S. Senate Special Committee indicate the message also appeared in the *Daily Times Herald*, presumably on the same date.
9. "Help Wanted," *Dallas Morning News*, October 2–5, 1943.
10. "Time Costs Lives" (advertisement), *Dallas Morning News*, October 3, 1943.
11. "In No. 1 Critical Area," *Dallas Morning News*, October 2, 1943.
12. "Labor Ruling on Dallas Unfair, Senate Probing Committee Told," *Dallas Morning News*, October 10, 1943 "Truman Investigators to Arrive Saturday for Secret Hearings," *Dallas Morning News*, October 8, 1943 (quotes); U.S. Senate Special Committee to Investigate the National Defense Program, "Investigation of the National Defense at Dallas, Texas, Transcripts of

Hearing Taken at Dallas, Texas, Beginning October 9, 1943," 1–3 [78ᵗʰ Congress, 1ˢᵗ Session].

13. *Handbook of Texas Online*, Robert S. La Forte, "Davidson, Thomas Whitfield," accessed August 8, 2022, http://www.tshaonline.org/handbook/online/articles/fda29; Senate Special Committee, "Hearing at Dallas, Beginning October 9, 1943," 6.

14. Senate Special Committee, "Hearing at Dallas, Beginning October 9, 1943," 6.

15. Ibid., 6–7.

16. Ibid., 10.

17. "Labor Ruling on Dallas Unfair, Senate Probing Committee Told," *Dallas Morning News*, October 10, 1943 (first quote); Senate Special Committee, "Hearing at Dallas, Beginning October 9, 1943," 13–14 (second quote), 22.

18. Senate Special Committee, "Hearing at Dallas, Beginning October 9, 1943," 22–24.

19. Ibid., 26–28.

20. Ibid., 28–45. Questioning about the certificates of availability was lengthy, as the committee members sought to understand the complexities of the process.

21. Senate Special Committee, "Hearing at Dallas, Beginning October 9, 1943," 29–31.

22. Ibid., 46–47.

23. Ibid., 49.

24. "Housing Official Requests 1,000 Temporary Units," *Dallas Morning News*, July 27, 1943; Senate Special Committee, "Hearing at Dallas, Beginning October 9, 1943," 50–58.

25. Senate Special Committee, "Hearing at Dallas, Beginning October 9, 1943," 58–59.

26. Ibid., 60–65.

27. Ibid., 66–67.

28. Ibid., 68–71.

29. Ibid., 73.

30. Ibid., 74.

31. Ibid., 75.

32. Ibid., 75–76. The officer in question was Capt. Donald E. Eggleston, the Army contract officer at the NAA plant. It is possible that Eggleston was in emotional distress at the time; he had a newborn son who died in November at the age of six weeks. "Infant's Rites Set," *Dallas Morning News*, November 2, 1943.

33. Senate Special Committee, "Hearing at Dallas, Beginning October 9, 1943," 76–78. To compare, North American Aviation at Inglewood had only delivered its first Merlin-engine Mustang in May, even with the long experience that facility had in building the earlier models. Ray Wagner, *American Combat Planes*, 3rd ed. (Garden City, NY: Doubleday, 1982), 282.

34. Senate Special Committee, "Hearing at Dallas, Beginning October 9, 1943," 78–79.
35. Ibid., 82–95.
36. Ibid., 95–100.
37. Ibid.
38. Ibid., 98–101.
39. Ibid., 101–103.
40. Ibid., 103–104.
41. Ibid., 105–108.
42. Ibid., 108–111.

Notes for Chapter 17

1. Ibid., 112–115.
2. Ibid., 115–119.
3. Ibid., 119–128.
4. Ibid., 129–135.
5. Ibid., 136–143.
6. Ibid., 144–162.
7. Ibid., 163–188 [first, second, third, and fourth quotes], 193–196 [fifth quote], 250–265 [sixth quote].
8. Senate Special Committee, "Hearing at Dallas, Beginning October 9, 1943," 351–376.
9. Ibid., 265–280.
10. Ibid., 280–291 [quotes], 293–308, 327.

Notes for Chapter 18

1. James H. Kindelberger, "To All Employees of the Texas Division," *Take Off*, October 8, 1943 (first four quotes); "Texas Division of NAA Wins Third Army-Navy E," *Take Off*, October 8, 1943 (last two quotes).
2. A version of the *Our Job* booklet was released to the California Division on September 30. The two versions are similar, with some differences in the text to account with matters specific to each plant. It is reasonable to assume that a third version was prepared for Kansas City.
3. North American Aviation, *Our Job (A Letter from the President)* 1–4, Central Subject Files, Records of the War Manpower Commission (Record Group 211, National Archives and Records Administration, Ft. Worth, TX [Box 1]).
4. NAA, *Our Job*, 4–7.
5. NAA *Our Job*, 8. Kindelberger mentions the engine switch and delivery delay. The quantity of Dallas B-24s with greenhouse noses is from Ray Wagner, *American Combat Planes*, 3rd ed. (Garden City, NY: Doubleday, 1982), 216.

6. NAA, *Our Job*, 9–10.
7. Ibid., 11 (first quote), 6 (second quote, italics in original).
8. Ibid., 12.
9. "Senators Tour Plane Plant, Demand Output Increase," *Dallas Morning News*, October 12, 1943.
10. U.S. Senate Special Committee to Investigate the National Defense Program, "Investigation of the National Defense at Dallas, Texas, Transcripts of Hearing Taken at Dallas, Texas, Beginning October 9, 1943," 304–305, 406–417 [quotes; 78th Congress, 1st Session].
11. Senate Special Committee, "Hearing at Dallas, Beginning October 9, 1943," 417–428.
12. Ibid., 429–454.
13. Ibid., 455–467.
14. Ibid., 468–474.
15. Ibid., 476–478.
16. Ibid., 482.
17. Ibid., 483–484.
18. Ibid., 485–490.
19. Ibid., 498–502.
20. Ibid., 502–503.
21. Ibid., 503–506.
22. Ibid., 506–514.
23. Ibid., 515–518, 520–524, 537.
24. Ibid., 525–534.
25. Irving B. Holley Jr., *Buying Aircraft: Material Procurement for the Army Air Forces* (Washington, DC: Office of the Chief of Military History, Department of the Army, 1964), 390, 372 (first quote), 412 (second quote).
26. Senate Special Committee, "Hearing at Dallas, Beginning October 9, 1943," 534.
27. Ibid., 534–536.
28. Ibid., 537–539.
29. "Senators Tour Plane Plant, Demand Output Increase."

Notes for Chapter 19

1. Ibid.
2. U.S. Senate Special Committee to Investigate the National Defense Program, "Investigation of the National Defense at Dallas, Texas, Transcripts of Hearing Taken at Dallas, Texas, Beginning October 9, 1943," 627–645 [78th Congress, 1st Session]. The transcripts are incomplete, as court reporter John H. Bond became ill before he completed the transcription. A note in the records stated that some testimony would not be available until Bond

recovered. Unfortunately, he died at Baylor Hospital on 27 October 1943, at age 51. It is uncertain whether the rest of his notes were transcribed. See "Bond Death Said Due to Truman Work," *Dallas Morning News*, October 28, 1943.

3. Senate Special Committee, "Hearing at Dallas, Beginning October 9, 1943," 548–577.

4. Ibid., 577–591.

5. "Housing Mismanaging and NAA Inefficiency Hinted at Probe's End," *Dallas Morning News*, October 13, 1943.

6. Senate Special Committee, "Hearing at Dallas, Beginning October 9, 1943," 592–596.

7. Ibid., 600–601.

8. Ibid., 601–604.

9. Ibid., 605–608. The meeting described by Orville Erringer appears to be the same one described by witness James Hereford in testimony on Monday.

10. Senate Special Committee, "Hearing at Dallas, Beginning October 9, 1943," 609–617.

11. Ibid., 617–625.

12. "Housing Mismanaging and NAA Inefficiency Hinted at Probe's End."

13. U.S. Senate Special Committee to Investigate the National Defense Program, "Investigation of National Defense Program, Closed Hearing on War Manpower Commission, October 14, 1943," 8–9 [78th Congress, 1st Session].

14. Senate Special Committee, "Closed Hearing on War Manpower Commission, October 14, 1943," 27–33.

15. U.S. Senate Special Committee Investigating the National Defense Program, *Investigation of the National Defense Program: Hearings, Part 21, 78th Congress, First and Second Sessions* (Washington, DC: Government Printing Office, 1944), 8, 545–8, 551.

16. Senate Special Committee, *Hearings, Part 21*, 8, 566–8, 567.

17. Ibid., 8, 568-9.

18. Ibid., 8, 550; "Use of Manpower at NAA Is Added to Production Study," *Dallas Morning News*, October 24, 1943.

19. Senate Special Committee, *Hearings, Part 21*, 8, 545 [quote]; "WPB Production Chief to Investigate NAA Manpower Shortage," *Dallas Morning News*, October 22, 1943; "Army Men WPB Inspect NAA Factory," *Dallas Morning News*, October 27, 1943.

20. Senate Special Committee, *Hearings, Part 21*, 8; 554–8, 555 [quotes]; "Change Order Due Monday," *Dallas Morning News*, October 29, 1943.

21. "NAA Makes Changes to Speed Output," *Dallas Morning News*, October 29, 1943 (first quote); "Straight from the Shoulder," *Take Off*, November 5, 1943 (second and third quotes).

22. "Schwedes Announces New System of Selecting Supervisory Staff," *Take Off*, November 19, 1944 [first, second, third quotes]; "Supervisory

Staff at NAA Is Increased," *Take Off*, November 26, 1943; "Straight from the Shoulder," *Take Off*, December 10, 1943; "NAA Employees to Have Sundays Off," (fourth and fifth quotes) *Take Off*, December 10, 1943.

23. Senate Special Committee, *Hearings, Part 21*, 8, 558.

24. North American Aviation, "Annual Report to Stockholders, 1941," The Museum of Flight, Seattle, WA; Irving B. Holley Jr., *Buying Aircraft: Material Procurement for the Army Air Forces* (Washington, DC: Office of the Chief of Military History, Department of the Army, 1964), 397, 404, 415.

25. Holley Jr., *Buying Aircraft*, 374, 385, 391.

26. "Kindelberger Explains Texas Division Contracts," *Take Off*, November 5, 1943.

27. "Fixed Price Contract for B-24 Signed," *Take Off*, December 31, 1943.

28. Holley Jr., *Buying Aircraft*, 415–416.

29. "WPB Finds Lumber to Speed War Housing," *Dallas Morning News*, October 15, 1943; "Grand Prairie Building for War Workers," *Dallas Morning News*, October 24, 1943.

30. "Education Office Sets Classes for Post-Holiday," *Take Off*, December 17, 1943.

31. Senate Special Committee, "Hearing at Dallas, Beginning October 9, 1943," 304–305, 406–417 [quotes], 497.

32. "Plane Plants Form Joint War Council," *Dallas Morning News*, April 6, 1942.

33. John C. Lee to Richard C. Palmer, March 18, 1944 [includes text of Lee's letter to James H. Kindelberger], Records of the National Aircraft War Production Council, Harry S. Truman Presidential Library, Independence, MO.

34. "Dallas-Made Bombers" (photo caption), *Dallas Morning News*, November 20, 1943; Patrick W. Timberlake to Julius H. Amberg, June 28, 1944, Investigation Files: Julius H. Amberg, Records of the Office of the Secretary of War (Record Group 107, National Archives and Records Administration, College Park, MD [Box 863]); "Unit Production," Records of the National Aircraft War Production Council, Truman Library.

Notes for Chapter 20

1. "This Was Said for You," *Take Off*, February 4, 1944.

2. "FBI Charges Two Workers in Theft of Tools," *Take Off*, November 19, 1943.

3. "Time Frauds at NAA Face Jury Scrutiny," *Dallas Morning News*, January 23, 1944; "8 Surrender in Time Clock NAA Charges," *Dallas Morning News*, January 28, 1944; "Time Card Charges Net Guilty Pleas," *Dallas Morning News*, January 29, 1944; "Conditions at NAA Castigated by Judge in Fixing Sentences," *Dallas Morning News*, February 3, 1944.

4. "Federal Fraud Issue Attacked in Wage Case," *Dallas Morning News*, February 1, 1944; "Jury Ponders Verdict in NAA Time Cards," *Dallas*

Morning News, February 2, 1944 (quote); "NAA Workers Freed in Time Card Case," *Dallas Morning News*, February 24, 1944; "NAA Machine Theft Brings Prison Term," *Dallas Morning News*, January 26, 1944.

5. "3 Sentenced, 2 on Trial in NAA Time Fraud Case," *Dallas Morning News*, February 22, 1944.

6. "Workers for New Plane Plant Here to Learn Quickly," *Waco Tribune-Herald*, October 3, 1943 (first quote); "Leases Signed for North American's Plane Plant Here," *Waco Tribune-Herald*, November 7, 1943 (second quote).

7. Training Starts for NAA Workers in Waco Factory," *Waco News-Tribune*, December 14, 1943; "Waco Wage Scale Set Temporarily," *Take Off*, December 17, 1943.

8. "Photo Caption," *Take Off*, January 21, 1944; "Photo Caption," *Take Off*, March 31, 1944; "Texas Plants Deliver 1,310 Planes in 90 Days," *Take Off*, April 7, 1944 (quote).

9. "NAA Sets Up Production Unit in Town," *Dallas Morning News*, January 13, 1944.

10. "Texas Division Has Downtown Production Unit," *Take Off*, January 14, 1944.

11. U.S. Senate Special Committee to Investigate the National Defense Program, "Investigation of the National Defense at Dallas, Texas, Transcripts of Hearing Taken at Dallas, Texas, Beginning October 9, 1943," 607–608 [78th Congress, 1st Session].

12. "Kindelberger Praises Texas L-M Groups," *Take Off*, March 31, 1944.

13. Phone call, Charles E. Branshaw to Julius H. Amberg, October 28, 1943 (Transcript), Investigation Files: Julius H. Amberg, Records of the Office of the Secretary of War (Record Group 107, National Archives and Records Administration, College Park, MD [Box 863]).

14. "5,500 Planes Built by U.S. In February," *Dallas Morning News*, March 5, 1943; Plane Output Hits Peak in July, but Manpower Shortage Faces Plants," *Dallas Morning News*, August 8, 1943; "Straight from the Shoulder," *Take Off*, December 10, 1943 (quote).

15. "NAA Employees to Hold Open House," *Take Off*, February 25, 1944 (first quote); "First Family Day Plans Completed," *Take Off*, March 3, 1944 (second quote).

16. "Thousands See Dallas Bombers," *Dallas Morning News*, March 6, 1944 (quote); "NAA Employees to Hold Open House," *Take Off*, February 25, 1944; "Texas State Guard to Participate in NAA Family Days," *Take Off*, March 3, 1944.

17. "Family Day at NAA," *Take Off*, March 10, 1944.

18. "'It was Really Swell' Is Employees' Opinion of North American's First Family Day Tour," *Take Off*, March 10, 1944 (first and second quotes); "Thousands See Dallas Bombers," *Dallas Morning News*, March 6, 1944 (third quote).

19. "Photo Captions," *Take Off*, March 17, 1944.

20. "Texas Population Grows 10.1 per Cent in Decade, Final Census Total Shows," *Dallas Morning News*, January 11, 1941.

21. NAA, *Plants People Planes*, 11; "Problems for Post-War Dallas Relating to Employment and the Labor Force: A Report for the Dallas Chamber of Commerce and the Committee for Economic Development," February 1945, 41, DeGolyer Library, Southern Methodist University, Dallas, TX.

22. "Production and Workers Lauded by Maj. Seversky," *Take Off*, March 24, 1944.

23. "'Blue Streak'" Crew to Talk Here Tuesday," *Take Off*, March 24, 1944; "NAA Workers Lauded by Crew of '*Blue Streak*'," *Take Off*, March 31, 1944; "Photo Captain," *Take Off*, April 7, 1944; "Work and Attitude at NAA Praised by Admiral Foote," *Take Off*, May 5, 1944.

24. "Unit Production," Records of the National Aircraft War Production Council, Harry S. Truman Presidential Library, Independence, MO; Senate Special Committee, "Hearing at Dallas, Beginning October 9, 1943," 478.

25. Ray Wagner, *American Combat Planes*, 3rd ed. (Garden City, NY: Doubleday, 1982), 283; Roger A. Freeman, *Mustang at War* (Garden City, NY: Doubleday, 1974), 107; North American Aviation, "A Brief History of Operations Immediately Prior to and during World War II," 43, 55, General Aviation Collection, History of Aviation Archives, Special Collections, University of Texas at Dallas.

26. Senate Special Committee, "Hearing at Dallas, Beginning October 9, 1943," 478.

27. Ibid., 476–478; "Unit Production," Records of the National Aircraft War Production Council, Truman Library; North American Aviation, "Brief History of Operations," 53–54.

28. North American Aviation, "Brief History of Operations," 53; "646 Planes in May Sets Record for Texas Plants," *Take Off*, June 16, 1944.

29. "Ford Claims One Plant to Build B-24," *Dallas Morning News*, June 3, 1944.

30. "Liberator Production to Increase," *Dallas Morning News*, June 4, 1944.

31. "B-24 Production Will Go On," *Take Off*, June 9, 1944.

32. "H-Hour Finds City Tense, Prayerful," *Dallas Morning News*, June 6, 1944; "Dallas Greets D-Day Calmly and Solemnly," *Dallas Morning News*, June 7, 1944; "NAA Workers Take Invasion News Calmly, Have Confidence in Allies, Expect Long Fight," *Take Off*, June 9, 1944 (quotes).

33. L-M Groups Take Part in Safety Drive," *Take Off*, May 26, 1944; "NAA's Bond Buyers Win Right to Raise 'Minute Man' Flag," *Take Off*, July 7, 1944.

34. "Plants to Shut Down for 3-Day Inventory in July," *Take Off*, June 9, 1944; "July 3, 4 NAA Days at Blood Bank," *Take Off*, June 23, 1944; "Letter from A. N. Boggs to H. F. Schwedes," *Take Off*, June 30, 1944 (quotes).

35. "Letter from H. F. Schwedes to A. N. Boggs," *Take Off*, June 30, 1944.

36. "Letter from H. F. Schwedes to A. N. Boggs," (first three quotes); Senate Special Committee, "Hearing at Dallas, Beginning October 9, 1943," 488;

"Texas Plants Still to Make B-24 Bombers," *Dallas Morning News*, July 19, 1944 (last quote).

37. NAA Press Release, D42-8-44, August 10, 1944, Records of the National Aircraft War Production Council, Truman Library.

38. "Outline of information procedure followed by North American Aviation in connection with B-24 cutback," Records of the National Aircraft War Production Council, Truman Library.

39. "Army Orders Liberator Output Cut," *Dallas Morning News*, August 11, 1944.

40. NAA Press Release, D43-8-44, August 11, 1944, Records of the National Aircraft War Production Council, Truman Library.

41. "Outline of information procedure followed by North American Aviation in connection with B-24 cutback," Records of the National Aircraft War Production Council, Truman Library; "New Jobs Await 3,689 To Be Laid Off by NAA," *Daily Times Herald*, August 13, 1944.

42. "NAA Cutback Forces Going to New Jobs," *Dallas Morning News*, August 15, 1944.

43. "Problems for Post-War Dallas Relating to Employment and the Labor Force: A Report for the Dallas Chamber of Commerce and the Committee for Economic Development," February 1945, 41, DeGolyer Library, Southern Methodist University, Dallas, TX; "NAA Cutback Forces Going to New Jobs."

Notes for Chapter 21

1. "Dallas Gets Big Plane Factory," *Daily Times Herald*, August 17, 1940; "17,000 More Workers at NAA Face Layoff by Mid-November," *Dallas Morning News*, August 17, 1944.

2. "Differences between W-11 & W-11 Revised," Records of the National Aircraft War Production Council, Harry S. Truman Presidential Library, Independence, MO; "Reduction at NAA," *Dallas Morning News*, August 18, 1944 (quote).

3. War Production Board, "Dallas: Preview of Postwar Problems," *War Progress*, September 16, 1944, 9–11, President's Secretary File (PSF), Series 5 – Subject File, Box 173, War Production Board – *War Progress*, February 12, 1944 – September 30, 1944, Franklin D. Roosevelt Presidential Library [online archive].

4. War Production Board, "Dallas: Preview of Postwar Problems," 9–11.

5. Ibid.

6. Ibid.

7. "Texas Division to Make B-25's Eight Gun Nose," *Take Off*, September 15, 1944; "Photo Caption," *Take Off*, January 19, 1945.

8. "NAA To Manufacture B-29 Superfort Units," *Daily Times Herald*, September 28, 1944 (quote); "Plan Revision Results in Decision Not to Build B-29s at This Time," *Take Off*, November 3, 1944.

9. "NAA Builds 30,000 World War II Planes, *Take Off*, October 13, 1944.

10. "Last Liberator Rolls Out at Dedication Ceremony," *Take Off*, November 3, 1944.

11. "Problems for Post-War Dallas Relating to Employment and the Labor Force: A Report for the Dallas Chamber of Commerce and the Committee for Economic Development," February 1945, 41, DeGolyer Library, Southern Methodist University, Dallas, TX; "NAA to Reduce Waco Personnel," *Dallas Morning News*, November 7, 1944.

12. "NAA Waco Project to Close Dec. 29," *Dallas Morning News*, December 9, 1944; "Part of Waco Work Will Be Moved to Dallas," *Take Off*, November 10, 1944 (quote).

13. "NAA Plans Lay-Off of 600 Workers," *Dallas Morning News*, November 24, 1944; "Workers Jump on Bond Wagon This Week," *Take Off*, November 17, 1944. An example of these photos can be viewed at *The Portal to Texas History*, accessed August 8, 2022, https://texashistory.unt.edu/ark:/67531/metapth28945/m1/1/.

14. "Texas Division to Manufacture New Ship," *Take Off*, December 8, 1944.

15. "New Cargo Ship Revealed to Be C-82," *Take Off*, December 15, 1944 (quote); North American Aviation, Analysis of Performance 1945 Fiscal Year (July 1946), 6; John Leland Atwood Collection, National Air and Space Museum Archives, Chantilly, VA; Records of the National Aircraft War Production Council, Truman Library.

16. "Military Restrictions Are Lifted to Allow Description of C-82," *Take Off*, December 15, 1944.

17. "Dallas Plant Builds 30% of Midwest's Output," *Take Off*, January 12, 1945.

18. "Bob McCulloch Named Division Manager," *Take Off*, January 12, 1945; "I Shall Always Be Proud of You," *Take Off*, January 12, 1945 (quotes).

19. J. L. Atwood to Army Air Force, January 11, 1945, Engineers' Reports and Appendices for Plancor 25, Defense Plant Corporation Files, Records of the Reconstruction Finance Corporation (Record Group 234, National Archives and Records Administration, College Park, MD [Box 20]).

20. G. H. Moriarty to Defense Plant Corporation, February 14, 1945, Elijah Ketchum to Frank Shaw, February 19, 1945, Engineers' Reports and Appendices for Plancor 25 [Box 20].

21. Atwood to Army Air Force, January 11, 1945, Engineers' Reports and Appendices for Plancor 25 Park [20].

22. "First Phases of C-82 Work Foreshadow Big Job Ahead," *Take Off*, January 19, 1945.

23. "17,500 Planesmen to Get Service Pins," *Take Off*, January 26, 1945.

24. "Downtown Dallas Workers Meet McCulloch, Get Pins," *Take Off,* February 2, 1945.
25. Ibid. An internal company document reports that African Americans represented 6.7% of the Dallas workforce in September 1944. See North American Aviation, "A Brief History of Operations Immediately Prior to and during World War II," General Aviation Collection, History of Aviation Archives, Special Collections, University of Texas at Dallas.
26. "C-82 Tool Makers Finish First Jigs This Week," *Take Off,* February 2, 1945.
27. "Photo Caption" *Take Off,* February 23, 1945; "Lofting Course Starts; C-82 Class Being Organized," *Take Off,* February 23, 1945; "C-82 Program Advances on Time-Table Schedule," *Take Off,* March 23, 1945 (quotes).
28. "Mustangs Smack Hirohito and Hitler," *Take Off,* April 13, 1945; "We of the AAF Salute You," *Take Off,* February 9, 1945.
29. "Air Forces Exhibit to Feature Robomb," *Dallas Morning News,* March 3, 1945 (quotes); "Thousands See Shot from Sky Now under Way at Fair Park," *Dallas Morning News,* March 9, 1945.
30. "Photo Caption," *Take Off,* March 9, 1945.
31. "Spectator Questions Burst Like Flak at NAA Air Show Exhibit," *Take Off,* March 16, 1945, (quotes); "Photo Caption," *Take Off,* March 16, 1945.
32. "Workers to See Own Planes, Enemies' in AAF Show," *Take Off,* March 9, 1945; "Photo Captions," *Take Off,* March 16, 1945; "Spectator Questions Burst Like Flak at NAA Air Show Exhibit," *Take Off,* March 16, 1945.
33. "A Message from Dutch," *Take Off,* April 6, 1945.
34. "NAA Family Listens, Stunned and Silent, When Tragic News Comes," *Take Off,* April 20, 1945.
35. "Future Schedules Don't Change C-82," *Take Off,* April 20, 1945.
36. Ibid.
37. "B-25 Nose Unit Production to End Next Week," *Take Off,* May 4, 1945; "We Pray for An Early Victory Against Japan," *Take Off,* May 11, 1945 (quotes).
38. "Third White Star to Be Added to Army-Navy Flag," *Take Off,* May 11, 1945; "Layout of C-82 Departments in Unit B Begins as Tooling Develops," *Take Off,* May 18, 1945; "Employees to Inspect Fairchild C-82 Packet," *Take Off,* June 15, 1945; "Photo Captions," *Take Off,* June 22 and 29, 1945.
39. "AAF Schedules Revealed Friday Now in Effect," *Take Off,* June 1, 1945; North American Aviation, Analysis of 1945 Performance, 8, Atwood Collection.
40. "Plant Produces 1–3 Planes in Midwest," *Take Off,* July 13, 1945; "17,861 War Planes Built Here since Dec. 7, 1941," *Take Off,* June 29, 1945; "Pistol Team Wins Second Quarterly Meet," *Take Off,* July 6, 1945; "Shangri-La Is Summer Utopia for NAA Picnickers," *Take Off,* August 10, 1945 (quote); "Mustang Pilots Seek NAA Girl To Be P-51 Pin-Up," *Take Off,* May 18, 1945; "P-51 Pin-Up Contest Closes," *Take Off,* July 6, 1945.

41. "First NAA Packet Makes Maiden Flight," *Take Off*, August 3, 1945; "C-82 Production Building Up in Unit B," *Take Off*, August 10, 1945; "Photo Caption," *Take Off*, August 3, 1945.

42. Samuel E, Morison, *History of United States Naval Operations in World War II, Volume 14: Victory in the Pacific*, (Boston, MA: Little, Brown, 1984), 344–349; "It Was the Blaringest, Howlingest, Happiest Celebration," *Dallas Morning News*, August 15, 1945 (quote).

43. "North American Receives Shutdown Order," *Dallas Morning News*, August 16, 1945.

44. Irving B. Holley Jr., *Buying Aircraft: Material Procurement for the Army Air Forces* (Washington, DC: Office of the Chief of Military History, Department of the Army, 1964), 578.

45. Holley Jr., *Buying Aircraft*, 560–561, 578. If output is considered in terms of airframe pounds, then NAA ranks fourth, producing 10.5% of total airframe weight, ranking below Douglas, Consolidated, and Boeing. Those three companies all produced large numbers of four-engine bombers, accounting for much of the difference in rankings.

Notes for Chapter 22

1. "To North American Aviation Employees," *Dallas Morning News*, August 19, 1945.

2. "NAA to Start Preclosing Inventories," *Dallas Morning News*, August 21, 1945; "Plant to Complete 3 Cargo Planes," *Dallas Morning News*, September 20, 1945.

3. "Peace Sends NAA P-51s to Grave," *Daily Times Herald*, November 15, 1945.

4. "U.S. Planes Obsolete, Leaders Told," *Dallas Morning News*, October 2, 1945.

5. "Metal Firm Leases Part of NAA Plant," *Dallas Morning News*, October 28, 1945.

6. E. C. Barksdale, *The Genesis of the Aviation Industry in North Texas* (Austin: Bureau of Business Research, University of Texas, 1958), 13–14.

7. "Globe Aircraft Trustees Named," *Dallas Morning News*, January 6, 1947; "Temco Gains Revealed to Stockholders," *Dallas Morning News*, April 6, 1947; "Temco Plans Swift Output, Buys Assets," *Dallas Morning News*, June 22, 1947.

8. "General Motors Leases NAA Plant at Kansas City," *Dallas Morning News*, November 8, 1945; Information Brochure: Aircraft Manufacturing Plant (Plancor 25), Pamphlets Relating to Manufacturing Facilities, Defense Plant Corporation Files, Records of the Reconstruction Finance Corporation (Record Group 234, National Archives and Record Administration, College Park, MD [Entry A1-E76]).

9. "Motors Seeks Space at NAA," *Dallas Morning News*, July 10, 1947.

Endnotes

10. "WAA Offices Merged, Set Up at NAA Plant," *Dallas Morning News*, February 5, 1947; "WAA Advertisement," *Dallas Morning News*, April 17, 1947; "NAA Floor Space Two-Thirds Taken," *Dallas Morning News*, November 9, 1947.

11. U.S. Senate Special Committee to Investigate the National Defense Program, *Third Annual Report*, Senate Report 10, Part 16, 78th Congress, 2nd Session (Washington, DC: Government Printing Office, 1944), 38; U.S. Congress, *United States Statutes at Large, 1947* (Washington, DC: Government Printing Office, 1948), 774–776 (second quote).

12. "Navy Seeks NAA Tenant," *Dallas Morning News*, October 17, 1947; "Aircraft Firm Considering Transfer to Grand Prairie," *Dallas Morning News*, November 22, 1947.

13. "Suburb Asks City Not Add Site of NAA," *Dallas Morning News*, October 1, 1947; "Plant Annexation Suit Faces Dallas," *Dallas Morning News*, October 9, 1947; "Mayor Vetoes Annexing Suit," *Dallas Morning News*, October 11, 1947; "NAA Action Made Final," *Dallas Morning News*, October 15, 1947.

14. "Navy Takes Over at Stand-By Plant," *Dallas Morning News*, December 5, 1947; "NAA Plant's Name Changed," *Dallas Morning News*, December 13, 1947; "TEMCO Gets Plant Lease," *Dallas Morning News*, December 12, 1947.

15. "Moving of Chance Vought Plant Waits Only Navy OK, Says Official," *Dallas Morning News*, December 18, 1947; "Plant Lease Way Cleared," *Dallas Morning News*, December 20, 1947.

16. "Chance Vought Ready to Lease Dallas Plant," *Dallas Morning News*, March 21, 1948.

17. "Chance Vought to Move May 1," *Dallas Morning News*, April 18, 1948; "Chamber to Publicize Chance Vought Move," *Dallas Morning News*, April 18, 1948; "Labor Supply Ample to Fill Firm's Needs," *Dallas Morning News*, April 18, 1948; "1,000 Seeking Jobs with Chance Vought," *Dallas Morning News*, April 20, 1948; "Grand Prairie Gets Set for Big Building Spree," *Dallas Morning News*, March 24, 1948 (quote).

18. "Transfer of Chance Vought Taking Place Little by Little," *Dallas Morning News*, July 18, 1948 (first quote); "Unions Move to Organize Workers at Chance Vought," *Dallas Morning News*, September 25, 1948; "Part of Made-in-Texas Corsair," *Dallas Morning News*, December 27, 1948; Barksdale, *Genesis of the Aviation Industry in North Texas*, 18 (second quote).

19. "TEMCO to Hire 500 More for Army Transport Job," *Dallas Morning News*, May 16, 1948; "TEMCO Given Contract by Chinese Government," *Dallas Morning News*, July 27, 1948.

20. "TEMCO Speeding Planes to Berlin Blockade Run," *Dallas Morning News*, August 29, 1948.

21. "Classified Advertisements," *Dallas Morning News*, April 2, 1949; "Chance Vought's Moving Day Ends," *Dallas Morning News*, April 17, 1949; "Flying V Brand Put on Corsair," *Dallas Morning News*, April 21, 1949.

22. "Flying V Brand Put on Corsair."

23. Table adapted from "Problems for Post-War Dallas Relating to Employment and the Labor Force: A Report for the Dallas Chamber of Commerce and the Committee for Economic Development," February 1945, DeGolyer Library, Southern Methodist University, Dallas, TX.

Bibliography

Primary Sources

Archival Sources—Unpublished

Boeing Archives, Bellevue, WA
    North American Aviation Collection
Dallas Historical Society, Dallas, TX
    Radio Broadcasts on stations WRR (AM 1310) and KGKO (AM 570)
    James H. Doolittle, "Speech at North American Aviation Inglewood, June 1, 1942"
National Archives and Records Administration, College Park, MD
    Records of the Office of the Secretary of War, Record Group 107
    Records of the War Department General and Special Staffs, Record Group 165
    Records of the Reconstruction Finance Corporation, Record Group 234
National Archives and Records Administration, Fort Worth, TX
    Records of the War Manpower Commission, Record Group 211
National Air and Space Museum, Chantilly, VA
    John Leland Atwood Collection
Franklin D. Roosevelt Presidential Library, Hyde Park, NY
    President's Secretary's File
Southern Methodist University, DeGolyer Library, Dallas, TX
    "Problems for Post-War Dallas Relating to Employment and the Labor Force: A Report for the Dallas Chamber of Commerce and the Committee for Economic Development," February 1945
Harry S. Truman Presidential Library, Independence, MO
    Records of the National Aircraft War Production Council
University of Texas at Arlington, Special Collections
    John W. Carpenter Papers
University of Texas at Dallas, Special Collections, History of Aviation Archives
    General Aviation Collection

Archival Sources—Published

Dallas Public Library, Special Collections, Dallas, Texas
    Daily Times Herald (clipping file)
Dolph Briscoe Center for American History, University of Texas at Austin
    North American Aviation - *Take Off* (newsletter)
Museum of Flight, Seattle, Washington
    North American Aviation - Annual Stockholder Reports, 1940–1945

Government Documents

U.S. Bureau of Demobilization, *Industrial Mobilization for War: History of the War Production Board and Predecessor Agencies, 1940–1945, Volume 1, Program and Administration.* Washington, DC: Government Printing Office, 1947.

U.S. Bureau of the Budget. *The United States at War: Development and Administration of the War Program by the Federal Government.* Washington, DC: Bureau of the Budget, 1946.

U.S. Civilian Production Administration. *Industrial Mobilization for War: History of the War Production Board and Predecessor Agencies, 1940–1945, Volume 1: Program and Administration.* Washington, DC: Government Printing Office, 1947.

U.S. Congress. *United States Statutes at Large, 1947.* Washington, DC: Government Printing Office, 1948.

U.S. Senate. Special Committee Investigating the National Defense Program. *Investigation of the National Defense Program: Hearings, Part 21, 78th Congress, First and Second Sessions.* Washington, DC: Government Printing Office, 1944.

U.S. Senate. Special Committee to Investigate the National Defense Program. "Investigation of the National Defense at Dallas, Texas, Transcripts of Hearing Taken at Dallas, Texas, Beginning October 9, 1943." 78th Congress, 1st Session.

U.S. Senate. Special Committee to Investigate the National Defense Program. "Investigation of National Defense Program, Closed Hearing on War Manpower Commission, October 14, 1943." 78th Congress, 1st Session.

U.S. Senate. Special Committee to Investigate the National Defense Program. *Third Annual Report.* Senate Report 10, Part 16, 78th Congress, 2nd Session. Washington, DC: Government Printing Office, 1944.

Books

Arnold, Henry H. *Global Mission.* New York: Harper, 1949.

Hull, Cordell. *The Memoirs of Cordell Hull.* New York: Macmillan, 1948.

Nelson, Donald M. *Arsenal of Democracy: The Story of American War Production.* New York: Harcourt Brace, 1946.

Wilson, Eugene E. *Slipstream: The Autobiography of an Air Craftsman.* New York: McGraw-Hill, 1950.

Articles

"From Blueprints to Production," *Dallas,* April 1941.

"North American Comes to Dallas." *Southwest Business,* October 1940.

"North American's Success Story." *Southwest Business,* October 1940.

"Rivers to Head Dallas Plane Plant." *Dallas,* March 1941.

"Scenes from Texas Factory Shot For 'March of Time' Production." *North American Skyline,* October 1941.

"Texans Make 'Good Hands' for Aircraft Industry," *Dallas,* April 1941.

"Texas Workmen Build Finished Home in 58 Minutes." *Life,* June 9, 1941.
"Texas Unit Starts Independent Trainer Production." *North American Skyline,* October 1941.

Secondary Sources

Bacon, Edmund N. "Wartime Housing." *The Annals of the American Academy of Political and Social Science* 229 (September 1943): 128–137.

Barksdale, E. C. *The Genesis of the Aviation Industry in North Texas.* Austin: Bureau of Business Research, University of Texas, 1958.

"Boeing History—Products through Boeing History—Defense Products - T-6 Texan Trainer" https://www.boeing.com/history/products/t-6-texan-trainer.page

Burns, James MacGregor. *Roosevelt: The Soldier of Freedom, 1940–1945.* New York: Harcourt Brace, 1970.

Carew, Michael G. *Becoming the Arsenal: The American Industrial Mobilization for World War II, 1938–1942.* Lanham, MD: University Press of America, 2010.

Churchill, Winston S. *The Second World War, Volume 1: The Gathering Storm.* Boston: Houghton Mifflin, 1948.

_____. *The Second World War, Volume 2: Their Finest Hour.* Boston, MA: Houghton Mifflin, 1949.

Craven, Wesley F., and James L. Cate. *The Army Air Forces in World War II, Volume 6: Men and Planes.* Chicago, IL: University of Chicago Press, 1955.

Divine, Robert A. *The Reluctant Belligerent: American Entry into World War II.* New York: John Wiley, 1979.

Doenecke, Justus D., and John E. Wilz. *From Isolation to War, 1931–1941.* Arlington Heights, IL: Harlan Davidson, 1991.

Fairbanks, Robert B. *For the City as a Whole: Planning, Politics, and the Public Interest in Dallas, Texas, 1900–1965.* Columbus: Ohio State University Press, 1998.

Fairchild, Byron, and Jonathon Grossman. *The Army and Industrial Manpower.* Washington, DC: Department of the Army, 1959.

Fredrickson, John. *Warbird Factory: North American Aviation in World War II.* Minneapolis, MN: Zenith Press, 2015.

Freeman, Roger A. *Mustang at War.* Garden City, NY: Doubleday, 1974.

Galbraith, John K. "Review of *Arsenal of Democracy* by Donald M. Nelson." *Journal of Political Economy* 55, no. 4 (1947): 399–400.

Hagedorn, Dan. *North American's T-6: A Definitive History of the World's Most Famous Trainer.* North Branch, MN: Specialty Press, 2009.

Holley Jr., Irving B. *Buying Aircraft: Material Procurement for the Army Air Forces.* Washington, DC: Office of the Chief of Military History, Department of the Army, 1964.

Horne, Allister. *To Lose a Battle: France 1940.* Boston: Little, Brown, 1969.

Hunter, Louis C. "Review of *Arsenal of Democracy* by Donald M. Nelson." *Military Affairs* 11, no. 2 (1947): 120–121.

Jablonski, Edward. *Flying Fortress: The Illustrated Biography of the B-17s and the Men Who Flew Them.* Garden City, NY: Doubleday, 1965.

Kimball, Warren F., ed. *Churchill and Roosevelt: The Complete Correspondence, Volume I: Alliance Emerging.* Princeton, NJ: Princeton University Press, 1984.

Klein, Maury. *A Call to Arms: Mobilizing America for World War II.* New York: Bloomsbury Press, 2013.

Koistinen, Paul A. C. *Arsenal of World War II: The Political Economy of American Warfare, 1940–1945.* Lawrence: University Press of Kansas, 2004.

Morison, Samuel E. *History of United States Naval Operations in World War II, Volume 1: The Battle of the Atlantic.* Boston, MA: Little, Brown, 1984.

_____. *History of United States Naval Operations in World War II, Volume 3: The Rising Sun in the Pacific.* Boston, MA: Little, Brown, 1984.

_____. *History of United States Naval Operations in World War II, Volume 14: Victory in the Pacific.* Boston, MA: Little, Brown, 1984.

Naval History and Heritage Command, https://www.history.navy.mil/

Pate, J'Nell L. *Arsenal of Defense: Fort Worth's Military Legacy.* Denton: Texas State Historical Association, 2011.

Payne, Darwin. *Big D: Triumphs and Troubles of an American Supercity in the 20th Century.* Dallas, TX: Three Forks Press, 1994.

_____. *Dallas, An Illustrated History.* Eugene, OR: Windsor Publications, 1982.

Peterson, Sarah Jo. *Planning the Home Front: Building Bombers and Communities at Willow Run.* Chicago, IL: University of Chicago Press.

Prange, Gordon W. *At Dawn We Slept: The Untold Story of Pearl Harbor.* New York: McGraw Hill, 1981.

Sherwood, Robert F. *Roosevelt and Hopkins: An Intimate History.* New York: Grosset and Dunlap, 1950.

Smith, R. Elberton. *The Army and Economic Mobilization.* Washington, DC: United States Army, 1991.

Stafford, Edward P. *The Big E: The Story of the U.S.S. Enterprise.* New York: Random House, 1962.

Szylvian, Kristin M. "Avion Village: Texas' World War II Housing Laboratory." *Legacies: A History Journal for Dallas and North Central Texas* 4, no. 2 (Fall 1992): 29–34.

Texas State Historical Association: The Handbook of Texas Online https://www.tshaonline.org/home/

Trimble, William F. *Wings for the Navy: A History of the Naval Aircraft Factory, 1917–1956.* Annapolis, MD: Naval Institute Press, 1990.

University of California, Santa Barbara: The American Presidency Project https://www.presidency.ucsb.edu/

University of North Texas: The Portal to Texas History https://texashistory.unt.edu

Wagner, Ray. *American Combat Planes,* 3rd ed. Garden City, NY: Doubleday, 1982.

Watson, Mark Skinner. *Chief of Staff: Prewar Plans and Preparations.* Washington, DC: United States Army, 1985.

Welch, Courtney. "Evolution, Not Revolution: The Effect of New Deal Legislation on Industrial Growth and Union Development in Dallas, Texas." Ph.D. Diss., University of North Texas, Denton, 2010.

White, Gerald T. *Billions for Defense: Government Financing by the Defense Plant Corporation during World War II*. Tuscaloosa: University of Alabama Press, 1980.

_____. "Financing Industrial Expansion for War: The Origin of the Defense Plant Corporation Leases," *The Journal of Economic History* 9, no. 2 (November 1949): 156–183.

Winters, Willis. "Avion Village: Enduring Values of Community," *Texas Architect* (May-June 1988): 24–29.

Newspapers

Altoona Mirror
Camden News
Daily Times Herald
Dallas Morning News
Edwardsville Intelligencer
Jefferson City Post Tribune
[Jefferson City] *Sunday News and Tribune*
Neosho Daily Democrat
New York Times
Portsmouth Herald
Portsmouth Times
Stanford Daily
Waco Tribune-Herald

Index

A

AT-6 Texan trainer
    cost per aircraft, 263
    importance of, 57, 121–122, 153–154, 196
    initial delivery from Dallas, *124*, 125
    production figures (Dallas plant), 162–164, 264, 339
    specifications, 142
A. Harris department store, 35, 93–94
Adams, Nathan, 46, 61, 223
Adoue, J. B., 37, 46, 61, 63
Advisory Commission to the Council of National Defense. *See* NDAC, 50, 65
Aircraft Production Board, 215, 283, 307
Alexander, Charles H., 235
Allen, J. Floyd, 63
Allis-Chalmers Manufacturing Co., 106–107
Amberg, Julius H., 229–230, 299
American Federation of Labor (AFL), 128, 130, 210–212, 214, 251
Andrews, Frank M. (US Army), 21
Army-Navy "E" award, 195, 256, 319, 332
Arnold, Henry H. (US Army), 19, 22, 25, 50, 53, 67, 194
Atwood, John Leland (NAA), 18, 39, 50–51, 61, 108, 144, 154–155, 167, 172, 187, 195, 226, 262, 323
Avion Village housing development, 74, 77–85, 206, 209, 224

B

B-17 Flying Fortress bomber, 21, 33, 106
B-24 Liberator bomber, 57, 161, 173, 215–217, 258, 262, 269, 285, 299, 301, 304, 319–320
    contract awarded, 168–169
    contract termination, 311–312, 315–316
Baker Hotel, 61–62, 93–94, 155, 226, 260, 278, 344
Baker, H. T. (NAA), *189*
Ball, Joseph (senator), 282
Baruch, Bernard, 8, 21
Beck, Henry C., 78
Beisel, Rex B. (Chance Vought), 344, 347
Bell, Lawrence, 10–14, 21
Bellamy, John (NAA), 183–184
Black, James T. (WMC), 277